YVES SAINT LAURENT

Yves Saint Laurent

A Biography

ALICE RAWSTHORN

Nan A. Talese

DOUBLEDAY

NEW YORK   LONDON

TORONTO   SYDNEY   AUCKLAND

PUBLISHED BY NAN A. TALESE
an imprint of Doubleday
a division of Bantam Doubleday Dell Publishing Group, Inc.
1540 Broadway, New York, New York 10036

DOUBLEDAY is a trademark of Doubleday, a division of
Bantam Doubleday Dell Publishing Group, Inc.

First published in the United Kingdom by HarperCollins*Publishers* Ltd., London

Library of Congress Cataloging-in-Publication Data

Rawsthorn, Alice.
    Yves Saint Laurent: a biography / Alice Rawsthorn.—1st ed. in
the United States of America.
       p.   cm.
    Includes bibliographical references and index.
    1. Saint Laurent, Yves. 2. Fashion designers—France—Biography.
3. Costume design—France—History—20th century.   I. Title.
TT505.S24R38   1996
746.9'2'092—dc20
[B]   96-9206
                                                     CIP

ISBN 0-385-47645-0
Copyright © 1996 Alice Rawsthorn
All Rights Reserved
Printed in the United States of America
December 1996
First Edition in the United States of America

10 9 8 7 6 5 4 3 2 1

Contents

Prologue
The First Refusal

The audience always, but always, treated Yves Saint Laurent to a standing ovation when he mounted the catwalk for the finale of his *haute couture* collections. Yet there are ovations and ovations, and when he took his bow on the morning of 24 January 1990, the spectators not only rose to their feet to cheer him, but carried on clapping for a full thirteen minutes.

The setting was one of the most sumptuous in Paris, the ballroom of the Hôtel Intercontinental. Designed in 1878 by Charles Garnier, architect of the Paris Opéra, it was designated as a national monument by the French government and commandeered twice a year by the house of Saint Laurent for its *couture* presentations. Mottled mirrors lined the walls, chandeliers blazed from the ceiling. In the centre of the room was a raised runway, with a cascade of flowers framing an entrance at one end, and a phalanx of photographers snapping and flashing from the other. Row after row of spindly gilt chairs arched around it, with the names of their occupants written by hand on cards tied to the backs by ribbons. Saint Laurent smiled aimlessly at the cameras, his *couture* 'bride' beaming beside him, as the models behind them clapped courteously.

The applause was, as one would expect, partly for the clothes. Many people in the room had seen dozens of Yves Saint Laurent's *couture* shows during his three decades as the world's most famous fashion designer: but it was years since he had unveiled such a magnificent presentation. It was Saint Laurent's tribute to the artists who had inspired him throughout his career. There was a slither of fiery red lace over a hot pink tulle skirt for Maria Callas; a flurry of impressionistic printed silk for Marcel Proust; and a neat navy-blue suit trimmed with white piping for Coco Chanel. Yves also paid homage to some of the women in the audience. The actress, Catherine Deneuve, smiled at the sight of 'her' canary-yellow satin cocktail dress; and Zizi Jeanmaire, the famous French singer and dancer, laughed out loud at a slip of a black sequinned shift dress, as she sang along to one of her own songs on the soundtrack. On the front page of the next day's *International Herald Tribune*, the journalist, Suzy Menkes, decreed that Yves Saint Laurent had 'scaled a Himalayan peak of *haute couture*', under the headline 'Born Again Couturier: Saint Laurent Show Is Strongest in 10 Years'.

The audience was also applauding Yves himself. Some of the spectators had watched him blossom from the timid twenty-one-year-old in a tightly-buttoned suit who had succeeded Christian Dior in the late 1950s, into the insouciant hippy *de luxe* of the late 1960s. They had then seen him stumble through a masochistic cycle of addiction, illness and depression in the 1970s and 1980s, but that day they saw a different man. Saint Laurent had lost weight, his voice seemed clearer and his gaze steadier. Smiling delightedly, he greeted the well-wishers who dashed backstage to shower him with compliments and congratulatory kisses. 'I can't believe it!' cried the New York socialite, Nan Kempner, who had known him since his Dior days when she came shopping to Paris as a teenager with her mother. 'It's my darling Yves again!'

His spirits lifted, Yves asked his press officer, Gabrielle Buchaert, to invite a dozen or so 'friends' to dinner that night at his home at 55 rue de Babylone. *Couture* week was always a social affair, as other designers, such as Karl Lagerfeld at Chanel and Hubert de Givenchy, invariably threw dinners and parties for influential editors and wealthy *couture* clients, but it was years since Yves Saint Laurent had entertained on the evening after a show. During the past few years of neurasthenic retreat he had seen only a handful of old friends, mostly one at a time, and appeared in public so seldom that a glimpse of him at a Parisian restaurant was ritualistically reported in the gossip columns. Most of the people whom Gabrielle Buchaert telephoned already had plans for that evening, but as an invitation from Yves Saint Laurent was so very rare, they cancelled their arrangements to accept it.

Anna Wintour, the editor-in-chief of American *Vogue*, arrived with her opposite number on Paris *Vogue*, Colombe Pringle, and a slew of Parisian socialites led by Marie-Hélène de Rothschild, *doyenne* of the banking dynasty and a friend of Yves since the 1950s. The guests were greeted by the designer, who proudly told them how he had given up alcohol, and had not felt as happy, or as healthy in years, leaving his business partner, Pierre Bergé, to take them on a guided tour of the apartment that he had shared with Yves in the years when they were lovers.

It was an exquisite place, one of the most beautiful private homes in Paris, a duplex designed in the 1930s by Jean-Michel Frank, one of the French artisans whom Yves most admired. The rooms were cast in Frank's ascetically elegant style, looking out through white-shuttered windows on to a private garden arranged in the formal French manner with topiary and classical torsos on a manicured lawn. The contents of the duplex bore the stamp of immense wealth and rarefied taste, with exquisite Picassos, Matisses, Mondrians, a Goya, and a dozen or so portraits of Yves's beloved dog, Moujik, by his friend, Andy Warhol. 'It was like walking into another world, or another era,' said one of the guests. 'Almost unreal. One of the loveliest, most luxurious homes I've ever seen.'

The guests lingered on until after midnight. A few hours later Yves was woken by a fire in his bedroom, a minor blaze, caused by an electricity fault. The servants quickly put it out, and Yves was unhurt, but too distressed to stay in Paris, he was helicoptered off to Château Gabriel, the nineteenth-century castle in the Normandy village of Bénerville that he had decorated in *Belle Époque* splendour as a private tribute to Marcel Proust. After a few days there, Yves returned to Paris, where he seemed so frail and febrile, his nerves shot to pieces, that he was sent away again, this time in the company's Lear jet with Moujik and his servants, to Villa Oasis, his 1920s mansion in Marrakesh.

Yves had retreated to Morocco in the weeks between his collections since buying his first house there in the 1960s, and in recent years spent most of his time there, returning to Paris only for his fashion shows. He loved the sunny, sensual Moroccan city, the scene of his sybaritic youth, and felt at ease in the warm climate of his native North Africa. Sometimes Yves strolled around the *medina*, the old town, but often he spent his days in the privacy of Villa Oasis, writing or sketching among the Orientalist paintings in the *salons*, or beneath the shady palm trees around the terraces, his solitude protected by acres of palms, orange trees and water-lily ponds. Over the years he had grown to dread the day when Pierre Bergé sent word for him to return to Paris to complete the next collection; but he had always agreed to go.

This time was different. For years the servants at Villa Oasis had sent regular reports of his conduct back to Pierre Bergé, as much for Yves's protection as anything else. He had in the past been known to wander aimlessly in the *medina*, stumbling drunkenly into bars that he would have been ill-advised to enter even when sober. As the weeks went by on this visit, the reports became increasingly alarming. Monsieur Saint Laurent was drained, depressed and drinking heavily again. He had sealed himself off in a room, where he was downing two bottles of whisky a day, screaming hysterically if they broached his return to the fashion house. As the day of the Rive Gauche ready-to-wear show approached on 21 March 1990, nothing they said had any effect, and the servants asked for help. Someone would have to be sent over to Marrakesh to take Yves Saint Laurent back to Paris.

The Boy from Oran
1936–1955

Oran lies in a spectacular setting at the heart of a crescent bay with the blue water of the Mediterranean on one side and the snowy peaks of the Atlas Mountains on the other. Founded by Arab sailors in the tenth century, it was conquered by the Spanish, then the Turks, and finally by the French when they colonized Algeria in the 1830s. The French ransacked the old Arab quarters, rebuilt the city in the staid colonial style commonplace along the North African coast and tried to instil it with the same insipid spirit.

Algeria was so close to Europe that it was easy for the French to import their way of life there. They built schools, and hospitals, even country clubs. The *colons* went to universities in France and were eligible for conscription into the French army. They voted in the French elections: Algeria was divided into three *départements*, or electoral regions, so its residents were represented at the National Assembly in Paris. By the time Yves Saint Laurent was born in 1936, the life of a French settler's son in Oran was much the same as that of a young boy in provincial France.

His family, the Mathieu-Saint-Laurents, was one of the most prominent in Oran. Yves's great-grandparents had fled there in 1872 from Alsace, a region of eastern France annexed by Germany after its victory in the Franco-Prussian War. Given the choice of staying in Alsace under German rule, or remaining French citizens but being repatriated to Algeria, thousands of Alsatians had left France for North Africa. Many arrived there penniless, like the grandparents of the philosopher, Louis Althusser.[1] The Mathieu-Saint-Laurents were luckier. They had a distinguished record of public service as lawyers and judges back in Colmar, and boasted a titled ancestor in Baron Mathieu de Mauvières, who was ennobled by Napoleon after officiating over his marriage to his mistress, Josephine.[2] When they left France to build a new life in North Africa, they took with them the wealth and status they had enjoyed in Alsace.

Algeria was a comfortable country for its foreign residents and the family prospered, as Oran became a bustling commercial centre with cargoes of barley, wheat and fruit grown in the Atlas plains making the short voyage across the Mediterranean to the French and Spanish ports. Yves's father, Charles, was the fifth of the five children of Marie-Jules Mathieu-Saint-Laurent, a wealthy Orani businessman. After passing his *baccalauréat* examination at the local *lycée*, Charles spent a few years studying law in Marseille before returning to Oran where, despite being tempted to become a lawyer, he followed his father into business by setting up a small insurance agency and a chain of cinemas. In his mid-twenties, Charles was a handsome man with a grave but kindly face, a vigorous air and a sportsman's tan. His dark hair was combed neatly from a side parting and he was always smartly dressed. Never short of girlfriends, he showed no sign of settling down until, while out walking with friends in the centre of the city one afternoon, he was introduced to Lucienne-Andrée Wilbaux.

Lucienne was one of those young women whose features are a little too sharp for chocolate-box prettiness, but who play the part of a pretty woman so well that people are happy to treat them as one. At nineteen she took great pains with her appearance, making sure her make-up was immaculate, her soft brown hair set in gentle waves, and decking out her dresses with, perhaps, a little too much jewellery. As a baby she had been handed over by her parents, a Belgian engineer and his Spanish wife, to be brought up in Oran, the second city of Algeria, by her Aunt Renée, the widow of a successful architect. Renée indulged her niece with an expensive education and vacations with rich relatives in Paris and Cannes. After school there was no question of Lucienne earning her own living: all that was expected of an attractive young lady in the 1930s was to find an eligible husband to look after her as Aunt Renée had done, and Charles Mathieu-Saint-Laurent looked like a perfect prospect.

They were married on 4 July 1935. The groom was twenty-six, his bride twenty. After the wedding they settled into a spacious house looking out over the sea in Saint-Michel, a genteel area of Oran bordering on the Arab quarter. The young couple were very different in temperament. Charles had a rather reserved character that betrayed his Alsatian origins, while his wife had the warmth and exuberance of her Spanish mother. But they made an attractive pair, with Charles's solid masculinity complementing his wife's fussy femininity. Lucienne soon coaxed him into a busy round of dinners, cocktail parties and theatre trips with other young couples, and occasional balls for the foreigners who passed through the port.

A few months after their marriage, Lucienne became pregnant. She gave birth to their first child at the Jarsaillon Clinic in Oran on 1 August 1936. The baby was a boy, baptized Yves Henri Donat Mathieu-Saint-Laurent. Looking laughably like his father, with brown hair and wide blue eyes, little Yves became the darling of the aunts, great-aunts and grandparents in the extended families of the Wilbaux and Mathieu-Saint-Laurents. His parents doted on him, especially his mother. As the youngest of a large, lively family, Charles had happy memories of his own childhood and was thrilled to have a son; Lucienne, having grown up apart from her parents, longed for children of her own. Fiercely attached to Yves, she was anxious that he should have the emotional security that Aunt Renée, for all her indulgence, could not give her.

Often she was left alone with the baby, while Charles went off to settle insurance business in France, or to inspect his cinemas in Tunisia and Morocco. There were servants to attend to the household chores and a nanny to help her with Yves. Lucienne spent her days playing with her son and planning new outfits for her evenings out with Charles. As a young wife, she took as much trouble with her appearance as she had when she was single: trying out new make-up techniques, poring over French fashion magazines and discussing the details of new gowns with her dressmakers. During the day she wore prettily patterned blouses with full sleeves and crisply laundered skirts. Her outfits were more elaborate for the evening: long dresses with fitted bodices and full skirts, a sash around the waist, a stole for her shoulders and strappy high-heeled shoes. Yves loved to watch his mother dress, and insisted on seeing what she and his aunt were wearing before they left the house at night. Years later Lucienne liked to tell the story of how the four-year-old Yves objected to one of his aunt's outfits. 'I think he made her change her dress and her accessories at least five or six times before he was satisfied. He had such authority and was so sure of himself that we accepted it.'[3]

Yves's childhood photographs show a lively, smiling toddler nestling confidently against his pretty mother. In family portraits he is invariably the centre of attention with one or both parents fussing fondly over him, cajoling him into smiles with a favourite toy or a posy of flowers. When Yves was three, France went to war against Germany in World War II, but the family's leisurely life was unaffected. As a married man with a child, Charles was exempt from military service and Algeria was far enough away from France to be spared the worst of its defeat and the German Occupation.

During the War Charles and Lucienne had two more children: Michèle was born in 1942 and Brigitte in 1945. They were pretty little girls. Michèle looked like Lucienne, and the baby, Brigitte, resembled her father and brother; but their arrival did little to threaten Yves's sense of supremacy. By the time Michèle was born he had enjoyed Lucienne's undivided attention for six years. He was the eldest, the only boy, and besides, there was never any doubt as to who was their mother's favourite. 'I love my daughters, of course,' said Lucienne. 'But for Yves there has always been something very strong and very special.'[4] As for Charles, he was a fond, if rather remote presence in the Saint-Michel household, returning home from business trips to hear his wife's accounts of their clever son's latest accomplishments.

The Mathieu-Saint-Laurents had a pleasant routine of spending their summers in a villa by the beach at the nearby resort of Trouville, where Yves played with Simone Tronc, a girl of his age whose parents were friendly with Charles and Lucienne, before returning to Oran in September for the children to start the new school year. During the winter, they took trips inland to stay with Charles's parents, who owned a country house on the Atlas plains, travelling there by car with the children staring out of the windows at the peasants toiling in the vinefields.[5] It was on these journeys that Yves glimpsed the natural beauty of the Algerian landscape: the white sands of the coastline, the blue of the Mediterranean and the silhouette of the Atlas ranges towering above the vines. He saw another side of the country while walking with his mother and sisters in Oran's colourful Arab quarter with the vivid scents of the spices and oils in the market and chanting from the mosques. Although he led the *bourgeois* life of a French settler's son, the backdrop to Yves's childhood was the visual drama of North Africa.

On the cusp of adolescence Yves was as much his mother's darling as when he was a baby. The most studious of the three children, he spent hours alone in his room, sketching and scribbling. Reading and writing came easily to him, but from an early age it was evident that he had a gift for art. Lucienne encouraged him by buying the paints, pastels and paper he needed to practise. She showered affection on her son, applauding his achievements and taking him out for treats to the opera, circus and the cinema where his favourite films were melodramas with glamorous heroines, like *Gone With The Wind*, *A Streetcar Named Desire*, or any other movie starring Vivien Leigh.

The outings Yves enjoyed most were trips to the theatre. Oran had its own theatre company, which stuck to a predictable repertoire of dramas and farces. Occasionally there were more sophisticated productions performed by travelling French companies on tours of the North African colonies. Having pestered his mother into taking him to see the latest plays, Yves then re-enacted them at home. He built a toy theatre with elaborate handmade sets, creating paper puppets by pasting faces cut from magazines on to cardboard torsos and sewing costumes from scraps of old sheets or Lucienne's discarded dresses. His parents let him use an empty room to act out impromptu performances of Molière and Giraudoux for an admiring audience of sisters and cousins.

Yves read about the latest Paris plays, operas and ballets in Lucienne's fashion magazines. In those days *Vogue* reported on the theatre as well as *haute couture*, giving detailed descriptions of the costumes and scenery with illustrations by the great theatrical designers of the day, Bérard, Cocteau and Clavé. Yves had never been to Paris but he could visualize exactly what the sets looked like in the theatres and how his favourite actresses were dressed. At thirteen he was taken to see a touring production of Molière's *L'École des Femmes*, directed by the actor, Louis Jouvet, who played the lead role of

Arnolphe, with sets designed by Christian Bérard. *L'École des Femmes* had run for years at the Théâtre de l'Athénée in Paris, but it was rare to see a production of that calibre in Oran and Yves was mesmerized by it, particularly by the designs. 'Bérard knew how to fashion a character, how to create a costume, to reinforce the spirit of the production,' he recalled. 'If the stage had been plunged into darkness you could still identify each character just by looking at Bérard's silhouettes – Tartuffe or Don Juan.'[6] He tried to replicate the visual effects in his own theatre and resolved to become a theatre designer 'just like him'.[7]

The thoughtful, artistic boy who seemed so sweet to his mother and aunts, was seen very differently by his schoolmates at the local *lycée*. The Orani took an old-fashioned view of sexual stereotypes. Women were expected to be sweetly submissive, and men to be strong and sporty. Most of Yves's schoolfellows were typical Orani to whom he looked suspiciously like a sissy. Every school has its bullies and they soon sniff out their victims. Yves Mathieu-Saint-Laurent was cast in that role on the first day he set foot in the *lycée*. 'Maybe I didn't have what it took to be a boy,' he recalled. 'As soon as my schoolmates realized I was different, I became their whipping boy.'[8]

If he was lucky he got away with jeers and abuse. If not, his classmates thumped or jostled him, laughing cruelly as he scrambled on the floor for his books. The worst of the bullies beat him up in the schoolyard, or dragged him off to the lavatories where they left him locked inside one of the cubicles. Too puny to defend himself, Yves tried to hide from the other boys. He invented excuses to stay in the classroom when lessons were over, or sneaked off to the chapel hoping to spend his breaks there alone. Sports lessons were torture; Yves stood shamefaced while the teams were picked, knowing that he was bound to be the last one to be chosen. Once the game began he dreaded the insults from his team-mates when he let them down as usual. His parents and teachers were pleased with his academic grades, but Yves's cleverness made his classmates tease him even more. 'I was full of sadness and fear, even terror. I was sick before going to school each morning. It was psychological torture.'[9]

Back at home he buried himself in his sketches, books and his theatre. 'I began to lead a double life. On one side was our home, happiness with my family and the world that I invented with my drawings. And on the other in school . . . I was mocked, intimidated and beaten by my classmates.'[10] Like most lonely, precocious adolescents he fantasized about escaping to a place where he would be appreciated. His favourite fantasy was imagining his name up in lights on the Avenue des Champs-Elysées in Paris. 'Whenever they picked on me, I'd say to myself, "One day you'll be famous." That was my way of getting back at them.'[11]

But the bullying took its toll. The bright-eyed little boy in Yves's childhood photographs became an ashen-faced adolescent with a skinny frame that accentuated his least flattering features, the prominent nose and jutting ears he had inherited from his father. Alone with his mother Yves chatted happily for hours, but he was awkward to the point of dumbness in company. While his gung-ho classmates pose confidently in school pictures, he seems to shrink away from the camera. Even his clothes proclaim his insecurity; the other boys loll confidently in open-neck shirts and raffish blazers, but Yves's jacket is nervously buttoned up to the top and his tie tightly knotted. In family snaps he clings uncertainly to Lucienne, blurring into the background behind his smiling sisters and Bobinette, their perky terrier.

Yves did not tell his parents about the bullying. 'I didn't confide in anyone, not even my mother.'[12] Pride must have played a part in his decision to remain silent. He was anxious not to disappoint his parents, particularly Charles, who seemed to him to be the epitome of everything an Orani man was expected to be. Yves might also have thought it simpler to ignore his problems, hoping that they would go away. But the main reason for his silence was guilt; he had sensed from an early age that one of the main 'differences' between him and his classmates was something that he dared not discuss with his parents – his sexuality. 'I wasn't like the other boys,' he admitted as an adult, in an interview with *Le Figaro*. 'I didn't fit in, no doubt because I was homosexual.'[13]

Homosexuality was taboo within the conservative circle of the Mathieu-Saint-Laurents, condemned as a sin by the Catholic Church and treated as a criminal offence by the authorities. Attitudes were more permissive in French artistic and literary circles, where there was a long tradition of homosexuality, from the nineteenth-century poets, Arthur Rimbaud and Paul Verlaine, to twentieth-century figures such as André Gide, François Mauriac and Jean Cocteau. But life was harder outside their rarefied Parisian set. One of the prime political concerns in postwar France was boosting the birthrate, which had dropped dramatically during the War, and the country adopted a family-oriented culture that became progressively more conservative. The police cracked down on gay clubs and bars with raids on pick-up places like parks and steam baths in France and the North African colonies.[14] The boys at Yves's school swapped horror stories about *pédés*, the derisory French slang word for homosexuals which literally translates as paederasts and was one of the worst insults among the *colons* at the Oran *lycée*.

The Arabs in the Islamic society around them had a different attitude. Sexual contact between unmarried men and women is strictly forbidden in Islamic culture, but sex between adolescent boys is tacitly tolerated in the hope that it might stop them from preying on young women. Similarly it is acceptable for Arab boys to be physically attracted to white men, the unwritten rule being that there is no shame attached to sex with a Westerner – providing the Arab adopts the dominant role.

There was no shortage of teenagers in the Arab quarter of Oran willing to have sex with wealthy French boys like Yves. He heard his schoolmates whispering about the streetboys in the *medina*, the old town, and sneering at the *pédés* who went to them. On walks around the Arab quarter, he noticed the streetboys gossiping and laughing as they lounged outside bars and cafés. Yves started creeping off there to watch the boys, and eventually screwed up the courage to approach one. It was there that he had his first sexual experiences, furtive encounters shrouded by shame and secrecy. 'I was ashamed,' he told the French writer, Laurence Benaïm. 'It was all poisoned by fear and anxiety. A terrible fear that stayed with me for a long time. To be homosexual in Oran was tantamount to being a murderer.'[15]

Yves hid his secret from everyone, dreading what would happen if Charles or Lucienne found out. Perhaps they came to their own conclusions about the sexual preferences of their sensitive, highly-strung son. If so, like most parents of their generation, they chose not to mention them and Yves did little to arouse their suspicions.

He even had a girlfriend, Simone Tronc, his playmate from the Trouville beach, who accompanied him to dances and parties, coming round to the house so they could practise their dance-steps beforehand. His school reports were excellent and he seemed happy enough at home. He had found a dog, Zou Zou, straying around the Arab quarter and brought her back for the Mathieu-Saint-Laurents to look after. When Zou Zou had a puppy they adopted her too and Yves christened her Églantine. For the rest of his free time, he was cheerfully absorbed by his art.

As his technique improved Yves's drawing and painting became more ambitious. By his teens he was dashing off portraits, cartoons and elaborate frontispieces for favourite novels, which he drew in a Hollywoodesque 1950s style, making Flaubert's Madame Bovary look suspiciously like Vivien Leigh. His toy theatre was destroyed when the flames from Joan of Arc's stake blazed uncontrollably during a performance of George Bernard Shaw's *Saint Joan*, but still set on becoming a theatrical designer Yves spent hours scribbling sets and costumes in his sketchbooks. He carried on reading the theatre reports in the fashion magazines and was particularly struck by the articles about Roland Petit, a brilliant young choreographer whose 1950 version of Bizet's *Carmen* caused a sensation. The ballerina, Zizi Jeanmaire, had her hair cut scandalously short like a boy's to play the lead role and the chorus of cigarette girls outraged the critics by coming on stage smoking.

At first Yves had read Lucienne's copies of *Vogue* and *Paris-Match* for the theatre reviews, but he soon moved on to the fashion pages where the latest looks from the Paris *couturiers* were shown in photographs and illustrations. He began by copying the cocktail dresses and ballgowns on his sketchpads, and then dreamt up designs of his own. Shortly after his seventeenth birthday he spotted a competition entry in *Paris-Match*: it was for an annual contest for young fashion designers organized by the International Wool Secretariat. The competition was highly regarded in fashion circles; the judges included famous Paris *couturiers*, such as Christian Dior and Pierre Balmain, and the winner stood a chance of being hired by one of them. Yves posted off his entry: three black and white sketches of a coat, a dress and a suit. A few weeks later he received a letter saying that he had won third prize and inviting him to attend the awards ceremony in

Paris that December. He set off from Oran for his first visit to the French capital accompanied by Lucienne.

The Paris of the early 1950s offered everything Yves had longed for in Oran. The intellectual life of the city had exploded after the rigours of the Occupation, and there was a resurgence of interest in the work of his favourite pre-war novelists and dramatists, André Gide and Jean Anouilh. A new generation of younger writers was emerging: Jean-Paul Sartre, Simone de Beauvoir and Albert Camus. The decorative arts were thriving. Yves's hero, Christian Bérard, had died in 1949, but Cocteau and Clavé were still prolific. Roland Petit had breathed new life into ballet and French fashion was flourishing after the success of Christian Dior's 'New Look' in 1947 and the work of his peers, Pierre Balmain and Cristóbal Balenciaga. Even the social scene regained a whiff of its pre-war grandeur in the opulent *soirées* of the great hostesses, Marie-Laure de Noailles and Marie-Louise Bousquet, where France's oldest families mingled with the brightest young artists and any interesting American who was visiting the city: from the writers, Ernest Hemingway and William Faulkner, to the conductor, Leonard Bernstein.

Yves and Lucienne were outsiders in Paris. People from Algeria, even those with money and old Alsatian names, were *pieds noirs* to the French. The name *pieds noirs*, or 'black feet', came from the clumpy black shoes that poor French farmers wore in North Africa. Lucienne and Yves spoke with the accents of wealthy *pieds noirs*, which, in Parisian eyes, placed them rather low in the social pecking order. But they were happy to be there and Lucienne showed Yves the city she remembered from childhood holidays with Aunt Renée, taking him for walks along the riverbank and for strolls around the shops. As was customary for the wife of a wealthy French businessman on a visit to the capital, she treated herself to a new outfit at one of the *haute couture* houses by ordering a gown from Jean Patou.

Before leaving for France, Lucienne had asked a family friend to arrange for Yves to meet Michel de Brunhoff, editor-in-chief of Paris *Vogue*. Yves was to show him his sketches and ask his advice about his chances of pursuing a career in theatrical design; or, in the wake of his success in the International Wool Secretariat competition, as a *couturier*. The interview was as much for Charles's benefit as for Yves's. Charles was happy to tolerate his son's passion for art as a hobby, but not as a career. Yves had always done well academically and his father wanted him to follow the family tradition – and to fulfil his own adolescent ambition – by becoming a lawyer. Knowing that Yves was determined to work in the arts, Lucienne hoped that the endorsement of an eminent man like Michel de Brunhoff might persuade her husband to change his mind.

Michel de Brunhoff was one of the most powerful figures in French fashion and a member of the artistic Parisian circle that seemed so enticing to Yves. His brother, Laurent, was the author of the Babar children's books and Michel himself a confidant of Christian Dior, Jean Cocteau and, before his death, of Christian Bérard. He had ruled the roost at Paris *Vogue* since the 1930s and under his editorship it became the arbiter of French chic. '*Vogue* was very élitist,' observed Marie-José Lepicard, one of his young writers. 'Michel de Brunhoff insisted that everything was done absolutely correctly. The fashion editors were expected to dress immaculately, like models. We wore tailored suits with gloves buttoned up to our elbows, full make-up and Joy perfume, probably because it was the most expensive. When I went to work for *Vogue* the first things I bought were a pair of gloves and a bottle of Joy.'[16]

Despite his lofty status, Michel de Brunhoff was a kindly man who was happy to help talented youngsters. He had a bluff, almost comical appearance, with a round face, bushy eyebrows and tufts of white hair around his bald pate. Too short and plump for conventional elegance, he dressed like Winston Churchill in double-breasted suits with a white handkerchief sprouting out of the breast pocket, occasionally topped off by a bowler hat. It was typical of him to have found the time to see the wife of an obscure Orani businessman and her shy seventeen-year-old son. He thought Yves's sketches were excellent and said so, but advised him that, although he might well have a dazzling career in Paris, he should first go back to school and pass his *baccalauréat*. If he was serious about a career in fashion, Yves could then return to Paris and enrol in one of the design courses run by the industry body, the Chambre Syndicale de la Couture. Lucienne was thrilled. Her son was as talented as she had thought, but she would not have to part from him; at least, not for a while. They returned to Oran hoping Charles would be swayed by Michel de Brunhoff's encouragement.

Charles knew when he was beaten. He found it difficult enough to stand up to his wife, but Yves was impossible; even as a child, he had an imperious side. Besides, the opinions of a man like Michel de Brunhoff were not to be taken lightly, his advice to Yves seemed sensible and all Charles had ever really wanted was for his children to be happy. 'Yves was never influenced by anyone,' he told American *Vogue* years later. 'I'd say it was his mother who was influenced by him. As for me, I've always believed that a child should be allowed to do what he wants in life. What matters is that he wants to do something.'[17]

Yves reapplied himself to his studies – with escape in sight, even school did not seem so grim. He spent his evenings and weekends working on new sketches of dresses and theatre sets, sending off a batch of drawings to Michel de Brunhoff in early 1954, a few months after their meeting in Paris. De Brunhoff wrote back in a kindly but constructive manner. 'Dear sir, I find your designs most interesting, and can only repeat what I told you when you were in Paris, that your gift for fashion is beyond doubt. I have marked with a cross those of your designs that I find most successful. If I were you, I should take advantage of this year when you are relatively free of other commitments to work from nature – landscape, still life, portraits, as well as fashion models. As a matter of fact, I am rather afraid that your particular talents do not encourage you to work hard enough on your drawing. I can see that you are still influenced by Bérard. All to the good – he was one of my oldest friends, and you could not choose a better master. But I should tell you that he did work hard at his drawing, and the few wonderful portraits he left behind him – remarkable portraits – are inclined to make one sorry that he devoted the end of his life solely to scenery and costume for the theatre and to fashion.'[18]

Yves waited to reply until he had received the results of his *baccalauréat*. 'Dear sir, I am sorry not to have written back sooner, but I wanted to wait for the results of my examination before doing so. As I had hoped, they proved entirely satisfactory and I am to move to Paris at the beginning of the autumn. Perhaps my plans are too ambitious. Like Bérard, I want to focus on a number of different activities which are really all parts of one thing – that is, scenery, costumes, decoration and illustration for the theatre. On the other hand, I am very much drawn to fashion. No doubt my career will develop naturally out of one or the other of these areas. In any case do you still think I should start by attending the Chambre Syndicale de la Couture? If you think otherwise, I should be grateful if you would tell me.'[19]

Charles enrolled his son in the Chambre Syndicale course starting in autumn 1954. Michel de Brunhoff had convinced him that Yves really did have a flair for design, and Charles had abandoned any hope of his going into the law. He had another reason for sending his eighteen-year-old son away from Algeria – the violent clashes between Muslim nationalists and the French forces, which threatened to plunge Algeria into a colonial war.

Until then Algeria had seemed more stable than France's other colonies. There had been nationalist protests in Morocco, Tunisia and Indo-China since the 1920s, but the French influence was stronger in Algeria as the European population was so large that it had been more difficult for the nationalists to build a political base there.[20] By 1954 Muslim militants were stepping up their attacks on French targets across North Africa and the violence had spread to Algeria. Early that year France retreated from Indo-China after a brutal defeat by the Vietnamese nationalists at the battle of Dien Bien Phu, and by summer it was preparing to withdraw from Morocco and Tunisia. The prospect of an independent Algeria no longer seemed improbable. Muslim militants were rallying behind the National Liberation Front, which was committed to expelling the French by force. Anxious to avoid seeing Yves conscripted into the French army, it seemed to Charles that sending him away to study in Paris was a sensible solution.

Yves set off for France that September; this time he travelled alone. Lucienne arranged for him to rent a room in the apartment of a family friend, the widow of a general, on Boulevard Pereire in the seventeenth *arrondissement*, a quiet residential district north of the Arc de Triomphe. He set off from there each day to his classes at the Chambre Syndicale school on rue Saint-Roch, a road running down to the Tuileries Gardens.

Yves disliked his lodgings and was bored by the course, 'learning about the right thread, the cut, all the little things like that'.[21] But he found a kindred spirit among his fellow-students in Fernando

Sanchez, an ebullient young Spaniard. A flamboyant figure, Fernando was as tall and spindly as Yves, with wiry curls and a foppish dress sense. His father had died when he was young, leaving him to be brought up by his Belgian mother, a wealthy woman who pampered him, just as Lucienne had her son. Fernando shared his new friend's interest in art and the theatre, but he was worldlier and more extrovert than Yves. Having persuaded his mother to let him live alone in Paris, he rented a studio on the fashionable Left Bank and took Yves under his wing, organizing escapes from the tedium of the Chambre Syndicale course by taking him off to nightclubs, art galleries, the opera and the theatre.

That autumn Yves re-entered the International Wool Secretariat competition. This time he was placed first, winning three of the seven prizes and easily beating the other finalists, including Fernando and Karl Lagerfeld, a German boy who was awarded first place in the coats section. Yves won the main prize with a sketch of a cocktail dress, which had an asymmetrical neckline and a slim tulip skirt tapering elegantly beneath the knee. At the ceremony, Yves looked younger than his eighteen years with his stern steel-rimmed spectacles and brilliantined crew-cut. His heavy woollen jacket gave him the gauche air of a schoolboy shuffled into his best clothes for a special occasion. L'Écho d'Oran, the Mathieu-Saint-Laurents' daily paper, sent a young fashion reporter, Janie Samet, to interview him afterwards at the Boulevard Pereire apartment. 'We were both very young and nervous about the interview – trembling like fawns,' she recounted. 'He was even younger and shyer than me. But what struck me about him was that, despite his shyness, he knew exactly what he wanted. His ambition was to be a famous *couturier*.'[22]

Yves returned to Oran in triumph that Christmas, elated by his competition success and talking excitedly about his future plans. On his return to Paris that January, his classes at the Chambre Syndicale school seemed even duller, as did life in the rented room on Boulevard Pereire. He told his parents that he was thinking of quitting the course. Charles was so concerned that on 14 January 1955 he wrote to Michel de Brunhoff appealing for help. The tone of his letter was sensible and sympathetic, showing how hard he was trying to understand his son and to do his best to advise him. 'We have received two letters from Yves since his return to Paris after his

Christmas holiday in Oran,' he wrote. 'It is clear to me that he has become very dejected after the thrill of his first term and, above all, his success in the Wool competition. He was full of enthusiasm and plans during the holidays. But I know all too well that the transition from home back to student lodgings can be depressing, particularly after spending a holiday with old friends. It would appear that he also feels disillusioned with his course work and does not find it sufficiently demanding to fill his time. He has pursued various other projects but they don't seem to fill the empty hours in his day and sometimes seem to make him even more depressed. You must have noticed his timidity, and his fear of intruding, so knowing of his great confidence in you, I am taking the liberty of asking you, when you see him, to give him a little help and advice.'[23]

Michel de Brunhoff replied a month later, apologizing for not having written sooner and explaining that he had been in hospital. He told Charles that he had sent Yves to see a friend at the Comédie-Française who had promised to try to find him work as a theatre designer. He concluded by assuring him of his high regard for Yves. 'I am extremely fond of your son and rate his talent very highly. I shall do all I can to ensure that he does find the right niche and that his stay in Paris is a real success.'[24]

He kept his word. A few weeks later Yves went back to see him with yet another set of sketches. De Brunhoff was astonished when he saw the drawings. They looked just like the 'A' Line that his friend, Christian Dior, had designed for his spring 1955 *couture* collection. Michel de Brunhoff had seen the collection privately that morning but it had not yet been shown to the public. A young Chambre Syndicale student could not possibly have known what Dior's designs looked like. De Brunhoff telephoned the *couturier*, knowing that he was about to leave Paris for a vacation, and told him that he had to find time to see Yves before he went. 'Dior agreed to meet me,' said Yves, 'looked at my designs and offered me a job.'[25]

The Dauphin at Dior
1955–1957

When Yves Saint Laurent arrived at Christian Dior's headquarters on 20 June 1955, his first task was to decorate the shop. It was a mundane assignment, but all he could expect as a nineteen-year-old design assistant who had not even completed his course at the Chambre Syndicale. As for Christian Dior, he was the world's most famous *couturier*. 'When I was little and my grandfather asked what I wanted to do when I grew up, I'd say that I wanted to be Christian Dior,' says Christian Lacroix, the fashion designer who was then a boy in Arles. 'He was so famous in France at that time. It was as though he wasn't a man, but an institution.'[1]

Fifty when he hired Yves, Dior was a short, portly man, with a pear-shaped face and doleful brown eyes, whom Cecil Beaton once described as looking like a 'country curate made of pink marzipan'.[2] Fastidious about his dress, he wore a crisp white smock when at work in the *couture* house and was so well-groomed that even his bald pate shone. Christian Dior was courted by the cream of Parisian society and had a client-list that read like a *Who's Who* of the gossip columns with names like Ava Gardner, Marlene Dietrich, Margot Fonteyn and the Duchess of Windsor. Yet he was so shy that he could barely bring himself to bow to the audience at the end of *couture* shows, and so superstitious that he insisted on consulting clairvoyants before taking any important business decisions.

Born in Granville, a lively seaside town on the Gulf of Saint-Malo in Normandy, Dior was the second of five children of Alexandre

Dior, a wealthy fertilizer manufacturer. At his father's insistence Dior enrolled at the prestigious École des Sciences Politiques (nicknamed *Sciences Po'*) in Paris to take a degree in politics. His parents hoped he would become a diplomat, but Dior, like Yves, had set his heart on a career in the arts and eventually persuaded his father to lend him enough money to open an art gallery with a friend. Alexandre Dior agreed but only on condition that the family name did not appear above the door. Galerie Jacques Bonjean opened in 1927 and quickly became an *avant-garde* haunt, exhibiting paintings by fashionable artists such as Georges Braque, Pablo Picasso, Jean Cocteau and Max Jacob, on walls decorated by Christian Bérard.

Disaster struck in 1931 when the death of Christian's elder brother was followed by that of his mother and then by the collapse of the family firm. The gallery closed and for the next few years he scraped a living by auctioning off his art collection and selling fashion sketches to the Paris *couturiers*. Finally he found a job as an assistant to Robert Piguet, who was a respectable figure in the fashion world if not as well known as Coco Chanel and Elsa Schiaparelli, the *haute couture* stars of the day. When war broke out in 1939, Dior was called up as an officer. After France's surrender the following year, there was no point in his returning to Paris as most of the *couture* houses, including Piguet's, had closed. Dior joined his father and one of his sisters at a farm in Caillan, a village in the Var region of southern France, where they eked out a living by selling produce at local markets until he was offered a job back in Paris by the *couturier* Lucien Lelong.

When the War ended France was in ruins, but it was a time of opportunities when new businesses were emerging to replace the old. Dior's chance came when he met an old friend from Granville, who was looking for a fashion designer to start a line of *couture* for a clothing company he managed, Philippe et Gaston. It was one of dozens of companies belonging to Marcel Boussac, the 'King of Cotton', whose business interests ranged from racing stables to newspapers, including *L'Aurore*, a racy tabloid that vied with *Le Figaro* as France's biggest-selling national daily. The son of a successful draper, Boussac had bought up dozens of bankrupt textile mills during the 1930s depression and made a fortune by selling their fabric and clothing to the captive markets of the North African colonies. He agreed to back Dior in his new *couture* venture which, at Christian's insistence, was to be called Christian Dior, rather than Philippe et Gaston.

New *couture* houses usually struggled along on shoestring budgets with a skeleton staff until they could afford proper premises and financial expertise. Pierre Balmain, one of Dior's colleagues at Lelong, set himself up in business after the War with 600,000 francs savings.[3] But Marcel Boussac launched his new business in style with an unprecedented budget of sixty million francs and a staff of eighty-five including Jacques Rouët, a thirty-year-old civil servant who was to be its administrator. The company moved into a modest mansion decorated in Dior's favourite colours of grey and white at 30 Avenue Montaigne off the Avenue des Champs-Elysées, and sent out invitations for its first *couture* show on 12 February 1947, one of the last slots on the spring schedule.

The *couture* trade was in a precarious state. Fabric was in short supply, as were fuel and food. Even the wealthy women who had bought *haute couture* before the War still wore the sharp-shouldered suits with knee-length skirts that they had cobbled together in the Occupation. Some of the Americans who used to come to the Paris fashion shows had returned for the 1946 collections, but not in the same numbers as before.

What Paris needed was excitement. Pierre Balmain had given the press a hint of a softer silhouette at his show that season, but Dior went further. Sensing that the public was ready for something new, he designed a collection reminiscent of the *Belle Époque* style his mother had worn, with soft shoulders, waspy waists and full skirts in luxurious fabrics. The most influential of the journalists there that day was Carmel Snow, the Irish-born editor of *Harper's Bazaar*, the American fashion magazine, who was famous for her tart tongue and her tendency to doze off during the shows. 'She was a drinker,' said a fashion editor of that era. 'We'd watch her snoozing in the front row after lunch. But as soon as *the* dress came on, her eyes snapped open.' Snow stayed wide awake during the Dior collection. 'It's quite a revelation, dear Christian,' she purred. 'Your dresses have such a new look. They are wonderful, you know.'[4]

Other journalists were equally appreciative. The *New York Herald Tribune* hailed the designs as 'the sensation of the season'[5] and Christian

Dior's 'New Look' made front-page news all over the world. 'The New Look wasn't modern,' said Katell le Bourhis, the French fashion historian. 'It was very traditional: a return to the *Belle Époque* ideal of femininity at the turn of the century when everything was so opulent with long skirts, tiny waists, curvaceous lines, beautiful fabrics and crafts. It was exactly what people needed. The War was such a psychological shock that all they wanted was to forget it.'[6]

It is no coincidence that the New Look swept across fashion at the same time as artists and designers in other media were developing new ideas. Jackson Pollock and Willem de Kooning were experimenting with the new school of abstract expressionism in painting. Charles and Ray Eames and the Castiglioni brothers were working with new forms and techniques in furniture design. Although only one expression of the new climate, Dior's fashion was arguably the easiest for the press – and the public – to grasp. His traditional image of femininity also suited the political agenda. While men were away fighting during the War, women had been mobilized to work on farms and in factories. In peacetime they were expected to return to their passive roles as home-makers, leaving their jobs free for the returning soldiers. The official paradigm of postwar womanhood was a caring, capable housewife who had happily forsaken her own career to look after her husband and children. Dior's clothes fitted the bill perfectly.

The new *couture* house was inundated with orders. Rita Hayworth picked out an evening gown for the première of her movie, *Gilda*, and the ballerina, Margot Fonteyn, chose a suit. The excitement generated by the New Look put Paris back on the fashion map and the Americans returned in force for the autumn 1947 shows.[7] The second Christian Dior collection was as well received as the first[8] and the designer was invited to stage a private presentation for the British royal family at the French Embassy in London, although King George V forbade his daughters, Princess Elizabeth and Princess Margaret, to wear the New Look lest it set a bad example to the public at a time when clothes rationing was still in force.

Season after season Dior stuck to the same successful formula. The opulent fabrics and rigidly structured silhouette of the New Look were wonderfully flattering for the middle-aged ladies who patronized the Paris *couturiers*. With each collection Dior made minor modifications to give his customers something new to try, but made sure that they still had their old favourites. 'Bobby', a suit named after his dog, was a best-seller for eight successive seasons.[9] As Jacques Rouët signed contracts with licensees to manufacture Christian Dior accessories, they were included in the shows too. 'Dior was the first *couturier* to present women with a total look,' said Katell le Bourhis. 'He would send a model out with everything: stockings by Dior, bag by Dior, shoes by Dior, even jewellery by Dior.'[10]

Thanks to Jacques Rouët, the house of Dior exerted nearly as much influence over the business side of fashion as it did over design. Before the War, a typical Paris *couture* house was a small operation which made most of its money by selling bespoke clothes to private clients. Some *couturiers* had moved into other areas. Coco Chanel and Jean Patou launched perfumes in the 1920s and 1930s, and in 1940 Elsa Schiaparelli signed a contract with Kayser, an American hosiery manufacturer, to sell stockings under her name, but Rouët was more ambitious for Dior. Within two years of the New Look show he had expanded into furs, opened a luxury boutique on Manhattan's Fifth Avenue and introduced a perfume, Miss Dior, named with the American market in mind.[11] Dior soon showed that he too had shrewd commercial instincts. When in 1948 Rouët thrashed out a contract with Prestige, a New York hosiery company, to manufacture Christian Dior stockings, for the then-enormous sum of $10,000, the *couturier* insisted on receiving a percentage of sales instead of the usual fee. That contract not only set a precedent for Dior's future licensing deals[12] but quickly became standard throughout the fashion industry and is now the main source of many contemporary designers' personal wealth.

By the time Yves arrived at Avenue Montaigne in 1955, Christian Dior was established as the biggest and best-run *couture* business in Paris. Neither of its closest rivals, Pierre Balmain, Dior's old colleague at Lelong, and the enigmatic Spaniard, Cristóbal Balenciaga, was as successful commercially and the pre-war *couture* stars had failed to regain their old stature. Even Coco Chanel received lacklustre reviews when she reopened her *couture* house in 1954 after returning from post-war exile in Switzerland. Her signature style, so popular in the 1920s and 1930s, seemed dated, and her reputation in France was sullied by the memory of her wartime liaison with a Nazi lover.

Yves had joined as Dior's most junior assistant, but he could not have been in a better place to learn how a well-run fashion business worked. Like most *couturiers* Dior operated from a townhouse originally occupied by an aristocratic family, as these were the only buildings in Paris big enough to accommodate everything a *couture* house needed, with enough room for the workrooms, offices, fitting rooms and a *grand salon*, usually the old ballroom, where the shows were staged. Christian Dior had started off at 30 Avenue Montaigne on the corner of rue François-Premier, but quickly expanded into the old houses on either side. By the time Yves arrived, Dior employed twelve hundred people spread across five different buildings and operated twenty-two workrooms.

The highlights of the Dior year were the two *haute couture* shows held in late January for the spring collection and early August for autumn, when more than two thousand people filed in and out of the Avenue Montaigne *salon*. The company staged a dozen or so showings each season. The first two were reserved for the most powerful members of the press and the highest-spending clients – everyone else had to make do with seeing one of the repeats which ran later in the week. Each lasted for up to two and a half hours and included as many as two hundred outfits. The presentations were beautifully staged with fresh flowers delivered each day to decorate the *salon* and crystal flutes of champagne for the audience. The spectators sat on little gilt chairs neatly arranged on the *salon* floor with a gap left in the middle for the models to walk along when they showed off the clothes. Handwritten name-cards were attached by ribbon to the backs of the chairs, to make sure that each member of the audience was sitting in the correct seat; the most important clients were placed at the front alongside journalists from influential publications such as *Vogue*, *Harper's Bazaar*, the *New York Times* and the *Herald Tribune*.

In the mid-1950s the biggest clients were still American, as they had been before the War. Hollywood movie stars and New York socialites stopped off in Paris for the January shows on their way to skiing holidays in St-Moritz and timed their summer holidays on the fashionable French Riviera to fit in with a trip to the July shows. After their first glimpse of the new season's styles at the show, they returned to the *couture* house for a closer look at the clothes and, having placed their orders, made a few more visits for fittings and alterations. Once a woman was established as a regular customer, Dior made a special dummy with her measurements to cut down the time required for fittings, but with every new order she was measured again in case her shape had changed between seasons. The *couture* houses worked hard at courting their clients, assigning a *vendeuse*, or saleswoman, to look after each one and inviting them to cocktail parties or dinners during *couture* week.

A big *couture* house like Dior made most of its money from commercial customers, department stores such as Bergdorf Goodman in New York and Marshall Field in Chicago, which negotiated for the exclusive rights to sell its designs in those cities. Each season the store buyers set sail for Paris on the liner *Île de France* (nicknamed the 'Seventh Avenue Special' in honour of the New York garment district) to place their orders which would be made up by their own *couture* operations, which were fully staffed with specially trained seamstresses and designed to look like replicas of the original Parisian *couture salons*. Marshall Field in Chicago had nine different *haute couture* workshops and a marble lined *salon*, 'The 28th Shop', where the clients went for fittings.[13] Discount chains, such as Ohrbach's, which sold cheap 'knock-off' copies of *couture* designs, were also allowed to attend the shows but only on condition that they guaranteed to buy a minimum number of outfits. On their return to the States, the discounters had to bond their *couture* purchases with US Customs and to promise not to resell them.[14] The originals were copied stitch by stitch into 'knock-off' garments before being given away to their wives, daughters or mistresses.

The models of the 1950s, or 'mannequins' as they were called, came from the same privileged backgrounds as the private clients. Often they saw modelling as an amusing interlude before marriage to wealthy men. Fiona Campbell-Walter, an English girl whom *Vogue* described as being as 'finely bred as a champion greyhound',[15] gave it up to marry the German steel tycoon, Baron Thyssen. Bronwen Pugh, one of Balmain's favourites, became Lady Astor. Dior had a team of a dozen mannequins, who were hired in various shapes and sizes to show how the clothes would look on different customers. Each model worked exclusively for one *couturier*. The schedule of repeat shows was so gruelling that they would not have had enough time to work for more than one, even had they wanted to. As well as appearing in the shows, they were expected to model for private clients when they came to place their orders. The mannequins stayed in the *cabine*, a room set aside for them to dress in, before coming out so the customers could take a closer look at the clothes. They unbuttoned the jacket of a suit to let them see the lining, or whisked off an evening cape, so they could inspect the embroidery.

Then there were the journalists. *Grandes dames*, like the somnolent Miss Snow of *Harper's Bazaar* and Bettina Ballard, the elegant fashion editor of American *Vogue*, spent *couture* week watching the shows from their front-row seats, but they brought teams of assistants and photographers with them to Paris to shoot the latest looks for the magazines. Star photographers worked exclusively for particular titles; Richard Avedon was under contract to *Harper's Bazaar* and Irving Penn to *Vogue*. Fashion assistants were expected to organize the shoots by running around Paris to collect the clothes, and to make sure that the models were ready to be photographed. 'Things were very different then,' said Susan Train, who was a junior on American *Vogue* in the 1950s. 'There'd be just the fashion editor and her assistant with a chauffeur to drive us backwards and forwards. There was no hair-stylist and no make-up artist. You had to do it all yourself. I got very good at a French twist. It was even difficult to get your hands on the clothes. The *vendeuses* wanted the best pieces for their clients. I made friends with the heads of the *cabines* and pleaded with them to lend me the clothes. I soon got to know the back stairs of every *couture* house in Paris.'[16]

The big *haute couture* houses, like Christian Dior, were rigidly hierarchical. At the bottom were the *mains-d'oeuvre* in the *ateliers*, or workrooms, many of whom had worked in *couture* since leaving school in their teens. Renée Cassart joined Dior as a trainee seamstress in the early 1950s at the age of fifteen. 'You started off as an apprentice. You did that for two years: fetching fabric and trimmings, little jobs like that. Then you worked for a year as a *petite main*, supervised by someone who was already qualified. After that you became a *seconde main* and then a *première main*. It usually took at least six years to become a *première main*. If you were very good you might be promoted to *seconde atelier* and then *première atelier*, which meant that you were in charge of the whole workroom.'[17] Different *ateliers* had particular areas of expertise, such as sewing, hat-making or embroidery. They were almost exclusively staffed by women, except for the male cutters in the tailoring workroom.

After the *mains-d'oeuvre* came the *vendeuses*, or sales assistants, who dealt directly with the customers and were expected to be on friendly terms with them. A good *vendeuse* did more than simply take the orders, she made sure that her clients had the pick of the best designs in each season's collection, and tipped them off whenever rare furs or particularly beautiful fabrics became available. Women often came to rely on their *vendeuses* to help with other aspects of their lives, everything from running errands, to recommending doctors or beauticians. Karl Lagerfeld, the German boy whom Yves and Fernando had met at the International Wool Secretariat competition, lodged with his mother's *vendeuse* at Molyneux when he was first sent away from home to study in Paris.

The Dior *vendeuses* came under the wing of Suzanne Luling, a childhood friend of Christian Dior's whom he appointed as his sales director despite the fact that she had never worked for a *couturier* before. Tall and brisk with short brown curls swept away from her face, Luling took care of the social side of the business leaving Dior to lead the quiet life he preferred: dining with old friends, such as Jean Cocteau and Michel de Brunhoff, or pottering with Bobby, his dog, in the gardens of his Fontainebleau mill and at his flower farm near Caillan. Luling was famous for the parties she threw for private clients at her Left Bank apartment on Quai Malaquais overlooking the Seine, and for taking American store buyers out dancing until the early hours of the morning. However late they stayed out, she always managed to report for work at the *couture* house by nine o'clock the next day.

There were three other women on whom Dior depended, the 'three Muses' who had worked with him since the beginning. He had met Raymonde Zehnmacker when he was an assistant at Lucien Lelong and persuaded her to come to Avenue Montaigne with him to take charge of the design studio. Apprenticed to a dressmaker at the age of fourteen, 'Madame Raymonde' learnt her trade the hard way and her practical approach to design often checked Dior's wilder flights of fancy. Invariably good-humoured, with her hair scraped back into a sensible bun, she was the first to step in whenever suppliers posed problems or a model threw a tantrum. After they had finished their work for the day, Yves and the other design assistants would try to coax her into reminiscing about the old days in the *couture* trade or into telling their fortunes with her tarot cards.

Madame Raymonde worked closely with Marguerite Carré, whom Dior had poached from Jean Patou to run his workrooms, together with an *atelier* of thirty skilled seamstresses. A pretty woman with blush-pink skin and heavy dark hair coiled neatly around her head, Carré wore simply-cut clothes, usually in dark shades, with a perfectly positioned brooch or a couple of carefully chosen strands of pearls. An excellent technician, she knew exactly how to execute Dior's instructions and laboured for hours over the tiniest detail of a sleeve, or a bodice, until it was perfect.

The third of the three Muses was Germaine 'Mitza' Bricard, a glamorous figure who had earned her living as a highly-paid call girl before being taken on by Captain Molyneux, one of Dior's favourite pre-war designers, and saw no reason to hide her *demi-mondaine* past. Rarely appearing at Avenue Montaigne before two o'clock in the afternoon, she wore a different outfit every day, usually an exotic creation with a plunging neckline, dramatic jewellery and a dinkily veiled hat. Officially she was employed as a hat designer, but her real role was to tell Christian Dior what was going on in the social scene and to run an exacting eye over his designs.

For Yves, the feminine world of Dior was both alluringly elegant and reassuringly familiar, reminding him of the times he had listened to Lucienne laughing and gossiping with his aunts in Oran. After the trauma of school and the tedium of his Chambre Syndicale course, he had found an adult version of his family home in Saint-Michel. The shyness and sensitivity that his schoolmates had scorned endeared Yves to the women at Dior, who felt tender towards the shy nineteen-year-old far away from his family in Algeria, always taking the trouble to seek him out and engage him in conversation.

Most of the staff were older than Yves, but he made a few friends of his own age. One was Anne-Marie Muñoz, a striking young woman with wavy dark hair and an olive complexion, who had worked there for a few years before his arrival. Her family were friendly with Christian Dior and asked him to give her a job. Anne-Marie was assigned to the workroom but often wandered up to the design studio when she had finished her work and met Yves there shortly after his arrival. She remembered going up one evening and seeing an unfamiliar figure standing beside a door. 'It seemed natural for us to become friends. We were the same age, which created a bond, and there was something about him that I liked as soon as I saw him.'[18]

Yves's other young friend was Victoire, the star mannequin, who had joined Dior in 1953 when she was sixteen. The daughter of a *couture* seamstress, Victoire was an oddball among the aristocratic beauties in the *cabine*, with the sultry look of a Left Bank student rather than their refined debutante features, and at five-foot-five, she was at least two inches shorter than the others. She had started modelling by posing for artists to earn a little extra cash and one of them sent her to see Michel de Brunhoff who bundled her off to Christian Dior with a letter of introduction. 'Monsieur Dior didn't even read it,' she recalled. 'He looked at me and hired me on the spot.'[19] Dior once said that he had taken on Victoire for her 'whiff of Saint-Germain'.[20] Some of his stuffier clients thought her looks were common, but she soon became a favourite of the press, which loved the idea of a working girl modelling for Christian Dior.

Always more comfortable with women than men, Yves had the same easy rapport with Anne-Marie and Victoire as he had with Simone Tronc back in Oran. He drew cartoons to amuse them, which were then passed round to the other employees. One of their favourites was his drawings of a little girl called Lulu, who got up to nasty tricks like setting fire to people's houses and stealing babies from their cradles;[21] soon even Christian Dior started asking to see the latest instalment.

Nan Kempner, the New York socialite, remembered meeting Yves at Dior when she went there in 1958 with her mother, who was a regular client. The teenage Nan spotted the outfit of her dreams: a white sheath dress with a matching coat trimmed with ermine cuffs. On being told that it cost more than her entire clothes allowance, she burst into tears – rather loud tears – only to spot a bespectacled young man poking his head round the door. He smiled sympathetically as Nan pleaded, successfully, with the *vendeuse* to reduce the price of the dress; Yves had come down from the design studio to see what the fuss was about.[22] Years later he remembered his early days at Dior as the happiest part of his career. 'There was laughter all the time. Our studio was just above Monsieur Dior's office. He'd hear us and sigh. "What are you up to again? I wish I could join in." '[23]

Yves felt the same instinctive admiration for Christian Dior as he had for Michel de Brunhoff. He was impressed by what he heard of Dior's lifestyle – the exquisite houses, magnificent art collection and his friendships with Jean Cocteau and Christian Bérard. Even Dior's insecurities struck a chord with the timid Yves who sympathized with his dependence on clairvoyants and the superstitious insistence that every collection had to include a coat called 'Granville' and at least one model wearing a sprig of his favourite lilies of the valley. And Yves respected him for the authority that made him the unchallenged head of the company. 'Dior was a rock, although he didn't always show that side of his character,' observed Anne-Marie Muñoz. 'On the surface he appeared to be gentle and slightly fragile, but underneath he had tremendous strength.'[24]

Dior also had a great deal to teach Yves, as his lengthy apprenticeships with Robert Piguet and Lucien Lelong had given him a formidable command of his craft. Although no fashion innovator, nor even a great technician, he had an unerring eye for proportion and knew immediately whether a fashion sketch was good or bad and what could be done to improve it. 'I had endless admiration for him,' Yves said of Dior. 'He was the most famous *couturier* of the time and had also managed to establish a unique *couture* house, surrounding himself with outstanding people.'[25]

Although courteous towards Yves, Dior was distant with him, as he was with most of his employees, never inviting him to his home, or engaging him in conversation.[26] But having recognized Yves's talent from the outset, he did his best to help by giving him more challenging tasks and taking time to discuss his work. Having started off by decorating the shop, Yves moved on to designing accessories for the licensees and then to submitting sketches for the *couture* collection. The final decision as to whether they would be included was still Dior's, but as the seasons went by more and more of Yves's ideas were deemed acceptable. One of his earliest designs, a long white evening gown, was photographed by Richard Avedon in a famous *Harper's Bazaar* session, 'Dovima with Elephants', shot in 1955 at the Medrano Circus in Paris with the statuesque Dovima posing elegantly, surrounded by circus elephants. While Avedon was finishing the shot, one of the elephants started chewing at the skirt – unfortunately for Dovima who was still wearing it.[27]

Yves settled into a pleasant routine, spending most of the year in Paris but returning to Oran for a few weeks before each show to work on his final sketches. His mother and sisters made a fuss of him, eager to hear about his life in France and the *couture* house gossip. Lucienne loved having a son who not only worked for the great Christian Dior, but also could tell her the Paris fashion news before her friends read about it in the magazines. Yves brought back presents for Michèle and Brigitte, then in their early teens, and special rolls of fabric for his mother. Lucienne took his fashion sketches to the local dressmakers and asked for them to be made up in the material Yves had given her. But the family was under strict instructions to leave him to work in peace during his visits. 'He'd lock himself away in his room and spend the whole day working away at his old school desk,' recalled his mother. 'We didn't dare disturb him and then on the day before his departure he'd show us his sketches.'[28] Yves's trips home were always productive. Anne-Marie Muñoz remembered meeting him in a Parisian bistro one evening on his return from Oran and being shown a suitcase full of sketches and drawings he had completed during his stay.[29]

Back in Paris he often spent his free time with Anne-Marie, or with Victoire, who accompanied him and Fernando Sanchez, his friend from the Chambre Syndicale school, on their evening outings. Less ambitious than Yves, Fernando had found a job as an assistant at Maggy Rouff, a second-string *couture* house, but he never resented his old friend's success and still hauled Yves off with him to Left Bank bars and bistros, and occasionally to formal balls or for weekend jaunts outside Paris.

Sometimes they were joined by Karl Lagerfeld, who had been taken on by Pierre Balmain. A stocky young man with heavy eyebrows, his dark hair slicked into a quiff, Lagerfeld was an only child whose father had made a fortune from the German licence for an American brand of condensed milk, but his parents were as cold and distant with him as Charles and Lucienne were tender towards Yves. His snobbish mother believed that she had married beneath her and had no qualms about reminding her son that he too did not meet her expectations. Karl attributed his quickfire speech to her scoldings. 'I can't bear to hear your ridiculous stories,' she would say when he tried to talk to her. 'Finish them before I get to the door.'[30] When he left Germany to study in Paris at the age of fourteen, his parents gave him a generous allowance, but left him to his own devices. Yves and Fernando often coaxed Karl into driving them around Paris in the convertible car his father had given him, and once he went on a trip to the South of France with Yves and Victoire. Lagerfeld remembered Yves at that time as being 'very cheerful, very funny, très drôle'.[31]

While Yves was enjoying himself, Christian Dior was growing wearier. The relentless round of collections and the burden of running such a big business had aggravated his old anxieties. Yves remembered that 'on the day of a show Monsieur Dior would become so upset that he couldn't even come to the *couture* house. We'd call his tarot card reader, whom he trusted completely, and she'd drive round and round the block with him until he finally agreed to get out of the car. He couldn't get used to the idea that his fashion house had become so big. In the end his success was too much for him.'[32]

The debilitated Dior became increasingly dependent on his prolific young assistant. Yves designed thirty-five outfits for the 1957 autumn collection, more than any Dior junior had done before. One of his designs was the 'chemise', a waistless dress which was absolutely the opposite to Dior's customary hourglass silhouette but was typical of the softer, more modern looks that Yves was persuading him to include in the collections. Lucienne came to see him in Paris that summer, arriving on the eve of the show. It was her first visit since Yves had joined Dior and he was thrilled to see her, whisking her off to dinner at a restaurant where they ran into Suzanne Luling. 'Why Yves,' she chided with professional tact, 'you should have told us you had such a pretty mother.'[33] The next day Luling mentioned the meeting to Dior who summoned Lucienne to see him. Yves ushered her up to Dior's office and was asked to leave them alone. 'I remember it perfectly,' recounted Lucienne. 'He made some complimentary remarks and then said "Yves is the one who'll succeed me." At the time I didn't really understand. Dior was still young, sixty at the most.'[34]

Dior was actually only fifty-two and his twenty-one-year-old assistant was not at all sure that he wanted to take over from him. Happy though he was at Dior, Yves was tiring of fashion, as Michel de Brunhoff had warned. He had seen what success as a *couturier* had done to Christian Dior and wondered whether he would be happier designing for the theatre. But he said nothing to his colleagues and when the fittings for the autumn collection were finished, Dior took off as usual for a rest cure at his favourite spa town of Montecatini in northern Italy. 'Don't worry,' he told Suzanne Luling the day before his departure. 'I'm leaving you with Yves.'[35]

Ten days after his arrival at Montecatini, Dior had a heart attack. After dining with friends one evening, he went up to his room to rest. His friends found him there, collapsed on the floor, and summoned a doctor and priest to see him. It was too late; by the time they got there, Christian Dior was dead.[36] Marcel Boussac sent his private plane to Montecatini to bring the body back to Paris.

The funeral was held on 29 October at the Chapelle Saint-Honoré d'Eylau in Paris. Some 2500 people attended the service, including Yves and the rest of the staff with hundreds of Dior's famous friends and clients led by the Duchess of Windsor as guest-of-honour. The coffin was covered with his favourite lilies of the valley and taken away to be buried beside his father's in the family vault at Caillan. *Le Monde* hailed Christian Dior as a man who 'was identified with good taste, the art of living and refined culture that epitomizes Paris to the outside world. One can thus claim that a significant part of France's prestige is due to this man.'[37]

The fashion world was rife with rumours about the future of the business. 'Dior's death was treated as a national tragedy,' recalled Susan Train of American *Vogue*. 'Everyone was very nervous and concerned about the future of the house. Dior had put Paris fashion back on the map after the war. The New Look had really brought the buyers and manufacturers back to France. When he died it was "Good God, what's going to happen to that house?" It was really important to the fashion world.'[38]

Marcel Boussac was tempted to cut his losses and close down the company. The Dior licensees, all of whom stood to lose lucrative businesses if he did so, gathered at Avenue Montaigne after the funeral pleading with Jacques Rouët to persuade Boussac to change his mind. After ten days' deliberation Boussac relented.

On 15 November 1957 Jacques Rouët called a press conference at the *couture* house and read out a formal statement to the reporters confirming that Christian Dior would stay in business. 'The studio will be run by Madame Zehnmacker, the *couture* workshops by Madame Marguerite Carré,' it said. 'Mitza Bricard will continue to exercise her good taste over the collections. All the sketches will be the responsibility of Yves Mathieu-Saint-Laurent.'[39]

3   On the Trapeze
                             1957–1960

No sooner had Jacques Rouët said the name Yves Mathieu-Saint-Laurent than the journalists turned to stare, pens poised over their notebooks, at the bespectacled twenty-one-year-old sitting shyly beside the three Muses. By then Yves had worked at Dior for three years, but he was barely known outside the company. Christian Dior had considered telling the press about his contribution to the last collection before he left for Montecatini, but had not found time to do so.[1] 'Nobody knew Yves but the Dior inner circle,' said Susan Train of *Vogue*. 'If you worked as an assistant in the design studio of a great *couture* house people didn't know who you were. And Yves was so terribly, terribly young. Paris wasn't youth-minded in those days. The people at Dior must have known they were taking a bit of a gamble.'[2]

Yves had nine weeks to prepare for the next show. He stayed in Paris for a few days after the press conference, and then left for Oran to work on his final sketches just as he had done when Christian Dior was still alive. He sealed himself away in his room with Lucienne and his sisters fluttering outside. For once he showed no signs of nervousness. 'I prepared that collection in a complete state of elation. I knew I was going to be famous.'[3]

He knew exactly what he was going to do. Dior had refined his designs over the years, but stuck to the same feminine silhouette and the luxurious fabrics that had sealed the success of the New Look. His middle-aged clients loved it, but the horsehair padding and starched skirts were too stiff and heavy for younger *couture* customers, who prefered the softer, less structured style of Cristóbal Balenciaga's 'sack' dresses. 'Christian Dior's collections looked amazing, but they had nothing to do with the practicalities of modern life,' recalled Anne-Marie Muñoz. 'Yves was always obsessed by making elegant, comfortable clothes which would be easier for women to wear.'[4] Yves had already introduced more fluid forms like the 'chemise' under Dior's supervision, now he had a chance to express his ideas more freely. But for his first collection he decided to compromise by finding a way of doing so without straying too far away from the traditional Dior repertoire.

By the time Yves returned to Paris, the frenzy of speculation about Christian Dior's successor had reached fever pitch.[5] On the day of the show, 30 January 1958, the Avenue Montaigne *salons* were packed with people. Cars were parked crazily on either side of the street outside. Scores of passers-by and hangers-on huddled on the pavement to ogle the celebrities as they arrived and to await the final verdict.

They did not wait for long. The applause started as soon as the first models strode into the *salon* wearing dainty dresses that dropped down from their shoulders to hover playfully at the knee. There were jaunty swing coats, ballerina ballgowns with organza skirts and slim suits with waist-length jackets. One ballgown was called 'Lily of the Valley' after Christian Dior's favourite flower. Yves's designs were as opulent as Dior's with the same impeccable proportions: but he had removed the padding, linings and stiffeners to reconstruct Dior's style in a lighter, livelier vein. He called it the 'Trapeze Line'. 'No one had done the trapeze dress since the early eighteenth century,' observed Katell Le Bourhis. 'Saint Laurent created change at Dior, but he did it within the house tradition. He kept the richness and luxury – the organza skirts, the magnificent fabrics and the elaborate embroidery that the clients loved. But he changed the lines.'[6]

The audience adored it. 'An American fashion editor sitting in front of me rose to her feet with tears in her eyes,' recalled Marie-José Lepicard. 'There were two French women next to me also crying. One turned to the other and said "My dear, France is saved. It's Joan of Arc." I remember thinking that was a ridiculous thing to hear from a woman who had lived through the War.'[7]

After the tears and cheers, so many people surged forward to congratulate Yves that he was led away to a tiny balcony looking down on to Avenue Montaigne to acknowledge the applause of the crowd below. Dozens of photographers perched perilously on other balconies to take his picture. A priest stood staring up at the *couture* house wondering what the excitement was about. 'The collection was a delight,' said the journalist, Janie Samet, who had interviewed Yves three years before for *L'Écho d'Oran*, and had since become a fashion editor on *L'Aurore*. 'He was *le petit prince* and everyone adored him.'[8]

Paris was plastered with newspaper placards the next day shrieking 'Saint Laurent has Saved France!' and 'The Great Dior Tradition Will Continue'.[9] The verdict of the international press was equally flattering. The *New York Times* declared that 'Today's collection has made a French national hero out of Dior's successor, Yves Saint Laurent and comfortably assures the future of the house Dior built.'[10] The *Herald Tribune* thought: 'It seemed impossible that Dior himself wasn't coming out at the end . . . Everybody was crying. It was the emotional fashion binge of all time.'[11]

Yves Saint Laurent (the 'Mathieu' and the hyphens were too much for the foreign press) was famous. On the evening after the show he was taken to dinner by the three Muses, Jacques Rouët and Suzanne Luling to Maxim's, a fashionable restaurant on rue Royale, to meet Jean Fayard, a diarist on *Le Figaro*. Fayard described Yves as '*le plus zaouï des zaouïs*', the 'hippest of all the hip cats' who was 'as tall as a reed and so thin in his pristine jacket, with shy eyes blinking behind his spectacles and a mouth always on the brink of a polite smile'.[12] The interview was clearly something of an ordeal for Yves, whose replies became progressively shorter until Suzanne Luling stepped into the breach and answered the questions for him.

Far from dampening the media's interest, Yves's reticence inflamed it. A self-effacing boy from Oran was more appealing to the press than a blustering boy-wonder, a real *zaouï*, would have been and Yves conformed completely to the French cliché of a shy, hypersensitive prodigy. Pictures of the new Dior collection were splashed across the covers of *L'Express*, *Paris-Match* and other weekly magazines. 'I have an incredibly clear image of the first time I saw the name Yves Saint Laurent,' recalled Christian Lacroix. 'I was about six years old and he appeared on the cover of *Paris-Match*, standing between two models – one in a bridal dress and the other in a red trapeze coat. At the time it was like being on the cover of *Time* magazine.'[13]

Twenty-one when he took the helm of Christian Dior, Yves was highly intelligent and imaginative but, in many respects, extremely immature. Despite having done well academically, he regarded his schooldays as a failure and had not managed to complete his Chambre Syndicale course; nor had he attempted the university degree or stint of military service which were regarded as the traditional rites of passage for young men of his age and class. The happiest periods of his life had been spent at home with his family as a child and as an apprentice among the affectionate women at Dior; but in both situations he was treated as a boy, not a man. Only a few years before, his father had written to Michel de Brunhoff expressing concern about his son's 'timidity'. Yves had grown in confidence since then, buoyed by his success at Dior and his friendships with Fernando, Anne-Marie and Victoire, but he was still ill-equipped to cope with his new role as one of the most famous men in France and the public face of a company with over a thousand employees.

Yves's first collection for Dior was an indisputable triumph, but the logistics of the *couture* business meant that he would have to repeat that success in six months' time – and then again and again. Each season he would be subjected to the same scrutiny from the press, the American store buyers and the Dior clients who did, of course, have plenty of other *couturiers* competing for their dress allowances. The speculation as to whether he could pull it off started immediately after the first show. 'There was always gossip about whether Saint Laurent had really done it all on his own, or if Christian Dior's other assistants had helped him,' said Marie-José Lepicard. 'He was very timid and he seemed so fragile. Everyone knew he was extraordinarily talented, but they wondered whether he'd be able to keep it up.'[14]

Yves had seen for himself how Christian Dior had buckled under the pressure. They shared the same nervous disposition, but Dior had founded his company at the age of forty after graduating from university, serving as an officer in the army and experiencing a tough but character-building period of poverty after his father's business collapsed. With all that behind him, he still struggled with the twin pressures of fame and his responsibilities to his employees. Yves Saint

Laurent had found himself thrust into a similar position at half Dior's age and with a fraction of his experience.

There were some compensations, one being an *entrée* to the glamorous Parisian social scene. Everyone, but everyone, wanted to meet the saviour of Christian Dior, including Marie-Louise Bousquet, one of the grandest *grandes dames* in Paris and an important client of the *couture* house. Fabulously rich and passionate about art, Marie-Louise held open house one evening each week at her mansion on Place du Palais-Bourbon behind the National Assembly building to which she invited anyone in Paris who attracted her interest, as well as any intriguing foreigners who happened to be passing through the city. A great friend of Christian Dior's, she was anxious to meet his successor and asked Raymonde Zehnmacker to bring Yves to dinner a few evenings after the show. Anxious that he should feel at ease, she invited two other young men to join them, the painter, Bernard Buffet, with his lover and business manager, Pierre Bergé.

Buffet was a rising Paris art star, whom Yves had long admired. He set off for dinner that evening looking forward to meeting the artist; but it was his companion who caught his eye. Pierre Bergé was a supremely self-confident young man of twenty-seven who was the opposite of Yves Saint Laurent in almost every respect. He was short while Yves was tall, and stocky while Yves was slender. Bergé had wiry brown hair combed back over a high forehead, an agile face with a long, pointed nose and an apparently inexhaustible supply of energy. He had opinions, strong opinions, about art, opera, politics, literature, the theatre, movies, music and absolutely no hesitation in expressing them. Having known Dior socially, Pierre was invited to attend Yves's debut show. 'I thought it was wonderful. I didn't know anything about fashion at the time, but it was obviously a triumph.'[15] As for Yves, he had the same delicate looks and soulful persona that Pierre had fallen for in Bernard Buffet: but unlike the artist, who irritatingly was becoming increasingly independent, the young *couturier* seemed engagingly vulnerable. Bergé's first impression of him was as 'a strange, shy boy' who 'wore very tight jackets as if he were trying to keep himself buttoned up against the world'.[16] For both men it was what the French call *un coup de foudre*, love at first sight.

Pierre Vital Georges Bergé was born on 14 November 1930 in Île d'Oléron, a prettily wooded island surrounded by sandy beaches and oyster beds off the coast of Vendée in western France. His mother was a schoolteacher and his father a tax inspector. When Pierre was a boy the family moved to the town of Lisieux in nearby Normandy, and then moved again to the port of La Rochelle where he attended the local *lycée*. He was a studious child, obsessed by literature and politics; his parents expected him to go to university and, if he did well there, to study for a second degree at one of the élite *Grandes Écoles* in preparation for a career in the law, medicine or the civil service. Pierre wanted none of it. After toying with becoming a doctor, he set his heart on a literary career. A few weeks before he was due to take his *baccalauréat* he left school and home, to go and live in Paris. 'I didn't want to get caught up in the system. I'd decided that I wanted to become a journalist or a writer. So I went to Paris to get on with it.'[17]

He rented a room near the Place de la République, a run-down area of eastern Paris, and eked out a living by buying and selling secondhand books. Early each morning he went to the *bouquinistes*, the little bookstalls clinging to the stone walls on either side of the Seine, to look for first editions that he could sell on at a profit to antiquarian bookshops. His evenings were spent rambling around the bars and cafés of Saint-Germain-des-Prés. It was the late 1940s, an exciting time to be in Paris, when American jazz stars, like Miles Davis and Lester Young, were playing in the jazz clubs and new books were being published by Jean-Paul Sartre and Simone de Beauvoir. Flinging himself into politics, Bergé joined a group of peace campaigners led by Garry Davis, an American actor and former bomber pilot who hit the headlines in 1948 when he renounced his United States citizenship outside a United Nations session at Palais de Chaillot. During one of Davis's demonstrations, Pierre was arrested and thrown into prison for the night with a cellmate, the writer, Albert Camus. When they were let out the next morning, the two men went off for breakfast together at Brasserie le Duc on nearby Place Trocadéro.[18]

After his release Pierre founded a political paper, *La Patrie Mondiale* (The Global Fatherland), to propound the merits of world peace and global citizenship, which had become a fashionable cause as a reaction against the nationalism that triggered World War II. *La Patrie Mondiale* was launched in 1949 as one of dozens of political periodicals surfacing in Paris at that time. Having persuaded Garry Davis to be its sponsor, Bergé begged, or bullied, other famous names to contribute. In later years he was wont to exaggerate the paper's influence, telling Jane Kramer of *The New Yorker* that Jean-Paul Sartre and Raymond Queneau had written for it, when in fact they had not.[19] Only two editions of *La Patrie Mondiale* were actually published and most of the articles were written by Pierre Bergé, although he did extract contributions from some well-known names: Albert Camus, Jean Cocteau, André Breton, Jean Giono and Bernard Buffet.

Born in Paris the year before Bergé, Bernard Buffet was then twenty-two and just starting to make his mark as an artist, having gleaned good reviews for the few exhibitions he had staged since graduating from the École des Beaux Arts. The two men met in a small Saint-Germain art gallery opposite one of the antiquarian bookshops where Pierre went to sell his *bouquiniste* finds. 'I thought I had met Rimbaud,' he said, convinced at the time that Buffet was a genius who had discovered 'a new language in painting'.[20]

He took charge of Buffet's career, applying the same energy he had once ploughed into *La Patrie Mondiale* to persuading art galleries to show his work and drumming up commissions. Bernard Buffet soon became one of the most sought-after artists in Paris, painting everyone from the dancers at the Paris ballet, to Christian Dior, who hung his portrait in pride of place in the *salon* of his Fontainebleau mill. His work had an angular, almost abstract style that gave the subjects a mournful air rather like the artist himself who, as one critic observed, 'looked just like one of his own paintings'.[21]

The talented artist and his amusing partner were welcomed by Paris society. Pierre drifted away from his Left Bank haunts to become a regular guest at the *soirées* held by Marie-Louise Bousquet and Marie-Laure de Noailles, the bohemian socialite whose grandmother, Laure de Chevigné, was the model for the Duchesse de Guermantes in Marcel Proust's *Remembrance of Things Past*. He and Buffet rented a *château* near Aix-en-Provence for the summer, where they held open house for friends and were invited to join a party of French artists travelling around the States on a *Vogue*-sponsored tour. 'We ended up in New York and Pierre invited us all out to lunch at some posh restaurant,' said Susan Train, who accompanied them on the trip. 'It was a really chic place, one of those *soi-disant* French restaurants in Manhattan where they make a point of snubbing everyone. Well, Pierre certainly snubbed them. He ordered wood-smoked salmon, but when they sent it over he was horrified. He sent it straight back. I just thought – wow!'[22]

When Pierre met Yves at dinner with Marie-Louise Bousquet that night, he fell for him with the same fervour he had once felt for Buffet. 'Pierre's a real Scorpio,' said Train. 'He does everything whole-heartedly. Things are either good or bad, black or white. Scorpios have a hard time seeing any of the shades in between.'[23] Besides, he and Buffet were already drifting apart. Bernard had met a young writer, Annabel Schwob, with whom he had begun an affair. 'Pierre and Bernard were together, then Buffet met Annabel,' said a friend of that era. 'They weren't going to be a happy threesome with Pierre for long – and then Yves came along.'

By the end of that year Buffet and Annabel were married: they later had three children. Pierre moved into an apartment on the Île Saint-Louis, the seventeenth-century island on the Seine in the heart of Paris, and began a relationship with Yves. Each was a perfect emotional complement for the other. Like many people who have grown up in cold, distant families, Pierre felt more comfortable providing emotional support than he did receiving it, and Yves was an eager recipient, needing someone to offer the unconditional love his family had given him. Like Yves, Pierre had known he was homosexual from an early age but he seemed to have found it less problematic. 'It's a question of environment. My family was fairly liberal and I came to Paris when I was eighteen. By the time I was twenty-one or twenty-two I'd met people like Jean Cocteau. If you moved in those circles it was perfectly acceptable.'[24] His attitude helped Yves to forget the humiliation of his encounters with the Arab streetboys in Oran, and gradually to feel more comfortable about his sexuality.

And Pierre was fun. He whisked Yves off to hear Maria Callas at the Paris Opéra, took him to see new plays, gave him the latest books to read and showed him off at the Paris *soirées*. They befriended the novelist, Françoise Sagan, whose first book, *Bonjour Tristesse*, was a huge hit in France.[25] A striking woman with strong *jolie laide* features and a thick blonde bob, she was only a year older than Yves but had published three novels by the time they met and become something of a celebrity. Pierre also introduced him to some of the people he and Bernard Buffet had known through Marie-Laure de Noailles and Marie-Louise Bousquet. Yves befriended Jean Cocteau, then in his late sixties. who gave him a drawing as a gift that Christmas; and he met Roland Petit, the young choreographer whose *Carmen* had caused such a sensation. Petit offered Yves the chance to fulfil his old ambition of designing for the theatre by asking him to create the costumes for his new ballet, a production of *Cyrano de Bergerac* at the Théâtre de l'Alhambra.

Most of Yves's time was taken up by his duties at Christian Dior. As soon as the fittings for the first collection were completed, he was sent off on a promotional tour of the United States, followed by trips to London, Brussels and even to Moscow, where the Soviets were slowly opening up to foreign trade in the Khrushchev thaw. Yves was well received wherever he went. 'He had real charm and grace,' said Claude Brouet, then a fashion editor on *Elle* magazine. 'He was young and handsome, in a rather romantic way. His rich clients and important journalists loved him. They were *femmes d'un certain âge* and he was their *petit prince* at Christian Dior.'[26] Within the company Yves was more popular than ever as the staff, many of whom had been fond of him since his arrival, were now grateful to him for saving their jobs after Dior's death. He did not have the same status, or power, as Dior, being restricted to the role of chief designer, with the three Muses left in charge of their domains; but that situation suited everyone, including Yves. 'He didn't change the working patterns of the house at all,' recalled Anne-Marie Muñoz. 'He couldn't have done even if he'd wanted to. Dior was a machine, an incredible efficient machine with these powerful women in charge of different areas. Yves had enough to do getting on with his own work, without crossing swords with them.'[27]

By the time he started work on the next collection for autumn 1958, Yves felt ready to be a little bolder with his designs. The result, the 'Arc' Line, was looser and lighter than the 'Trapeze', and considerably longer as he dropped the hems by three inches to below the knees. There was applause from the younger spectators at the show that July, but older clients were less enthusiastic and the other *couturiers* were livid. Yves Saint Laurent had broken one of the unwritten rules of the fashion industry – never, ever move hemlines by more than two inches in one season.[28]

The following season Yves played safe with the 'Long' Line, a classically pretty collection for spring 1959 which *Le Figaro* praised as 'a real triumph'.[29] Buoyed by that success,[30] he felt ready to be braver again when he tackled his fourth collection, which included 'hobble' skirts that hovered well above the models' knees. Eugenia Sheppard, a petite American blonde with a doll-like appearance that belied her occasionally poisonous prose, who had taken over as fashion editor of the *Herald Tribune*, described 'a moment of stunned silence' falling on the Dior *salon* when the first 'hobble' appeared and the 'Dior personnel went a little green about the gills'.[31] Rather than staying on to sip their customary glasses of champagne after the show, some journalists hurried out of the *salon* to telephone their editors with the news that there was another fashion sensation at Christian Dior.

The hullabaloo over the 'hobble' disguised a serious debate within the fashion world. For decades the Paris *couture* houses had created luxurious looks for their predominantly middle-aged customers, which were then copied into cheaper clothes for the public. By the late 1950s the fashion pendulum was swinging away from Paris and away from clothes for *femmes d'un certain âge.* The young consumers of Yves's generation were brought up in the buoyant postwar climate. They expected their lives to be different from those of their parents and to set their own agenda rather than accepting the *status quo.* Their main influences were the American images that blasted into postwar Europe through their record-players, televisions and radios. There was abstract expressionism in art, Elvis Presley's rock-'n'-roll in music, the Beats in literature, and the films of James Dean and Marlon Brando at the cinema. The mood of youth in the late 1950s was fresh, feisty and anti-establishment. It had everything to do with the *zaoui* lifestyle of Left Bank jazz bars and nothing to do with the rituals of *haute couture*.

The new mood was already filtering through to fashion. The casual clothes worn by Audrey Hepburn when she whizzed around Rome on the back of Gregory Peck's Vespa in *Roman Holiday* were copied in the Saint-Germain jazz clubs. The Paris *couturiers* faced a new source of competition from Valentino, Pucci, Capucci and the other

Italian designers whose sporty styles were more in tune with the times than elaborate French elegance. Gucci, the Florentine leather firm, became a cult among the 1950s jet-set for its leather loafers and cane-handled bags. The hottest new American designers, Anne Klein and Claire McCardell, worked in a similarly sporty vein. Even *Vogue* was moving away from the stylized perfectionism of photographers like Irving Penn, famous for flying plane-loads of equipment to another country just to work in a particular room, to the irreverent style of Antony Armstrong-Jones, Princess Margaret's future husband, who shot his *couture*-clad models in comical situations, tumbling off boats or falling asleep on deckchairs while the tide rolled in.[32]

Yves was not really a *zaouï*. He led a gilded life behind the closed doors of Christian Dior, at the *soirées* of Marie-Laure de Noailles and Marie-Louise Bousquet, with a wardrobe that ran to Ivy League suits and corduroy jackets, not motorcycle leathers. But he was young and perceptive enough to see the changes around him on the Paris streets and in the Left Bank bistros he visited with Pierre, Victoire, Fernando and Françoise Sagan. He took his work as a *couturier* far too seriously not to see it as a means of expressing his ideas and impressions; yet each time he moved closer to imposing his vision of modernity on the Dior collections, as he had with his 'hobble' skirts, he was attacked by the press, by the conservative Dior clients and by Marcel Boussac's managers. 'They were businessmen and they were very nervous about what Yves was doing,' said Anne-Marie Muñoz. 'They'd had ten years of incredible success with Christian Dior. Suddenly everything changed. They had to deal with someone new and they felt insecure.'[33]

Marcel Boussac had no hesitation in conveying his displeasure, not only to Yves but to the three Muses, who still exercised considerable influence over the collections They worked closely with him on his initial designs and sat in on the rehearsals for the shows when Yves decided what each model would be wearing. Photographs of Avenue Montaigne at that time show Yves sitting in the middle of a row of hard-backed chairs with a couple of matronly women on either side of him. After the 'hobble' furore his colleagues advised him to play safe again and he did so, creating an elegant but restrained look for spring 1960. 'The loveliest thing to hit Paris for years,' beamed Eugenia Sheppard in the *Herald Tribune*. 'It puts Saint Laurent out of reach of the gloom-mongers, who have been busy as bird-dogs since Dior died.'[34]

Not for long. The 'bird-dogs' were back when he unveiled his new line for autumn 1960, the 'Beat' collection which made even the 'hobble' seem tame. It was Yves Saint Laurent's homage to the Left Bank beatniks. He had adopted the styles that the art students were wearing in the Saint-Germain jazz clubs, but made them up in exquisite *couture* fabrics. There were skimpy bubble skirts in sleek wool, slinky black turtlenecks in finest cashmere and gleaming crocodile-skin jackets lined with mink. It was the first time that such a close approximation of street styles had been seen on an *haute couture* catwalk.

'*Liberté, liberté chérie!*'[35] clucked *Le Figaro* in a parody of beatnik slang, while hinting at its true opinion of the 'Beat' collection by burying the Dior report among a round-up of the previous day's shows, rather than splashing it across the front page as it usually did.[36] But the 'Beat' found a few fans among the young *Vogue* editors.[37] 'A black *blouson* with a fur collar – it was a pretty luxurious *blouson noir*!' enthused Susan Train. 'Though the "Beat" collection was a bit of a shocker for the *couture* clients, especially for Dior's *couture* clients.'[38]

They were horrified. Dior's customers were notoriously conservative. They had once boycotted one of Christian Dior's own designs just because he called it the 'Jean-Paul Sartre'. The middle-aged ladies in the Dior front row had no desire to squeeze into bubble skirts and, for them, a *blouson noir*, or black jacket, was slang for the hooligans who raced against their chauffeurs in the Paris traffic and made them feel nervous about wearing quite so much jewellery when they ventured out on the streets.

Marcel Boussac loathed the 'Beat' look too. Having been paid back handsomely for his investment in Dior when Christian Dior was alive, his profits were now imperilled by the whims of a stubborn young man in his early twenties. 'Those street inspirations all seemed very inelegant to a lot of people sitting on the gilt chairs of a *couture salon*,' admitted Yves years later. 'But this was the first collection in which I had tried hard for poetic expression in my clothes.'[39] His yearning for 'poetic expression' and Marcel Boussac's equally intense desire for profit were becoming increasingly incompatible. Crisis loomed. But the Boussac camp had already found a solution, as Yves

Mathieu-Saint-Laurent was to be called up to serve in the French army as a conscript in the Algerian War.

The situation in Algeria had deteriorated steadily during Yves's five years in Paris. The conflict between France and the Muslim nationalists was brutal, with both sides being accused of barbaric practices.[40] As the death toll rose, public opinion in France swung against the war; but the French army, still stung by its defeat in Indo-China, was determined to fight on in Algeria. When General de Gaulle returned to power in 1958 he was intent on ending the fighting swiftly; but in the meantime, anxious not to alienate the army, he stepped up the conscription campaign.

Technically Yves had been eligible for military service since he left the Chambre Syndicale course, but until then Christian Dior had been able to use its political influence, not least Marcel Boussac's power as a press baron, to stop him from being drafted on the grounds that, as Dior's chief designer, he was too important to the French economy to be lost to the army. Securing exemptions became much more difficult once De Gaulle's conscription drive got underway[41] and the conservative press, led by Boussac's L'Aurore, started to attack draft-dodgers, particularly famous ones. By early 1960 Marcel Boussac had decided that he could not – or would not – block Yves's call-up papers again. Yves Mathieu-Saint-Laurent was told to report for military service on 1 September 1960. Jacques Charrier, a pop star who was married to the actress Brigitte Bardot, received his draft at the same time. L'Aurore and other French newspapers hailed the news that two such prominent people were joining the war effort as a patriotic triumph.

Yves was in despair. After the misery of school he had enjoyed five happy years at Christian Dior, only to be forced to give up his glittering career and his relationship with Pierre to join the army. He knew exactly what it would be like – 'school all over again'.[42] Everyone in France had heard stories about the dreadful conditions that conscripts were subjected to, the dilapidated barracks, atrocious food and outbreaks of violence. And Yves had no illusions about how damaging it would be professionally. The fashion world was fickle. He would be in the army for at least two years, plenty of time for new *couture* stars to emerge and for his successes at Dior to be forgotten.

As 1 September approached, Yves grew more and more despondent. By the time Pierre took him away to the South of France for a few weeks in the sun after the 'Beat' show, he was inconsolable. They joined Susan Train who was staying at a rambling old family house owned by Alice Chavanne, an editor on *Elle* magazine, in the village of Le Cannet in the hills above Cannes. 'Poor Yves was in a terrible state. All he and Pierre could talk about was the army and his fears. We kept on trying to distract him by dragging him off on to boats, or to go swimming. But he just couldn't stop thinking about it. He was the most miserable boy I've ever seen.'[43]

The Ten of Clubs
1960–1962

The army was not like school: it was worse. Yves was sent to a regimental barracks outside Paris where he was to complete a military training course before being dispatched to Algeria. He had no illusions of being fit or tough enough to cope with the training and barrack life was unbearable. The buildings were squalid, cold and draughty, and the food virtually inedible. Forced to surrender all but a few of his personal possessions, Yves had to exchange his clothes for a rough army uniform and to sleep alongside his fellow conscripts in a communal dormitory.

He had nothing in common with them. At that time the French army lumped everyone together, regardless of education or social status. Most of the conscripts who were drafted with Yves were *mecs*, working-class men, who had never met anyone like him before and were not impressed with what they saw. Yves had lost some of his old timidity during his happy years in Paris, but only within the privileged circle around him at Dior. His reticence and frailty, even his job as a *couturier*, made him appear feeble and effeminate to his barrackmates. At best he was a figure of fun to them, at worst a suspected *pédé*, who was fair prey for whatever verbal assaults or physical abuse they chose to subject him to. The gulf between Yves and his barrackmates was even wider than it had been with the middle-class *colons* back at school in Oran; and whereas there he could count on the teachers to help fend off the bullies, the army officers had as low an opinion of their famous recruit as the national servicemen.

Worst of all was the threat of what might happen once they arrived in Algeria. The French army used conscripts for policing duties, leaving the fighting to professional soldiers. It seemed harsh enough to Yves that he would have no say in where he was sent to, or what tasks he would be asked to do, but he had no illusions about how dangerous his duties in Algeria might be. The French army might distinguish between civilians and soldiers, but the Muslim nationalists did not. They were notorious for their brutality towards the French. The bombing of civilian targets was commonplace, as were attacks on conscripts. One of their favourite forms of execution was known as *le grand sourire*, or 'the wide smile', whereby they slit their victims' throats and left them bleeding to death.

Yves did not even have the consolation of suffering in an honourable cause. The conduct of the French Army in Algeria was just as bad as that of the nationalists. Although reports of civilian casualties and the torturing of Muslim captives did not appear in conservative French newspapers, such as *L'Aurore* and *Le Figaro*, they were routinely reported in left-wing publications and by the international press. The intellectuals with whom Yves and Pierre mixed in Paris saw the Algerian War as a national disgrace, likening France's treatment of the African nationalists to the Nazi atrocities towards the Jews in World War II. Yves had lost a life he loved to find himself trapped in intolerable conditions, possibly risking death for a cause he despised.

He lasted in the barracks for nineteen days until 20 September 1960 when he broke down and was admitted to the Bégin Military Hospital at Saint-Mandé in the Bois de Vincennes on the eastern outskirts of Paris. The only news of his whereabouts to the outside world was a short statement in *Le Monde*. 'Mr Yves Mathieu-Saint-Laurent, who has for the past few seasons been a stylist at the house of Dior, was conscripted several days ago but is now under observation at the military hospital. Although the army refuses to disclose any information about one young man among so many others, it does confirm that the state of health of Mr Saint-Laurent, who had been suffering for several months from a nervous depression, rendered this step necessary.'[1]

None of his friends was surprised. 'Yves a soldier?' snorted Victoire. 'You might as well try to turn a swan into a crocodile.'[2] 'It was perfectly obvious he was going to have a breakdown,' said Susan Train. 'He'd been put into an impossible situation. It wasn't as though the French army in those days could find anything useful for him to do. He was put into uniform and forced to live rough with the butcher, the baker and the candlestick-maker. For a boy like Yves it was impossible.'[3]

Their sympathy turned to fury when Christian Dior announced that it was appointing a new chief designer. 'When Yves was in the hospital, Jacques Rouët arranged to see me early one morning saying he had something to tell me of great importance,' recalled Pierre Bergé. 'He said he'd done everything he could to help Yves, but it was no use. He had been told to call a press conference at eleven o'clock that morning to announce that Yves was to be replaced as he was too ill to continue working at Dior.'[4]

Yves's replacement was thirty-four-year-old Marc Bohan, who had made his name as a talented assistant at Jean Patou before being poached by Dior to be the designer at its London *couture* house. The appointment had an air of permanence. Bohan's style was more conservative than Yves's, closer to the grand Dior tradition and, to Marcel Boussac's relief, he was a calmer, more placable character. Reluctant to carry on working at Dior without Yves, Anne-Marie Muñoz resigned and found a job with another *couturier.* The fashion editors who had followed Yves's progress since his first collection were indignant too, convinced that Marcel Boussac had deliberately allowed him to be drafted into military service. 'People were very angry when Saint Laurent went into the army,' recalled Marie-José Lepicard. 'They were worried about him, worried about the effect on the house and furious at the way Dior replaced him so suddenly with Marc Bohan.'[5]

Yves spent fifteen days at the Bégin hospital before the doctors pronounced him fit to return to barracks. Anxious to avoid the risk of embarrassing publicity if he had another breakdown, the military authorities intervened and sent him off for further treatment at Val-de-Grâce, a mental hospital in southern Paris. It was there that his real nightmare began.

Val-de-Grâce was typical of the mental institutions of the early 1960s. It looked like a nineteenth-century house of horror, filthy and unheated with bars at the windows. Psychiatry was then one of the least fashionable forms of medicine and many of the doctors on the hospital staff were only there because they were too poorly qualified to get jobs elsewhere. The nurses were little better. Most subscribed to the old-fashioned school of psychiatry that considered patients to be clinically ill and a menace to society with no hope of recovery. Electric shock treatment was standard practice, as was sedating patients with huge doses of tranquillizers. Modern methods of treatment, such as psychotherapy and counselling, were virtually non-existent.

The staff had little sympathy with their charges, who ranged from people with critical conditions to unfortunates like Yves who had ended up there because of more mundane nervous disorders. Some of the inmates were seriously deranged, manic in their behaviour and prone to outbursts of violence; the staff were too busy dealing with them to bother with milder cases such as Yves's. Whereas his condition might have elicited sympathy at a more liberal institution, the people charged with looking after him at Val-de-Grâce probably despised him. He was, after all, an army drop-out, a famous one at that, who, given the political climate in France at the time, would have been seen as a cowardly draft-dodger deserving whatever was coming to him.

When Yves was first admitted to the hospital, he tried, half hysterical and half despairing, to escape; after that the doctors pumped him full of sedatives each morning. Many of the drugs routinely administered at institutions like Val-de-Grâce in the early 1960s have since been banned because of their dangerous side-effects. The mental hospitals of that era were so poorly regulated that there is no accurate record of the type of medication given to Yves, but it is probable that he received regular doses of drugs such as chlorpromazine, which was then commonly used as a tranquillizer or anti-depressant. Chlorpromazine is still used in cases of schizophrenia, but can be damaging if given to patients with other conditions, exacerbating their anxieties and sometimes causing alarming hallucinations. There is no record of the quantities of drugs Yves was given, but it seems likely that the doses would now be regarded as dangerously high. He recalled one of his doctors bragging about it. 'He told me that he had given me the strongest dose of tranquillizers that can be administered to anyone. He said to me: "Just watch, you'll be back on them." '[6]

Day after day Yves was left alone, too sedated to move, on a makeshift bed often with soiled sheets. He barely ate, or even drank anything, for weeks. As autumn set in and the temperature dropped, the room became damp and chilly. The final humiliation was the behaviour of the other inmates. Only the most violent were locked up all day, the others wandered around the hospital in varying degrees of mania. Yves remembered being 'stretched out in a room, alone, with people coming and going all the time. Crazy people. Real crazies. Some of them tried to fondle me, but I wouldn't let them. Others started screaming for no reason. It was enough to drive anyone to despair. I was so frightened that I only went to the bathroom once.'[7]

The contrast with the life he had left could not have been more marked. Only a few weeks before Yves had been surrounded by people who cared for him deeply and considered it their object in life to make him happy, but at Val-de-Grâce he was locked away in barbaric conditions, completely isolated from his friends. Visitors were banned by the hospital authorities. None of Yves's friends or relatives, not even his parents, were permitted to see him. Lucienne made a special trip from Algeria to plead with the general of Yves's regiment to help him, but to no avail.[8]

One friend refused to give in. Day after day since Yves's admission Pierre Bergé had driven down to Val-de-Grâce from the Île Saint-Louis to beg the hospital administrator to let him see Yves. When his pleas failed, Pierre resorted to bullying, telling him that Yves was a famous man with influential friends and leaving him in no doubt as to who would be blamed if anything went wrong. Eventually he was given permission to visit Yves on a daily basis and to take fruit, flowers and other presents into the institution. All the Mathieu-Saint-Laurents could do was wait for Pierre's bulletins, while he stepped up his efforts to get Yves out of Val-de-Grâce. He lobbied politicians, civil servants, military officials – anyone who he thought might be able to bring influence to bear on Yves's behalf. Finally he succeeded. Yves Mathieu-Saint-Laurent was released from hospital on 14 November 1960, the day of Pierre Bergé's thirtieth birthday, and discharged from the army on the grounds that he was too ill for military service.

Yves looked like a shadow of the distraught young man who had dreaded being drafted into the army less than three months before. His weight had dropped to eighty pounds, far too low for a man of his age and height; his face was drawn and gaunt, with dark shadows around the eyes. Fraught and fractious in the months before he went into the army, Yves now seemed steeped in depression, his speech still slurred from the after-effects of the shock treatments and the powerful shots of sedatives he had been given. Victoire remembered him seeming 'so distressed, so numb and alone'.[9]

The news from Dior did nothing to help. Yves had hoped to be able to go back to his old job there, at least for a short time; but Marcel Boussac was pleased with Marc Bohan's work on the spring collection and had no intention of replacing him. Jacques Rouët spoke up on Yves's behalf, suggesting that Boussac should set him up in business in his own *couture* house as he had done for Christian Dior. Boussac declined. His only concession was to offer Yves the position in London that Bohan had relinquished to return to Paris. He must have known that Yves would refuse.

Yves and Pierre had already discussed what to do if Dior did not take him back. 'He said that he'd have to set up his own *couture* house and that I should help him,' said Bergé. 'I'd never, ever wanted to be a businessman. But I agreed to do it for him.'[10] Pierre's first step was to take Yves to see his lawyer to find out whether he had grounds to sue Christian Dior for breach of contract. The lawyer assured them that Yves had a strong case and a writ was issued, demanding immediate reinstatement or financial compensation. It would be months before the case came to court, as the first hearing was scheduled for May 1961, so Pierre took Yves away on holiday, to convalesce in the Canary Islands.

The weeks of torment at Val-de-Grâce left an indelible mark on Yves Saint Laurent. Someone with a more robust constitution might have been able to cope, but Yves was too fragile. He had been sensitive as a child, and the bullying at school had aggravated the nervy, introverted side of his character. As an adult he had enjoyed a few happy years as an apprentice at Christian Dior, until Dior's death plunged him into a turbulent period, oscillating between pride in his achievements and panic at the pressures of fame and responsibility. The weeks of worry before he went into the army had ground him down and his misery in the barracks led inexorably towards a breakdown, but his incarceration at Val-de-Grâce was the final blow. It was too much for Yves at a time when his spirit was shattered and he was doped up by drugs, his physique weakened by weeks without proper food or sleep. The after-effects would haunt him for the rest of his life.

After his release Yves was in no condition to cope with the demands of daily life, relying on Pierre to make any practical arrangements on his behalf and to deal with the legal arrangements for the Dior court case. Pierre helped him to settle back into his apartment on Place Vauban, a pretty sandstone crescent near the gilded dome of Les Invalides in the seventh *arrondissement*, one of the smartest parts of the Left Bank, and dispatched Bernard, who had been his own manservant for nearly ten years, to look after Yves there.

Yves's last hope of reinstatement at Christian Dior vanished on 26 January 1961 when Marc Bohan unveiled his first collection, which was given the same rapturous reception that had greeted Yves's 'Trapeze' Line three years before. *Le Figaro* hailed the show as an 'unqualified success' and restored the Dior report to its old slot on the front page. The article did not mention Yves and ended with the wish that Marc Bohan would have 'a long and brilliant career at Dior'.[11] Yves had some friends left, notably Eugenia Sheppard, whose *Herald Tribune* column was now syndicated to scores of local papers across the States, making her by far the most influential journalist at the Paris shows. Sheppard had not forgotten her old favourite, although she too was full of praise for the new Dior designer. 'I never meant to like the Marc Bohan collection for Dior and I already had a poisoned typewriter ribbon ready. I was deeply pro-Yves Saint Laurent, the boy wonder designer who succeeded Dior and who may or may not have got a dirty deal from the boss when the army took him from his job. But Marc Bohan is wonderful. His new collection should be the commercial hit of all time. If I could just see a rosy future coming up for Yves Saint Laurent, I'd sit myself right down and have a good cry.'[12]

Yves soon tasted revenge by winning his legal case against Dior. The judge found in his favour, ordering Christian Dior to pay him 430,000 francs damages in lieu of notice and 250,000 francs for breach of contract. Yves and Pierre were jubilant, but 680,000 francs was not enough money to open an *haute couture* house. Marcel Bousssac had spent ten times as much on launching Christian Dior fifteen years before. Pierre set about raising more money in the hope of being ready to present the first collection at the spring shows the following January.

He found them temporary headquarters in a tiny two-roomed apartment at 66 rue de la Boétie, an inauspicious street running northwards from Avenue des Champs-Elysées to the Saint-Lazare railway station. 'It wasn't much, but at least it meant that Yves had somewhere to look at fabrics and people could come to see us.'[13] Victoire left her job in the Dior *cabine* to join them, as did Claude Licard, another of Yves's Dior colleagues, who was given Raymonde Zehnmacker's role as head of the design studio.

The rue de la Boétie offices were sparsely furnished with a couple of chairs that Pierre and Victoire had found at a flea-market and a desk rigged up by flinging a slip of fabric over a rickety old table. Neatly-framed sketches of Yves's costume designs for Roland Petit's *Cyrano de Bergerac* hung on the wall, as did the drawing that Jean Cocteau had given him. The only other ornaments were a portrait of Christian Dior and a photograph of Zou Zou and Églantine, the dogs that Yves had left with his family in Algeria.

He still showed the after-effects of his confinement at Val-de-Grâce. In photographs taken at that time, Yves looks thin and pale with a forlorn air that contrasts sharply with Pierre's purposeful vigour and Victoire's easy smiles. Even his clothes had become more ascetic. At Dior he had worn casual corduroys and jaunty reefer jackets, saving suits for formal occasions. Since his return to Paris he wore suits all the time, usually skinny tailored styles in sombre grey cloth with narrow-collared white shirts and dark silk ties. He swapped the steel-rimmed spectacles he had worn since school for heavier tortoiseshell frames with dark lenses to ward away the light on sunny days, and his hair had grown out of its old crewcut to be combed back above his forehead.

Old friends rallied round. Françoise Sagan, who had just had a success on the stage with her first play, *Château en Suède*,[14] often called at Place Vauban with her sister, Suzanne, in the evenings. After drinks they bundled Yves and Pierre into Françoise's little sports car to drive them to dinner at Maxim's or for more drinks at Régine's, the hot nightclub of the moment. Roland Petit lifted Yves's spirits by asking him to design the sets and costumes for another ballet, *Les Forains*. He had become fond of Yves since their collaboration on *Cyrano*, as had his wife, Zizi Jeanmaire, who invited him to create the costumes for her new show, the *Spectacle Zizi Jeanmaire*, due to open that autumn at the Théâtre de l'Alhambra.

Pierre ensured that each piece of good news was leaked to the press, making the most of their friendship with Zizi, who was one of France's most popular entertainers and a style icon of the era with her boyishly cropped hair and long, elegant legs. When Yves designed the outfits that Zizi and Victoire wore to the wedding of the banking heiress, Philippine de Rothschild, Pierre tipped off his newspaper contacts so that the name Yves Saint Laurent appeared in the gossip columns again. He even persuaded *Paris-Match* to publish a photograph of Yves and himself clinking celebratory glasses of champagne with Victoire and Claude over upturned packing cases when they first moved into rue de la Boétie.

But months went by and they still did not have enough money to produce a collection. Pierre kept the company afloat by selling the Île Saint-Louis apartment that had once seemed the perfect base for a fashionable young man-about-town and moved in with Yves at Place Vauban. 'The thing that no one but me seemed to realize was that Yves had nothing to live on. He hadn't earned a franc, not a *sou*, since he left Dior. So I sold my apartment. I didn't get much for it but it was enough to keep us going for a while.'[15] He knew that if they did not show that January, they might have missed their chance. By then it would have been eighteen months since Yves's last Dior show, the public would be beginning to forget him and it would be even harder to find a financial backer.

Pierre did his best to stop Yves from discovering how desperate things were, by spinning reassuring stories about how he was about to hook an important investor, or would soon start hiring more staff. It was he who had made most of the financial sacrifices, selling his apartment and some of the art he had amassed during his relationship with Bernard Buffet. Yves carried on living in comfort, looked after by his *valet de chambre*, Bernard, in the bright, sunlit rooms on Place Vauban with his theatrical commissions from Roland Petit and Zizi Jeanmaire to keep him busy during the day. But he knew that things were not going as well as Pierre was pretending and Victoire remembered him tumbling into bouts of despair, until Pierre tersely told him to 'pull yourself together'.[16]

Even Pierre's confidence was faltering. With only a few months to go before January *couture* week, he had already asked all their rich friends and acquaintances to lend them the money, or to rustle it up from other people on their behalf, but to no avail. One day he received a call from Suzanne Luling, who doted on Yves and had promised to help them, despite the fact that she still worked for Dior. She asked Pierre to join her for lunch with a Swiss financier, who was a friend of one of her cousins. The financier specialized in spotting investment opportunities in Europe for wealthy foreigners and had one client, J. Mack Robinson, an American businessman, who might be interested in backing them. The American had plenty of money to invest and was familiar with Yves's work, having heard about his success at Christian Dior.

There was a popular myth in postwar France that a long-lost 'American Uncle' might arrive at any moment to shower his French family with dollars. Jacques Tati made a film, *Mon Oncle*, about one of these apocryphal transatlantic philanthropists, but it looked as though Pierre Bergé had actually found one. Jesse Mack Robinson, or J. Mack as he liked to be called, was a tall, heavy man in his late thirties with an easy smile and an unmistakable Southern drawl. A self-made millionaire, he was a high school drop-out from Atlanta, Georgia, who had earned his own living since the age of twelve, when he got his first job as a route carrier for the *Atlanta Journal*. By the early 1960s J. Mack had made a fortune from his secondhand car dealerships and motor-loan companies.

He also owned a couple of small insurance businesses, one of which had some spare cash lying idle in a Swiss bank account. J. Mack instructed his lawyers to begin negotiations with Pierre Bergé and then arranged a meeting with him in Zurich. They thrashed out a deal whereby he would invest up to $700,000 in Yves Saint Laurent over the next three years in return for eighty per cent of the equity and a firm promise that his identity would be kept secret.[17] The deal was signed on 14 November 1961, Pierre's thirty-first birthday and a year to the day after Yves's release from Val-de-Grâce.

The 'American Uncle' arranged an overdraft facility for them at the First National City Bank of New York. Pierre no longer needed to concoct consoling stories for Yves, they could actually start putting the collection together. Never having run a fashion business before, he asked the *couturier*, Madeleine de Rauch, for advice. She sent one of her accounts clerks to help and arranged for them to move into the disused offices of Manguin, a small *couture* house on rue de Hanovre that had recently closed, while they searched for permanent premises.

Anne-Marie Muñoz handed in her resignation at the *couture* house she had joined after Yves's departure for the army. 'My boss there always said that my heart wasn't in it, and of course it wasn't. I told Yves I'd be waiting to join him whenever he was ready, so I left to go and work for him as soon as I could.'[18] Gabrielle Buchaert, one of the Dior press officers, called to see if Yves needed anyone to handle publicity. 'I'd really enjoyed working with him before. He was so charming and talented. Looking back I don't know how I had the nerve to do it, but I phoned him.'[19] Some of the Dior *mains-d'oeuvre* followed him too. Renée Cassart joined Yves Saint Laurent as a *seconde atelier* after Esther, her elder sister, was made a *première*. 'We all knew how talented he was. The move there meant promotion for me and it was an adventure.'[20] The defections became too much for Christian Dior, which slapped a writ on Saint Laurent accusing it of using underhand tactics to poach its employees. But by the time the writ arrived the damage was done; they had hired all the Dior staff they needed.

Yves and his new team started work on the spring collection in the old Manguin workrooms, while Pierre hunted for permanent premises. They needed a townhouse, something similar to the original Dior headquarters at 30 Avenue Montaigne, which would be big enough to house the workrooms and offices with a spacious *salon* where they could show the collections. Only a few suitable places were available in Paris at the time. One was Hôtel Forain, once the home of Jean-Louis Forain, a moderately successful turn-of-the-century artist best known for his caricatures. The building itself was fine, if a little higgledy-piggledy; but the location was a problem. Hôtel Forain was tucked away on rue Spontini, a dusty little street between Avenue Foch and Avenue Victor Hugo in the sixteenth *arrondissement*, only a stone's throw from the leafy Bois-de-Boulogne, but miles away from the other *couture* houses.

The sixteenth *arrondissement* is a residential district, the home of many of France's wealthiest financiers and industrialists. Some of Yves Saint Laurent's future clients doubtless lived in the expensive apartments along Avenue Foch and Avenue de Malakoff, but it was too far out of town for Pierre's taste. He was dead set against it, whereas Yves liked Hôtel Forain at first sight. His mind was made up when he went down to the cellar and spotted a playing card lying face down on the floor. It was the ten of clubs, one of his luckiest cards.[21]

One omen was enough. Yves was as superstitious as Christian Dior had been. Clubs were his lucky cards, diamonds and spades were unlucky. He adored dogs, but hated cats and was terrified of birds. 'Whenever I see them I think I'm in a remake of an Alfred Hitchcock movie.'[22] The ten of clubs was an excellent sign. Pierre protested, but Yves had his way as usual. They took the lease on Hôtel Forain.

There were only a few weeks to go before the show on 29 January 1962. The staff had to be transferred from Manguin, fabrics and finishings had to be ordered and the entire building redecorated. Yves had the walls painted white and the offices furnished in a simple modernist style with Mies van der Rohe's leather and chrome Brno chairs.[23] Cassandre, the famous French graphic artist, designed a logo entwining the letters Y, S and L in an elegant typeface. Yves sketched frantically while Pierre bullied the builders and chivvied suppliers. 'He seemed to be running around doing everything,' recalled Renée Cassart. 'I even remember him going out to buy food for us when we were working late at night.'[24]

Money was tight despite J. Mack Robinson's overdraft. Yves was a perfectionist and having only ever worked within the well-run machine of Christian Dior, he was used to having the best of everything at his disposal – from the finest fabrics to the most expensive trimmings – and Pierre would not have dreamt of refusing him. Then there were the bills for the show: flowers, champagne, make-up artists and Alexandre, Yves's favourite hairdresser. Pierre persuaded some people to work on the collection for nothing and pleaded with others to wait to be paid until the orders came in.

Even so they needed more money. One way that other *couturiers* raised cash to offset the cost of their collections was by charging an entry fee to commercial clients, or by asking them to guarantee to buy a certain number of outfits and to pay in advance. Pierre decided to ask for more money than their rivals: $1,000 as an advance, or a $400 entry fee for those that did not want to buy. No one baulked at the prices, even though there were rumours running around Paris that Yves Saint Laurent did not have enough money to complete the collection in time. Bergdorf Goodman, I. Magnin, Lord & Taylor, B. Altmann and the other big American stores snapped up tickets and by the end of December all the seats were taken. 'Everyone was so excited about it,' said Marie-José Lepicard, who had left Paris *Vogue* to become a fashion editor on *Jardin des Modes.* 'We were longing to see what Yves Saint Laurent would do.'[25]

On Thursday, 25 January, four days before the Saint Laurent show, Marc Bohan unveiled his third collection for Dior which, like the first two, was praised by the press.[26] 'Dior Changes Everything' trumpeted the headline in Marcel Boussac's *L'Aurore* above two photographs of ecstatic spectators racing to embrace Marc Bohan.[27]

The YSL team busied themselves with the final preparations for their show. Gabrielle Buchaert spent the weekend shepherding around a crew from *Life* magazine, which planned to publish a photospread on the dress rehearsal. Yves and Pierre snatched a few hours of sleep on Saturday night, but worked round the clock on Sunday as Yves agonized over the final details of his designs. Eventually Pierre hauled him off to a nearby bistro for a late-night dinner, only for Yves to beg to be taken back to the studio. 'We were beginning to feel tired. But at two o'clock in the morning Yves decided he wanted to add another design to the collection. It wasn't until six o'clock in the morning that we were even able to take a shower.'[28]

By half-past-eight that morning rue Spontini and the surrounding streets were choked with traffic. There were still two hours to go until the start of the show but spectators were arriving early to make sure of their seats and long lines of people queued up outside the door. The Comtesse de Paris, one of the most important women in French society, came at half-past-nine, accompanied by her two daughters, and Yves had to tear himself away from making last-minute adjustments to his designs to greet them. Zizi Jeanmaire appeared in a flash of paparazzi camera bulbs, clad in a crisp white duffel coat with Roland Petit at her side. Lucienne sat in pride of place in the front row, and Brigitte and Michèle, who had been treated to a special trip to Paris to see their twenty-five-year-old brother's first solo collection, were given seats outside in the gallery. Photographers snapped the celebrities as they arrived: Helena Rubinstein, the cosmetics tycoon, the nattily-dressed Françoise Sagan and Marie-Louise Bousquet, the woman who had brought Yves and Pierre together. She was seated in the front row, as were influential editors such as Edmonde Charles-Roux of Paris *Vogue* and the *Herald Tribune*'s Eugenia Sheppard.

The show started at half-past-ten when Victoire walked into the *salon* to a reassuring round of applause wearing a pink and green checked suit with Helena Rubinstein's 'Doll Pink' lipstick. Yves had not taken any chances. This was his first opportunity to do exactly what he wanted without Marcel Boussac and the three Muses looking over his shoulder, but he was not yet ready to make the most of his freedom. Still shaken by his experience at Val-de-Grâce, he had completed the collection in very little time under arduous circumstances and plumped for the quietly elegant vein of his most popular designs for Dior: youthful rather than young, and very, very chic. One of the mannequins wore a jewelled heart encrusted with false stones that he had adopted as his lucky talisman. After checking that each model was correctly dressed and accessorized, Yves darted off to stand beside a screen separating the backstage area from the *salon*, peering nervously through a tiny hole to see how the audience was responding.

Two hours – and 104 outfits – later the show was over. The audience clapped and cried 'Bravo'. Yves was pushed out into the *salon* to take a bashful bow. Zizi Jeanmaire raced to embrace him and he collapsed in tears on her shoulder surrounded by scores of photographers. So many people surged forward to congratulate him that he ran into a cupboard to hide. There were screams from the crowd as a potted plant wobbled precariously, threatening to topple over into the throng. Pierre Bergé climbed on to a chair and shouted out directions to friends who were trapped in the crush.

Reports of the first Yves Saint Laurent show were splashed across the front pages of newspapers all over the world. There was no clear verdict. 'Poor Yves!' wailed the *Daily Express* in Britain,[29] whereas *Women's Wear Daily*, the powerful American trade paper, argued that if there was a battle between Saint Laurent and his old employer,

Yves had won.[30] Patricia Peterson, the *New York Times*'s fashion editor, delivered a balanced judgement. 'Everyone wanted this young man to have a staggering success that would make fashion history. It is hard to live up to such high expectations and Saint Laurent, although he produced a very good collection, did not say anything new.' But – 'This morning's collection, while not as dazzling as his first, did prove that he can go it on his own without the vast machinery of Dior behind him.'[31]

The reaction of one paper was, in its way, more damning than 'Poor Yves!' in the *Daily Express*. Marcel Boussac's *L'Aurore* ran daily reports on all the Paris *couture* shows, but there was no mention of Yves Saint Laurent in the next day's paper. 'Perhaps the fashion editor genuinely didn't like the collection, or perhaps she was acting on Marcel Boussac's instructions. I honestly don't know,' said Janie Samet, who attended the rue Spontini show as part of the *L'Aurore* team. 'But it went down very badly with Pierre Bergé, Yves Saint Laurent and everyone else at that house.'[32] They started as they meant to go on. So what if *L'Aurore* was one of France's most powerful newspapers? Pierre Bergé sent a letter to *L'Aurore* banning its journalists from all future Yves Saint Laurent shows – exiling them from Hôtel Forain.

The Scent of Success
1962–1965

Once the fittings were completed Yves and Pierre took off for a fortnight in Marrakesh, the Moroccan city which was then becoming fashionable among young Parisians. After years of living in the beiges of sandstone and stucco Paris, Yves was happy to be back in North Africa. Marrakesh is a beautiful city with the highest of the Atlas Mountains looming above it, and the vestiges of colonialism were less oppressive there than in Algeria.[1] The French had restored the *medina*, the rosy-stoned old town, rather than ripping it down as they had done in Oran, and the daily life of the city seemed not to have changed for centuries. There were no streetlights or traffic lights; goats and sheep wandered around the narrow streets. The locals wore traditional robes in the vivid pinks, blues and violets of Delacroix's paintings. Yves and Pierre spent their days lounging on the leafy verandas of the Mamounia, the old Art Deco hotel where they were staying, and their evenings exploring the labyrinth of *souks* and alleyways that rambled down to Djemaa el Fna, the square at the heart of the *medina*.

On their return to France one topic dominated the newspapers and radio bulletins – Algeria. After seven years of conflict, the situation had hit crisis point. The war was never popular with the French, but public opinion swung firmly in favour of withdrawal when the OAS, *l'Organisation de l'Armée Secrète*, an underground movement of *pied noir* extremists, started attacking political targets on mainland France. The violence escalated after General de Gaulle started peace talks with the nationalists.[2] When the two sides finally agreed terms for a settlement in spring 1962, Algeria was flung into chaos as nationalist factions jostled for power and Muslim militants vowed revenge on the OAS extremists. Oran, long a right-wing stronghold, had been the scene of some of the most brutal OAS atrocities, and the mood there was particularly tense.

Recognizing that Independence was inevitable and frightened by the threat of reprisals, many of the Mathieu-Saint-Laurents' friends had already left Algeria, but Charles and Lucienne stayed on. At fifty-three, Charles had no desire to abandon his comfortable life in Oran to start again in France, a country he had never really liked, having been miserable there for much of his time as a student. But as Independence approached on 1 July 1962, even he had to accept that staying on in Algeria was too dangerous for a middle-aged French couple with two young daughters; one of whom, Michèle, was barely out of her teens, and the other, Brigitte, still only seventeen.

In the end they had no choice. Oran became a bloodbath as vengeful Muslims attacked the OAS extremists. The Mathieu-Saint-Laurents fled to safety in France, taking Bri-Bri, their pet mongrel, and the few possessions they could carry. Everything else, the contents of the Saint-Michel house and Trouville villa, were left behind with most of their money. They arrived in Paris, frightened and bewildered, turning to Yves for help. He and Pierre could do little for them financially. The *couture* house was only a few months old and, having sunk their savings into launching the business, all they had to live on were the salaries they had negotiated with J. Mack Robinson. There was not enough room at Place Vauban for the Mathieu-Saint-Laurents, and Yves was still terrified by the thought of Charles discovering his homosexuality, which he would have been bound to do had he lived with them. He and Pierre found a small rented apartment where the family could stay. Lucienne and the girls soon recovered their good humour, but Charles found it harder to adjust to the change in their circumstances, missing the warmth and vibrancy of North Africa.

For Yves, the family's flight from Oran marked the final break with his childhood. His feelings towards Algeria had always been confused, with nostalgia for his boyhood at Saint-Michel and love for the landscape clashing against miserable memories of school and contempt for the petty *colon* culture. During his first few years in Paris he had used his parents' house as a refuge, but he had gone there less often as he became absorbed by his life with Pierre. Now there was no home to return to, and his relationship with his family had changed irrevocably.

Lucienne's love for Yves was unquestioned, but it had always been Charles to whom he had turned for practical support. Their relationship had never been easy. It must have been hard for Charles to see his wife becoming so besotted by their son, and he may have found it difficult when the twenty-one-year-old Yves suddenly became so famous. But he had always done his best to help him and, as his letters to Michel de Brunhoff showed, Charles was not only well aware of Yves's emotional fragility, but had gone to great lengths to accommodate it. It is indicative of how heavily Yves depended on him that when he went to live in France he looked for another father-figure, eventually finding one in Pierre Bergé. Now Charles was too preoccupied by his own problems to play his old role as Yves's protector. As a prosperous businessman in his fifties, he had probably expected to be thinking about winding down towards retirement; instead he had lost much of his money and faced the challenge of building a new life in a foreign country. He was no longer capable of supporting Yves as he had done in the past and, in any case, Pierre Bergé was now fulfilling that role.

Pierre had gradually supplanted Charles as Yves's father-figure during the five years of their relationship. It was he, not Charles, who was responsible for getting Yves out of Val-de-Grâce, for orchestrating the legal battle against Dior and for setting him up in his own *couture* house. Charles's predicament now made his take-over complete. Emotionally Pierre was completely bound up by their relationship; friends say that he spoke constantly of Yves, but rarely mentioned his own family. 'He was totally, totally obsessed by Yves,' said one. 'His first and only objective was to protect him and make him happy.' It is a sign of how secure Yves felt within their relationship that, although distressed by his family's plight, he did not allow it to distract him as it might have done in the past. The Mathieu-Saint-Laurents arrived in Paris only a few weeks before the presentation of his second collection, but Yves was single-minded enough to press ahead with the preparations for the show.

This time he had started off relaxed and refreshed after the trip to Marrakesh, knowing that the rue Spontini staff would be able to plan a proper schedule for the collection, rather than cobbling it together in a hurry as they had done with the first one. Tellingly Yves felt ready to be more adventurous with his designs, creating a collection which was close in spirit to his most innovative work for Dior, rather than the subdued style of his debut.

The clothes were stunningly sophisticated with a hint of street chic. The highlight of the show was a series of suits with tubular tunics and slinky skirts hovering on the knee, made from black *ciré* satin and trimmed with mink. This time the reviews were unreservedly enthusiastic. 'There is no doubt that Saint Laurent stands head and shoulders above most of the *haute couture*,' reported the *New York Times*,[3] while the show was hailed as 'a smash hit' on the front page of the *Herald Tribune*.[4] The movie star, Elizabeth Taylor, placed an order; as did Helena Rubinstein, the cosmetics empress. When Paris *Vogue* hit the news-stands that September, the outfit on the cover was by Yves Saint Laurent. It was his second Paris *Vogue* cover since the 'Trapeze' collection at Christian Dior.

Yves Saint Laurent opened his *couture* house at a time when there was a thirst for something new on the fashion scene. American politics had skipped a generation when John F. Kennedy was elected president in 1960. Michel Foucault, Roland Barthes and Claude Lévi-Strauss were making waves among the French intelligentsia; as were the *nouvelle vague* directors, Jean-Luc Godard and François Truffaut, in films. The music scene exploded in 1962 with the release of the Beatles' first single *Love Me Do*, in Britain and Bob Dylan's first album in the States. A new wave of 'pop' artists breezed into the art world. *The New Realists*, a group show featuring the work of Andy Warhol, Roy Lichtenstein and Claes Oldenburg was the smash of the 1962 Manhattan art season. A few months later a group of British pop artists – David Hockney, Allen Jones and Peter Blake – took the Paris Biennale by storm.

The fashion industry needed its own star to epitomize the new era. The youngest, freshest looks came from the boutiques of Emanuelle Khanh in Paris and Mary Quant in London, but their clothes were cheap and casual, aimed at girls in their early twenties rather than at the *couture* market which was still seen by the press as the centre of the fashion scene. American and European newspapers carried daily reports of the *couture* shows, often running front-page stories if there was a really special collection. Yves had created plenty of front-page sensations with his controversial designs at Dior, but the *couture* scene became subdued after his departure for the army. There had been no real leader of the *couture* since Dior's death. Coco Chanel had regained a little of her old lustre since her disastrous comeback collection in 1954, but all she did was refine her old styles for the faithful customers who had patronized her for years. Marc Bohan's classic designs were still popular with Dior's clientèle, though too conservative to make front-page news. Stung by bad reviews in the mid-1950s, Cristóbal Balenciaga had banned the press from the first presentation of his collection, as did Hubert de Givenchy. Since then they had only allowed journalists to see them three or four weeks later, *after* the clients had placed their orders.

'It was a real problem,' recalled Susan Train of *Vogue*. 'We'd always covered the January collections in the March issue and the July collections in September. All of a sudden the clothes from those two houses weren't available in time. Screams, yells, etc. For years people had to come back to Paris to cover their collections. Even then, Balenciaga was terrible. He didn't want the press, didn't like the press, didn't need the press. Givenchy was easier. We just did lots of stories on Audrey Hepburn (the movie star who was one of his favourite clients) wearing the clothes. But the fact that two such big houses weren't showing gave a better shake to young designers. Saint Laurent benefited from that. He became the new leader of the pack.'[5]

Yves was also fortunate in that the opening of his *couture* house coincided with the arrival of new faces in some of the most powerful posts in the fashion press. Diana Vreeland, the imperious fashion editor of *Harper's Bazaar*, was poached by American *Vogue* in 1962 to remould the magazine for the 1960s.[6] It is always easier for a new editor to make their mark on a magazine when there is a dramatic change in taste, and Vreeland made the most of the explosion of energy in pop music and the art scene, hailing Yves Saint Laurent as the *couturier* for the pop generation. Beatrix Miller followed suit at British *Vogue* when she became its editor-in-chief two years later.

The most timely appointment for Yves and Pierre was that of John Fairchild as editor-in-chief of *Women's Wear Daily*. Tall and courtly, Fairchild looked and spoke like a preppy patriarch, rather than a rag-trade publisher. Born in Newark, New Jersey in 1927, he was educated at Kent, an expensive Episcopalian prep school in Connecticut, and then at Princeton. He had hoped to become a doctor, but was corralled into the family firm, a publishing company founded by his grandfather and, at twenty-four, was sent to Paris as a reporter for *Women's Wear*, one of its most profitable publications. When he arrived, the most accurate indication of the magazine's status was that its reporters were relegated to the back row of the shows, with those of other trade titles. By the time he returned to the States in 1960, with a string of scoops in his wake, it was elevated to the front row alongside *Vogue*, *Harper's Bazaar* and the *Herald Tribune*.

As editor-in-chief, John Fairchild turned *Women's Wear Daily* into a social gazette, as well as a trade paper, cataloguing the activities of the fashionable new First Lady, Jackie Kennedy, whom he dubbed 'Her Elegance', with the Duchess of Windsor and Audrey Hepburn cast in supporting roles as 'The Impeccables'. Like Diana Vreeland at *Vogue*, he needed a new *couturier* to embody the spirit of his editorship and Yves Saint Laurent fitted the bill.[7] Some of his best scoops had come from Yves's career at Christian Dior, and Fairchild got on well with him and Pierre, sharing their interest in art, politics and literature. His attitude to the fashion business was once described as 'professionally schizophrenic',[8] running it down to insiders but defending it to outsiders, and was not unlike Pierre Bergé's. The editor-in-chief of *Women's Wear Daily* was the only journalist allowed to see the Saint Laurent collection before the show, a privilege generally reflected in his glowing coverage.

'Friends' of the house, like John Fairchild and Diana Vreeland, were welcomed to Hôtel Forain by a rousing cry of '*Mon cher ami*', 'My dear friend', from Pierre Bergé, before being taken out to lunch or dinner at Maxim's. But there was another side to Pierre's character, as anyone who fell foul of him soon discovered. He had a peppery temper, which he lost all too easily, erupting into storms of sarcasm and shouting at whoever had offended him, or Yves.

For Pierre Bergé, the world was divided into two camps: one that believed Yves Saint Laurent to be a genius, and another that did not. He was merciless at dealing with miscreants, just like Christian

Dior, who routinely banned critical reporters from his shows, and Jean Patou, famous for firing off furious letters to Edna Woolman Chase, editor-in-chief of American *Vogue* in the 1930s, if she allocated more pages to Coco Chanel's collection than to his. Excluding *L'Aurore* from Hôtel Forain after the first show was only the start. Any journalist with the temerity to devote too little space to an Yves Saint Laurent collection, too much to a competitor, or to convey the slightest hint of criticism, was subjected to a telephone tirade from Pierre Bergé, often followed by a letter of complaint to their editor. He even insisted on good behaviour at the *couture* presentations. Marie-José Lepicard remembered arriving a few minutes late to see an early YSL collection. 'When I walked in Pierre Bergé shouted loudly, so everyone could hear: "Marie-José Lepicard, you're late! We've all been waiting for you!" I blushed. But I never dared be late for one of their shows again.'[9]

Although he scoffed at the thought of being a businessman, Pierre was proving to be remarkably efficient at it, ensuring that Hôtel Forain ran like clockwork along classic *couture* lines. The staff were instructed to address him and Yves as '*Monsieur Bergé*' and '*Monsieur Saint Laurent*'. Secretaries were expected to dress smartly and forbidden to drink tea or coffee at their desks. Pierre prided himself on being a fair employer, boasting to other *couturiers* that YSL paid better rates than its competitors, but he was as censorious with his workforce as he could be with the press. If he came across anything that did not meet his expectations, the staff soon heard about it. 'He was always starting arguments or taking umbrage at something,' said an employee of that time. 'If he was in a bad mood, everyone knew it. You'd hear him storming through the building, shouting at people and banging doors behind him. The staff used to raise their eyebrows and say "*Bergé a le cafard*" ("He's in a black mood").'

Pierre's experience as an art dealer stood him in surprisingly good stead when it came to dealing with private clients. The wealthy women who patronized promising young Parisian artists were, after all, often the same ones who dressed in *haute couture*. But he swiftly realized that although an impressive client-list was important for the company's cachet, its future lay with the commercial buyers who placed larger orders and with licensing deals along the lines of those that Jacques Rouët had negotiated for Christian Dior. He and Yves persuaded Yvonne de Peyerimhoff, one of Suzanne Luling's sales team, to leave Dior and join them as sales director. An imposing woman with crisply classic taste in clothes, De Peyerimhoff arrived at Hôtel Forain in autumn 1962, bringing the impressive Dior client-list with her and leaving Pierre with more time to attend to other areas of the business.

Most of the commercial customers he dealt with were the same American and European stores that had been dealing with Paris *couturiers* for decades, but Yves Saint Laurent was also approached by a less conventional source, Seibu-Saison, a Tokyo department store. At that time it was virtually impossible to buy French fashion in Japan; most women still wore kimonos during the day, as did men for formal occasions. But the wealthy Japanese had acquired a taste for American luxuries from the imports shipped in by the GIs in the late 1940s, and the young people born after the War did not share their parents' distrust of the West. A new wave of entrepreneurs was emerging who sensed a desire for something new among Japanese consumers.

One of them was Seiji Tsutsumi, who was put in charge of Seibu-Saison, a dowdy store in the Tokyo suburb of Ikebukuro, by his father, Yasujiro, one of the richest men in Japan.[10] Seiji asked his sister, Kuniko, to help him spruce it up. Too wild to conform to the conventions of Japanese society, Kuniko had been sent away by their father to live in Paris, where as the daughter of an Asian millionaire, she was invited to the *couture* shows. Yves had been her favourite designer since his Dior days. 'His clothes were very different from anything we'd seen in Japan. But they were beautiful and very elegant, qualities that the Japanese have always been sensitive to.'[11]

The Tsutsumis negotiated for the rights to reproduce the YSL *couture* line in Japan. Yves flew to Tokyo to sign the contract in 1963, leaving Pierre behind in Paris. Few Westerners had visited Japan at the time,[12] and the Tokyo jungle of grey and beige concrete towers was as incomprehensible to Yves as the ideograms on the street signs. But he was fascinated by traditional Japanese art, which had been a strong influence over the early modernists he admired, such as Eileen Gray and Le Corbusier. The Tsutsumis took him around the Tokyo museums and arranged a special trip to Kyoto, the ancient capital of Japan, so he could see its famous Zen temples.

Unlike the American stores, which employed skilled European *émigrés* in their *couture salons*, there were no seamstresses or tailors for Seibu to hire in Japan, so they sent a team of workers to Paris for two years of training before bringing them back to Ikebukuro. Each season Kuniko chose a selection of outfits from the YSL collection and ordered two samples of each to be flown out to Tokyo. Once the clients had placed their orders, the Seibu team made up the garments, sending them back to rue Spontini to be checked at least three times before being handed over to the customers. It was a costly and complex process, but the 'Yves Saint Laurent for Seibu-Saison' *salon* slowly attracted a cult following among actresses and singers, helping to establish the Ikebukuro store as a fashionable place for affluent Tokyoites to shop.[13]

Pierre was also keen to develop more conventional sources of income and in early 1963 he flew to New York to talk to prospective licensees. During his visit he was told that Richard Salomon, president of Charles of the Ritz, one of the leading American cosmetics companies, wanted to see him. They arranged to meet for lunch at the Savoy, an old hotel on 59th Street that later became the Playboy Club. Then in his early fifties, Richard 'Dick' Salomon had been at the top of the beauty business for a quarter of a century. Born in New York to a Belgian father and American mother, he had been an ardent francophile since spending his junior year at Brown University in Paris. At twenty-four he was made chairman of Charles of the Ritz by an uncle, who left the business to him after his death. By the early 1960s, he had turned the company into a $50 million concern by positioning it at the top of the cosmetics market, where his diplomatic skills earned him the nickname, 'King Salomon'.[14] He always paid close attention to what was happening on the French fashion scene and had admired Yves's work since seeing his first shows at Christian Dior.

Salomon was an urbane, intelligent man whom Pierre took to immediately. To his relief the president of Charles of the Ritz spoke fluent French, which was just as well as Pierre's English was weak. 'Richard Salomon was a wonderful man. He loved France and he was a democrat – not a republican – that was very important to me. We both really admired Roosevelt. He said he'd like to do a perfume with us. We'd had other offers. Helena Rubinstein, for instance. But for one reason or another they didn't seem right.'[15]

Perfume was a small, but growing business. The American cosmetics giants, Revlon[16] and Avon,[17] dominated the market for cheap chemical scents, and women who wanted something more exclusive generally bought it from the 'beauty queens', Elizabeth Arden[18] and Helena Rubinstein.[19] But the most sought-after perfumes were the 'real' French fragrances which bore the names of the *couturiers* and were made from the flowers, herbs and spices grown in the Grasse region of southern France.[20]

The first *couturier* to launch a perfume was Paul Poiret in 1910, but the turning point came in 1921 when Coco Chanel introduced No. 5, the first 'modern' scent with a distinctive, stable smell. Until then French perfume was made wholly from natural ingredients and was hopelessly unstable with the smell fading away after a few hours. By the early 1920s chemists were experimenting with ways of stabilizing scents and Chanel asked Ernest Beaux, one of the most eminent perfume chemists, to create a new fragrance for her. No. 5 was invented by accident when one of Beaux's assistants forgot to dilute the fatty aldehyde he added to a sample scent.[21] Diluted aldehyde was used to accentuate the smell of perfumes, but had the side-effect of destabilizing the scents. The undiluted aldehyde not only enhanced the smell, but fixed it too. When Chanel tried out the samples she liked the undiluted one best and, as it was the fifth she had been shown, called it No. 5. Other *couturiers* then adopted similar formulae for their scents: Jeanne Lanvin with Arpège and My Sin, and Jean Patou with Joy.[22]

For years French perfume was regarded as a rarity, the preserve of wealthy women most of whom only wore it on special occasions, but ordinary American women were introduced to it after World War II when the GIs brought it back as souvenirs from Europe. Even so Christian Dior counted himself lucky to sell two hundred bottles of Miss Dior in 1948, its first year on sale, and Nina Ricci did little better with L'Air du Temps, when it came out the same year. The first French perfume to really take off in the States was Chanel No. 5 in the 1950s, after Marilyn Monroe told a reporter at Tokyo airport that 'the only thing I wear to bed is a little Chanel No. 5'. It was not an original remark – she had stolen the line from a 1930s advertising slogan – but it had a dramatic effect on sales.

Chanel's success with No. 5 convinced Dick Salomon that there was a larger market for French perfume. He bought the rights to Jeanne Lanvin's 1920s classics, Arpège and My Sin, and hatched plans to develop a new scent for the younger women who wanted something more fashionable. Yves Saint Laurent would make an ideal figurehead: young and stylish, roaring around Paris in his little MG sports car, and receiving rave reviews for his collections.

Salomon presented Pierre with a proposal whereby Charles of the Ritz would manufacture and market a perfume bearing Yves Saint Laurent's name in return for giving them a royalty of five per cent of its sales. The scent was to be called 'Y'; it would be launched in France in spring 1964 and in the States the following year. 'He told me at our first lunch that we could create a perfume worth $25 million a year,' recalled Bergé. 'I didn't believe him. At the time it just didn't seem possible.'[23]

In *couture* circles Pierre was becoming known as a bright young businessman and one evening Coco Chanel invited him to dinner, telling him that he could name his price if he agreed to leave Yves Saint Laurent to run her company for her. Chanel was well past her heyday, but it was a flattering offer; thanks to No. 5, her *couture* house was one of the most profitable in Paris, and Coco was famously fussy about whom she worked with. Unfortunately she was equally famous for being impossible,[24] and Pierre sent his regrets the following day with a bouquet of her favourite white roses.

His hard work at Hôtel Forain was finally bearing fruit. The company had lost money in its first year, as they expected, but made a modest operating profit in the second.[25] The perfume deal with Charles of the Ritz, coupled with other licensing contracts for women's stockings and men's ties, augured well for the future and there were no complaints from the genial J. Mack Robinson, who had always regarded Yves Saint Laurent as a long-term investment. 'I never ever had to worry about money,' said Bergé. 'He set up a credit facility for us with his bank and that was that.'[26] Mack was of little use to Pierre when it came to giving him advice about the fashion business – once describing his decision to back Yves as 'like picking a winner in a horse race'[27] – but Dick Salomon's lengthy experience of dealing with department stores and expensive beauty brands made him an invaluable counsellor. Finally Yves's reputation as a designer was going from strength to strength. He garnered the same glowing reviews for his third collection as for the second,[28] and the press was equally enthusiastic in its initial response to his fourth line for spring 1964.[29]

But a new star surfaced that season. After training as a tailor at Balenciaga, André Courrèges had opened his own *couture* house in 1961.[30] His first few shows were modest successes, but the silver and white 'Space Age' look that he unveiled for spring 1964 caused a sensation. It was an exquisite collection of skinny silver sequin hipsters tied with narrow white ribbons, white *faille* coats and daringly short skirts. The Courrèges *salon* on Avenue Kléber was painted white, to convey the same futuristic feel as the clothes, and the models marched up and down to the beat of tom-tom drums.

Courrèges' space age aesthetic struck a chord with a society obsessed by the race between the American and Soviet astronauts, and matched the iconoclastic mood of the mid-1960s. It was the age of the 'youthquake' when civil rights protests erupted across the United States, and snappily dressed 'mods' clashed with 1950s throwback 'rockers' on the British beaches. Beatlemania spread across the Atlantic when thousands of hysterical fans greeted the Beatles on their arrival at Kennedy Airport for their first trip to the States in February 1964. Three months earlier John Lennon had summed up the anti-establishment mood when he interrupted the band's spot at a Royal Command Performance in London to ask the wealthier members of the audience to 'rattle your jewellery' in such a cheekily charming manner that even the Queen Mother smiled.

The youth market had rarely seemed so lucrative and fashion got the youth bug, like every other area of contemporary culture. The models in *Vogue* no longer looked like twenty-year-old versions of well-coiffed *couture* clients, but were tousle-haired waifs who looked and acted their age. One was Twiggy, the angelically pretty daughter of a London carpenter, and another Jean Shrimpton, alias *'The Shrimp'*, once the girlfriend of *Vogue*'s favourite photographer of the moment, David Bailey, a working-class London-boy-made-good in his twenties.

Yves Saint Laurent had always been seen as the most audacious of the *couturiers*, but he worked within the confines of *couture*; whereas André Courrèges aimed his 'Space Age' collection directly at the young women who usually shopped at Emanuelle Khanh's boutique. Yves's spring 1964 line, with its quilted skirts and cheeky kerchieves tied around the models' heads, was fresher and livelier than those of the older *couturiers*, but it seemed almost staid compared to Courrèges' uncompromisingly futuristic style. Only a year before Eugenia Sheppard had praised Yves in the *Herald Tribune* for creating 'the kind of uncontroversial collection the world's press has been pining for', but by 1964 'uncontroversial' was not enough any more.[31] The newspapers, which had been so flattering when they first saw the YSL collection, now shifted their allegiance from Saint Laurent to Courrèges, as did the spring issues of *Vogue* and *Harper's Bazaar*.

Instead of trying to win back his laurels as an innovator, Yves retreated into traditionalism. Six months later he unveiled the most subdued collection of his career to date in a show that had none of the chutzpah his clients had come to expect. The models wore deliberately demure make-up, and one had her hair plaited into schoolgirl braids. 'With the rest of the world on a youth kick, Yves is suddenly designing for the most lady-like ladies,' reported the *Herald Tribune*.[32] The review was respectful, but scarcely scintillating and the account of his show was shorter than usual. Other press reviews were in the same unenthusiastic vein.

It was Yves's first serious setback since his rejection by Christian Dior and the limp reviews had an immediate impact on the business. One of its main sources of income came from the deposits that store buyers paid to see the repeat shows held later in the week after the press and private clients had seen the first presentation. The money was eventually deducted from the buyer's orders, but it helped to cover the cost of producing the collection and eased the company's cashflow. In previous seasons Hôtel Forain had been inundated by last-minute requests for seats after buyers read the glowing newspaper reports of the debut show. Pierre was able to raise the price of the deposits from $1,000 in 1962 to $1,500 by 1964. But after the lacklustre reviews of the autumn line, Hôtel Forain received a stream of cancellations from buyers who had decided that it was not worth seeing the collection that season. Some $100,000 of deposits were withdrawn, a heavy blow for a company with an annual turnover of only $1 million.[33]

A few weeks later Pierre issued a statement saying that Yves Saint Laurent, like Hubert de Givenchy and Cristóbal Balenciaga, would not be admitting journalists to the first presentation of the spring 1965 collection. They would be invited to attend another show, a month later. The decision was perfectly understandable from a personal perspective – negative reviews were wounding for Yves and bad for staff morale – but it was absurd from a commercial standpoint. Well aware of how valuable a good rapport with journalists could be, Pierre had gone to great lengths to court them and must have known how difficult it would be to woo back the commercial buyers who had withdrawn their deposits, particularly without the benefit of favourable press reports. He and Yves knew that they had benefited from the vacuum created by the Givenchy and Balenciaga bans. Now Yves was banishing the press at the very moment when he was most vulnerable with André Courrèges' star in the ascendant.

Common sense dictated that Pierre should have insisted that Yves stick it out and win back his old supporters. But then, as in the future, Pierre bowed to Yves's wishes, even if it was bad for business. 'Yves is a strong character – very steely,' said a friend from that era. 'He's a Leo. He knows exactly what he wants and what he doesn't want. But he needs a rod and Pierre is that rod. Whenever problems arise Yves sits back in his sweet way pretending he hasn't seen anything. But Pierre is only doing what Yves wants. If he barks, you can be pretty sure it's because Yves told him to.'

When the doors of Hôtel Forain opened on 1 February 1965 for the first showing of the Saint Laurent spring collection, the only people present were friends and private clients. The fashion editors were a few miles away in another part of Paris watching the comeback collection of the veteran *couturier*, Captain Edward Molyneux, after his fifteen-year retreat to the Riviera.[34] The next day's papers merely mentioned that the YSL show had taken place,[35] although Diana Vreeland later described the collection in *Vogue* as 'ravishing, subtle, polished. French, and very feminine.'[36]

The timing of the press ban could not have been worse financially. Until then J. Mack Robinson had hoped that the company would make a small operating profit in its third year, as it had in the

second, so he could start to recoup his investment; but the loss of
$100,000 of deposits had put paid to that. Mack was a wealthy man,
but not rich enough to continue to lose money on a Paris *couture*
house, particularly as it had nothing in common with his other
businesses.[37] After three years as the backer of the hottest *couturier*
in Paris, he only spoke a few hundred words of French and still
styled himself as a gangling Atlanta businessman who had stumbled
into fashion by mistake. He visited Paris twice a year to check on
his investment, but had stopped attending the shows after the first
few seasons. 'Everybody's too busy,' he told the *New York Times*. 'I
prefer going a few weeks later when things are quieter.'[38]

Mack was fond of Yves and Pierre. A framed photograph of Yves
signed *'Pour Mack avec toute mon affection'* ('For Mack with great
affection') was one of two pictures hanging in his Atlanta office; the
other was an architect's sketch of the new headquarters of his finance
company. But by the beginning of 1965, his investment in Yves
Saint Laurent must have seemed like a luxury he could no longer
afford. 'Y' had come out in France the previous spring and was such
a success that Pierre, spurred on by Richard Salomon, was talking
of diversifying into other products – furs, shoes, maybe even make-up.
The business was becoming too big for J. Mack Robinson's taste;
the last thing he wanted was to become so preoccupied by his sleeping
partnership in a loss-making French fashion house that it took time
away from his main interests in Atlanta. He told Pierre that he
wanted to sell his shares, as soon as they found a suitable buyer. 'He
was very generous about it,' said Bergé. 'He said he wasn't in a
hurry, that he could take his time, and it was up to us to choose
who would buy the shares from him.'[39]

The final point was crucial. The last thing Yves and Pierre wanted
was to exchange the affable 'American Uncle' who allowed them to
run the company as they wished for an intrusive investor like Marcel
Boussac or Charles Revson, the president of Revlon, once described
as 'the epitome of the hard-driving, exasperating and demanding
American executive'.[40] But there was an ideal candidate at hand in
Richard Salomon. He offered the financial clout of Charles of the
Ritz, as well as the strategic expertise that J. Mack Robinson lacked
– and they liked him. Pierre asked if he would be willing to
buy Mack's eighty per cent stake and after a few weeks of discreet

negotiations, Salomon agreed terms with J. Mack Robinson. On 13 July 1965 Pierre Bergé issued a press statement announcing that Lanvin-Charles of the Ritz was buying the shares for a little less than $1 million. Pierre, whom the *New York Times* presented to its readers as the 'tough, highly intelligent, protective man, who is believed to have steered the designer to his present enviable position',[41] insisted that things would stay the same under their new owner and Richard Salomon was characteristically courteous about his new acquisition.[42]

J. Mack Robinson returned to Atlanta where he diversified into banking. He remained friends with Yves and Pierre and returned to Paris from time to time when invited to special events at the house of Yves Saint Laurent. By the early 1990s he was one of the richest men in Atlanta with a fortune 'conservatively estimated' by *Forbes Magazine* at $365 million. 'One doesn't always keep the right things,' he replied when asked whether he regretted selling his Yves Saint Laurent shares for $1 million.[43]

*

On the Left Bank
1965–1966

For years Richard Salomon had gone over to Paris for each *couture* week, but this time he stayed in Manhattan, telling friends that Yves had quite enough to worry about without his new backer being there.[1] It was nearly a year since the criticism of Yves's autumn 1964 collection, and whereas in the past if he got bad reviews one season he could win over the critics the next, his spring line had generated less coverage than usual because of the press ban and, as *couture* week approached, Yves grew edgy and uneasy.

The dress rehearsal did little to lift his spirits. The shift dresses and slim-fitting suits he had designed were cleverly conceived, but not dramatically different from anything he had done before. With only a fortnight to go before the show, he decided to add another series of simple woollen shifts, this time emblazoned with the bold black lines and brightly-coloured blocks of the paintings he had seen in a monograph of the Dutch artist, Piet Mondrian, that Lucienne had given him for Christmas. The seamstresses at Hôtel Forain were accustomed to Yves asking for last-minute changes to particular pieces; occasionally he even added a few extra designs, but never before had he introduced as many new pieces with so little time to go before the show. The *mains-d'oeuvre* stayed on late in the *ateliers* to finish the new dresses. 'We did tiny, tiny stitches,' recalled Renée Cassart, one of the seamstresses. 'We followed the grains of the fabric so that the seams between the coloured panels were almost invisible.'[2]

The extra effort was worthwhile. The shifts were a perfect mix of a flattering form with a dash of visual drama reminiscent of Mondrian's abstracts and the Op Art paintings that a young British artist, Bridget Riley, had shown in London the previous year. To the more discerning members of the audience the Mondrian shifts were also a technical feat, as Yves had designed and cut them so cleverly that they accommodated the curves of the female form while appearing as perfectly flat as the original oil paintings. Cheers resounded around the Hôtel Forain *salon* when the dresses appeared, and a standing ovation greeted Yves as he was coaxed out from his backstage peep-hole to take a curtain call. By lunchtime, word had spread around Paris about the sensational new Saint Laurent line, and journalists, who were not due to see the collection for another few weeks, were forced to resort to quizzing private clients for eye-witness accounts of the show.[3]

Besieged by pleas from journalists to see the clothes, Pierre Bergé agreed to bring the press presentation forward to 6 August, four days after the debut show. Yves drove himself to rue Spontini that morning in his MG sports car, arriving so early that the front door was still locked and he had to slip round to the trade entrance at the back. As the spectators filed into the *salon*, he stood on a balcony staring down at the crush of people on the street below. A few favoured clients were wearing the Mondrian silk scarves he had given them as gifts after the first presentation; he handed a scarf to Lucienne when she came backstage to greet him, and another to Yvonne de Peyerimhoff. As the spectators settled into their seats Yves stood shyly in a corner, gingerly fingering his good-luck talismans: a string of African worry beads and a toy Bugs Bunny.

His nervousness was extraordinary. The early 'eye-witness' reports in the press had been unreservedly positive, and he did not have to worry about making last-minute changes to the collection, as it had been finished four days before in time for the debut. Yves's behaviour showed how hurt he had been by the criticism of the past few seasons, and that his reaction ran far deeper than pique. 'It's as though he has a layer of skin missing,' observed Susan Train. 'He's very sensitive to whatever is going on and feels things very, very deeply.'[4]

His concern was, of course, completely unnecessary. 'Saint Laurent has bounced back higher than ever,' wrote Gloria Emerson in the *New York Times*, pronouncing the new line to be 'the brightest and freshest he has ever done'.[5] Hôtel Forain was bombarded by orders, not only from private clients, but from commercial buyers who were convinced that the Mondrian shifts would be *the* mass-market look that autumn.[6] Pierre Bergé relayed the good news to Richard Salomon's New York office by telephone, quietly tipping off John Fairchild that he had decided to lift the ban and journalists would be allowed to see the first show again that summer.

With Yves's reputation restored and the business secured by Richard Salomon, Yves and Pierre could enjoy their life together. They still lived in Yves's old apartment at Place Vauban, which was light and bright with wide windows looking out across a leafy garden to the sandstone of Église du Dôme. It was furnished in a simple modernist style with white walls, potted palms, Isamu Noguchi's paper light sculptures and a couple of chrome and leather Barcelona chairs by Mies van der Rohe, who had designed the Brno chairs at Hôtel Forain. Most weekends they went antiqueing in the Paris flea-markets and Saint-Germain des Prés dealers, in search of paintings or sketches for Yves, and the first edition books that Pierre still collected.

Another of their passions was music. Yves enjoyed the *'yé-yé'* records of Johnny Hallyday and Françoise Hardy, France's answer to the Rolling Stones and the Beatles, and the old-fashioned French songs sung by Charles Trenet, playing them over and over on the record-player at Place Vauban, but his real love was opera. Already regulars at the Palais Garnier opera house in Paris, he and Pierre started making special trips to the music festivals at Strasbourg and Bayreuth. Their idol was Maria Callas who, by the 1960s, had become a highbrow camp icon, playing the same role for the gay intelligentsia as Judy Garland did for working-class men. Opera, with its extremes of emotion, melodramatic plots and expressionistic imagery, had a special significance in homosexual culture, and Callas attracted a fanatical following as her life – her struggle from humble origins, unconventional beauty and unhappy love-affair with the Greek shipping tycoon, Aristotle Onassis – conformed completely to the camp cliché of an outsider struggling for acceptance by society. Even her voice, with the telltale vibrato that infuriated opera purists, was lionized by her gay fans. Yves and Pierre went to hear Callas sing whenever they could. Years later Yves remembered her performances in Paris. 'The hall was waiting for her to make a false note, divided between those who wanted her to sing beautifully and others who wanted her to hit the false note.'[7] The parallel with his perception of the audience's attitude to him at his *couture* shows was obvious.

He found similar parallels with a more accessible icon, Rudolf Nureyev. Two years younger than Yves, Nureyev was hailed as the most brilliant male dancer since Nijinsky and was one of the few men of their age to be as famous as he was. Just as Yves had to submit his reputation to public scrutiny with each collection, so Nureyev had to prove his worth with each performance. Although he had been the Royal Ballet's star since his defection to the West in 1961, he was still employed on contract rather than being made a permanent member of the company like his partner, Margot Fonteyn.[8]

And like Yves, Nureyev was homosexual. They were part of the new generation of wealthy, successful gay men who were sufficiently self-confident to be open about their sexuality in private and, although they were not entirely frank about it in public, at least they did not feel the need to lie. Their temperaments were very different. Nureyev was much the more extrovert of the two, with the mischievously playful character that Yves enjoyed in Fernando Sanchez; and whereas Yves's public persona was shy and self-effacing, Nureyev's was gregarious and unashamedly arrogant. Stories of his tantrums were legion in the ballet world: from the 'spaghetti incident' when he tossed a plate of pasta at an Italian waiter screaming 'Nureyev never serves himself', to the wintry night in Toronto when, on being refused admittance to a restaurant for not wearing a tie, he thrust his fur coat at the *maître d'* shrieking 'Feel this! If this coat isn't worthy of your restaurant, nothing is!' and pelted the windows with snowballs.[9]

Pierre had met Nureyev on the dancer's first trip to Paris with the Kirov Ballet before his defection from the Soviet Union, and introduced him to Yves during that visit. Their friendship continued after Nureyev went to live in London, as he returned regularly to Paris, often coming to perform in Roland Petit's productions. Whenever he was there he sought out Yves and Pierre, joining them for dinners with Roland, Zizi and their friends, the ballerina Claire Motte and her publisher husband, Mario Bois, rounding off the night at chic nightclubs such as New Jimmy's and Régine's.

Another addition to their circle was Clara Saint, a pretty young heiress in her mid-twenties whom Yves and Pierre had met through Nureyev's ballet partner, Margot Fonteyn, a regular client at Hôtel Forain. Fonteyn stayed with Clara during her trips to Paris, and one day she took her along to lunch at Maxim's to meet two friends, Yves Saint Laurent and Pierre Bergé. 'It was a *coup de foudre* – a friendly *coup de foudre*,' said Clara. 'We had so much in common, the same likes and dislikes, it was as though I'd known them for twenty years. Sometimes you meet people and it's like that. We arranged to meet again the next day and it went on from there.'[10]

A bastion of the young Paris arts scene, Clara was born in Chile but moved to France with her parents, both artists, when she was five. Classically pretty with long, straight blonde hair, she had a petite, slightly rounded figure and a sunny demeanour. 'Mellow is the word for Clara,' said one of her friends. 'She's so serene and capable that it's lovely just to be around her. Whatever happens she carries on smiling and laughing.' She had been engaged to Vincent Malraux (the son of André Malraux, the novelist who became General de Gaulle's culture minister) but he died in 1960 in a Riviera car crash. Clara settled back into her old life of art and ballet, until the next summer when she had a brief burst of fame after helping Rudolf Nureyev to defect from the Soviet Union.

Nureyev had befriended Clara during a Kirov Ballet trip to Paris, when Claire Motte took her backstage to meet the Russian dancers after one of their first performances, *La Bayadère*. 'I'd noticed him during the performance because he danced so beautifully and when Claire took me backstage he jumped forward saying "I speak English." He was the only one of the Kirov dancers who did.'[11] At the end of the Paris season Nureyev was told to leave for Moscow rather than going on to London with the other dancers and he telephoned Clara from Le Bourget airport asking for her help. Having made contact with the French authorities on his behalf, she took Nureyev back with her to Paris, and found him a place to stay and a studio where he could practise.

By the time she met Yves and Pierre, Clara had a new boyfriend, Thadée Klossowski, an aspiring writer from one of France's most eminent intellectual families. Improbably handsome with thick curly hair and shabby chic clothes, Thadée was the son of the painter, Balthazar Klossowski de Rola, known as 'Balthus', and the nephew of Pierre Klossowski, the writer known for his work on the Marquis de Sade, and a close friend of the philosopher, Michel Foucault. He and Clara slipped into Yves's and Pierre's social circle, introducing them to their friends in the art and dance world.

Yves continued his collaboration with Roland Petit, designing sets and costumes for five of his ballets between 1962 and 1965. It was a huge addition to his workload at the *couture* house, as set design called on completely different skills from fashion, and creating the costumes for a ballet alone involved designing hundreds of different pieces, each of which had to be made to the tightest technical specifications, so that the dancers could move freely and the fabric withstood the physical pressure of their movements. Intellectually it was more demanding for Yves than designing a *couture* collection, as the details of each costume and every piece of scenery had to convey the spirit of the ballet and Roland Petit's interpretation of it.

His work for the theatre freed Yves from the commercial constraints of *couture*, allowing him to play with abstract forms and historical styles which were inappropriate in contemporary clothes. It enabled him to use his imagination in a way which would have been impossible had he been restricted to fashion, and doubtless helped stave off the nagging frustration he had started to feel at Christian Dior. Yves took on more theatrical projects with other collaborators, designing two operas, *The Marriage of Figaro* and *Il Faut Passer Par Les Nuages*, directed by Jean-Louis Barrault in 1964, and a play the following year, *Des Journées Entières Dans Les Arbres*, written by the novelist, Marguerite Duras. He also created the costumes for Catherine Deneuve, a young French actress, in her new film *Belle de Jour*, directed by the Spanish surrealist, Luis Buñuel.

Yves had met Deneuve when her husband, the *Vogue* photographer David Bailey, took her to Hôtel Forain to order a dress for a reception in London at which she was to be presented to the Queen. Already a star in her early twenties, Deneuve arrived clutching a scrap of old newspaper with a photograph of a gown from the previous season's collection. Yves made a long white dress with an elaboratedly embroidered bodice which she loved so much that she asked him to design her entire wardrobe for *Belle de Jour*. Reticent with each other at first, they gradually opened up during the long round of fittings. 'We spoke of films, of clothes, of people in a professional context,' said Deneuve. 'Then we began to talk of other things which, little by little, created a bond between us.'[12] In the film she played the part of Séverine, the beautiful but bored wife of a young Parisian surgeon who seeks distraction by working as a call girl. Yves dressed her in a snappy military style, with a double-buttoned red suit, a boxy coat with epaulettes and a stunning mini-trench in gleaming black patent leather. 'Ooh!' exclaims another girl in the brothel when she sees it. 'Oh well. I can always get a copy made.'[13]

The inspiration for the military style came from the American uniforms Yves had seen that autumn on a trip to New York for the launch of 'Y' perfume. He spent hours browsing around the Army & Navy Store on 42nd Street, fascinated by the neat little naval pea-coats and officers' jackets with their half-belts and epaulettes, that he remembered seeing on the naval crews passing through war-time Oran. Just as Yves had refined the leather jackets of the Left Bank beatniks into the luxurious 'Beat' look for Dior, so he reworked the clearly-defined forms and crisp detailing of the Army & Navy uniforms into boxy suits and coats for Catherine Deneuve in *Belle de Jour*, and into pretty pea-coats with slinky bell-bottoms for his spring 1966 *couture* collection.

Only a few days before the Saint Laurent show, the fashion press raved about the futuristic dresses covered with geometric plastic discs designed by a new *couturier*, Paco Rabanne,[14] and about Pierre Cardin's sculptural shift dress suspended from circular collars with dinky pillbox hats.[15] But Yves emerged as the star of *couture* week with his nautical look, which the *New York Times* reckoned had 'just as much sizzle' as the previous season's Mondrian shifts.[16] Catherine Deneuve watched the show from the front row flanked by two other movie stars, Leslie Caron and Elsa Martinelli, and the usual Hôtel Forain mix of Yves's arty friends, Zizi Jeanmaire and Françoise Sagan, with socialites such as Marie-Hélène de Rothschild and the perfume heiress, Hélène Rochas. Paris *couture* week always attracted star-studded crowds, but that season's YSL show marked a new departure: from then onwards the audience at Hôtel Forain would attract almost as much press attention as the clothes.

Rave reviews and paparazzi-packed shows were exactly what Pierre

Bergé and Richard Salomon needed to seal the success of their latest venture, the launch of a Left Bank boutique to sell a special *prêt-à-porter* collection designed by Yves. The shop was to be called Rive Gauche, in honour of its Left Bank location to distinguish it from the *haute couture* houses on the other side of the Seine, and would stock a full range of clothes and accessories selling at far lower prices than the YSL *couture* line, so that younger women could afford to buy them.[17]

Prêt-à-porter, or ready-to-wear, was a controversial topic among the Paris *couturiers*. The concept of selling inexpensive, off-the-peg clothes dated back to the 1920s when Madeleine Vionnet sold the rights to reproduce some of her designs to Eva Boex, a dressmaker on rue de Castiglione. Lucien Lelong followed in 1934 when his business was hit by the depression, opening a small shop inside his *couture* house where his clients could buy a simplified version of the *couture* collection. After the War, other *couturiers* opened similar shops to sell *confection* lines, clothes based on original *couture* designs, which were cheaper to produce, being simpler in style with less elaborate materials and made partly by machine rather than hand-sewn in the *ateliers*. Not only was *confection* less expensive for the clients, it was easier to buy, as it only involved one fitting or, if they were in a hurry, no fittings at all.

Yet the bulk of the business was still *haute couture*, which was run in the traditional way under the aegis of the Chambre Syndicale de la Couture. Anyone could set up in business as an ordinary *couturier*. There were hundreds of local dressmakers all over France, like the ones Lucienne had patronized in Oran, who mostly made copies of the *haute couture* outfits their clients had seen in fashion magazines. An *haut couturier* had to be licensed by the Chambre Syndicale and to abide by its rules which stipulated that they must employ a minimum number of people and show a certain number of outfits each season, all of which were made-to-measure for individual clients. This system helped maintain high standards, but burdened the *couturiers* with hefty overheads and made buying *haute couture* an expensive and time-consuming affair. Diana Vreeland once complained that she had to go for a couple of fittings just to buy a nightdress.

By the mid-1960s fewer and fewer women were able, or willing, to spend over $1,000 on a cocktail dress, and to find time for four or five fittings, particularly when the clothes they could buy in the new wave of fashion boutiques were cheaper and more exciting. Bazaar in London sold the 'Chelsea Girl' look of skinny jumpers and mini-skirts designed by Mary Quant, a former art student who had started making her own clothes from sewing patterns and fabrics she bought in Harrods department store. The boutique played pop music all day and stayed open late on Friday so its customers could blow their weekly wages on new clothes to go out in that evening.[18] Its arch-rival, Biba, opened in 1964 on Kensington High Street selling a jumble of old and new clothes with antique beads and ostrich feather boas chosen by its owner, Barbara Hulanicki. The bill for a coat, dress, shoes and hat from Biba rarely came to more than £15, about the same as the price of a Mary Quant dress.[19]

Young French designers were choosing to work for Parisian versions of Bazaar and Biba, rather than serving lengthy apprenticeships with *hauts couturiers*, as their predecessors did in the 1950s when Yves joined Dior.[20] 'I would never have dreamt of becoming involved with *couture*,' recalled Sonia Rykiel, who started designing clothes in the early 1960s for a Parisian boutique called Laura. 'It had no appeal for my generation. The 1960s was a time when people started to break down taboos and change things.'[21] The younger elements in the Paris fashion establishment, Pierre Bergé among them, argued that the Chambre Syndicale must move with the times and relax its rules if *haute couture* was to survive. The old guard, led by Raymond Barbas, the Jean Patou chairman who frequently bickered with Bergé over industry issues, argued that this would make matters worse by imperilling their prestige and encouraging yet more clients to switch to ready-to-wear.[22]

Financial pressure was mounting on the *couturiers*. One by one the American and European department stores closed down their *couture salons*, and by 1965 the number of *hauts couturiers* licensed by the Chambre Syndicale had fallen to forty, from over a hundred just after the War.[23] Most of the survivors were losing money; they even found it difficult to replace retiring employees because young people were unwilling to work for long hours on low pay when it was easy to find jobs in other industries. Lanvin, one of the older houses, announced that it was reducing the size of its collection to cut costs,[24] and André Courrèges was talking about abandoning *couture* to concentrate on *prêt-a-porter*.[25]

Ever since his Dior days, Yves had tried to make clothes which were more in tune with the times and easier to wear than cumbersome *couture* classics. *Prêt-à-porter* looked like the next logical step; but he wanted to create a proper ready-to-wear collection, with its own identity, rather than a diluted version of his *haute couture* designs and to sell it from its own boutique, not an adjunct of Hôtel Forain. The idea was to combine the fun of Biba with his own brand of bohemian glamour. 'At that time no *couturier* had done *prêt-a-porter* properly,' said Pierre Bergé. 'Some had tried but it hadn't worked because all they'd done was a cheaper version of *haute couture*. Yves was the first to think of creating a collection with a life of its own.'[26] But they had to act swiftly. The last thing Pierre wanted was to see André Courrèges stealing a march over Yves Saint Laurent by moving into *prêt-à-porter* first, leaving them behind with the *couture* old guard. With J. Mack Robinson as their backer it had been difficult to see how they could raise the necessary capital, but that was no longer a problem with Richard Salomon and Charles of the Ritz behind them. They announced a date for the opening of the first Rive Gauche boutique in Paris on 22 September 1966.

'When Yves Saint Laurent started Rive Gauche. Gosh! To me and my friends it was so exciting,' recalled Katell Le Bourhis, the fashion historian who was then a student. 'We knew the clothes were going to be expensive, but not as expensive as *couture*. Suddenly it was possible to think about buying these wonderful things that we'd seen and read about in the magazines. We wouldn't have to buy copies any more. Also Saint Laurent was an incredible cult figure. He was very young and we'd all seen pictures of him with his long hair and his amazing clothes. He had such an aura.'[27]

Yves started work on the design of the boutique with the decorator, Isabelle Hebey. They found a suitable site in an old bakery at 21 rue de Tournon, a narrow street in the sixth *arrondissement* running between the lovely old Saint-Sulpice church and the Luxembourg Gardens. It was an unusual location for a fashion boutique. Most of the other shops on the street sold antiquarian books and it was a brisk ten-minute walk from the bustle of Boulevard Saint-Germain,

Born in Oran, Algeria, in 1936, Yves Saint Laurent had a privileged upbringing as the son of a wealthy French businessman and a member of one of the most prominent French families in the city, but the backdrop to his childhood was the natural beauty of north Africa.

Lucienne Mathieu-Saint-Laurent and her son at his Place Vauban apartment in 1960. 'I love my daughters, of course,' she said. 'But for Yves there has always been something very strong and very special.' She is wearing one of the dresses he designed for Christian Dior.

(*Above*) The twenty-one-year-old Yves on the Dior balcony after his debut in January 1958.

(*Clockwise*) Yves in the Dior workrooms; Christian Dior at his Fontainebleau mill; the 'Trapeze' line that 'saved' the house of Dior.

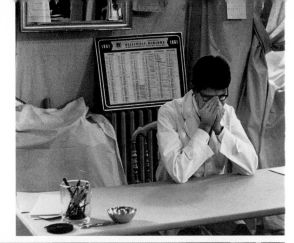

(*Left*) Pierre Bergé, Yves, Victoire and Claude Licard in 1961, at their temporary offices on rue de la Boétie.

Yves, Pierre and their staff in January 1962, preparing for the first YSL *couture* collection at Hôtel Forain.

The paint was barely dry on the walls when the spectators took their seats in the Hôtel Forain ballroom for the first YSL *couture* show on 29 January 1962. The collection drew mixed reviews, with 'Poor Yves' from one newspaper, but compliments from others.

(*Left*) Yves backstage at the Théâtre Nationale Populaire, Paris, in 1962 with a dancer wearing one of the costumes he designed for *Les Chants de Maldoror*, choreographed by his friend, Roland Petit.

GIRL

ïNO DE FARIS

(*Above*) Helping Zizi Jeanmaire dress for her 1961 *Revue*. She and her husband, Roland Petit, did their best to raise Yves's spirits after his army discharge by asking him to work on their theatrical projects.

Yves on the balcony at Place Vauban in 1963. The photographer, Archie Parker, was accompanied by his wife, Una Mary, who acted as an assistant. She remembered Yves as being 'beautiful, slender and very elegant; but so timid, he barely uttered a word'.

but the building was perfect, with spacious ground-floor rooms opening on to a picturesque courtyard at the back.

Clara Saint agreed to come and work for them to handle publicity, and they asked a young clothing manufacturer, Didier Grumbach, to produce the collection. Clever and energetic, Grumbach was a childhood friend of Clara's who had taken over C. Mendès, his family's clothing company, in 1964 when he was still in his twenties. The company had started as a coat manufacturer in the early 1900s, and began making *confection* coats for the *couturiers* after the War. Didier Grumbach expanded the *couture* side of the business by negotiating new contracts with Jean Patou and Castillo, but when Pierre Bergé asked him to supply Yves Saint Laurent's new *prêt-à-porter* line, he declined, worried about the risk of becoming too dependent on one customer.

A few days later he was astonished to be shown a cutting from *France-Soir*, the Paris evening paper, announcing that Mendès was to manufacture the new Yves Saint Laurent ready-to-wear line. Pierre had leaked the 'news' to the press, without telling Grumbach, who had already sent him a polite letter of refusal. The man who showed Grumbach the newspaper report was Raymond Barbas of Patou, who disliked Pierre and was furious that Mendès had taken on such a big commitment to another customer without telling him first. Grumbach was angry too, but started to reconsider when other people called to congratulate him on the new venture.[28] The next day he received a note from Richard Salomon inviting him to dine at Calvet, a restaurant on Boulevard Saint-Germain, later that week. Pierre Bergé was to be present, as were Yves Saint Laurent and Claude Bernheim, their head of licensing.

Dick Salomon mapped out a blueprint for the new business, telling Grumbach about his plans to turn it into a chain of boutiques. He sketched a scenario whereby Didier Grumbach and Mendès would each own twenty-five per cent of the new company, Saint Laurent Rive Gauche, with Pierre Bergé and Yves Saint Laurent holding the remaining fifty per cent. Salomon himself would retain two special shares, allowing him to cast the deciding vote if the two camps clashed. A twelve per cent royalty would be payable on sales of Rive Gauche products, five per cent of which would go to the Yves Saint Laurent *couture* house with the rest being ploughed back into Saint

Laurent Rive Gauche. Pierre Bergé had nearly blown the deal by trying to put pressure on Grumbach through the press, but Richard Salomon was a persuasive man and the concept was compelling. Didier Grumbach said 'yes'.[29]

The first inkling of what the new Rive Gauche range would look like came that July when Yves unveiled his autumn 1966 *couture* collection, inspired by the work of two artists he had befriended. One was Nikki de Saint-Phalle, a sculptor friend of Clara's with whom he had collaborated on a Roland Petit ballet. Yves loved the vivid colours and dramatic shapes in her *Nanas*, voluptuous female figures sculpted from lacquered papier-mâché, and he admired her clothes, particularly the slinky trousers suits with the same androgynously elegant effect as those worn by Marlene Dietrich in her early films. Yves added a couple of tailored trouser suits like hers to his *couture* line.

His other influence was Andy Warhol, the most successful of the new American pop artists. Born in Pittsburgh, the youngest son of Ondrej and Julia Warhola, who emigrated to America from a Ruthenian village on the Russo-Polish border, Warhol made his name as a commercial artist in New York in the late 1950s and resurfaced in the early 1960s 'pop' wave with his repetitive images of Campbell's soup cans and dollar bills. He paid his first visit to Paris in May 1965 to open an exhibition of flower paintings at the Ileana Sonnabend gallery, swapping the return sea ticket that Sonnabend sent him for four airplane tickets so he could take his assistant, Gerard Malanga, his *gamine* 'girl of the year', Edie Sedgwick, and her on-off boyfriend, Chuck Wein. Warhol hit the Paris clubs with his entourage and posed with Edie Sedgwick for photographic sessions in *Paris-Match* and Paris *Vogue*. Yves and Pierre enjoyed the Sonnabend show and seized their chance to meet the artist when he returned to France the following summer. 'Andy was one of the few artists to be doing something new and different with painting,' recalled Bergé. 'All his work – his Maos, his flowers, his use of photographic images – made a big impression on us.'[30] The three men hit it off; Warhol, like them, was openly homosexual, and he was as besotted by fashion as they were by art.

Yves added to the *couture* collection a line of woollen dresses emblazoned with Warholesque images with ruby red lips, cartoon-book

88

faces and brightly coloured hearts. The younger members of the audience squealed approvingly, but the older ones were less impressed. The *New York Times* suggested that the 'Pop Art' dresses might have been better off being 'saved as a private joke for a few friends to wear to New Jimmy's.'[31] However, the *Herald Tribune*'s Eugenia Sheppard detected a serious sub-text. 'With this collection I have a feeling that Yves tore up more than some half-finished fashions. He washed his hands once and for all of the old-time concept of Paris Couture that involves dresses built to last for ever, multiple fittings and a look carefully modified for women with gorgeous bank accounts but less than gorgeous figures.'[32]

The 'Pop Art' dresses reappeared on the rails of the Rive Gauche boutique when it opened the following month, alongside vinyl raincoats, suede skirts, skimpy 'baby doll' dresses and new versions of Nikki de Saint-Phalle's trouser suits. Prices ranged from $75 for a simple jersey tunic, to $120 for a long crêpe evening dress. The walls were lacquered in red, and acid orange rugs thrown on the floor, alongside futuristic furniture designed by Olivier Morgue, a young Frenchman who was starting work on the sets for Stanley Kubrick's sci-fi epic, *2001: A Space Odyssey*. A life-size portrait of Yves by the artist Arroyo hung on the wall, next to a blinking electronic heart that the Hôtel Forain staff had given him for his thirtieth birthday that August. A couple of Nikki de Saint-Phalle's colourful *Nanas* were on display inside the boutique and another stood outside in the courtyard.

The Hôtel Forain *couture* crowd showed up in force for the opening, clutching orange and purple invitations that bore the Rive Gauche logo of two pop art squares, one in red, the other pink. Arriving early with Richard Salomon by his side, Yves greeted Zizi Jeanmaire and Marie-Hélène de Rothschild, both loyally wearing Yves Saint Laurent *couture*, before giving a guided tour to his guest of honour, Catherine Deneuve. She appeared in a military-style coat like the one he had made for her in *Belle de Jour* with oval-shaped sunglasses, and her long blonde hair swept away from her face by a black velvet band. Yves helped Deneuve to pick out a few pieces: a red coat, black jersey dress, a trouser suit and three suede mini-skirts that she asked to be made even shorter. By four o'clock on its first afternoon, the boutique had sold $24,000 of clothes.[33]

The Hippy De Luxe
1967–1968

'Everyone went to Rive Gauche, absolutely everyone,' said Susan Train of *Vogue*. 'It was so exciting. You could buy an entire wardrobe there: everything you needed.'[1] 'The clothes just walked out of the shop,' recalled Clara Saint. 'Yves did these chain belts with medallions that everybody wanted to buy. We were selling forty a day. The customers left with their bags going chink, chink, chink.'[2]

One of the most popular styles was the tailored trouser suit that Catherine Deneuve had bought on the opening day. Yves had included a few in the previous season's *couture* collection, but they had slunk past the press virtually unnoticed, so for spring 1967 he made them the main theme of the show. The models were decked out like gangsters with crisply-laundered shirts, ties, fedora hats and handkerchieves poking out of their breast pockets. He called the jackets *les smokings*, after the French word for tuxedos, and this time his trouser suits were hailed as the hit of the season.[3]

Until then a woman in a trouser suit was associated with the butch look of lesbian writers like Radclyffe Hall and Gertrude Stein, or the libidinous Lakey in Mary McCarthy's *The Group*.[4] Yves changed that, by softening the mannish silhouette of his suits with a smooth cut that made them wearable for formal occasions. 'He used traditional men's tailoring in a completely new way,' said Jean-Pierre Derbord, one of the tailors who worked on the first *smokings*. 'All the other *couturiers* tried to copy us. But they couldn't do it because they didn't understand our technique.'[5] The final touch was Yves's choice of accessories – spindly stiletto heels, siren make-up and dramatic jewellery – to create a sophisticated, yet very feminine effect.

His timing was perfect. The Paris of the mid-1960s was not as louche as swinging London, nor as wild as Andy Warhol's world in New York, but attitudes were changing. The De Gaulle government passed laws to improve the legal rights of married women and then legalized contraception for anyone over eighteen. Feminism was surfacing on the academic agenda, and women were carving out careers in the media, education and the arts. Even wealthy Parisian housewives, such as Catherine Deneuve's Séverine in *Belle de Jour*, were no longer willing to play the same submissive roles as their mothers.

An Yves Saint Laurent *smoking* became the uniform for the new generation of women who, by appropriating a masculine style, were signalling that they did not intend to defer to men as second-class citizens. The political message was not lost on a manager at the Plaza Hotel in Manhattan who banned a woman from eating in the restaurant because she was wearing a YSL trouser suit. 'It was absolutely revolutionary for a woman to wear trousers at the time,' said Maïmé Arnodin, a Parisian art director who bought some of the first Rive Gauche *smokings*. '*Elle* magazine ran article after article on Yves Saint Laurent and his *smokings*, but it wouldn't let its own journalists wear trousers to work. Imagine! And Yves's trousers were so beautiful.'[6]

No one looked better in a *smoking* than Yves's new best friend, Betty Catroux. Twenty-three when they met, she was androgynously slim with apparently endless legs, an angular face and heavy blonde hair hanging nonchalantly over her cheekbones. They ran into each other one night at Régine's. 'He picked me up! He was so beautiful. That's what I noticed about him at first. He had long hair with such big eyes and a beautiful body – broad shoulders and long legs. I looked a lot like that. It was very narcissistic. We started talking and there we were! Best friends!'[7]

Betty was a model, albeit a reluctant one, having started work at Chanel when she left school at seventeen. 'I hated modelling. I only did it to earn money so I could go out and have fun. That's all I cared about. I'd do a bit of work, then stop and go back to work when the money ran out.'[8] She and Yves made a striking couple, looking as alike as Andy Warhol and Edie Sedgwick did when she cropped her hair and sprayed it silver to resemble his. But whereas Edie was literally a 'girl of the year' for Warhol,[9] the bond between Yves and Betty was stronger. 'We were like brother and sister, like twins. We were so alike. We had fun together, doing crazy things and being silly. And we were both full of anguish at that age. So we shared that too.'[10] Another thing they had in common was a cosmopolitan background. Betty was born Elisabeth Lage in Rio de Janeiro, where her Irish-American father was posted as a diplomat. She came to Paris at the age of four when her parents split up and her Italian mother married a Frenchman. Although educated in France, Betty never felt entirely at home there; like Yves, she was always an outsider, albeit a privileged one.

Yves had the same easy intimacy with Betty as he had with Simone Tronc in his teens and with Victoire in his Dior days. Their friendship even survived her marriage to François Catroux, a boyishly handsome interior designer whom she met shortly after Yves. 'There wasn't any real difficulty, maybe a little resentment at first. It was hard work for me. I had to make a double effort so they'd both be happy. Then Yves realized that things would still be the same way between us and François loved him too.'[11] After her marriage Betty stopped modelling, apart from occasional jobs for Yves. Each season he asked her to do the *couture* collection, but she always declined, although she did agree to do odd bits of photographic work for him and to accompany him on his foreign trips.

The circle of friends – Pierre, Fernando, Clara, Thadée, Betty and François – formed a protective ring around Yves whenever he went out in Paris. Their evenings began with drinks at Yves's and Pierre's on Place Vauban, or at the Catroux's modernist apartment on Quai de Béthune overlooking the Seine on the Île Saint-Louis, followed by trips to the opera or the ballet, with dinner at Maxim's or La Coupole, and then dancing at Régine's, New Jimmy's or Castel, a more conservative club in Saint-Germain des Prés where the older members chatted over dinner in the ground-floor restaurant while the younger ones dived down to dance in the basement. Sometimes they went to Fernando's apartment near the Delacroix museum on pretty Place Fürstenberg in Saint-Germain des Prés for one of his Spanish dinners, and they were there every Sunday when he held open house with friends and friends of friends dropping by all afternoon. 'All we cared about was having fun and good times,' said Betty. 'There was a tremendous sense of freedom. The Algerian War was over. Life was easy. We were carefree, with no worries like illness or lack of money. We led charmed lives.'[12]

Yves's life seemed charmed indeed. At thirty he looked better than he did at twenty; his body had rounded out to become slender rather than skinny and his face had acquired the distinguished air of his father's. His hair had grown fashionably long until it curled over his collar, and he had swapped the severe suits he wore on his return from the army for soft velvet jackets and long leather coats. Calmer and more confident, he seemed to have shaken off his old anxieties, as Gloria Emerson, the *New York Times'* fashion editor, noted when she interviewed him in Paris. 'Once a shy, sad-eyed person who seemed to quiver at the sound of strange voices, he is now much more open, more lively – and much more sociable. Like a few of the other French designers, Mr Saint Laurent shows up at the season's posh parties and seems to like it.'[13]

Yves threw a party of his own at New Jimmy's in May 1967 to celebrate the publication of *La Vilaine Lulu*, a book of the cartoons he had been drawing since his Dior days.[14] For years Françoise Sagan had been urging him to publish them, and finally he agreed, dreaming up a new set of adventures for Lulu in the contemporary Paris fashion scene. In one story she visits André Courrèges' boutique on rue François Premier and sprays black ink at the sales assistants – all dressed in white tunics and pants, with matching boxing gloves – before fleeing to see Yves at Hôtel Forain.[15]

The Mathieu-Saint-Laurents had settled into their new life in France. Lucienne lived with Bri-Bri, the family dog, in an apartment in the sixteenth *arrondissement*, not far from rue Spontini, where the walls were filled with photographs of Yves, his sketches and paintings. Once or twice a week they lunched together, and she was a familiar figure at Hôtel Forain, often calling in to chat to the staff, or to see her son in his studio. 'It was obvious that she adored him,' said one employee. 'She'd come in beaming with pride at her wonderful son and everything he'd achieved. It just shone out of her. He was sweet with her, affectionate and attentive. And she was friendly with the staff, always making a point of saying something nice or asking how you were.' Lucienne sat in pride of place in the front row of the *couture* shows, immaculately made-up – 'maybe a little *too* made-up', as one observer put it – dressed from head to toe in Saint Laurent *haute couture*.

Charles made a point of seeing the collections too, but he preferred slipping into one of the quieter shows later in the week. The staff remembered him as a 'good-looking man, rather distinguished, quiet but very polite. Yves seemed slightly nervous when he was around, pleased to see him, but a little on edge.' Disliking the chilly Paris climate, Charles had fled south to the Riviera where he now spent most of his time living in a villa near Antibes. Lucienne visited him there in the summer and once a month Charles travelled to the capital to attend the board meetings of a property company of which he had become a director.

Professionally Yves's reputation was higher than ever. He took his theatrical work to a new level with his Warholesque designs for Roland Petit's production of *Paradise Lost.* The sets and costumes were more daring than anything he had attempted before. At the end of the first act Rudolf Nureyev dived into a gigantic pair of scarlet lips, wearing nothing but a skimpy pair of ballet tights.

After rave reviews for three successive seasons, he scored another hit with his autumn 1967 *couture* collection,[16] an affectionate homage to the eighty-four-year-old Coco Chanel, and his version of the retro look popularized by the hit film of the year, Arthur Penn's *Bonnie and Clyde.*[17] It was a series of Chanel's 'little black dresses' complete with swirling skirts, low-slung belts, dinky white collars and signature gardenias, which Eugenia Sheppard regarded as his best collection to date. 'All the promise that Yves Saint Laurent showed ten years ago when he took over after Christian Dior's death came true,' she wrote in the *Herald Tribune.*[18] Coco Chanel responded a few months later by naming Yves as her heir apparent on French television because 'one day, someone will have to take over from me'.[19]

Rive Gauche had not only given Yves an opportunity to design clothes for younger women, free from the financial constraints of *couture*, as he had always wanted, but was a roaring success financially. Kuniko Tsutsumi remembered people coming into Seibu-Saison in Tokyo just to look at the clothes, even if they could not possibly afford to buy them.[20] Richard Salomon was talking about turning

Rive Gauche into a chain by opening other shops, starting with one in New York.

By 1967, Yves and Pierre could contemplate buying a house in Marrakesh, to give Yves the North African refuge he longed for. Like his father, he missed the sun and colour of Africa, and had become particularly attached to Marrakesh after returning several times since his first visit with Pierre in 1962. They looked for a place to buy there and eventually found a simple stone house build around a shady courtyard in the heart of the old town, called Dar el-Hanch, or the 'House of the Serpent'.

North Africa had a romantic resonance for European intellectuals; a haven for nineteenth-century bohemians, it had been a source of inspiration for writers and painters from Gustave Flaubert and Eugène Delacroix to André Gide and Henri Matisse. It also held a special place in homo-erotic folklore as it was there that Gide acknowledged his homosexuality after a chance meeting with Oscar Wilde and his lover, Lord Alfred Douglas, in Algiers.

The bohemian tradition continued after the War when Tangier, designated as an International Zone free from French rule, became a haven for dissolute Americans and Europeans. David Herbert, the English aristocrat, bought a crumbling palace in the old town, as did Barbara Hutton, the Woolworth heiress whose brother-in-law, Maurice Doan, was later to sell Dar el-Hanch to Yves and Pierre. A motley assortment of American writers and artists linked to the Beat movement converged on Tangier in the 1950s: Paul and Jane Bowles, William Burroughs, Allen Ginsberg, and Brion Gysin.

When the International Zone was abolished, the expatriates drifted south to Marrakesh. It was more picturesque than Tangier with a lovelier setting, finer architecture and a culture which was friendly and permissive, even by Moroccan standards. Marrakesh was founded by Berber tribesmen who drifted there from the Sahara desert and Atlas ranges, with a more relaxed attitude to life than the *Fassis* in northern Morocco. The city was steeped in Berber superstitions with sorcerers and medicine-men setting up stalls in the *souks* to sell herbs, magic stones and home-made elixirs. The Marrakesh brothels were famous, particularly among gay men who found it easy to find willing partners there, like the streetboys the teenage Yves had sex with in Oran. Another attraction was *kif*, or cannabis, which was smoked openly and sold in *hookah* pipes on the markets. The Moroccans believe in two worlds: one ruled by reality, the other an imaginary world where the individual re-orders reality to suit their subconscious desires by smoking *kif*. Other drugs were readily available too, including opiates, like heroin, and over-the-counter drugs long banned in Europe and America, which were sold in Moroccan pharmacies.[21]

By the time Yves and Pierre bought Dar el-Hanch, Marrakesh was known among young Europeans as a beautiful, unspoilt city, free from tourist hotels and souvenir shops, where the locals took a tolerant attitude towards the vices of their fashionable foreign visitors. The philosopher Michel Foucault had been going there since the late 1950s,[22] and Brian Jones of the Rolling Stones made his first trip in 1966 with his girlfriend, Anita Pallenberg. He brought the rest of the band with him on his next visit to see some friends who had just bought a house in the *medina*: the American oil heir, J. Paul Getty Jr, and his wife, Talitha Pol.

The third of the five sons of J. Paul Getty Sr, the Oklahoma oil baron who was one of the richest men in America, J. Paul Jr was brought up by his mother, Ann Rork, who left his father after three years of marriage. He grew into a shy, artistic young man who married his college girlfriend and after an unhappy stint as a conscript in the Korean War, spent a gruelling period 'proving himself' by pumping gas for $100 a week at one of his father's oil companies, before moving to Rome to run Getty Oil's Italian operation.

Paul Jr met Talitha Pol in 1965 at a London party hosted by Claus von Bülow, one of his father's assistants. Born in Java to Dutch parents, Talitha spent her early years in a Japanese prisoner-of-war camp with her mother, while her father, the painter William Pol, was held in another camp. After the war she went to England where her father married a daughter of the artist Augustus John. By the time she met Paul Jr, Talitha was a strikingly beautiful woman in her early twenties with long auburn hair and almond-shaped brown eyes. After their marriage in 1966, they divided their time between a rooftop apartment in Rome and a dilapidated palace in Marrakesh.

The Gettys soon ran into Yves and Pierre in the tiny foreign community, inviting them back to their home where they held court to a steady stream of guests. The Rolling Stones, Mick Jagger, and his girlfriend Marianne Faithfull often stayed there, as did

Christopher Gibbs, a London antiques dealer, and Bill Willis, a young American decorator whom the Gettys had met in Rome and brought with them to Marrakesh. They threw parties at their palace which went on for days, and set off on treks into the mountains where they picnicked beside waterfalls on antique carpets that their servants spread out on the ground.[23] Sometimes the Getty set descended on Dar el-Hanch for the night, sprawling on the terrace with Maria Callas's voice blasting from the record-player, and trying out the herbal *hookah* pipes and magic potions they had bought from the sorcerers' stalls in the *souks*.

Yves was captivated by the Gettys, particularly by Talitha, whom he saw as a contemporary incarnation of F. Scott Fitzgerald's brittle, beautiful 1920s heroines. His taste in people had always veered towards hedonists, such as Fernando Sanchez, Rudolf Nureyev and Betty Catroux; but under Pierre's influence he had joined the purposeful artistic circle of Roland Petit, Zizi Jeanmaire, Claire Motte and Clara Saint, who mixed their fun with creative projects. The Gettys led the exquisitely idle lives of the effortlessly rich and gave Yves an *entrée* into that world. 'Everyone talked about Yves as this lucky, lucky man who'd been given all the gifts,' commented one friend. 'Well he was, in a way; but he also worked incredibly hard and had to be fantastically disciplined. Always pushing himself, with Pierre pushing from behind. Suddenly he met these madly glamorous people who didn't have to put up with any of that. No wonder he found them so seductive.'

Marrakesh was like an adult playpen of light and sun, where Yves spent his time with people who were young, rich and beautiful, free to do whatever they wanted with no risk of censure. The locals were warm and welcoming, but the city was still so far off the tourist trail that even Yves could wander around the *souks* unrecognized. For someone whose face had been plastered across newspapers since the age of twenty-one, it must have been a tremendous relief to be treated like any another young European, able to go out in public without being stared at or pestered. He had become expert at warding off strangers in Paris, responding to chance remarks with smiles and courtesies that invariably left them thinking how polite he was, when actually it was a ploy to keep them at bay; but in Marrakesh none of that was necessary.

Occasionally Yves flew to Rome to stay with the Gettys, and sometimes they came to Paris to see him and Pierre. One evening he hosted a dinner for them after a performance of Roland Petit's *Notre-Dame de Paris*, with Rudolf Nureyev and Claire Motte dancing the leading roles. When the meal was over they walked Nureyev back to the Ritz Hotel and, eager to impress Talitha, he treated them to an impromptu performance of *Petrouchka*, dancing across the cobbles of Place Vendôme.[24]

It was a time when other people were seeking refuge in simpler, unspoilt societies. The late 1950s and early 1960s had been an energetic period of rapid change, but it was a materialistic era devoid of political idealism. The turning point came in 1966 when Mao Tsetung's Cultural Revolution in China gave Western intellectuals a new cause to believe in after a decade of disillusion since their faith in communism was shattered by Khrushchev's exposure of Stalin's brutalities. Events in China made Western society seem barren, an impression reinforced by the rising tide of anger in the United States against the Vietnam War. The art world turned against the extrovert imagery of pop, towards the work of the Fluxus artists – such as Joseph Beuys, Nam June Paik and Yoko Ono – who combined conceptual art work with politically engaged 'happenings'. Exploring an exotic culture like the one Yves and the Rolling Stones had found in Marrakesh, and that the Beatles were looking for when they bolted to the Maharishi Mahesh Yogi's meditation centre in Rishikesh, meshed with the desire to escape from a spiritually impoverished society.

The other escape route was the hallucinogenic drugs that had suddenly become popular. William Burroughs and Allen Ginsberg had been tripping for years on obscure substances, such as *ayahuasco*, which they found in Latin America; but hallucinogens did not become fashionable, or readily available, until a Harvard academic, Dr Timothy Leary, tried LSD (acid) in 1961,[25] and started publicizing its mind-expanding properties. Leary saw himself as a psychic pioneer with a duty to enrich his followers' lives by introducing them to acid. He and his disciples, among them the writer Ken Kesey, fostered a climate in which taking LSD and other hallucinogens, such as magic mushrooms, was seen as *de rigueur* for anyone with artistic or intellectual aspirations.

Leary's message had a strong appeal for Yves, who drew parallels between the acid culture of the 1960s and the drug experiments of nineteenth-century poets such as Coleridge, Shelley, Baudelaire and Gautier. The self-exploratory aspect of LSD struck a chord with the introspective, conceptual side of the Fluxus movement, and for anyone as visually aware as Yves, the sensory experience of an acid trip was extraordinary. He genuinely believed that it opened up his mind, enabling him to explore new creative avenues in his work.[26] By the late 1960s he was tripping regularly, adding LSD to the cocktails of opiates and *kif* he and his friends dabbled with in Marrakesh.

Just as acid culture influenced the music of the Beatles and the Rolling Stones, so it spilled over into Yves's fashion. The 'homage to Chanel' was to be his last classic collection for some time, and for the next few seasons he jumbled together dozens of iconoclastic styles. His spring 1968 show alone included a string of innovations: an all-in-one jumpsuit, a transparent silk chiffon blouse and the safari jackets he had spotted on his Moroccan trips. The *pièce de résistance* was the appearance of one of Yves's favourite models, a stunning redhead called Danielle, wearing a sheer black silk chiffon dress with ostrich feathers encircling her hips, both breasts clearly visible through the fabric. Around her waist was a gold belt in the shape of a serpent, a private reference to Dar el-Hanch, the 'House of the Serpent'.

It would be overly simplistic to describe such a collection as purely a product of acid culture, but the cacophony of styles and colours displayed some characteristics of other LSD-inspired exercises, such as the Beatles' *Sergeant Pepper* album. Years later these collections would be hailed as among the most creative of Yves's career, but at the time the fashion editors were as sceptical about the designs as they were about his appearance in the Hôtel Forain *salon*, with long hippy curls straggling his shoulders and a couple of wispy silk scarves draped around his neck.[27] Danielle hit the headlines the next day for having bared her breasts in a *couture salon*, but Gloria Emerson took Yves to task in the *New York Times* for displaying 'too much honky tonk, and not enough signs of hard work and long thought'.[28]

The reviews were even less enthusiastic six months later[29] when Yves dedicated his autumn 1968 collection to the French students who had battled against the riot police in *les événements* of May 1968.[30]

Hundreds of students fought for days in the narrow streets around the Sorbonne in the fifth *arrondissement*, hurling stones, debris and home-made Molotov cocktails against the police riot shields. By the time the unrest was quelled at the end of May, millions of French trade unionists had gone on strike or marched in sympathy, and the television images of the Parisian demonstrators triggered copycat protests all over the world.

Les événements polarized France, as the country divided between the conservatives who abhorred the violence, and the *soixante-huitards*, or 'sixty-eighters', who saw the rioters as heroes. Yves had played no part in the protests, but he admired the students' courage. By creating a *couture* collection composed of the duffel coats and cowboy-style fringed suede suits they had worn during the protests, he was signalling his sympathy with their cause, just as the Beatles did by recording various versions of *Revolution* that summer, and the Rolling Stones by writing *Street-Fighting Man.*

Whereas the establishment had been willing to tolerate the pretty-boy pop stars in their smart suits who had symbolized the early 1960s youthquake, the violence of *les événements* made the generation gap seem unbridgeable. The middle-aged fashion editors in the Hôtel Forain *salon* found Yves's reincarnation as an idealistic hippy as hard to accept as they did the Beatles' metamorphosis from mischievous moptops into acid-dropping radicals. As for Yves, having spent his twenties struggling with the dilemma of interpreting the ideas of his generation for the wealthy women who bought his clothes, he could now design for his own generation, for the 'flower children' who wore Afghan coats over their Rive Gauche jumpsuits. Whenever his collections were criticized in his early years at Dior it was because he was deemed to have 'gone too far'; now he was a mature designer at a time when the only crime, at least in the eyes of his peers, was not going far enough.

The Beautiful and the Damned
1968–1971

It was a balmy day in late September and Manhattan sweltered in the last of the summer heat. By the middle of the afternoon a straggle of students, models and hangers-on had gathered outside a clothes store at 855 Madison Avenue. More people arrived until, by early evening, so many had squeezed on to the pavement that they were blocking the entrances to neighbouring shops and spilling out on to the street. Chequered cabs swerved to avoid them, the drivers honked their horns and hollered. People hung out of apartment windows to see what was happening, wondering where the noise was coming from. Eventually the police arrived and swept the kids back on to the sidewalk, erecting crowd-control barriers along the kerbside to keep them off the road and away from the long black limousines pulling up outside the shop.

The paparazzi flashed their cameras at the men and women crawling out of the limos. 'Is it YSL?' yelled one of the photographers when Lauren Bacall appeared in a slinky black jersey jumpsuit. 'Of course it's a Saint Laurent,' she drawled. 'If it's pants, it's Yves's.'[1] Another limousine drew up, ejecting a slender young man dressed in a baggy paisley cossack shirt and low-slung pants with a cascade of chains around his hips. He was accompanied by a woman with long blonde hair wearing a black satin sequinned jumpsuit slashed open to her waist. The crowd went wild when they realized that Yves Saint Laurent had arrived, with Betty Catroux by his side. 'It was incredible,' she recalled. 'They behaved as though we were the King and Queen.'[2]

Yves and Betty had flown to New York for the opening of the new Rive Gauche boutique. For months Pierre Bergé had been beseiged by offers from people who wanted to launch Rive Gauche in other countries, but Richard Salomon had insisted that the second shop should be in Manhattan. He found a suitable site in an abandoned Gristede grocery store on Madison Avenue, between 70th and 71st street, at the southern end of Central Park. The other shops on that stretch of Madison were antique dealers and neighbourhood groceries, but it was only a few blocks away from the big department stores, Bergdorf Goodman and Bloomingdale's, and a short taxi ride from the museums around Central Park. The old Gristede was gutted, and the building refurbished in a futuristic style using the Rive gauche colours of red, pink and orange, with an aluminium tunnel at the entrance and acid orange carpet climbing up the wall.

The launch party was as pandemoniac as the scene outside on the pavement. So many people crowded into the boutique that the staff had to take the clothes away to a storeroom for safekeeping. The chaos continued the following day as hundreds of New Yorkers turned up early to grab the best pieces. Within half an hour the police were called out again to control the crush. By closing time the new Rive Gauche boutique had sold $25,000 of clothes and its stocks were so depleted that the staff had to cable to Paris for fresh supplies. The daily papers and weekly news magazines ran story after story on the Rive Gauche phenomenon. 'In the fashion world Yves's name is magic,' wrote *Time* magazine. 'At the age of 32, Yves is a celebrity's celebrity.'[3]

He and Betty spent the rest of their visit hanging out with Andy Warhol at his new studio on Union Square West and hitting the New York clubs with him at night. The new studio was called The Factory like the old one, and Warhol had moved there after being shot the previous summer by a feminist activist, Valerie Solanas, at the shabby silver-painted Factory on East 47th Street. Badly injured by the shooting, he had drifted away from his old downtown haunts and swapped his grungier hangers-on for a new entourage led by Fred Hughes, a Texan art dealer who had a fling with Clara Saint a few years before while he was working at a Paris gallery, and two good-looking Californian twins, Jay and Jed Johnson. Yves and Betty slotted straight into the new Warhol world. 'Yves felt very comfortable with Andy,' she said. 'They didn't say much to each other as Yves's English was never very good and Andy hardly spoke French at all. But we all had such fun together.'[4]

Back in Paris, a couple of new faces joined their circle. One was Paloma Picasso, the twenty-year-old daughter of the artist Pablo Picasso and his mistress, Françoise Gilot. Paloma, named after the Spanish word for 'dove', and Claude, her brother, were largely brought up by their mother, a forceful woman who was a talented painter in her own right, and their stepfather, the pioneering medical scientist, Jonas Salk. Paloma had the standard ingredients of a glamour girl, with gleaming black hair and a porcelain complexion which she was careful to keep out of the sun, but she also had an original sense of style and strength of character that set her apart from the superficial socialites hovering hopefully on the fringes of the Saint Laurent set.

Paloma liked to mix the *couture* outfits her mother bought her with flea-market finds and treasures unearthed from the trunks in the Salks' attic. Andy Warhol said she would still have been famous even if she had not been Pablo Picasso's daughter, a sentiment with which Yves and his friends agreed. 'There's something very special about her,' said one. 'She has a warmth and an honesty that you sense straightaway.' Paloma turned up out of the blue at Hôtel Forain one day, when her mother made an appointment for her to look at the *couture* collection. Yves took to her at once, inviting her to join him for dinner; she was adopted by the rest of the clique and soon became close friends with Clara Saint.

They met their next recruit at Fernando Sanchez's one Sunday afternoon. Yves, Pierre, Betty and François arrived at Place Fürstenberg to find the usual scene of people lolling on low white sofas with candles burning, incense smouldering and the latest in a long line of Fernando's unexpected house-guests, Loulou de la Falaise. The daughter of Comte Alain de la Falaise, a member of one of France's most distinguished families, and Maxime Birley, an English debutante who had modelled for Elsa Schiaparelli in Paris, Loulou's background was as eccentric as it was grand. Born in the English country home of her grandparents, the court portraitist, Sir Oswald Birley, and his Anglo-Irish wife, Rhoda, she lived with both parents until she was three, when her father returned to France, leaving her mother to rip between London, Paris and New York, where she wrote recipes for Diana Vreeland's *Vogue*. Loulou was sent away to school in Switzerland, but was expelled for bad behaviour and landed back in London where she met, and quickly married, Desmond FitzGerald, the glamorous young Knight of Glin. It took her very little time to discover that a quiet life at his Irish country seat was not to her taste, so she filed for divorce and headed for Paris, turning up on the doorstep of her mother's friend, Fernando, to ask if she could stay.

At twenty-one Loulou was caffeine-slim with a classically pretty face and a cloud of light-brown curly hair, which looked distinctly like her host's. Fernando thought of her as a fairy or a gypsy, and she dressed the part, wearing long fringed shawls with heavy ethnic jewellery and antique dresses.[5] 'She was the most captivating woman I've ever met, so pretty that you couldn't stop staring at her,' said a friend who met her at that time. 'She dressed fabulously in clothes that looked as though they'd come from a magical dressing-up box. And she had real *joie de vivre*, always lively and laughing. You couldn't ever imagine Loulou being bored.'

Loulou and Fernando looked as alike as Yves and Betty, Andy and Edie. He took her under his wing, taking her out dancing in the Paris clubs, and introducing her to his friends. When Loulou was told that 'Yves and Pierre' were coming round to Place Fürstenberg that Sunday afternoon, she realized that 'Yves' was Yves Saint Laurent and assumed 'Pierre' must be Pierre Cardin. The real Pierre, who had never got on with Cardin, thought it a huge joke when she explained her mistake. 'We all fell in love with her at once,' said Betty. 'She was so beautiful and so funny. So she became part of our little family.'[6]

Loulou and Paloma posed for the paparazzi in their flea-market finds in the front row of the Saint Laurent *couture* shows, and the gossip columns were filled with snippets about Yves's appearance at social events with fashionable young friends in tow. Loulou caused a stir by arriving at the Palais Garnier opera house for the gala première of Pier Paolo Pasolini's *Medea* swathed in one of her favourite heavily-fringed shawls. All the other women at the theatre were wearing *couture*, including the guest of honour and star of the film,

Maria Callas, who arrived with her lover Aristotle Onassis on her arm. Paloma provoked a similar rumpus in London when she turned up for a Royal Ballet opening night at Covent Garden dressed in a ballerina's tutu.

The highlight of the night at chic Parisian nightclubs such as Régine's and New Jimmy's was the arrival of Yves and his clique. Sometimes he showed up with the Gettys, if they had flown in from Rome, or from London, where Talitha was spending more of her time; other nights he was accompanied by Rudolf Nureyev or Andy Warhol. But Yves could only take so much of Parisian society and whenever he could he stole off to Marrakesh, to hide away at Dar el-Hanch and spend time with Talitha.

Once work had been his chief concern, but now he was wearying of it, longing to find time for other things. The Gettys' wealth gave them the freedom to go to Marrakesh whenever they wished and Yves wanted to be able to join them there more often, or to take off and travel without being tied to the *couture* house. Even at the start of his career, he had been ambivalent about fashion, unable at first to decide between *couture* and the theatre, and after a few years at Dior he toyed with abandoning it altogether once he realized the limitations of working as a *couturier*. Dior's death and Yves's sudden promotion had settled the matter for him then, and after the trauma of his army breakdown he had gone back to the field he knew best, being in no psychological state to try his luck at something new. Now Yves was locked into the *couture* cycle, which left him with no choice but to go back to Hôtel Forain every six months to prepare his collections and to take on the extra responsibility of designing for the burgeoning Rive Gauche chain. The only area of his work where he could cut down was the theatre.

During the mid-1960s Yves had stepped up his theatrical projects, designing a couple of productions a year. It was a hefty addition to his duties at the *couture* house, but one that he welcomed as he found it so satisfying. Now he wanted to work less. His mood was probably influenced by the drugs he was taking. Acid often has a sedative effect on its users, leaving them in a benign, but dreamily listless state. John Lennon stopped songwriting for weeks at a time during the height of his acid trips in the late 1960s and doubtless it had a similar impact on Yves. He took on two theatrical projects in 1968

– designing costumes for one of his favourite actresses, Madeleine Renaud, in *L'Amante Anglaise*, a new play by Marguerite Duras, and for Zizi Jeanmaire in her latest show at the Théâtre de l'Olympia – but he did none the following year. It would be the first year he had not worked in the theatre since 1960.

Ironically, Yves was cutting himself off from the aspect of his work that he found most stimulating at a time when his creativity was heightened by his drug experiences. Years earlier Michel de Brunhoff had warned him about falling into the same trap as Christian Bérard, who had frittered away his talent on illustration, rather than applying it to painting. One of the reasons why Yves had taken on so much theatrical work in the mid-1960s was because he found it more intellectually stretching than *couture*, and without that distraction, his frustration with fashion intensified.

All around him other people were breaking down barriers and flirting with freedom. *Les événements* had acted like a lightning rod for France. General de Gaulle survived a snap election after the student riots, only to be toppled the following spring and replaced by the reformist president, Georges Pompidou. The copycat strikes and sit-ins in other countries continued well into the following year. Czech students occupied Prague University in autumn 1968 to protest against the Soviet occupation, and the following February the British authorities were forced to close the London School of Economics. Women formed protest movements, the Women's Liberation Front in the States and the Mouvement de Libération des Femmes in France. Gay rights activists mobilized all over the world after a group of New York drag queens fought a pitched battle against the police when they tried to close the Stonewall, a bar in the West Village. 'It was an extraordinary time,' recalled the fashion designer, Sonia Rykiel. 'Suddenly there seemed to be no constraints and we had so much freedom. Change was everywhere. All the old taboos were breaking down.'[7]

The changes aggravated Yves's sense of restlessness. He told friends that he was thinking of giving up fashion to spend more time on painting, writing and to go back to the theatre. 'There was a bit of a spoilt-brat syndrome,' said a friend of that era. 'Yves would complain and say he was tired of it all and everyone screamed "Oh no!" "How could you?" "You're so brilliant!" But it wasn't just affectation. Part of him really wanted to move on. He's highly intelligent and extremely creative. Right then he really thought that he'd gone as far as he could with fashion. Then there was the whole hippy thing. If you're spending half your time floating around Morocco in God knows what state with Talitha Getty you don't suddenly want to be told to stop and to go back to work. The people he was mixing with didn't have those constraints and Yves didn't want them either.'

Yves stayed on at the *couture* house as his friends urged him to, not least Pierre Bergé who, as he did not hesitate to remind Yves, had only become a businessman for his sake. And ironically, at the moment when he felt most inhibited by his role as a *couturier*, Yves found himself hailed as a cult figure by the young and fashionable. Despite his disaffection with fashion, he played the part to the full, posing for *Elle* magazine with his youngest sister, Brigitte, for the German photographer, Helmut Newton, in identical safari suits, Yves with his arm draped nonchalantly around Brigitte's shoulder. During *couture* week Hôtel Forain was besieged by young Parisiennes, who parked their little sports cars and battered old Citroên 2CVs on rue Spontini, so they could jump up on to the bumpers to see what Loulou, Paloma, and the rest of the audience were wearing as they filed in to the shows.

Yves's cult status was not restricted to France. When he and Betty flew to London for the opening of the first Rive Gauche there in 1969, they were greeted by a mob, just as on the previous year's trip to New York. Miuccia Prada, the Milanese fashion designer who was then a young drama student, remembered racing off to Rive Gauche in Milan as soon as it opened to pick out a pink puff-sleeved dress. After that she treated herself to a new Rive Gauche outfit each season, even wearing her Saint Laurents for political demonstrations. 'I'd stand on street corners handing out left-wing leaflets in my YSL outfits. Maybe it looked a little strange to other people, but I didn't care, I loved the clothes so much.'[8] Paul Smith, later to become one of Britain's most successful men's wear designers but then also a student, travelled to Paris each season for the *couture* shows with his wife, Pauline, and they slipped into Hôtel Forain to see one of the quieter presentations at the end of the week. 'If you waited until then, it was surprisingly easy to get in. One time there were six nuns from a local convent sitting in the row behind us. We saw all the great YSL collections. The *smokings*, and the first transparent blouses. The model walked in wearing a jacket, then she opened it and revealed her breasts. Fireworks! You never saw anything like that in the 1960s.'[9]

Yves aimed his designs directly at his young fans, with no concessions to the older *couture* clients. The collections at Hôtel Forain became *pots-pourris* of styles, many of which were never intended to be made up as *couture* outfits but were destined for the Rive Gauche rails. 'He is the hero of a whole generation,' decreed the *New York Times* after seeing the long sweeping maxi-dresses, mixed with super-short minis, he had designed for autumn 1969. 'The young in Paris wear him with the same private passion that an older, sadder generation read Camus.'[10]

Where Yves had once been at pains to refine his own ideas so that they stayed within *couture* conventions, he now parodied the rituals he had once respected. The next season's show ended with the traditional *couture* bride sweeping into the *salon* wearing a white wool trouser suit with a lacily veiled hat.[11] It was too much for the press, who accused him of becoming obsessed with headline-hitting gimmicks.[12] Unabashed, Yves took the parody a step further six months later by ending a show featuring brazenly bra-less models with a bride bearing the motto 'Love Me Forever Or Never' emblazoned on her velvet patchwork dress. 'Yves's new clothes are madly original,' wrote Eugenia Sheppard in the *Herald Tribune*. 'They are full of high voltage excitement that comes straight from today's times.'[13] The only serious competitor for the press's attention that season was Paloma Picasso who arrived at Hôtel Forain in a 1940s-style outfit of a short yellow skirt and orange satin coat with multi-coloured platform shoes amid an audience of women in pretty peasant flounces.

Yves's fans leapt hungrily on each innovation, as did the boutiques and department stores that slavishly copied his ideas. Having flourished in the 1960s by selling 'Here today, gone tomorrow' fads, from vinyl raincoats to paper dresses, the mass market needed designers like Yves to set new trends each season if consumers were to be persuaded to chuck out their old clothes and buy new ones. Before Rive Gauche the 'knock-off merchants' had ordered samples of the *haute couture* originals from Hôtel Forain; now they sent their junior designers to the boutiques to buy armfuls of clothes and rip them apart at the seams before reconstructing them in cheaper fabrics.

Sometimes the copies were too close for comfort. Yves Saint Laurent took out a writ against an Italian department store, claiming that it had pirated one of its designs and sold it with a fake YSL label; but mostly the company relied on Yves's ability to stay ahead of the copyists by coming up with new ideas the next season.

'He was completely in tune with the times,' said the designer Christian Lacroix, who was then avidly following the YSL collections as a student. 'It was a glamorous, sensual era when there were no barriers and no limits. There was unbridled sex and very chic drugs. There was a type of woman then who was clever and beautiful, but with a real audacity and she dressed in Yves Saint Laurent.'[14] Richard Salomon encouraged Yves's innovations, partly because he admired his talent and partly because he realized the publicity value of bra-less models and trouser-suited brides. He also urged Yves, Pierre and Didier Grumbach to plough the money they made back into the business by opening more Rive Gauche boutiques[15] and launching a new Rive Gauche for men.

The old taboos of what men could and could not wear had broken down steadily in the 1960s, starting with the self-consciously stylish suits worn by Britain's 'mods' and the French '*yé-yés*', and culminating in the androgynous psychedelic look. Acid culture was all about self-discovery, and its sartorial role-models were pretty-boy pop stars such as Brian Jones and Mick Jagger of the Rolling Stones, or Jim Morrison of the Doors who did not flinch from expressing the feminine side of their characters in their clothes, even if it raised questions about their sexual preferences. After the Stonewall riot, those questions were addressed directly by the increasingly vocal gay groups. Rudolf Nureyev summed up the changing sartorial *mores* by becoming the first man to be allowed into the '21' club in Manhattan when not wearing a tie.[16]

Yves modelled his men's collection on his own hippy *de luxe* wardrobe of velvet jackets, kaftans, gabardine safari suits, printed silk shirts and chain belts.[17] Nureyev was one of his most enthusiastic customers, plumping for outlandish designs, such as the pony-skin jacket with matching thigh-length boots he wore for a night on the town with Princess Margaret.[18] Another fan was Andy Warhol who, at Fred Hughes's prompting, kitted himself out in a new wardrobe of tailored Rive Gauche jackets and Levi jeans which he wore with the same unwavering loyalty as his old downtown uniform of battered black leathers and grungy T-shirts.[19]

The Warhol set was coming over to Paris more frequently, spurred on by Loulou de la Falaise, who divided her time between there and New York, where she did stints at The Factory between modelling jobs for Diana Vreeland's *Vogue*. Loulou had a brief fling with Fred Hughes until she dumped him for Eric de Rothschild, one of the younger members of the banking clan, but they remained friends and he looked her up, along with Clara Saint, whenever he was in Paris with Warhol and Jed Johnson, one of the Californian twins whom Yves and Betty had met in Manhattan the previous summer.

As a fashionable American artist allied to the Saint Laurent set, Andy Warhol had an *entrée* to levels of society in Paris that still eluded him in New York.[20] His work sold well in France, and he exhibited regularly at Parisian galleries, often asking Clara to take time off from Rive Gauche to organize interviews with the French critics for him. And Paris was a treasure trove of the Art Deco *objets* he was collecting, offering richer pickings than New York. Yves and Pierre were also buying Art Deco pieces for the new apartment they were renovating on rue de Babylone. They tipped off Warhol if interesting auctions were coming up and took him off antiqueing when he was in town, sometimes inviting Karl Lagerfeld, Yves's friend from his Dior days, to come along with them.

The Factory crowd decamped to Paris for a couple of weeks in autumn 1970 when Paul Morrissey, one of Warhol's collaborators, was shooting a film, *L'Amour*, in Karl Lagerfeld's Left Bank apartment. It was The Factory's version of the 1953 Hollywood classic, *How To Marry A Millionaire*, and told the story of an American innocent abroad who spent most of her time in Paris complaining about how much she was missing her favourite television shows back home. Karl Lagerfeld had a cameo role as an insouciant German aristocrat, and the leads were played by Jane Forth, Patti D'Arbanville and Donna Jordan, a teenage trio who hung out at The Factory. Andy Warhol spent most of his days out antiqueing with Yves, leaving the filming to Paul Morrissey with Jed Johnson as camerman, but at the end of each afternoon he and Yves dropped in on the film set to see how things were going.

Yves was struck by Donna Jordan's clothes, which she had copied from the 1940s shoulder-padded dresses, platform shoes and bright red lipstick worn by the Factory drag queens. Her look was similar to Paloma Picasso's at that summer's *couture* show, and to a 1940s outfit Paloma had worn one evening that autumn when she turned up for dinner in a black *crêpe* Joan Crawford dress she had found on a Portobello Road junk stall in London with a grey-feathered pink turban that one of her mother's friends had thrown away. Yves had asked Paloma to come to his studio the next day so he could sketch her in it.[21]

The 1940s was one of Yves's favourite periods, rekindling memories of Christian Bérard's work in the postwar Parisian theatre and of Elsa Schiaparelli's sharp-shouldered fashions. It reminded him of Lucienne's clothes in Algeria, in particular of an outfit she had worn for a dance one summer night when she was staying in the country with the children. Charles was away on business, and Lucienne went out on her own. Yves had persuaded the servants to take him and his sisters after her. 'We wanted to see *maman* dancing. The windows were so high that one of the servants had to lift me up so I could see her. She was wearing a black *crêpe* dress with square shoulders and a pointed neckline. The dress stopped just below her knees and on it she had pinned a bouquet of daisies, cornflowers and poppies. She was wearing a white cross on a black velvet ribbon around her neck. It was exquisite.'[22] His memories of Lucienne in the 1940s were as evocative to him as the image of his mother's *Belle Époque* dresses had been to Dior when he was working on the New Look. 'It's a funny thing,' said Christian Lacroix. 'But if you look at the best work of many designers, it's almost always the style that their mothers wore in their prime.'[23]

The pretty peasant styles of the late 1960s seemed inappropriate in the darker climate of the early 1970s. The hippy idyll was over. The United States was mourning its Vietnam War victims, and the British army had started using rubber bullets against the IRA in Northern Ireland. The psychedelic drugs that Yves and some of his friends had found so illuminating were showing a darker, sinister side as the toll of acid casualties mounted. Brian Jones left the Rolling Stones when his drug habit spiralled out of control and was later found drowned in his swimming pool. The pregnant actress, Sharon Tate, and three of her friends were butchered by the cult leader,

Charles Manson, after a party at the Hollywood home of her husband, Roman Polanski. The stark 1940s silhouette with its harsh make-up and clunky shoes seemed better suited to the cynical climate of the early 1970s.

When the spectators settled into their little gilt chairs in the Hôtel Forain *salon* on 29 January 1971, they saw a collection of *crêpe* dresses, palazzo pant suits, dinky hats and platform sandals that Lucienne Mathieu-Saint-Laurent might have worn in her heyday. To Yves they rekindled happy memories of his childhood, but to most of the audience they harked back to one of the cruellest periods of French history – the Occupation.

Silence fell as the first models entered the room. 'It was an extraordinary occasion,' said Marie-José Lepicard, who covered the show for *Jardin des Modes*. 'Some of the older French journalists had lived through the War. They were appalled. Saint Laurent had gone too far for them, beyond the boundaries of good taste. They were so angry that they couldn't see the clothes.'[24] Knowing that the collection would be contentious, Yves had begged Paloma Picasso to come in one of her 1940s outfits so the spectators could see how to wear the look; but he had not realized quite how angry they would be. Some people stalked out of the *salon* before the end of the show and the atmosphere was so hostile that, for the first time in his career, Yves did not come out for the finale.

France-Soir, the Paris evening paper, ran a scathing report under the headline, *'Un Grand Farce!'* *Le Figaro* took up the gauntlet the following day, accusing Yves of tricking his audience with *'Un long gag'*. The British press was equally vociferous. The *Daily Telegraph*'s verdict was 'Nauseating!' The *Guardian* described it as 'A *tour de force* of bad taste.' Even Yves's old champion, *Women's Wear Daily*, urged him to 'shake off the weird and kooky influences'.[25] 'What a relief, at last, to write that a fashion collection is frankly, definitely and completely hideous,' pronounced Eugenia Sheppard in the *International Herald Tribune*. And that was just for starters. 'Yves has picked the ugliest, harshest period in fashion to recapture. Other designers have been toying with the 1940s, but leave it to Saint Laurent to bring the whole period back alive . . . If you ask me to sum up the whole European *couture* trend in one adjective I'd say it's suicidal.'[26]

Not everyone hated the 1940s look. When Bianca Pérez Mora de Macías married Mick Jagger in the Riviera village of Saint-Tropez that spring, she arrived for the ceremony four months pregnant and naked under an icy white Saint Laurent 1940s *couture* suit. The Rive Gauche version of the style proved equally popular with Yves's young fans, many of whom had no recollection of the War, and had already caught glimpses of the harsher 1940s silhouette on trendsetters, like Paloma Picasso.

Christian Lacroix thought it was the most exciting fashion collection he had ever seen. 'Sublime! I didn't live through the War years. I'd only heard about them from my parents and grandparents. I'd always been fascinated by the aesthetics of that period – possibly because it was so taboo. Saint Laurent based his collection on the look that the French call BOF – Beurre, Oeufs et Fromages, or Butter, Eggs and Cheese – because those were the things that the black marketeers got rich by selling during the War. A BOF was someone who was wicked and vulgar, who had made lots of money, often by selling things they'd taken from Jews sent to the concentration camps. Platform shoes, floral dresses and big shoulders were symbolic of everything about the time which had since become taboo. It was an incredibly daring thing for him to have done.'[27]

The older members of Yves's audience did not want him to be daring that season. Coco Chanel had died a few weeks before on 10 January 1971. Having dominated French fashion in the 1920s and 1930s, she had restored her reputation after her disastrous postwar comeback to rule the roost as a *grande dame* in the 1960s. By the time she died Chanel was treated as a monument, rather than a living designer, attracting more attention for past achievements than for her current work. 'Just her name was enough to describe a pair of shoes, a hat, a pocketbook, a suit, perfume, jewelery – an entire look,' read her obituary in *Time* magazine. 'It conveyed prestige, quality, impeccable taste and unmistakable style. It was a sign of excellence. Coco Chanel had no patience, and too much taste, for anything else.'[28]

Her death left Yves unrivalled as the world's most famous living fashion designer. Chanel herself had named him as her successor on television only a few years before. None of his contemporaries could match Yves's achievements. André Courrèges, who had once seemed like a serious threat, had faded after a few seasons, never having succeeded in matching the triumph of his 'Space Age' look. The fad for Paco Rabanne's plastic sculptures proved to be short lived, and Pierre Cardin seemed more interested in licensing his name to a string of conspicuously uncouture-ish products, such as chocolates, than in fashion. Hubert de Givenchy still had a loyal coterie of clients, as did Marc Bohan at Dior; but their classic styles were too restrained to excite the mass market, or to hit the headlines as Yves's did. Emanuel Ungaro, a Provençal tailor who had trained with Balenciaga, was praised as a gifted colourist, but had neither the range, nor the stature of Yves Saint Laurent.[29] Names like Emanuelle Khanh, Sonia Rykiel and Michèle Rosier were virtually unknown outside the trendy ghetto of *prêt-à-porter*. After Chanel's death the fashion establishment had hoped that Saint Laurent would produce a collection worthy of his coronation as the king of *couture*, not one which would be dismissed as 'weird', 'kooky' and 'completely hideous'.

There was another reason for the stormy response to the show. Yves's 1940s look was not simply an exercise in nostalgia, but a tribute to the self-consciously camp style of the drag queens who hung out at Andy Warhol's Factory. The hipper fashion magazines were starting to write about drag, but Yves was the first designer to pay public homage to the homosexual underworld in an *haute couture salon*. His 1940s collection conformed completely to the criteria defined in Susan Sontag's 1964 essay, 'Notes on Camp'. 'Camp asserts that good taste is not simply good taste; that there exists, indeed, a good taste of bad taste,' she wrote, concluding with 'The ultimate camp statement: it's good because it's awful.'[30]

The sexual sub-text of Yves's 1940s look was inescapable at a time when the gay movement was gathering force, as the Gay Liberation Front spread from the States to Europe after the Stonewall riot.[31] It made the 1940s collection seem more threatening than past *couture* controversies such as André Courrèges' silver sequinned hipsters, or Yves's beatnik leathers at Dior. *Time* magazine blamed his 'good chum', Andy Warhol, for the 'campier influences' over the collection in an article entitled 'Yves St Debacle'.[32]

Even Lucienne was drawn into the fray, leaping to her son's defence in a *New York Times* interview entitled 'Criticize Yves Saint Laurent

– and It Hurts His Mother'. Photographed in her Paris apartment with Bri-Bri the dog by her side, she looked the epitome of *couture* chic in a neat little navy blue crêpe dress from the infamous collection, claiming not to understand what the fuss was about. 'I can't help it. I'm simply not capable of being critical where he's concerned.'[33] Yves broke his habit of leaving public comment to Pierre, by telling a reporter that his critics were 'narrow-minded and reactionary, petty people paralysed by taboos' who did not understand the 'revolutionary spirit' of his work.[34]

Yves's instincts were correct; the climate was becoming chillier. A few months after the 1940s show Talitha Getty flew to Rome to see her husband, from whom she had separated that spring. The Gettys' drug experiments had ended with both Talitha and J. Paul Jr becoming hooked on heroin. In a desperate attempt to beat her addiction, she left him, taking their toddler son, Tara Gabriel Galaxy Gramaphone, with her. The trip to Rome was a final effort at reconciliation. Talitha arrived there on 10 July 1971, and was found in their apartment the following afternoon – dead from a heroin overdose.

End of An Era
1971–1972

When Yves Saint Laurent arrived at Jeanloup Sieff's studio to pose for a new portrait, he knew exactly what he wanted to do. A friend of Loulou and Clara, Sieff had hung out with the Saint Laurent set for a couple of years; Yves felt comfortable with him and was familiar with his studio, an artist's loft at the top of an apartment building on rue Ampère, not far from Boulevard Pereire, where he had lodged when he first came to Paris. Yves settled into the open-plan area under a glazed roof that Sieff used as a workspace and issued his instructions for the portrait, which was to be used as an advertisement for the new YSL men's perfume. 'He told me to photograph him in the nude,' recounted Sieff. 'He said he wanted to create a scandal.'[1]

A scandal was what he got. Jeanloup Sieff shot Yves sitting cross-legged on a leather cushion wearing nothing but his spectacles. It is a beautiful backlit composition. Yves's face falls into shadow, bordered by shoulder-length curls and a casual beard, with the details of his body flung into focus, even the veins on his hands and the texture of his flesh. 'It was all Yves's idea,' recalled Sieff. 'The only thing I changed was that he wanted to sit with the perfume bottle between his legs. I explained why I didn't think *that* would work. We finished the shoot very quickly in about an hour.'[2]

Nudity was hardly a novelty in the early 1970s. Flower children had romped naked at the 1960s rock festivals in Woodstock and on the Isle of Wight, and each summer the paparazzi flashed as the French police chased nude sunbathers off the Riviera beaches. Images of naked women were a familiar feature in advertising, but they were almost always pictures of anonymous models. It was absolutely unheard-of for a man as prominent as Yves Saint Laurent to be photographed nude for an advertisement.

Some publications refused to run it. *Jours de France* rejected the ad on the grounds that children might see it. Others made the most of the scandal. The evening paper, *France-Soir*, described Yves as looking like a 'bespectacled Christ', and Hélène de Turckheim, *Le Figaro*'s fashion editor, called him a 'cherub'. Coming so soon after the 1940s collection, it sealed Yves's reputation as the most iconoclastic of the Paris *couturiers* and enhanced his cult status. 'It added to the Saint Laurent myth,' said Claude Brouet, who was then fashion editor of *Marie Claire* magazine. 'Posing nude made him seem even more daring and glamorous to young people. But it's a beautiful photograph and something as lovely as that can never really be scandalous.'[3]

By causing a stir in the press, Yves had generated free publicity of far greater value than the advertising his company actually paid for. After the newspapers and magazines had finished with the furore, more people knew that Yves Saint Laurent was bringing out a new men's perfume by reading about it in the press, than from seeing the advertisement.[4]

The decision to commission a naked portrait says a great deal about Yves at that time, not least how aware he was of the extent of his fame. His picture had been plastered across the international press since he was twenty-one. Having shied away from publicity in the early years of his career, Yves now seemed to enjoy exploiting it; by posing with Brigitte for *Elle* magazine, and styling himself as the role model for his men's collection. Being photographed in his own designs was one thing, but appearing nude, literally stripped of his professional accomplishments, quite another. Few other fashion designers would have dreamt of publicizing a new product by using their own image, nor would they have been able to. The public might have recognized the names and the clothes of Pierre Cardin or Hubert de Givenchy, but not what they looked like; whereas Yves Saint Laurent was instantly recognizable.

Even so it was an extraordinarily narcissistic act from someone described only a few years before as 'a shy, sad-eyed person who seemed to quiver at the sound of strange voices'.[5] It showed how Yves liked to see himself, and wanted others to see him. Thirty-five when the advertisement came out, he often quipped that although he did not like his face, he was proud of his body. Rightly so; Jeanloup Sieff's portrait shows a slender, perfectly proportioned torso that might have belonged to a man in his early twenties. Yves had always played the boy in his personal and professional relationships: as Lucienne's only son, the *petit prince* at Dior, Pierre Bergé's younger lover and the playmate of Betty Catroux and Talitha Getty. By posing naked for Jeanloup Sieff, he was flaunting his youthfulness and signalling that, as an adult in his mid-thirties, he had no intention of abandoning the boy-wonder role.

The naked Yves was also brandishing his sexual self-confidence by casting himself as a desirable man like Rudolf Nureyev or Andy Warhol's boyfriend, Jed Johnson. Yves's homosexuality was an open secret in the Paris fashion world, as was Nureyev's among balleto-manes. The portrait sent a tacit signal to the growing group of sexually-aware gay men and became a homosexual icon of the 1970s: a picture that gay teenagers tore out of magazines to pin on their bedroom walls, or to paste into secret scrapbooks.

The same sexual self-confidence was evident in Yves's private life. He was spending more time with Rudolf Nureyev who, like Betty and Talitha, appealed to the wayward side of his nature. Obnoxious though he could be, Nureyev was sometimes enchanting, as he had been on the night that he treated Yves and the Gettys to an impromptu performance of *Petrouchka* across the moonlit Place Vendôme. He could talk about anything – art, opera, physics, philosophy – and was extraordinarily sexy with his superb dancer's body. The consensus in gay circles was that Rudolf Nureyev was one of the world's most desirable men. When he first met Yves in the 1960s Nureyev had begun an affair with the Danish dancer, Erik Bruhn, and after separating from him in 1968, he found another long-term lover in the young American film-maker, Wallace Potts. But he was unfaithful to both of them, indulging in a string of casual flings. He and Yves had a flirtatious relationship, that some of their friends think went further than flirtation.

Yves had also become close to François-Marie Banier and Jacques Grange, two beautiful young men whom he and Pierre had taken with them to Marrakesh that Easter. Banier was an impish figure with a wicked sense of humour and misleadingly cherubic looks, who had befriended Parisian *grandes dames*, like Marie-Laure de Noailles and Marie-Hélène de Rothschild, through his job as Pierre Cardin's press officer. They doted on him and on the equally handsome Jacques Grange, a sunnier, more serene character adept at smoothing things over when François-Marie made a barbed remark or caused a scene. Grange worked for Didier Aaron, one of the great Paris antique dealers, and shared Yves's love for the work of 1930s artisans such as Jean-Michel Frank, Jean Dunand and Christian Bérard. In many ways he was a lighter version of Yves, coming from a similar wealthy provincial background with many of the same enthusiasms, but free from his neuroses.

The Saint Laurent set found a new nocturnal haunt, Club Sept, or 'Le Sept' as they called it, which was wilder than their old dives. It was run by Fabrice Emaer, who filled the club with people from the fashion, art and literary worlds, rather than the middle-aged socialites who congregated at Régine's and New Jimmy's. Yves and his friends went there nearly every night.[6] After finishing work at the Rive Gauche press office, Clara Saint would go home and take a long bath before ringing round to arrange when and where they would meet that evening, knowing that they were bound to end up at Le Sept. Betty and François Catroux danced for hours on end there, as did Loulou de la Falaise with Fernando Sanchez, or Kenzo Takada, the Japanese fashion designer. Pat Cleveland, a beautiful black American who was one of Yves's favourite models, was famous for dancing naked *à la* Josephine Baker on the Le Sept table-tops. Andy Warhol insisted on going whenever he was in Paris. Clara Saint remembered him turning up with the leftovers of his evening meal tucked into his jacket pocket to give to his dogs the next day. 'One evening he had fish for dinner and forgot to take it out. When he wore the jacket again a few nights later, it smelt terrible!'[7]

Their long nights at Club Sept were fuelled by drink and drugs. Yves had always been a drinker; like many shy people he found that alcohol made socializing seem easier, but by then his drinking had become heavier. 'He was really hitting the bottle,' said a friend. 'But so was everyone else. It was a wild time, very heavy, not as innocent as the 1960s, but much more extreme. And Yves was a charming drunk – never obnoxious. He'd start telling funny stories but would forget the punchline before he'd finished, slurring his words and saying silly things like a little boy.'

He had other crutches too. Having smoked *kif* in Marrakesh since the early 1960s, Yves tried any other drugs, opiates or acid, that floated in and out of fashion. At first he and his friends did not know about the darker side of the drugs they were taking; that only became apparent at the end of the 1960s when the toll of fatal overdoses, like Talitha Getty's, mounted. But even the tragedy of Talitha's death did not stop him. After *kif*, opiates and acid, Yves moved on to cocaine, the chic drug of the early 1970s. Cocaine had been around for decades but only in short supply and at very high prices; suddenly it became more easily available, at least for those who could afford the going rate of $1,500 an ounce. It was the ideal drug for the era: clean, discreet and easy to take at nightclubs and parties, without any of the fiddly preparations needed for marijuana or the ugly syringes used for heroin, and it had an immediate, exhilarating effect. 'There were lots of uppers and downers around then,' said a friend. 'And whatever went down in those days was going on in Yves's life in spades.'

Many drug-takers are saved from toppling into addiction because they run out of money, or their supplies dry up; but none of these constraints applied to Yves Saint Laurent, who could afford to buy as much cocaine or anything else as he wanted. His wealth saved him from the most dangerous aspects of drug-taking. He did not have to resort to cheap, doctored drugs, or to come face to face with violent dealers, as nothing was too expensive and there was always someone else to buy drugs for him. But wealth left fewer barriers between Yves and addiction, which in his case was particularly dangerous. Not only was he the type of intense, visceral character that tends to be most prone to drug dependency, but his maltreatment at Val-de-Grâce had worn away his natural defences.

Even before going into the army, Yves had taken prescription pills, mainly sedatives and anti-depressants, to soothe him when he became tired and enervated in the run-up to the Dior shows. Throughout his confinement at Val-de-Grâce he was subjected to heavy doses of sedatives, so heavy that one of the doctors there warned him they would have a lasting effect. After his discharge, the anxiety attacks worsened and he needed higher doses of tranquillizers to calm him down and help him sleep. The years of sleeping pills and anti-depressants aggravated the damage done at the hospital, locking Yves into a vicious cycle that made it all too easy for him to get hooked.

Whenever he could he took himself off to Marrakesh where, after Talitha's death, he found new confidants in Bill Willis, the handsome young American decorator whom the Gettys had brought there from Rome, and Boule de Breteuil, a French countess who had a house in the city. Boule was a vivacious elderly woman, with a wavy white bob swept away from her face, whom Yves treated as if she was an indulgent and engagingly errant aunt.

Yves made other trips too, going to music festivals with Pierre and to Venice, with which he had fallen in love after seeing Luchino Visconti's film of Thomas Mann's *Death in Venice*. Infected by his enthusiasm, Andy Warhol set off with Clara for a Venetian weekend during one of his European trips. Yves had raved about the art and architecture, but all Warhol wanted to do was celebrity-spot on the terrace of Harry's Bar. 'There we were in Venice with all these beautiful buildings around us and Andy would have happily sat in Harry's Bar all day,' recalled Clara. 'I had my nose buried in the Blue Guide telling him about all the things we could do. Once I suggested going to see a wonderful Veronese in a nearby church. And Andy said, "Oh gee! Virna Lisi! Let's go see her!"[8] He thought Veronese was an Italian movie star!'[9]

Yves's relationship with Pierre seemed stable enough. Rumours ran around Paris that one or other of them was having affairs, but that was deemed perfectly acceptable among the gay and straight couples in their circle. They were still living together at Place Vauban with their dogs – Yves's chihuahua, Hazel, and Pierre's pug, Ficelle – sharing the main part of the apartment, but each having their own bedroom. Yves's was a small, sparse room tucked behind an inconspicuous door in the *salon* with a bed and a tiny television set as the only pieces of furniture, and one of the walls covered with magazine clippings of his favourite images: fragments of landscapes and sunsets, swatches of colour, sketches of *La Vilaine Lulu*, a pencil portrait of Hazel and a photograph of the Rolling Stones. He told visitors that he loathed the apartment, but he and Pierre would soon be moving into the new home they were renovating at 55 rue de Babylone, a few streets away in another part of the seventh *arrondissement*.

Having outgrown Place Vauban, they had looked at dozens of different places, none of which seemed right, until they found rue de Babylone and Yves fell in 'love at first sight'.[10] It was a remarkable apartment, a duplex designed in the 1930s for Marie Cuttoli, a wealthy art collector, who commissioned Jean-Michel Frank to create a home for her collection of Picassos, Braques, Mirós and the African art she had bought in Algeria when her husband was a senator there. Frank arranged the apartment in his ascetically elegant style as a series of large, light rooms around a private garden, a rarity in central Paris and the perfect playground for Hazel and Ficelle. Rue de Babylone was a quiet street of apartment blocks and government buildings punctuated by the greenery of a small public park, the Jardin de Babylone, and the private garden of the prime minister's residence, the Hôtel de Matignon. Next door to the duplex was La Pagode, a pretty Japanese pagoda shipped over to France in the late 1800s by a director of the nearby Bon Marché department store who used it as a private ballroom until it was converted into a cinema in the 1930s.

The Place Vauban apartment had the hallmarks of two men who had moved there at a time when they had exquisite taste, but little money; by the time they bought 55 rue de Babylone in 1969, Yves and Pierre were affluent enough to decorate their home exactly as they wished. Teams of builders and decorators were hired to renovate the duplex, and to restore its original features, the Jean-Michel Frank radiators and a Jean Dunand chimney. The construction work took three years and during that time Yves and Pierre roamed the Paris antique dealers searching for Art Deco art and furniture in the same spirit as Frank's designs.

They turned 55 rue de Babylone into a private enclave in the heart of Paris. Visitors walked through a classic Parisian façade of black lacquered door under a wrought-iron and glass canopy, into an entrance hall painted in Diana Vreeland's favourite shade of lacquer red. The hall opened on to a drawing room decked out as an Art Deco showcase with a collection of Jean Dunand vases and a vividly coloured 1930s carpet. Yves placed his collections of African carvings and tribal masks there, with an imposing Senufo bird sculpture, one of the first works of art he had treated himself to when the business took off.

The most decadent part of the apartment was an Oriental Room lined with smoked mirrors and encircled by long, low sofas in glittering *lamé* with 1930s motifs picked out in pinks and blues. The centrepiece was a sixteenth-century Chinese Ming buddha in heavy gold flanked by a pair of elaborate candelabra. Yves designed it as a refuge, where he could languish with friends after Club Sept had closed for the night. Another room was set aside as a daytime den for sketching and reading, and he furnished it in the simple modernist style of Place Vauban with white walls, leafy plants, plain white sofas and Chinese *objets* on wooden bookshelves. On the carpet stood a couple of life-like sheep sculptures made by Claude Lalanne, an artist whom Yves had befriended when she made a series of gold-dipped breastplates for one of his collections. All the main rooms of the duplex looked out through white-shuttered windows on to the garden arranged in the formal French manner with neatly trimmed topiary, a shady terrace and a flock of Claude Lalanne's sheep 'grazing' on the lawn.

It was a place where Yves could retreat from the pressures of work, just as he did at Dar el-Hanch. He still spoke of his desire to break away from fashion, but did nothing about it, although he had evidently lost any inclination to pander to the Paris fashion establishment. A decade of designing two collections a year had drained his interest in *haute couture* and the storm over the 1940s look was the final straw. Shortly afterwards he dismissed *couture* as 'a museum' that had become 'bogged down in a boring tradition of so-called good taste and refinement',[11] and talked openly of wanting to be free to experiment with *prêt-à-porter*. The next season's YSL *couture* show was a sober affair. Only a handful of journalists was allowed to see it. *Le Monde* and the *Herald Tribune* were among those banned because of their scathing reports of the 1940s collection.

Three weeks later Pierre Bergé issued a formal statement saying that there would be no more *haute couture* shows at Hôtel Forain. The *ateliers* would remain open to accept orders from private clients, but the YSL shows would in future be devoted to Rive Gauche ready-to-wear. The sub-text to his announcement was the decline of *haute couture*. The number of houses registered with the Chambre Syndicale had fallen from thirty-seven in 1966 to nineteen by 1967, the year after rue de Tournon's opening.[12] By the end of the decade all the New York department stores had closed their *couture salons*, except Bergdorf Goodman and Saks Fifth Avenue. The economic pressure on the *couturiers* intensified as French inflation escalated and labour costs rocketed. The finances of *couture* did not add up. By the early 1970s Yves Saint Laurent was spending $250,000 to produce and present each *couture* collection, when the bulk of its income came from *prêt-à-porter* and perfume.[13]

All the creative excitement was in ready-to-wear. Rive Gauche's success[14] had prompted other *couturiers* to launch their own boutiques,[15] but the real innovations came from outside the *couture* circle. Kenzo Takada, one of Loulou de la Falaise's Le Sept dancing partners, rented a space in Galerie Vivienne, a glazed nineteenth-century arcade near the Bibliothèque Nationale,[16] and opened a boutique, Jungle Jap, to sell clothes made from cheap fabrics he bought from the Saint-Pierre market in Montmartre. Sonia Rykiel sold her 'poor boy' knitted separates from a boutique in Saint-Germain des Prés,[17] and Yves's old friend, Karl Lagerfeld, was making his name at Chloé for his floaty hippy *de luxe* printed dresses.[18]

Even the *prêt-à-porter* shows were gaining momentum. Until then they had been scrappy affairs. It was too late for the ready-to-wear designers to show their collections during *couture* week in January and July, as it did not give them enough time to manufacture their clothes before the start of the season. But by the late 1960s a couple of designers had started showing their autumn ranges in April and spring collections in October, and the *couturiers* staged impromptu presentations of their *prêt-à-porter* lines at the same time. Clara Saint began by inviting a few journalists to see the latest Rive Gauche range at rue de Tournon after the boutique had closed for the day, later arranging more formal presentations in a showroom off Place des Victoires.

Didier Grumbach, Yves's and Pierre's partner in Rive Gauche, formed a new organization, Créateurs & Industriels, to help young designers to manufacture and show their work. The decorator, Andrée Putman, organized the first show at C. Mendès' headquarters in April 1971. It featured the designs of Emanuelle Khanh, a friend of

Grumbach's whose country house was close to his in Normandy, and Ossie Clark, a young British designer who Grumbach had met through Clare Rendelsham, the woman behind Rive Gauche in London. A friend of the artist David Hockney, Ossie Clark was known for his inventive cut and the delicate prints he designed with his wife, Celia Birtwell. He arrived in Paris with an entourage of hip hangers-on including the Warhol starlet, Donna Jordan.

Realizing that the future of French fashion lay with *prêt-à-porter*, Pierre Bergé was anxious to distance Yves Saint Laurent from the dying *couture* trade.[19] The decision to stop the *couture* shows was not as dramatic as it seemed. Yves would still design a small *couture* collection and even present it during *couture* week, albeit on a smaller scale than before to an invited audience of private clients and carefully selected journalists. But just as he had billed the opening of the first Rive Gauche boutique as an important innovation, Pierre hailed the start of the ready-to-wear shows as a significant departure. Aware that other *couture* houses were toying with the same idea, he made sure that YSL was seen to take the lead by being the first to announce it publicly.

His strategy worked perfectly. Yves Saint Laurent's announcement was plastered across the next day's newspapers. Some of the older *couture* houses criticized Bergé for having taken unilateral action, arguing that he should have waited for the Chambre Syndicale to vote on the issue; but by the end of the day Pierre Cardin and André Courrèges had announced that they too were scrapping their formal *couture* presentations.[20]

The first Yves Saint Laurent *prêt-à-porter* show took place in Paris on 28 October 1971. It included three hundred different pieces ranging from palazzo pants and artists' smocks, to black satin tuxedos and platform-soled espadrilles. The *New York Times* hailed it as 'Saint Laurent's Giant Step Away From Couture';[21] and *Harper's Bazaar* as Yves's 'best collection in many years'.[22] A few days before Pierre Bergé had taken pride of place at C. Mendes' showroom to cheer on Fernando Sanchez when he unveiled his collection at the second Créateurs & Industriels show together with the British designer, Jean Muir.

The next season's *couture* week was an uninspired affair. Yves Saint Laurent, the only designer who could be relied on to hit the headlines, was conspicuous by his absence. Christian Dior, Chanel, Hubert de Givenchy and a dozen or so other houses staged their shows as usual, but many of the American editors and buyers did not bother to make the trip to Europe. Even Bergdorf Goodman and Saks Fifth Avenue stayed away, missing the Paris *couture* shows for the first time since the War. *Couture* week had lost its old *élan*. Hebe Dorsey of the *International Herald Tribune* described the Chanel show, once conducted in a respectful silence, as being 'like a picnic on the beach' when 'people coughed, chatted, scratched or put on lipstick' with a rabble of paparazzi and a CBS camera crew in attendance.[23] Business was so bad that season that the surviving *couturiers* had to raise their prices to compensate for the fall in orders.

Even the press corps was changing to reflect the new mood, just as it had in the early 1960s. James Brady, John Fairchild's jocular lieutenant at *Women's Wear Daily*, took over the editorship of *Harper's Bazaar* and the imperious Diana Vreeland was fired from American *Vogue* to make way for the capable, but more casual style of Grace Mirabella. The grand old days seemed to have gone for good. 'The question was raised last week: "Can *couture* last?"' asked Hebe Dorsey in the *Herald Tribune*. 'As much as one hates to admit it, this week's answer: "It can't."'[24]

Yves Saint Laurent cast its vote for *prêt-à-porter*. It named its latest new perfume after the Rive Gauche boutiques and aimed it at the women who shopped, or wanted to shop, there. Yves designed a blue, black and silver box for the perfume, which struck a deliberate contrast to the daintily packaged crystal bottles of classic French scents. The advertising campaigns featured a Rive Gauche-clad woman photographed on the bustling square outside Les Deux Magots, one of the most famous Left Bank cafés, with the Église Saint-Germain des Prés in the background. The advertising slogan was *'pas un parfum pour les femmes effacées'*; 'not for unassuming women'.

The launch of the ready-to-wear shows meant more responsibility for Yves. Over the years he had built up a team of design assistants, who worked on designs for the licensed lines and suggested ideas for the main collections, as he had done at Dior, but in 1972 he brought in a new recruit, Loulou de la Falaise. After a few years of flitting between France and the States, Loulou wanted to settle down. Her New York flatmate, the photographer Berry Berenson, was moving to the West Coast to marry the *Psycho* star, Anthony Perkins, and Loulou decided to spend more time in Paris with her new boyfriend, Ricardo Bofill, the Catalan architect. She moved into his apartment on rue des Grands-Augustins, a narrow street running down to the Seine in the sixth *arrondissement*, and started work at Hôtel Forain.

Most of the rue Spontini staff had served long apprenticeships there or at another *couturier*, as Anne-Marie Muñoz had done at Dior. Even the rawest recruits to the design studio had undertaken some form of training, such as the Chambre Syndicale course that Yves attended with Fernando Sanchez. Loulou had no training at all, but she did have great style. Some glamorous women, like Bianca Jagger, took days to prepare for their entrance at a party, but Loulou could go out in a shawl, as she did to the *Medea* première, or wear denim jeans with her YSL *smoking*, and still hit the gossip columns. 'I used to look forward to seeing her walk up the stairs when she came into work each day,' observed Julia Kennedy, who worked at YSL as a secretary in the 1970s. 'You never knew what she was going to look like. One day she'd come in as a gypsy, then a glamorous hippy, and then a business woman. It wasn't just the clothes, but her whole manner. She was so clever that she could dress in different characters.'[25] Yves hired Loulou to play Mitza Bricard to his Christian Dior.

As Loulou was settling into Hôtel Forain, Richard Salomon was nearing the end of his career. After thirty years in business he wanted to devote more time to politics and to his voluntary work for Brown University and the New York Public Library. Having promised his wife, Edna, that he would retire by his sixtieth birthday in 1972, a few years before he started thinking about what would happen to Charles of the Ritz after his departure. The company had thrived under his management, but the beauty business was changing. Sales soared throughout the 1960s,[26] when companies like Revlon[27] and Estée Lauder[28] went from strength to strength. The old beauty queens, Helena Rubinstein and Elizabeth Arden, had died – Helena Rubinstein insisted on being buried in one of her favourite Yves Saint Laurent *couture* outfits – and both businesses had struggled since their death. Elizabeth Arden was up for sale, reportedly in take-over talks with Eli Lilly, the pharmaceuticals group. Richard

Salomon was anxious to prevent Charles of the Ritz ending up the same way. Realizing that the company would need a powerful partner if it was to compete against Revlon and Lauder, he decided to find one before he retired, rather than risk it floundering without him.

In summer 1969 he started negotiations with Squibb-Beech Nut, an American industrial group that owned a motley assortment of food and pharmaceutical products, the best known of which was Beech Nut chewing gum. Squibb was the type of company that the democratic Salomon respected, with a sound reputation for corporate ethics, a progressive employment policy and active arts sponsorship programme. By the end of the year it had agreed to buy Charles of the Ritz for $197.5 million in shares, leaving the Salomon family with a large tranche of Squibb stock and giving seats on the board to Richard Salomon and two of his fellow directors.

At first the change of ownership made little difference to Yves and Pierre. Having bought Charles of the Ritz for its cosmetics interests, Squibb had little or no interest in fashion and Pierre Bergé continued to report to Richard Salomon on anything concerning Hôtel Forain. Squibb raised no objection to their decision to stop showing *haute couture* and even sanctioned a plan to expand Rive Gauche in the States.[29] Life was more difficult when it came to the perfumes; although Richard Salomon had the final say over important issues, Pierre was expected to deal on a daily basis with the Americans who ran Squibb's cosmetics division. He had never worked in a corporate structure before, having been a free agent as an art dealer and then dealing directly with J. Mack Robinson and Richard Salomon. Hot-tempered and fiercely independent, he was hopelessly ill-suited to a conventional business environment. Arguments flared whenever the Squibb executives queried his decisions, or he challenged theirs, and Richard Salomon was often called in to defuse the tension.

Salomon was as fond of Yves and Pierre as they were of him. He admired Yves's creativity and Pierre's business skills, and was proud of what they had achieved with Rive Gauche.[30] For their part, Yves and Pierre appreciated how valuable his advice and contacts had been when they were building up the business, but most of all they enjoyed his company, as he chatted in fluent French to Pierre about politics, or to Yves about art. As his sixtieth birthday approached, Richard

Salomon became concerned that their relationship with Squibb would deteriorate after his retirement.

He knew that there was no question of their being able to afford to buy the business, or of Squibb's agreeing to give up the YSL perfumes at a time when they were selling so well.[31] But he did think that Squibb might be persuaded to relinquish the fashion house, giving Yves and Pierre a degree of independence. 'I told him it was a wonderful idea – but impossible,' said Pierre. 'We didn't have any money.'[32]

But they did have shares in the company which they had been given in their original agreement with J. Mack Robinson, as well as entitlements to various fees and royalties on sales of YSL products. Richard Salomon persuaded Squibb to accept an elaborate deal whereby Yves and Pierre exchanged those shares and entitlements, in return for full ownership of the fashion house and a small royalty on the perfumes.[33] They also agreed to pay Squibb the sum of $1.1m, which Salomon arranged to take the form of a loan repayable over fifteen years at a low rate of interest. As a safeguard Yves retained a right of veto over the YSL scents, which meant that Squibb could not introduce new products without his permission and that he could reject any advertising or publicity material he did not like.

The deal suited both sides. Squibb had rid itself of a truculent subsidiary in fashion, a business it knew nothing about, and had gained sole ownership of the perfumes. As for Yves and Pierre, they had forfeited their share of one of the most lucrative parts of the YSL empire, but would still receive royalties on the perfumes and, for the first time, they had complete control of the fashion house.

The New Cycle
1973–1976

Eugenia Sheppard, fashion editor of the *International Herald Tribune* and syndicated columnist to scores of newspapers across the United States, was in excellent humour as she settled into her gilt chair in the Hôtel Forain *salon* on 25 January 1973. 'Let's face it,' wrote the woman who had been banished from that room two years before for an article best remembered for the headline 'Truly Hideous'; 'It's nice to be back in the Saint Laurent showroom, sitting in the same old seat and, after two years absence, finding things changed just enough, but not too much.'[1] The spring *couture* collection, she decided, was a 'smash hit', with skinny sequinned cardigans, floaty organza prints and soft white linen suits, that 'managed to make lots of the other new Paris clothes look fashiony and fussy'.[2]

Three months later Eugenia Sheppard and the rest of the fashion press were watching another Yves Saint Laurent show several miles west of rue Spontini in the more ascetic environment of Porte de Versailles, the commercial exhibition centre where the French designers were presenting their autumn *prêt-à-porter* ranges. The reviews were as enthusiastic as they had been for the *couture*.[3] 'The French ready-to-wear collections have a new star,' pronounced Bernadine Morris, the fashion editor of the *New York Times*. 'It's the same as the old star: Yves Saint Laurent.'[4]

Yves was showing *haute couture* again. He had slipped into the new Paris fashion cycle of presenting four collections a year: *couture* at the traditional times of January and July, and ready-to-wear in

April and October when, in deference to his stature, he was given the final slot in the show schedule to ensure that the most influential buyers and editors stayed on in Paris until the end of fashion week to see which of the season's trends had been given the Saint Laurent stamp of approval.

He handled the two collections very differently. *Haute couture* was organized in the old-fashioned way, with Yves preparing sketches of the clothes a couple of months before the show, when he selected fabrics and finishings helped by Loulou and Anne-Marie Muñoz. Some of the fabrics were imported from Switzerland, but most of the buttons, embroideries, ribbons and other trimmings were made to order by the Parisian cottage industry of highly skilled artisans that had supplied the *couturiers* for decades.

With three or four weeks to go, Yves booked the models for the show. Many *couturiers* knew exactly what their collections would look like at the sketching stage, but Yves did not refine his ideas until later in the design process when he fitted the clothes on the mannequins, by draping the fabric over their bodies and pinning it into place. His final designs were invariably influenced by what the models looked like in the clothes, so the choice of mannequins was important to him. By the mid-1970s he was working regularly with a group of models from different ethnic backgrounds: Marie Helvin, a Hawaiian-American; Iman, a statuesque Somalian; the Japanese-American Tina Chow; and Yves's favourite, Mounia from Martinique. Each woman had an exotic look that enlivened the sophisticated but subdued styles that had dominated fashion since Yves's 1940s collection and was perfect for the intense, almost melodramatic style of fashionable photographers such as Helmut Newton, Guy Bourdin and Chris Von Wangenheim. It was unusual for such a prominent *couturier* to work with so many African and Asian models but Yves relished the clash of cultures in the *cabine* which reminded him of his childhood in cosmopolitan Oran. 'Yves liked to talk to us during the fittings, always asking how we'd wear this or that,' said Marie Helvin, who worked for him for ten years from the mid-1970s. 'That's why the ethnic mix was important, because we all had different attitudes to dress.'[5]

The models were hired to work at YSL for fourteen days during *couture* week. Before the show they had to be at the *couture* house from 9 a.m. to 6 p.m. for fittings. On a typical day there were four fitting sessions, including one with Yves, when he insisted that they wore full make-up with their hair done just as it would be in the show. 'Yves was very good to his models,' said Helvin. 'He paid the highest rates and put us up in nice hotels. All we had to do was sign the bills. And we were treated well at the *couture* house. We'd go up to the staff canteen for lunch and in the afternoon there was always a good tea. At the end of the afternoon Loulou would come down and fix me a whisky and soda. I'd look forward to it as a nice way of ending the day. There were other designers that I was fond of, who were fun to work with, but I never thought of them in the same way. I was captivated by Yves and wanted him to respect me.'[6]

The *couture* collections were shown in the Hôtel Forain *salon* with an audience of a few hundred people, but the ready-to-wear shows were larger affairs with over a thousand spectators packed into a tent at Porte de Versailles. The design process was different too, as the clothes were made up by machine in factories from the sketches sent from Yves's studio, rather than fitted by hand. All the *couture* models appeared in the *prêt-à-porter* shows, together with a dozen or so others who were chosen from casting sessions held at the start of fashion week.

A couple of days before the show the finished garments were delivered to the *couture* house and Yves, flanked by Loulou and Anne-Marie Muñoz, assembled outfits from the different pieces and decided which models would wear them. 'It was very efficient,' said Helvin. 'You always knew exactly what you'd be wearing before the day of the show, and how Yves and Loulou were going to accessorize it. Some of the other shows were more chaotic. Karl Lagerfeld used to put all the clothes for Chloé on a rail in the middle of the room and the models took one or two things off them. Also some designers let photographers come backstage and take pictures. Yves would never have let anything like that happen.'[7]

The company threw a cocktail party after both sets of shows, to which the models and staff were invited with a few favoured journalists and clients. Everyone who had worked on the collection was invited to a lunch hosted by Yves with Lucienne, still applauding proudly from her front-row seat each season, in attendance. When the Rive Gauche shows started, Pierre held his own 'thank you' lunches at Maxim's, or the Hôtel de Crillon restaurant, for the scores of licensees who had converged on Paris to see the collections. The restaurant tables were wired with microphones so the licensees could discuss the state of trade and comment on the clothes. 'They started off with compliments, congratulations and cries of pleasure,' recalled Didier Grumbach. 'But soon they were grumbling and arguing. It was unbearable.'[8] After a few seasons Pierre announced that he was scrapping the lunches.

By then *prêt-à-porter* was by far the biggest part of the fashion business,[9] while *haute couture* was shrinking,[10] with only about three thousand *couture* customers left, compared to fifteen thousand after the War.[11] Many of the old clients were badly affected by the 1973 oil shock, when the price of oil rocketed, heralding years of hyper-inflation in the West; others were shaken by the volatile political scene. America was scarred by the storm over the Watergate cover-up. Strikes and stoppages hit Britain as trade unionists clashed with the government. Terrorism became a serious threat when the Baader-Meinhof group struck in Germany and the Red Brigade in Italy. J. Paul Getty Jr's son, J. Paul III, was kidnapped by the Red Brigade in the summer of 1973 and imprisoned in Calabria, where he was chained to a stake, for five months while his family procrastinated over whether to pay the ransom. Eventually they paid it, but only after a parcel containing J. Paul III's rotting ear was delivered to a Rome newspaper office.

At a time of terrorist attacks and rising unemployment, even the wealthiest Americans and Europeans felt uneasy about flaunting their wealth. Many of them preferred to sneak into the *couture* houses for private presentations rather than risk recognition at the shows, or started shopping at ready-to-wear boutiques instead. The *couturiers* found a few new customers among the oil-rich Arabs, but the daughters of their old European and American clients were too heavily influenced by the hippy ethos of the late 1960s to be tempted by anything as ostentatious as *haute couture*. They preferred the *prêt-à-porter* interpretations of the fashionable Glam look inspired by the nostalgic films of Luchino Visconti and Bernardo Bertolucci, and the stylized androgyny of the pop stars Roxy Music and David Bowie.

Yet the Chambre Syndicale still clung to the illusion that *couture* was the most important part of the industry, refusing to relax its rules and embrace ready-to-wear. This created practical problems for the Paris designers who needed a strong central body to organize the shows at a time of growing competition from other cities. Paris had ruled supreme in the *couture* age as nowhere else could match its cottage industry of embroiderers, ribbon-makers, silk-weavers and button-makers. The best of the French *couturiers* showed there, as did the cream of the foreign designers, from Elsa Schiaparelli and Cristóbal Balenciaga, to Karl Lagerfeld; the advantage of having such a strong artisanal base was eroded in the *prêt-à-porter* era. All that was needed to make ready-to-wear was well-equipped factories, making it easier for fashion designers to operate from other cities. Valentino's star was rising in Italy. *Women's Wear Daily* dubbed him the 'Sheikh of Chic' and his clients 'Val's First Ladies'. Bill Blass, Geoffrey Beene, Oscar de la Renta and Ralph Lauren were gaining ground in the States, as was Roy Halston Frowick, known as Halston, or 'H' to the Warhol crowd, whose sleek clothes had become a uniform for Manhattan socialites.[12]

If Paris was to retain its reputation as *the* international fashion centre, the ready-to-wear designers needed to be as well-organized as the *couturiers*, a point that Pierre Bergé frequently tried to impress on the traditionalists in the Chambre Syndicale. Otherwise they would all suffer, even Yves Saint Laurent, as the journalists and buyers drifted away to see the shows in Milan or New York. 'It was a crazy situation,' he recalled. 'The old Chambre Syndicale was clinging on to the part of the industry which was dying, and ignoring the new designers. So I did something about it.'[13] On 15 November 1973, the day after his forty-third birthday, he announced the creation of Groupement Mode et Création, a new organization under the aegis of the Chambre Syndicale that included Yves Saint Laurent, Christian Dior and Emanuel Ungaro from the *couture* world with Chloé, Kenzo, Dorothée Bis, Sonia Rykiel and Emanuelle Khanh from *prêt-à-porter* – under the presidency of Pierre Bergé.

Although a vocal figure in fashion politics, who rarely shrank from voicing his views on industry issues,[14] until then Pierre had no official power base. His only weapon was Yves's status as the star of French fashion. The other *couturiers* had seen how Yves's absence had affected the 1972 shows, and although new talents were rising in ready-to-wear, he was still the only designer guaranteed to draw an international audience to Paris. After years of manoeuvring by threatening to withdraw Saint Laurent's support from various ventures if he did not get his way, Bergé had finally found a political platform in Groupe Mode et Création. He used it as a springboard to win the following year's election for the presidency of the Chambre Syndicale and then quietly folded it to concentrate on his new responsibilities.

At the same time he was making the most of the commercial opportunities created by the Squibb deal. Rive Gauche women's wear was thriving; Yves even achieved his adolescent ambition of seeing his 'name up in lights on the Champs-Elysées' when they opened a boutique there, and Pierre was keen to expand the men's range. In 1974 he reached agreement with Maurice Bidermann, who had taken over Marcel Boussac's mantle as France's largest clothing manufacturer, to make Rive Gauche men's wear in the States. Yves and Pierre had known Bidermann for years; his sister, Régine, the 'Queen of the Night' as the French press called her, owned two of their favourite Paris nightclubs, New Jimmy's and Régine's. Bidermann was born Maurice Zylberberg in Brussels and brought up in a poor Jewish quarter of Paris. He got his first job at seventeen in a clothing factory owned by an uncle, whose surname he later adopted. After taking over the factory, he bought a string of rival companies and expanded into North America by manufacturing Pierre Cardin men's wear there. In the deal with Pierre he agreed to switch those factories over to Yves Saint Laurent. The Paris gossips were convinced that Pierre, who was known to dislike Cardin, had insisted on Bidermann dropping him. 'Bah!' replied Bergé. 'Bidermann ditched Cardin because it wasn't selling.'[15] But taking over Pierre Cardin's infrastructure was a real bonus for Saint Laurent, giving it huge production capacity and an instant *entrée* to the big American stores. The YSL men's wear line mustered sales of $50 million in North America during its first year.[16]

Pierre was also building up the licensing side of the business as, under the terms of their agreement with Squibb, he and Yves now owned the rights to license any product other than perfume and cosmetics. In the old days a regular source of conflict between Pierre and Squibb executives was his refusal to sanction YSL licensing deals on the grounds that they might imperil the prestige of the *couture* house. His attitude changed sharply once he and Yves had sole ownership of the rights and they were inundated with offers from prospective licensees. The mid-1970s was a profligate period when high inflation triggered such steep price rises that consumers felt more comfortable spending money than they did saving it, on the grounds that the things they bought might cost more in a few months' time. In such an uncertain economic climate they wanted their purchases to last, and the *imprimatur* of a famous French *couture* house provided the reassurance they needed. Bergé signed licence after licence, selling the YSL name for sunglasses, scarves, belts, ties, even cigarettes.[17] One of the few deals he declined was for Yves Saint Laurent car tyres.

As the company became more commercial, so did Yves's designs. He still changed the themes of his collections each season, but the changes were less *staccato* than in the past, and the familiar forms – *smokings*, soft chiffon blouses, tailored trouser suits, jumpsuits and evening tunics – were starting to recur. If his designs were less iconoclastic than before, that seemed apt at a time of oil shocks and terrorist threats, when youth culture was infused by the knowing irony of Glam. By the mid-1970s, there were fewer sartorial barriers to be broken down than in the late 1950s and early 1960s when Yves started his career and dress codes were still rigid.[18] And after two decades as a designer, Yves felt in command of his craft. Confident that he had defined a style of his own, he was anxious to perfect it.[19]

It was exactly what the YSL *couture* clients, and the women who shopped at Rive Gauche, wanted to see.[20] 'His clothes are a pleasure to behold,' wrote Bernadine Morris in the *New York Times* after seeing the Rive Gauche range for autumn 1975. 'No straining for effects. No wandering in an ethnic morass. Just nice, clean, casual clothes.'[21] While the *Herald Tribune*'s Eugenia Sheppard reported approvingly that the following autumn's *couture* collection 'couldn't have been more suave, sophisticated or adult'.[22] John Fairchild of *Women's Wear Daily* was more succinct when *Newsweek* asked for his opinion. 'Yves Saint Laurent is the most influential designer I've ever seen.'[23]

The company was becoming so big that they needed new headquarters. This time Pierre insisted that they be closer to the other *couture* houses and, as money was no longer a problem, they looked for a larger *hôtel particulier* in the *haute couture* heartland around

Avenue Georges V and Avenue Montaigne, south of the Champs-Elysées. Finally they found one in 8 Avenue Marceau, an opulent townhouse built in Napoleon III's reign. Victor Grandpierre, the veteran French decorator who had redesigned the interior of 30 Avenue Montaigne for Christian Dior, was commissioned to restore it to its former glory.

A smartly-dressed receptionist welcomed visitors at the entrance to 8 Avenue Marceau from a desk beside a sweeping central staircase that led up to a secretariat on the first floor with Pierre's office on one side and Yves's studio on the other. To the right of the staircase on the ground floor was the room where they staged the *couture* shows: the *grand salon* with mirrored walls, chairs and couches covered with ruby red brocade and pale green *moiré* carpet. Other floors were filled with offices and *ateliers*. A whiff of Rive Gauche wafted around the building, as the secretaries were instructed to spray it in every room at the beginning of the day. The Mies van der Rohe Brno chairs that Yves and Pierre had bought for rue Spontini went with them to Avenue Marceau, as did an Eero Saarinen table and a couple of Eileen Gray leather *chaises* from Place Vauban. Yves insisted on taking the 'lucky' ten of clubs playing card he had found in the Hôtel Forain basement with them, as well as the bejewelled heart that still appeared in each of his shows. Hanging on the walls were the silkscreen portraits that Andy Warhol had done of Yves on a recent trip to New York.

Warhol had taken up portraiture a few years before at Fred Hughes's prompting, and by the time Yves sat for him he had perfected his technique, but had not yet tired of the medium.[24] Most of his portraits, particularly the later ones, have a harsh, parodic quality in which the subjects are flattered into bland anonymity; but the series of Yves is sympathetic in tone and executed with great delicacy. Both Clara Saint and Betty Catroux remembered Yves as being light and playful, almost skittish, in Warhol's company; yet the portraits emphasize the mournful side of his character. Warhol's subjects usually stare straight out of the canvas at the artist and viewer, but Yves is depicted mostly in half-profile with his eyes downcast. Even in the few poses where he looks outwards, he seems lost in thought and his eyes do not connect with those of the viewer. By casting him in such a self-absorbed manner, Warhol seems to be indicating that Yves is not someone whom he, or anyone looking at the portrait, could expect to comprehend.

The portraits show Yves as he entered his late thirties, just after he had cropped his long hair into a spruce shoulder-length cut, and swapped his hippy *de luxe* kaftans for a smarter wardrobe of striped shirts and dandyish bow ties. On the day that he posed for Andy Warhol, he was wearing contact lenses instead of his signature spectacles. But he soon gave up, finding lenses too painful, and went back to his heavy black glasses again.

Outwardly Yves led the charmed life of France's most famous fashion designer. The Saint Laurent set was at the centre of the social circle around the Rothschilds – Baron Guy and his wife, Marie-Hélène – who ruled Parisian society from Hôtel Lambert, their seventeenth-century *hôtel particulier* on the Quai d'Anjou, one of the prettiest parts of the Île Saint-Louis. Marie-Hélène was the closest that contemporary Paris came to a hostess of the stature of Marie-Laure de Noailles and Marie-Louise Bousquet. Famous for her parties, she followed the triumph of her 1971 Proust Ball, when all the guests came dressed as characters from *À la Recherche du Temps Perdu*, with a Surrealistic Ball at which Salvador Dali made a dramatic entrance in his wheelchair. Elaborately dressed in the slightly over-coiffed style of a 1950s glamour queen, Marie-Hélène loved the company of bright, beautiful young men. Jacques Grange was one of her favourites, as was Rudolf Nureyev, and she adored Yves, insisting on being fitted for her *couture* outfits in his design studio, rather than in a fitting room like the other clients. Yves and Pierre were regular guests of the Rothschilds at Hôtel Lambert and were also close to Hélène Rochas, the perfume heiress who was friendly with Marie-Hélène and often took them away for weekends to her house on the Riviera.

There was no love lost between the Rothschild-Saint Laurent circle and the cliques around other *couturiers*. One faction was led by Bergé's old enemy, Pierre Cardin, and his partner, André Oliver. Another younger crowd had congregated around Karl Lagerfeld, since he had made his name at Chloé. But their arch-rivals were Hubert de Givenchy and his socialite champion, São Schlumberger. Whenever Andy Warhol and his friends came to Paris, they spent their time with the Rothschild-Saint Laurent axis knowing they would be dropped if they mixed with any of the other camps.[25] Yves and Pierre took the Warhol set off with Loulou and Betty to lunch with the Rothschilds at Hôtel Lambert, or entertained them at rue de Babylone. After dinner they repaired to the Oriental Room with their guests, and at lunchtime they went into the garden with the dogs. Marie Helvin remembered Yves being 'great fun' on those occasions. 'He was so endearing. He loved to tell jokes and funny stories, but never seemed to get the punchline right. He did it so sweetly that it was charming.'[26]

Yet it was becoming more and more difficult for Yves to go out in public. His face was recognized wherever he went, and Pierre's licensing deals made his name seem more familiar to people now that they saw YSL stamped on beach towels and ballpoint pens. Strangers rushed up to ask him for autographs, or shouted out comments. 'The situation was becoming unbearable,' said Clara Saint. 'Wherever he went, people came up to pester him. Usually they meant to be pleasant, but it was very intrusive. Yves never had any privacy, it was as though he was living in a strange kind of prison.'[27]

For a long time he tried to ignore it by carrying on as normal, refusing to have a bodyguard and insisting on driving himself around Paris in his black and white Volkswagen Beetle convertible. But as his fame became intrusive Yves went out in public less often, finding it easier to dine privately with friends in their homes rather than going out to eat in restaurants, and shunning formal events in favour of late-night appearances at Le Sept or Régine's, where Fabrice and Régine could be relied upon to keep strangers at bay. For years he had depended on his circle of friends to form a protective ring around him in public, but by then Yves rarely risked venturing out without them. *Newsweek* likened the 'ever-present entourage' that accompanied him on a 1974 trip to New York to 'a Byzantine court where everyone is vying for the emperor's attention', with Pierre Bergé cast in the role of 'chamberlain'.[28]

Bob Colacello, editor of Andy Warhol's *Interview* magazine, came to much the same conclusion when the Warhol crowd decamped to Paris that year for the opening of an exhibition of Andy's Mao paintings at the Palais Galliéra. 'I liked the Saint Laurent group, but I wasn't sure if they liked me. It was hard to tell who they liked, except each other, and even then I wasn't sure. Yves hardly talked, except in whispers and in French. Pierre never stopped talking, in barks and in French . . . Loulou was nice one minute, not the next. Clara was always nice, always laughing, but did she also laugh behind your back? And Thadée was like Yves, the weak, silent type. Or so it seemed. I wondered if Yves and Pierre had an Andy-and-Fred act going, and if when no one was around, Yves drove Pierre crazy as Andy did Fred. Everyone said that Yves was so pure and sweet and fragile, but I wasn't so sure.'[29]

Sometimes the tension bubbled up in public. When Yves discovered that Andy Warhol had accepted commissions for portraits of two rival designers, Halston and Valentino, he was so angry that he threatened to burn his own silkscreens in an act of vengeance. Unfortunately he confided his intention to a *Women's Wear Daily* reporter who splashed it across the magazine and asked the other designers what they thought of the threat. Both were furious, but Warhol forgave Yves, even though he often fell out with other friends over far slighter rifts.

Such outbursts were becoming more common as the strain of the four-season fashion cycle started to show. Once Yves flung himself into such a fury that he smashed his hand against a wall and broke it. In the old *régime* there had been six months between each *couture* show, and Yves could usually take a couple of weeks off between finishing work on one collection and beginning the next. The new cycle left him with three months between each presentation, giving him less time to rest and adding considerably to the physical and psychological demands made on him.

Among Yves's friends were people like Rudolf Nureyev and Andy Warhol who were as famous and as successful in their fields as he was in fashion. Like him, they were under constant pressure to prove themselves, but at least they had some control over their work schedules. Warhol was expected to exhibit regularly, but he did not have to submit a completely new series of paintings every three months and have his reputation reassessed by the art critics. Rudolf Nureyev could decide when, and where, he danced and, if the worst came to the worst, could always cancel a performance. But the commercial constraints of the fashion industry meant that Yves had to come up with a new collection every three months, regardless of whether he had anything new to say. 'I've made a rope to hang myself with,' he said at the time. 'I'd love to be able to do fashion when I want to, but I'm a prisoner of my own commercial empire.'[30]

In 1973, the first year of the new fashion cycle, Yves revived his theatrical work by designing two ballets for Roland Petit, *La Rose Malade* and *Shéhérazade*, and the costumes for a couple of plays. But the pressure proved too much, and he gave up the theatre again the following year. Even so, the work involved in preparing for four fashion shows was overwhelming, all the more so as Yves no longer had the stimulus of the theatrical projects he so enjoyed. He had talked of his desire to give up fashion for literature and the theatre since the late 1960s, but by then he seemed to have accepted that he would never actually do anything about it.

Pierre's views were doubtless an issue. Having worked so hard at building up the business, he was hardly likely to sit back and allow Yves to throw it away at the moment when they were starting to make money. Another consideration was Yves's loyalty to his staff. Some of them had worked with him since the first Hôtel Forain show, and by the time the company moved to Avenue Marceau hundreds of people relied on him for their livelihood. 'If he'd been a total spoilt brat he'd have said "To heck with them" and left,' observed Susan Train of *Vogue*. 'But he felt a tremendous loyalty to those people. They all depended on him, everyone from the simplest seamstress, to the messenger boy. He couldn't do it.'[31]

As his fortieth birthday approached on 1 August 1976, Yves faced the prospect of spending the rest of his career in a field that, creatively and intellectually, he had long since exhausted. His age made matters worse. For a man who had spent his entire adult life being treated as a boy-wonder, the prospect of middle age was bound to be daunting. Yves had clung on to the vestiges of youthfulness in his thirties, by posing nude for Jeanloup Sieff's camera and surrounding himself with younger friends, such as Loulou, Paloma, Jacques Grange and François-Marie Banier. But no one can play the prodigy in their forties and, with his fortieth birthday approaching, Yves did not know which new role to play.

For years he had sought solace in the nocturnal world of Le Sept; but as his depression mounted, the physical effects of the drink and drugs he was taking, the late nights and his workload became harder to hide. Gerry Dryansky of American *Vogue* remembered seeing him

shaking visibly as they went up in an elevator together to the Rive
Gauche show at Porte de Versailles that spring.[32] A few weeks later
Yves collapsed and was admitted to the American Hospital, an expensive private medical institution in Neuilly-sur-Seine, a wealthy
suburb of western Paris. He worked on his sketches for the next
couture collection from his hospital room until, in the weeks before
the show, the doctors allowed him to go to his Avenue Marceau
studio in the afternoons. After a couple of hours working there, Yves
was driven back to Neuilly for the night.

It did not seem like the most auspicious start to the new *couture*
season, but the discipline of the hospital routine allowed Yves to
devote more time to his designs than he had done for years. His
initial inspiration for that season's collection was Johannes Vermeer's
portrait, 'Woman With A Pearl', which he had seen on a trip to
Amsterdam before his breakdown. The subject of the painting was
sumptuously dressed in a black bodice with powder-blue sleeves and
a rose-pink skirt, topped off by a turban. Taking that as his starting
point, Yves designed the collection as if dressing his models as
theatrical heroines,[33] drawing on the orientalist costumes that Léon
Bakst had created for Sergei Diaghilev's *Ballets Russes* in pre-
revolutionary Russia. A pile of books on Russian costume sat in his
Neuilly hospital room, as Yves patiently sketched the billowing
skirts, shawls and harem pants of Bakst's designs and issued instructions for the Avenue Marceau *ateliers* to recreate them in magnificent
couture fabrics with elaborate embroidery, layers of petticoats and
masterful mixes of colour.

Anne-Marie Muñoz remembered the excitement of the
mains-d'oeuvre as they worked on the clothes. She thought it was
Yves's most beautiful collection in the twenty years they had worked
together. 'Magical! When he put the finishing touches to the models,
they were perfect.'[34] The cost of the collection was colossal. The bill
for making the clothes and staging the show came to $500,000, the
most that the house of Saint Laurent had ever spent on presenting
a collection and almost twice as much as it usually paid. Pierre even
booked the ballroom of the Hôtel Intercontinental on rue Castiglione
for the occasion, rather than using the *grand salon* at Avenue Marceau.

When the spectators arrived at the Hôtel Intercontinental on 28
July 1976, they were expecting to see Yves's variation of the crisply

classic clothes other *couturiers* had shown that week, and that he had presented in the past few seasons of enthusiastically reviewed, but comparatively conservative collections. The theatricality of his 'Bakstian' vision caught them completely by surprise and they sat through the first half of the show in awestruck silence. The applause only started when the first evening dress appeared: a long black velvet top over a billowing black taffeta skirt with a glimpse of green petticoats. More evening dresses followed in jewel-coloured silks and satins, with beautiful braiding, embroidery and gold brocade. The clapping and cheering continued until Yves mounted the runway for an emotional finale. 'I wouldn't have believed it if I hadn't seen it,' said Grace Mirabella, editor-in-chief of American *Vogue*, afterwards.[35] 'I don't think any of us will see a presentation like that again. It's been a long time since we had that sense of excitement about clothes. In fact, I'm not sure I've ever seen it.'[36]

The *New York Times* ran its report of the *Ballets Russes* show on the front page alongside the news of an earthquake in the Chinese city of Tangshan and an account of the progress of the Viking I spacecraft's search for life on Mars. 'Yves Saint Laurent presented a fall *couture* collection today that will change the course of fashion around the world,' it began. 'It is as stunning in its impact as the collection Christian Dior showed in 1947, the one that came to be known as the New Look and affected the way women dressed everywhere.'[37] The paper rushed out a profile of Yves on an inside page accompanied by a photograph of him with his arm around a radiant Lucienne.

The American press flung itself into a furore as the New York fashion designers debated the merits and demerits of the *Ballets Russes* collection.[38] Ralph Lauren dismissed it as having 'no relationship to what's happening to women today',[39] and Geoffrey Beene wrote it off as 'self-indulgence far beyond the realms of reality'.[40] Even Yves's most ardent admirers did not deny that his designs were self-indulgent, but they saw that as a virtue, not a vice, convinced he had created something so beautiful that it transcended traditional definitions of fashion, taking his work on to a higher artistic plane.[41]

Yet by creating costumes, rather than clothes, Yves was tacitly acknowledging that *haute couture* no longer had a place in women's daily lives. He had turned *couture* into a form of escapism from a society haunted by unemployment, homelessness, sex crimes and drug abuse. Anyone who wanted to see fashion confronting contemporary issues, as his work had once done, could go to Sex, a boutique on London's Kings Road where the British designer, Vivienne Westwood, was selling parodies of sex shop clothes fused with images of 1950s Teddy Boy costumes. The bondage trousers and rubber T-shirts worn by the Sex Pistols, a band managed by Westwood's husband, Malcolm McLaren, reeked of reality; whereas Yves's billowing skirts and beaded bodices were a retreat into fantasy.

Realistic or not, the *Ballet Russes* collection was a financial success. Marie-Hélène de Rothschild, Hélène Rochas, Jacqueline de Ribes and Bianca Jagger all placed orders at the *couture* house. The Rive Gauche boutiques were besieged by women hoping to cobble together ready-to-wear versions of the *Ballets Russes* look with $1,050 taffeta evening skirts and $470 braided jackets, rather than spending $7,000 or $8,000 on an *haute couture* ballgown. The Madison Avenue boutique rang up sales of $20,000 on the day after the *couture* show, ten times as much as the same day the previous year.[42] And while it had looked like commercial lunacy for the house of Saint Laurent to spend $500,000 on a fashion show when *couture* was such a small part of its business – generating sales of $2 million a year at a time when the licensed lines were making $200 million – it made sound commercial sense in the light of the millions of dollars of free publicity it provided for the YSL brand name.[43]

And, despite the doubts of the American critics, ordinary women were influenced by Yves's 'Bakstian' fantasies. That autumn the department stores were filled with fur-trimmed boots, flounced skirts and peasant shawls, and when Marie-José Lepicard, the French fashion journalist, went to visit a sick relative in Rouen that winter she was struck by the sight of a woman waiting beside a bus stop. 'She was a working-class woman dressed in a cheap version of the Russian style in boots and a fake fur hat. I'd seen the originals at the show and they were wonderful, very rich, very pretty. The clothes this woman was wearing looked dreadful. Fake fur really wasn't very nice in those days. But there she was a Russian princess, *à la Saint Laurent*.'[44]

A Living Death
1976–1977

The first thing Julia Kennedy was asked to do when she started her new job in Yves Saint Laurent's headquarters on Avenue Marceau in 1977 was to take dictation for a letter from Pierre Bergé to the chairman of Air France. It was a complaint, rather a long complaint about the unsatisfactory standard of the caviar he had recently been served on Concorde. 'It went on,' she recalled, 'for pages and pages.'[1]

An Irish graduate in her early twenties, Kennedy was taken on as Pierre Bergé's new personal secretary in place of Madame Elisabeth, who had recently retired after years of service. At the time it was considered chic for successful French businessmen to have bilingual secretaries and she suspected that was the reason why Bergé hired her. The Concorde complaint was the first of many irate letters she was to dispatch for her boss. 'Nothing was ever quite good enough for him. He'd complain about bad service. He was incensed if anyone snubbed him. He didn't suffer fools gladly and had to have his own way. He had a terrible temper. There was a row about something or other almost every day. If anything happened that he didn't like he'd rant and rave about it, slamming doors and kicking things.'[2]

There was nothing, but nothing, Pierre Bergé disliked more than missing out on an invitation from Baron Guy and Baronne Marie-Hélène de Rothschild. He had other famous friends. Catherine Deneuve, Hélène Rochas, Jeanne Moreau and Paloma Picasso's mother, Françoise Gilot, often called the office to ask if he would like to accompany them to dinner, or to the opera, but the Rothschilds were his favourites. Having been introduced to them first as Bernard Buffet's agent and then as Yves Saint Laurent's partner, Pierre now knew them well enough to be invited to dine alone without Yves under the seventeenth-century Charles Lebrun frescoes on the galleried ceiling of their quarters at Hôtel Lambert. 'It was his oxygen,' said Kennedy. 'He had dinner with them most weeks and he loved it. If he wasn't invited he'd be in a terrible mood. He went round the *couture* house slamming the doors even harder than usual.'[3]

The Rothschilds epitomized everything that Pierre Bergé aspired to. Although born with a grand name and dynastic connections, Baron Guy had made his own fortune as the head of the family bank, and Marie-Hélène, his second wife, spent their money in a rarefied manner that reeked of culture and connoisseurship. The fur-lined plates among the table settings at her Surrealist Ball did not simply tell her guests that she and her husband were so very rich that they could afford to fritter their francs on such an extravagant gesture, but hinted at a higher sensibility that expected them to recognize the plates as a reference to the work of the surrealist sculptor, Meret Oppenheim.

As the son of a provincial schoolteacher and tax inspector, Pierre's background was very different to that of the Rothschilds, but he had won a place in their gilded circle because, like them, he combined wealth with a passion for culture. Proud of his intellect, Pierre peppered his conversation with observations about Proust, Flaubert, Wagner, Verdi and obscure French poets, and expected his friends to reciprocate. French society is imbued with the values of the middle-class intellectuals who reconstructed the country after the 1789 Revolution,[4] and the Rothschilds respected Pierre both for his wit and for having worked his way up from nothing. For his part Pierre never tried to conceal his humble origins; on the contrary, he delighted in having achieved so much through his own efforts, but he rarely saw, or spoke of his family.

His attitude towards the way he earned his living was equally complex. Pierre made no secret of his contempt for the fashion scene, once describing Yves to American *Vogue* as 'a man of exceptional intelligence practising the trade of an imbecile'.[5] He was similarly scathing in his attitude to business, only deeming it to be acceptable if it was linked to a higher artistic purpose. 'I have never, never, been impressed by businessmen. Not by Marcel Boussac, not by Monsieur X, Monsieur Y, or Monsieur Z.'[6] Although he had created, and now presided over, a multi-million-dollar business empire, Pierre preferred to present himself as an artist *manqué* who had sacrificed his literary ambitions to nurture Yves Saint Laurent's genius.

Undoubtedly Pierre believed that he had made a considerable sacrifice for Yves's sake, but the reality was that he was already a businessman of sorts, an artist's agent, when they first met and all his literary achievements amounted to were a few issues of *La Patrie Mondiale* and a monograph on Bernard Buffet. The final irony was that despite his scorn of business in general, and the fashion industry in particular, Pierre Bergé made an excellent president and chief executive of Yves Saint Laurent.

In many respects Pierre's achievements in the fashion business matched Yves's as a designer. He could not have functioned in a conventional corporate environment, as his difficulties with Squibb illustrated, but he had an extraordinary aptitude for the idiosyncrasies of the fashion industry. From the beginning Pierre had shown that he had the strategic vision to see beyond the narrow boundaries of the traditional French *couture* trade, by steering the company into North America and then into Asia. Among the first people in the industry to appreciate the importance of *prêt-à-porter*, he turned Rive Gauche into a role model for the ready-to-wear boutiques which now provided the bulk of most designers' income. Equally quick to realize the commercial potential of licensing, Pierre had helped to launch a series of perfumes which were not only successful in sales terms, but genuinely innovative in their approach to advertising.

One of the most valuable lessons that Pierre had learnt from Richard Salomon was to take a long-term view of the business. For years he had reinvested most of the money they made into opening new Rive Gauche boutiques, or staging extravaganzas like the $500,000 *Ballets Russes* show. He and Yves had drawn generous salaries, and had another source of income from their shares in Rive Gauche,[7] but Pierre ploughed so much cash back into the company that it did not produce a profit until 1977. By then the YSL empire was so enormous, with annual sales of over $250 million, that the profits for him and Yves were substantial.

Pierre also excelled at the minutiae of running a fashion house.

Priding himself on being a philanthropic employer in the French tradition of the '*grand patron*', or 'big boss', he knew all the staff by name and enjoyed boasting to his Chambre Syndicale colleagues that there was no trade union at Yves Saint Laurent because the workforce did not need one. He paid well by fashion industry standards and working conditions at Avenue Marceau were excellent. The company canteen was heavily subsidized and the quality of the food so high that even the models chose to eat there during *couture* week. Employees were entitled to discounts at Rive Gauche and allowed to rummage through the occasional boxes of 'seconds' which were delivered to Avenue Marceau. A few particularly privileged members of staff were given permission to borrow *couture* outfits for special events, like family weddings or opening nights at the theatre.

The workforce still dreaded the explosions of temper on the days when '*Bergé a le cafard*', but even those who disliked Pierre respected his authority and others found him to be a solicitous employer. 'He was a good manager,' said Julia Kennedy. 'If ever there were problems he'd sort them out. And although he went round barking at the staff, every so often you'd hear that he'd helped someone. Maybe one of the older employees was in a hole and Bergé had given them some money, or paid a hospital bill for them or a member of their family. It was always done very discreetly.'[8]

But Pierre Bergé's most successful role was looking after Yves Saint Laurent. He handled all the practical details of Yves's life: dealing with his financial and business affairs, paying the bills, even signing cheques on his behalf. It was Pierre who made sure that rue de Babylone was run smoothly by Bernard and their two other manservants, and that Dar el-Hanch was taken care of in their absence. He fussed over the tiniest details: vetting the seating plans for other people's dinners to make sure that Yves would be sitting next to someone who would amuse him, and diplomatically sending one of the younger design assistants home to change when she arrived at Yves's birthday party wearing a dress from a rival *couturier*. When Rudolf Nureyev went shopping on trips to Paris, he charged his purchases to Pierre Bergé's office. The shops phoned through to Julia Kennedy at Avenue Marceau to check whether they would pay for the goods. 'There was a fur anorak from Revillon and some other things. We paid the bills. Bergé didn't question any of them.'[9]

Pierre's critics claimed that he deliberately discouraged Yves from assuming responsibility for his own affairs, as a means of ensuring that he remained dependent on him. If this was so, Yves did nothing to change the situation, and it seems likely that it suited him as much as it did Pierre. Yves had been looked after by other people all his life; first by his parents and then, for the past twenty years, by Pierre Bergé. Not only did he show no inclination to take charge of his own affairs, but latterly his drinking and drug-taking would probably have rendered him incapable of doing so.

Although his life was still entwined with Pierre's, their relationship had changed. After the *Ballets Russes* show, Yves returned briefly to the American Hospital before moving back into rue de Babylone, where he and Pierre now lived in different parts of the duplex with Yves occupying the upper floor and Pierre the lower part of the apartment. Yves also took over a penthouse on the seventh floor of an apartment building on nearby Avenue de Breteuil, and asked Jacques Grange to decorate it for him. Pierre told friends that the penthouse was intended as a private retreat where Yves could work in peace, but he already had a study at rue de Babylone, as well as his Avenue Marceau studio. Yves used the penthouse as a place where he could entertain friends, and occasional lovers, in privacy.

As for Pierre, after years of devoting himself to Yves, he longed for a wider role than that of Yves Saint Laurent's boyfriend and business partner. Thanks to his share of the company's profits, he was able to publicly indulge his love of the arts. He began by producing a French version of Peter Shaffer's play, *Equus*, the story of a psychologist and a teenage boy who has killed half a dozen horses, which was a critical and commercial hit in London and New York. Some novice theatrical producers would probably have been willing to sign the cheques and leave any important decisions to the director, but Pierre insisted on being involved with every aspect of the production, starting with the cast. A succession of young men trotted up the stairs of Avenue Marceau to introduce themselves to the secretaries with '*Je suis un cheval*', 'I am a horse', before being ushered into Pierre's office for their auditions.

Equus was such a success that Pierre went further by buying Théâtre de l'Athénée, the famous Paris theatre where Louis Jouvet, whom the teenage Yves had seen in *L'École des Femmes* in Oran, played many of his greatest roles. The Athénée was in a dilapidated state and Pierre paid for its restoration. After the reopening he launched a series of *Lundis Musicaux*, 'Musical Mondays', to which he invited famous singers, including Placido Domingo, Montserrat Caballé and Joan Sutherland, to perform their favourite pieces. Before long he had acquired a reputation as a patron of the arts. When Christian Lacroix left university and was considering a career in theatrical design, a friend suggested that he take a portfolio of sketches to show him. 'Pierre Bergé was known in Paris as someone who might help you get started in the theatre. I hadn't met him before, but I called his office and he agreed to see me. He was very kind, taking time to go over my work and making helpful comments.'[10]

Pierre enjoyed the trappings of wealth. He was driven to Avenue Marceau each morning in a chauffeured Rolls-Royce and whenever he ate out in a restaurant he insisted on being given the very best table. 'Nothing else would do,' said Julia Kennedy. 'It wasn't enough to eat at the best places, he would only sit at certain tables. There was a list of restaurants that he liked. If I tried to book Maxim's and the Round Table was taken, I'd have to see if the best table was free at Le Grand Véfour.'[11]

A familiar figure in the Paris antique shops, where he bought expensive baubles such as the sixteenth-century vermilion lion with ruby eyes that he gave to Yves for his forty-first birthday, Pierre was becoming as well known in the New York auction rooms. He had taken an apartment in the Pierre Hotel, where he liked to stay on business trips to Manhattan. Peter Marino, a young American architect who had worked at Andy Warhol's Factory, was hired to remodel it as a *pied-à-terre*, and Jed Johnson was asked to assemble a collection of the early American furniture that Andy Warhol had been collecting since the 1960s. Helped by a friend, Judith Hollander, Jed searched the sale-rooms for American Empire pieces from the 1820s and 'Neo Grec' work from the 1860s and 1870s. Both periods were so rare that Pierre paid high prices for the few pieces that came up at auction.[12]

Yves's personal tastes were relatively simple. He enjoyed driving himself around in his seven-year-old Volkswagen convertible, smoked Kool cigarettes, an inexpensive brand bought from street-corner kiosks, and had little interest in food. His favourite snack was a club sandwich, and when the *New York Times* asked half a dozen *couturiers* where they liked to eat in Paris, the others listed the city's finest restaurants, but Yves fantasized about being able to fulfil his nutritional needs by taking a pill.[13] And he had adopted a very different approach from Pierre to his latest architectural project, the renovation of Dar es Saada, a new villa that he and Pierre had bought in Marrakesh. Dar es Saada, or 'House of Happiness', was a 1930s colonial building in the grounds of the family home of Louis Majorelle, one of the great Art Deco furniture makers, in an area of the city called *La Zahia*, or 'Serenity'. Helped by Bill Willis, Yves restored the gardens, with their palms, orange trees and lily pond, and salvaged the Majorelle façade, which was the villa's only distinguished feature. They redesigned the rest of Dar es Saada in the idiosyncratic blend of Art Deco and local *Marrakchi* craftsmanship that Yves had loved at the old Mamounia Hotel, where he and Pierre stayed on their first visit to Morocco. While Pierre was bidding high in the New York auction rooms, Yves and Bill Willis scoured the *souks* for bargains. They paid $5 for each of the terrace chairs, and even less for a splendid 1930s carpet in the *salon*. The rest of the furniture was made up by local crasftsmen in *Marrakchi* materials to Yves's and Bill's designs. The window grilles were based on an image that Yves remembered seeing in a silent movie years before. Even the art collection was a snip: the walls of the villa were hung with paintings by gifted, but obscure Orientalist artists.

Despite their differences Yves and Pierre were still seen as a 'couple' on the Paris social scene and often entertained together at rue de Babylone. In his diaries Andy Warhol described a Sunday lunch there with Fred Hughes, when they went out into the garden with the dogs, and the conversation took on a camp tone with Pierre confessing that he liked to wear a cock ring.[14] Marie Helvin remembered another lunch at rue de Babylone with her then-husband, the photographer David Bailey, Diana Vreeland and Andy Warhol. 'Diana told the most wonderful stories. Andy said silly things like "Oh gee, Marie, what's it like to be on the stage?" And Yves just giggled and tried to tell his jokes. Bailey took a picture of us on the steps when we were leaving, all smiling and waving gaily. That's how I like to think of Yves.'[15]

Behind the smiles, Yves was in a fragile state. The rapturous reception of the *Ballets Russes* collection had made him more than usually anxious about the fate of his show the following season. Presenting his designs had always been a psychological strain for him, but as his reputation rose, so did the public's expectations, and after the triumph of the *Ballets Russes* show, disappointment seemed unavoidable.

Yves started work on the next collection for the October *prêt-à-porter* show immediately after the *couture* presentation. He designed hundreds of different outfits, before whittling them down to three hundred for the show. The theme for the season was *Carmen* and the first models marched on to the catwalk to the strains of the opera wearing black bullfighter shirts with cigarette pants and cummer-bunds. The presentation lasted for three hours, a record for Paris. For the finale the models danced along the runway in frilly *señorita* shirts with black velvet bodices and the bride came out doing the can-can. The spectators rose to their feet to cheer Yves when he came out to acknowledge their applause, but he was so drained by his ordeal that he could not stand up straight, barely managing a bow before being helped off stage.

The next day's newspaper reports were sympathetic, but scarcely scintillating, and would probably have been harsher had Clara and Pierre not taken the trouble to brief the journalists about Yves's nervous state of mind.[16] Sympathy was wearing thin by the time he showed his spring *couture* collection in January and Eugenia Sheppard noted tartly in the *Herald Tribune* that the audience sat 'waiting for the explosion that never happened'.[17] Yves survived that show intact, but looked so frail at the cocktail party afterwards that Pierre Bergé was overheard telling him to sit down and rest.

Rumours about his health ran around Paris that winter. One set of gossips suggested that Yves had an incurable illness, another blamed drink and drug abuse. The speculation reached a crescendo on the weekend before the *prêt-à-porter* show in March, when a story surfaced that Yves Saint Laurent was dead. Avenue Marceau was swamped by calls from reporters and, despite the denials, the rumour refused to subside. There was no consensus on the cause of death: the most popular theories were that Yves had committed suicide, or been stabbed to death in a Marrakesh brawl.

One fashion editor turned up at the *couture* house and sat down in the foyer, refusing to leave until she had proof that he was alive. 'There was a real houha,' recalled Julia Kennedy. 'Saint Laurent was there all the time. He was working away in his studio. But, of course, it would never have occurred to him to pop his head around the door so she could see him and leave. That would have been much too practical. He stayed in his studio and she stayed downstairs – until Bergé threw her out.'[18]

A British journalist telephoned incessantly demanding an exclusive interview with Yves and when Pierre Bergé refused she badgered the British Ambassador into making a special plea on her behalf. The answer was still 'no'. 'He didn't give a toss,' said Kennedy.[19] Eventually Pierre permitted Hélène de Turckheim of *Le Figaro* and Barbara Larcher of the German magazine, *Stern*, to peek into Yves's studio and see for themselves that the rumours were false. But on the morning of the show on 29 March 1977, the usual complement of fashion journalists were almost outnumbered by the foreign correspondents and television crews who had requested special tickets so they could verify whether the world's most famous fashion designer was dead or alive.

At the end of the show Yves paced along the catwalk with more vigour than he had mustered in the two preceding seasons, and he was at pains to assure the journalists who surged backstage afterwards that he was in excellent health. He tried to carry on as usual for the rest of the day, attending the post-show cocktail party and the lunch before spending the evening with Clara, Thadée, Loulou, Betty and Paloma. They ended the night, as was their custom, at Le Sept, but Paloma Picasso was struck by how hurt Yves had been by furore over his 'death'. 'The rumour was the proof that he was becoming a living myth and it seemed to him very difficult to accept.'[20]

Other celebrities had been subjected to similar apocryphal stories. When Paul McCartney was injured in a moped accident in 1966, a rumour spread that he had died and been replaced by an actor who posed as 'Paul' for the rest of the Beatles' career. Conspiracy theorists claimed to find numerous 'clues' in the band's work to support the story, insisting that there was a sinister significance in the words 'Bury my body' at the end of the song, *I Am The Walrus*, and that the letters 'OPD' on a badge McCartney wore for the cover of the *Sergeant Pepper* album meant 'Officially Pronounced Dead' when, in fact, they stood for 'Ontario Police Department'.[21] Paul McCartney was able to laugh off the rumours, but Yves could not. For such a painfully private man, it must have been deeply wounding to discover that a false report of his death would be splashed across the world's newspapers.

As an isolated incident, Yves might have found it easier to bear, but the 'death' story came at a time when he was already very vulnerable. Having achieved so much at such a young age, it was hard to see what more he could do in his forties. There was little further he could go as a fashion designer. After being billed as a great innovator in the 1960s, and the supreme classicist of the 1970s, Yves's talent seemed to have culminated in the *succès fou* of the *Ballets Russes* collection, when his work scaled such a height that, judging by the lacklustre reviews of subsequent shows, he might well be unable to match it again. Even before the *Ballets Russes* show, Yves had felt frustrated with fashion, the 'trade of an imbecile' as Pierre Bergé had called it;[22] now he was trapped in it, whether out of loyalty to his staff, because of his debilitated state, or a combination of the two. The macabre speculation over his 'death' was crushing to a man whom Bergé had described to a journalist that summer as having been 'born with a nervous breakdown'.[23] 'Before the death rumour Yves had been hyper-sensitive and self-indulgent,' said a friend. 'But after that the drink and drugs got completely out of control. He seemed hellbent on self-destruction.'

He stole into Avenue Marceau, hoping that no one would see him. Julia Kennedy remembered him 'driving up in his Beetle and going straight to his studio. Most of the time he was so quiet that you hardly knew he was in the building.'[24] As the shows approached she noticed a change in his behaviour. 'He got very worked up, really worked up. He'd stay in his studio round the clock and absolutely exhaust himself.'[25] Once she was called by a *valet de chambre* at rue de Babylone and asked to dispatch Pierre's chauffeur to buy Tranxyne, a powerful tranquillizer, for Yves and to send it over with a syringe in the Rolls-Royce.

After a prolonged bout of drinking and drug-taking, Yves broke down again and Pierre arranged for him to be readmitted to the American Hospital to be treated for alcohol and cocaine addiction. It was the first of what was to become a regular round of stays there.

Betty Catroux was enrolled on the same course of treatment by her husband, François and once she and Yves ended up in hospital at the same time. 'Yves and I have always behaved like naughty children. My husband is more sensible. He's like Pierre Bergé. They're the parents who try to stop the children, Yves and me, from doing crazy things. I don't know what would have happened to us without them.'[26]

Addiction and depression were not the only clouds over the Saint Laurent set. Loulou de la Falaise surprised them all that spring with the news of her sudden marriage to Thadée Klossowski, who had been Clara Saint's lover for almost a decade. Clara only found out about it when she saw the official announcement in Le Figaro. Even the self-absorbed Andy Warhol noticed how unhappy she seemed when he saw her for lunch with Paloma Picasso at Angélina's in Paris that May. Although Clara was already recovering her good humour, managing to laugh at Warhol's suggestion that they should outdo Loulou and Thadée by announcing their own wedding in Le Figaro.[27]

One of Yves's and Pierre's closest friends for fifteen years, Clara had been a great source of support to Yves during his depressions and was one of the few people whom Pierre trusted in a crisis. Thadée's desertion was a cruel blow to her, and it split the younger end of the Saint Laurent set, as Paloma sided with Clara. Yves's loyalties were less clear-cut. Fond though he was of Clara, he adored Loulou and offered to host a ball to celebrate her marriage to Thadée at the Châlet des Îles, a castle on an island in a lake in the Bois de Boulogne. The island was specially decorated for the night and the four hundred guests were taken across the lake in lantern-lit boats with swans trailing behind them. Thadée's father, the painter, Balthus, attended with his second wife, Setsuko, alongside the other Klossowskis and de la Falaises, including Loulou's mother, Maxime. The Rothschilds were there; as were Karl Lagerfeld, Kenzo, Manolo Blahnik and Bianca Jagger, who flew over from New York for the night only to make the diplomatic gaffe of wearing a pink Dior gown which Yves festooned with ferns. Paris Vogue set up a makeshift studio with a white backdrop to photograph the guests, who lingered on until dawn when Pierre Bergé was the first to leave, rowing himself across the lake with a pair of swans in stately pursuit.[28] Clara did not go to the Châlet des Îles celebration, but she carried on with her job in the Rive Gauche press office where she worked alongside Loulou each day.

That summer the novelist Anthony Burgess made a special trip to Paris from his Monte Carlo home to interview Yves for the *New York Times* magazine. Burgess arrived at Avenue Marceau with only a day to go before the autumn 1977 *couture* show. He watched Yves working on the final fittings in his Avenue Marceau studio and then spent time with him alone at rue de Babylone. His observations of Yves and of the *couture* house are intriguing, all the more so because Burgess came fresh to his subject with no prior knowledge of the fashion world.

'I was told by ladies of deliberate dowdiness that I would have to wait before I could see the master at work,' he wrote. 'This, I had expected. So I waited. Beyond that mirrored door, I was breathlessly told the final preparations for the *défilé* of the next day were proceeding; nerves were like overtuned E-strings; work would have to go on all night; the master (and I thought of Mozart composing the overture to *Don Giovanni* while the audience was arriving) had left things a little late. Ladies of the entourage peeked in to see how things were going. At length. Now you may enter. I don't want to stay long, I said (meaning it). So I went in. It was as though I was being admitted to a royal accouchement, or some delicate ancient ritual of erotic initiation. Actually it wasn't as frightening as I'd expected.'[29]

Once inside, Burgess saw Saint Laurent putting the final touches to 'what looked like a plaid travelling rug' draped over a model's shoulder. 'I would have put it on her like an old coal sack, but the master, with deft twists of hands I could see were both strong and delicate made an instant sonnet of it.'[30] As for Yves himself: 'The smile was shy. He is fair, slight and very myopic. Thick glasses rest on a John Gielgud nose that bespeaks strong will. The mouth is wide, the chin firm. In handling his *jeunes filles* he exhibited a respect for the female body not far from worship.'[31] Later he asked Yves how he saw women, and thought that he replied 'as dolls', until Saint Laurent corrected him. What he had actually said in his halting *franglais* was 'as idols'.[32]

At the end of their interview Burgess, who was fascinated by palmistry, asked Yves to show him his hands. Palmistry posits that the lines on the left hand illustrate a person's potential, the character traits that shape their life, while the lines on the right signify their fate and how they have moulded those traits. Most people's left and right palms are strikingly different. An aptitude for music might be evident on the left hand, but not on the right because it was never allowed to develop, or the right hand might show a gift for writing, which was not apparent on the left. Yves was a rare case, in that his palms were virtually identical. 'As I'd expected,' wrote Burgess, 'the right hand was almost an exact duplication of the left. His career had been worked out in the stars.'[33]

The Opium Wars
1977–1978

What Anthony Burgess saw in the Avenue Marceau studio that summer was a *couture* collection inspired by Yves's vision of eighteenth-century China. Yves had loved Asian art since seeing the Zen temples in Kyoto in the 1960s, and collected antique Chinese *objets* at rue de Babylone. That season he dressed his models in satin kimonos and mandarin tunics as though they were imperial concubines, and had them made up with scarlet lips and porcelain faces. The collection was an elegant expression of Yves's passion for Chinese aesthetics, and a perfect platform for the launch of Opium, the new Yves Saint Laurent perfume.

Opium was the product with which Yves, Pierre and Squibb hoped to capitalize on the acclaim for the *Ballets Russes* collection the previous summer, and the wave of publicity that followed it. Perfume sales had soared throughout the 1960s and 1970s, and the profits from the handful of best-selling scents were stupendous, largely because it cost so little to make the fragrance itself, the 'juice' as the industry called it.[1] If a 14ml. bottle of perfume went on sale for $80, the 'juice' cost roughly $4, with $6 going on packaging and $8 on advertising, leaving a profit of $22 from the wholesale price of $40. If Opium succeeded in matching Chanel No. 5's annual sales of $100 million, it would produce around $25 million a year in profits.

Ever since Marilyn Monroe's 'the only thing I wear to bed . . .' quip in the 1950s, the perfume market had been dominated by classic French fragrances, such as Chanel No. 5 and Nina Ricci's L'Air du Temps, but by the mid-1970s they were losing sales to the new genre of American 'concept scents', the products of lengthy research and aggressive marketing. When a French *couturier* or *parfumier* introduced a new perfume, they drew on the centuries of expertise of the Grasse *nez*, the 'noses' who invented the 'juice', and sold it on old-fashioned Parisian prestige; American cosmetics companies, such as Revlon and Estée Lauder,[2] did not have that heritage to draw on, and had to work harder at discovering what sort of perfumes consumers wanted, and at creating images likely to persuade them to buy the product.

The breakthrough was the introduction of Charlie by Revlon in 1973. Revlon's research showed that women, particularly younger women, preferred stronger, more extrovert scents to the gentle, floral smells of French fragrances. The company instructed a *nez* to develop such a perfume, and devised an advertising campaign featuring an attractive, uninhibited 'Charlie Girl' striding along a busy city street in a tailored trouser suit, epitomizing everything that its research said the women who would buy the fragrance wanted to be. Revlon then spent an unprecedented $10 million on advertising the launch in North America. By 1975 Charlie had joined Chanel No. 5 and Nina Ricci's L'Air du Temps at the top of the best-seller list, proving that it was possible to create a successful scent by inventing an appealing and appropriate image.

Charlie's success encouraged Squibb to go one step further with the next Yves Saint Laurent perfume. Picking up on the sexual ambiguity in Charlie's name and advertising imagery, Eau Libre was introduced in 1975 as a 'genderless' scent with a cool, slightly crisp smell intended to appeal to both sexes. Selling the same fragrance to men and women was an iconoclastic concept, but one that seemed to make sense at a time when pop stars such as David Bowie boasted openly about their bisexuality, and gay rights groups were becoming more active. Yves collaborated on the advertising with two Parisian art directors, Maïmé Arnodin and Denise Fayolle, whom he had met through Clara Saint. Then in their fifties, Maïmé and Denise worked in fashion journalism and interior design before founding an advertising agency, Mafia (Maïmé Arnodin Fayolle International Associés) in 1968.[3] Devotees of Yves's *smokings*, they ripped around Paris at breakneck speed in their tiny car, living and working from a pretty sandstone villa in an artists' quarter in Montparnasse.

The result of their collaboration was a stark photographic image of a black hand and a white one grasping a bottle of Eau Libre. There was a fierce debate in the press about its racial undertones, and some publications refused to carry the advertisement, just as they had the 'naked Yves' four years before. Whereas the controversy over the nude portrait increased sales of the men's scent, Eau Libre did not catch on commercially.[4] 'We didn't really know why,' said Clara. 'It smelt wonderful, but it was too far ahead of its time. People weren't ready for it.'[5] A decade later Benetton, the Italian clothing company, caused a furore with an advertising campaign featuring similar juxtapositions of black and white flesh, including one shot of a black and a white arm handcuffed together and another of a white baby suckling on a black breast. And twenty years after Eau Libre's launch the New York designer, Calvin Klein, introduced a 'genderless scent' with an identical product premise, CK One, that became an instant best-seller, unlike the Saint Laurent fragrance which was quietly withdrawn from the market.

Eau Libre's failure was particularly galling for Yves and Squibb as another new perfume associated with a fashion designer launched in the same year was so successful. Halston, like Charlie, was the result of lengthy research and an expensive advertising campaign, paid for by Norton Simon, the industrial group which owned Halston's fashion company. The sub-text to the advertising was that by buying a bottle of his perfume, American women could tap into the heady Halston lifestyle they read about in the gossip columns. A charismatic man with photogenic friends such as Bianca Jagger and Liza Minnelli, Halston was a firm favourite of the American press, and although he could not match Yves Saint Laurent's creative achievements, he was a formidable rival in commercial terms with his sleek, simply-cut clothes, such as *lamé* pyjamas and ultra-suede shirtdresses.[6] Yves's feelings on the subject were probably best summed up by his threat to destroy his Andy Warhol silkscreens when he discovered that the artist had also done a series of the American designer.

If Squibb's confidence in the Yves Saint Laurent name was dented by Eau Libre's failure, it was swiftly restored by the triumph of the

Ballets Russes collection the following year, which presented Yves to the public in a new light. Until then he was still seen as the hippy *de luxe* whose outrageous designs scandalized the *couture* establishment in the 1960s and early 1970s, an image reflected in Eau Libre. The rapturous reception for the *Ballets Russes* redefined Yves as an artist, or the closest that a fashion designer came to being one. Yves and Pierre persuaded Squibb that a new YSL perfume reflecting the themes of opulence and exoticism that had proved so popular in that collection might be able to match the sales of Chanel No. 5 and Halston.

Traditionally the invention of a new scent started when the *nez* produced a promising new 'juice', followed by the choice of an suitable name and advertising image to suit the smell. Opium was developed along modern American lines, beginning by dreaming up a name and image for the fragrance, and then creating a 'juice' to match them. Once Squibb had secured the legal rights to use the name Opium for which it paid a fee of $200 to the two elderly *parfumiers* who had registered it years before, it issued instructions to half a dozen *nez* to create a fragrance with a spicy, oriental smell. The 'juice' that Yves and Squibb chose was created by Jean Amic of Roure Bertrand Dupont, one of the most successful *nez*, who then liaised with them to refine the final formula. The perfume was constructed in the American proportions of one part oil to four parts liquid, giving it a stronger smell than classic French fragrances, and Squibb decided to price it at $100 an ounce, putting it right at the top of the market above Rive Gauche, Halston and Charlie.

The packaging Yves designed for Opium seemed innocuous enough. Inspired by the Chinese *objets* in his collection at rue de Babylone, it was a replica of a Mandarin lacquered bottle encased in a brown box embossed with gold lettering and sprigs of Chinese flowers. But the advertising was unashamedly provocative: a Helmut Newton portrait of the Texan model, Jerry Hall, lying languidly on a *lamé* sofa in the Oriental Room at rue de Babylone, with the slogan, '*Opium, pour celles qui s'adonnent à Yves Saint Laurent*'; 'Opium, for those who are addicted to Yves Saint Laurent'.

Sprawled across the *lamé* beneath an inscrutable Ming buddha and a riot of longine lilies, Jerry Hall, one of Marie Helvin's best friends and the future Mrs Mick Jagger, wore a black and gold mandarin jacket lined with red satin over a gold vest and purple satin harem pants with a red braid belt ruffling her hips. On her feet were high-heeled strappy gold sandals, and she was laden with jewellery, a heavy gold necklace and pendant earrings, broad bangles on each arm and knuckle-dusting rings on her fingers. Yves styled the advertisement himself, insisting that it be shot in his apartment, designing a special outfit for Jerry Hall, and even showing her how to lie on the *lamé* cushions. Maïmé Arnodin remembered him 'adjusting the bracelets while Helmut Newton was taking the photograph to make sure they were in the right position'.[7]

The choice of name, the *double entendre* in the advertising slogan and the decadent image of Jerry Hall looked like a chic joke to anyone on the Paris fashion scene, who would have been bound to have known about Yves's drug use and doubtless dabbled in drugs themselves, but they caused a furore in the press when Opium went on sale in Europe that autumn. Yves Saint Laurent and Squibb were accused of glamorizing drug addiction and trivializing the Opium Wars, a tragic period in China's history. This time the controversy worked in their favour, as it had with the 'nude Yves', with the storm over the 'scandalous' new Yves Saint Laurent perfume fusing perfectly with the dissolute climate of the late 1970s.

A new nightclub, Studio 54, opened in New York that spring, occupying a disused television studio on West 54th Street where CBS once filmed *What's My Line?* and *The $64,000 Question*. It was run by Steve Rubell and Ian Schrager, who had made their names as the owners of the Enchanted Garden, a nightclub set in a deserted Queens country club, where they threw gigantic theme parties that thousands of disco-crazed kids flocked to each weekend. On the morning after Studio 54's opening, the front page of the *New York Post* featured a picture of the pop star, Cher, standing on the eleven-thousand-square-foot dance-floor beneath a neon 'man on the moon' suggestively sprinkling shiny white stars up his nostrils. The club hit the headlines again the following month when Halston threw a birthday party there for Bianca Jagger at which the guest of honour, dressed in white and gold, was led on a white horse across the glitterdust-strewn dance-floor to an explosion of paparazzi flashbulbs.

After oil shocks, terrorist threats, hyper-inflation and Watergate, New York socialites flung themselves into the cocaine-crazed hedonism of Studio 54, just as young suburbanites like the one John Travolta played in the film *Saturday Night Fever*, headed for their local discotheques. The extremes of the gay scene made even Studio 54 seem tame; bath houses, such as the Castro in San Francisco and St Mark's in New York, were opening where men could pick up partners for casual sex, and more esoteric fare was on offer at hard-core sex clubs, like Plato's Retreat in Manhattan with its notorious urinal where men lay down to be urinated on by strangers.

Opium, with its opulent image and druggy undertones, packaged discomanic decadence in a manner palatable to the general public. It achieved higher sales in Europe during the month before Christmas 1977 than Chanel No. 5 did in the entire year,[8] and although it was not due to go on sale in the States until the following autumn, Opium quickly became a 'must have' souvenir for Americans who stocked up on it at airport shops on their way home from Europe. The new line of Yves Saint Laurent make-up proved just as popular when it came out in spring 1978, particularly the strongest colours, such as a purple lipstick, Number 19, which sold out straightaway. Anna Sui, the New York fashion designer who was then a student, remembered being asked by friends in the States to bring back bundles of Number 19s whenever she travelled to Europe.[9]

The highlight of the American launch was to be a party in New York on 19 September 1978 organized by Marina Schiano, who ran the YSL press office there. Buoyed by Opium's success in Europe, Squibb agreed to spend $300,000 on the party and Schiano hired a Chinese junk, the *Peking*, moored beside Brooklyn Bridge on the East River, for the night. Invitations were dispatched to over a thousand people including Diana Vreeland, Oscar de la Renta, Andy Warhol, Cher, Truman Capote and Halston, with whom Yves had recently staged a very public *rapprochement* by kissing him on the Studio 54 dance-floor under the watchful eye of a *Women's Wear Daily* reporter. The party was billed as the first important event of the autumn social season when New Yorkers returned to the city after the Labor Day holiday.

The Saint Laurent set flew over from France for the event, except for Clara Saint, who had a phobia about flying. Yves arrived at the *Peking* in a double-breasted evening suit with satin lapels, a crisply-laundered white shirt and a black satin bow tie. At his side were Loulou de la Falaise, wearing a black velvet *haute couture* jacket with a red and green opium poppy embroidered across it, and Thadée Klossowski in the same classic style of evening dress as Yves's with a bright red cummerbund at his waist and a red cotton peasant handkerchief tucked in his breast pocket. Half a dozen models accompanied them, wearing mandarin jackets and harem pants in the reds, purples and golds that Jerry Hall had worn in the advertisement.

The cream of New York society showed up, along with thirty-three television crews, but without Andy Warhol, who was visiting his West Coast art dealer and moaned in his diary about having to miss the Opium party.[10] The *Peking* looked exquisite, festooned with hundreds of Yves's favourite white orchids, and pretty Chinese paper lanterns strung around the rigging. Up on the main deck people sipped champagne and helped themselves to *hors d'oeuvres* and strawberries, staring out over the water, from the surreal splendour of the Manhattan skyline to the urban debris of Brooklyn. Other guests dived down to the lower decks to sample the unofficial menu of cocaine, before returning to the main deck to report on who was *in flagrante delicto* with whom in the bathrooms. Diana Vreeland held court from a makeshift perch on a pile of wooden crates, picking daintily at a plate of caviar. When a reporter asked her what she thought of the new perfume, she replied: 'I like the smell of money.'[11]

One guest remembered the party as being: 'Just perfect. It was one of those lovely, lazy early autumn evenings, when Manhattan seems like the centre of the world. Everyone looked fantastic, fresh from the holidays, excited to see each other again with lots of talk about. So there we all were. Beautiful people, great drugs, fabulous food, champagne and a spectacular setting. It was wonderful.' At the end of the evening, the guests assembled on the main deck to watch a firework display spelling out the words 'Yves Saint Laurent' and 'Opium' in $30,000 of explosive sparks and flashes across the inky sky above the East River. As the party-goers filed off the boat, Yves slipped away with Loulou, Thadée and Marina Schiano to West 54th Street for an impromptu celebration at Studio 54, where he perched on a banquette in the VIP area with Loulou, Nan Kempner and Halston, while Potassa, a transvestite who hung out at the club, hovered hopefully at his shoulder.

Stories about the *Peking* party swamped the gossip columns for weeks; no sooner had they died down than the controversy over Opium flared up again. A Chinese activist group in Queensland, Australia, caused such a furore that the perfume was banned from being sold there, and the fracas spread to the United States, even before it went on sale. At Squibb's annual general meeting in May, one of the shareholders tabled a question for the chairman, Richard Furlaud, asking whether he thought Opium was an appropriate name for a perfume.[12] He replied in the affirmative, but the protests escalated when Opium went on sale, with anti-drug abuse campaigners and Chinese-American groups calling for it to be banned, as it had been in Queensland.[13]

James Tso, chairman of the Committee for Equal Opportunity of the Organization of Chinese Americans, wrote a formal letter of protest to Squibb describing the commercialization of the word Opium as 'psychological pollution'[14] and demanding that the company either change the name, or take the product off the market. The protests rumbled on through the winter, and flared up in the spring when James Tso's organization joined forces with Franklin Williams, a prominent New York politician who often campaigned on drugs issues, to form an 'Opium War 1979' campaign.[15] On the day of Squibb's next annual general meeting that May they staged a demonstration outside its corporate headquarters at which protesters, wearing 'Kill Opium' and 'Boycott Squibb' badges, brandished banners and placards calling for a ban on all the company's products.

Squibb was in an unenviable position. A genuinely progressive organization, it prided itself on sound corporate ethics and a liberal reputation which was now sullied by the choice of name for a perfume that, however successful, would only ever represent a tiny proportion of its turnover and profits. Some of the anti-Opium lobby's complaints seemed petty, but there was no doubt that the name had, albeit unintentionally, offended members of the Chinese community and that the drugs undertones in the advertising were frowned upon by anti-drug abuse campaigners. Yet Squibb continued to support Yves and his choice of name. At the annual general meeting Richard Furlaud dismissed the anti-Opium protest as 'commercial and artistic censorship'.

What else could he say? The $300,000 that Squibb had sunk into the *Peking* party was only part of its multi-million dollar investment in Opium's launch. A change of name might imperil that investment and, as Squibb was well aware, the publicity generated by the controversy had probably increased sales of the perfume. Diana Vreeland's prediction was correct; Opium was as successful in North America as it had been in Europe, shooting straight into the top ten above Charlie and Halston.[16] Squibb had succeeded in creating its $100-million-a-year perfume, leaving it with the prospect of $25 million in profits and annual royalties of at least $2.5 million for Yves Saint Laurent. If Squibb's board was unnerved by the furore, Yves seemed to relish it. 'He loved it,' recalled Maïmé Arnodin. 'He used to say that he wished they'd come and protest outside his windows on rue de Babylone.'[17]

The Retreat to Babylone
1978–1980

It was generally a treat for the people in the audience to see what Yves Saint Laurent was wearing when he walked along the runway to accept their applause at the end of his shows. The length of his hair became a minor obsession for the fashion editors of the 1960s, who reported on its progress each season as it crept over his collar to curl around his shoulders. His clothes changed too, as Yves swapped the tightly-buttoned suits he had worn in the early 1960s for beatnik corduroys and hippy *de luxe* kaftans, and finally for a dandyish wardrobe of white linen suits and foppish bow ties with a glint of Cartier gold bracelets. A very different figure appeared on the catwalk at the end of his *couture* presentation in January 1978; the most fashionable fashion designer in Paris was wearing a smart, but undeniably boring business suit.

Yves's stints at the American Hospital and a new course of psychotherapy had done little to unlock his cycle of drink, drugs and despondency. For years his favourite game had been the Proust questionnaire, in which the players ask each other questions about their likes and dislikes. Yves's answer to 'What is your greatest fear?' was always 'Solitude', but now he seemed obsessed by it. The evenings when the Saint Laurent set congregated at rue de Babylone were becoming rarer; even his mother saw less of him, although she still tried to coax Yves out to lunch each week, usually on Sundays when his sisters and their children came to her apartment. 'I often feel incapable of communicating with people,' he said that summer, 'even with those that I love and admire profoundly, because they don't have the time and I am in a frenzy.'[1]

Social outings were kept to a minimum. The *Peking* party was one of the last of Yves's wild nights. Sometimes he was too drunk or too stoned to go, but mostly he felt too wretched. As Yves withdrew from view, lurid stories about him swilled around Paris, saying that he had been banned from leaving rue de Babylone by Pierre Bergé, or spotted in one of the seedier Pigalle bars. On the odd occasions when he did attend dinners or galas, Yves was invariably the centre of attention, surrounded by acquaintances, often by people he barely knew. Loulou, Clara and Betty tried to fend them off, but in the process often shielded Yves from the old friends who genuinely cared for him and were concerned about his condition.

'The people in that inner circle loved him very deeply, but they wanted to keep others away,' said a woman who had known Yves since the 1950s. 'Suddenly he wasn't around any more and when he came to a party or a dinner, it was so rare that everyone wanted to talk to him, so they'd protect him. They never left him alone. He came over to talk to me at a party once and I could see one or two of them looking over nervously to see what was going on. Then they came to join us. Now Yves could have politely moved away if he'd wanted to, but he stayed. He felt safe with me, he knows I'm fond of him, and he was perfectly happy gabbing away about the good old days.'

Yves still had tremendous charm, the crux of which was his courtesy. Much as he disliked being assailed by strangers, he smiled and thanked them, invariably leaving a pleasant impression. Diana Vreeland once described him as having an 'extraordinary sweetness'[2] and Anthony Burgess noted that 'there seemed to be no malice in this Yves'.[3] Few of his employees, except for Loulou, Clara, Anne-Marie and Marina Schiano, were intimate with him, but Yves was unfailingly polite to all of them. Julia Kennedy remembered him as 'a lovely man' who 'although he was so shy, always made an effort to say "hello" or make a pleasant remark' when he passed her desk outside Pierre's office in the Avenue Marceau secretariat.[4]

His courtesy was partly a ruse to keep people at bay by curtailing conversation and enabling him to escape. François-Marie Banier remembered Yves deploying the same tactic on the Paris social scene, fobbing off his hosts at social events by complimenting them on their good taste, even if the *décor* was dreadful, and remaining sweetly silent when people said something he disagreed with rather than going to the trouble of arguing.[5] Yet those who knew him well were touched by unexpected acts of thoughtfulness. Susan Train of *Vogue* remembered a conversation in the late 1970s when he suddenly said, 'Susan, I remember exactly what you were wearing the first time I ever saw you,' and then described the outfit she had worn on the day in 1955 when he went to Paris *Vogue* to show his fashion sketches to Michel de Brunhoff. 'Well, that was years and years before! And I was Little Miss Nobody. I was this junior fashion editor trying so hard to look like a fashion editor in my Balenciaga suit on sale; but he remembered!'[6]

Yet mostly he stayed out of sight, sealing himself off in his rooms at rue de Babylone, or Dar es Saada. Yves romanticized his depressions, just as he had his drug-taking, by drawing parallels between his plight and that of the French romantic poets, such as Charles Baudelaire and Arthur Rimbaud, who drew on their suffering in their writing. Most of all he was moved by the work of Marcel Proust, burying himself in *À La Recherche du Temps Perdu*, the series of novels he had first read in his teens and now read again and again, poring over Proust's descriptions of creative anguish and his characters' struggles for acceptance in the seductive but superficial world of the aristocratic Faubourg Saint-Germain. Yves always stopped before the end of the final volume, *Le Temps Retrouvé*, which he added to his superstitious tally of taboos after birds, cats, diamonds and clubs. 'I often pick it up but never finish it. I need to have it close to me. But some superstition tells me that if I reach the end something will happen. Nothing good.'[7] Framed quotations from *À La Recherche* were pinned above his desk at Avenue Marceau, Yves described himself in conversation as a member of Proust's 'magnificent and pitiful family of the hyper-sensitive', and littered letters to friends with such passages as 'One can almost say that works of art, like Artesian wells, rise that much higher if suffering has dug more deeply into the heart.'[8]

When in Paris he withdrew to his Avenue de Breteuil penthouse, where he spent hours scribbling pages of prose and poetry, and writing long letters, among the Jean-Michel Frank furniture and

Diego Giacometti lamps. Friends, such as Marie-Hélène de Roths-child and Diana Vreeland, cherished Yves's letters, and when Anthony Burgess, who wrote and spoke French fluently, was being shown around rue de Babylone he sneaked a look at a piece of prose. 'I didn't take in much of the content,' he observed, 'but I was pleased with the intricacy of the sentence construction, the love of rare words, the hints of a mental complexity not usually associated with a dress designer.'[9] For years Yves had talked of publishing his work, but did little about it, apart from *La Vilaine Lulu*, which was really a cartoon book, and a tribute to Maria Callas that appeared in *Le Monde* after her death in September 1977.[10]

Nor did he pursue his passion for the theatre, despite the entreaties of Roland Petit and Zizi Jeanmaire. Yves agreed to design a revue for Zizi in 1977, his first theatrical project for four years, and created sets and costumes for the production of Jean Cocteau's *L'Aigle a Deux Têtes* with which Pierre reopened the Théâtre de l'Athénée the following year, but he spurned other offers. His theatrical designs were highly acclaimed, and Roland Petit considered him one of the most gifted people in the field since Christian Bérard.[11] Once Yves had enjoyed his collaborations with actors, dancers and directors, relishing the challenge of intricate commissions, but now he told Bernadine Morris of the *New York Times* that he found it 'impossible' to design for the theatre in addition to fashion because it was so 'much more demanding'.[12]

Yves saw his work as the source of his problems, describing it as 'quite horrible – a system of meshing cogs, a cycle that one is caught up in which cuts short many relationships one could have with friends, family . . . lots of things.'[13] The French are attached to the notion of the tormented genius spurred on by suffering to greater creative triumphs and, as Yves's depressions deepened, the official company line from Pierre Bergé, Loulou de la Falaise and Clara Saint was that he had become another tortured artist in the tradition of the Rimbauds, Baudelaires, Verlaines and Prousts. The summer after the 'death' rumour Pierre described Yves as 'an artist with an artist's anxieties of constantly seeking perfection'; while Loulou cast him as 'someone who doesn't really belong to daily life' as it was 'too flat, too ordinary for him'.[14]

As he retreated, Loulou became the public face of the fashion house. Other than Yves and Pierre, she had been its most visible employee since her arrival in the early 1970s and the press reports of fashion week almost always carried an account of what Loulou was wearing at the YSL show, generally theatrical outfits in rich colours with dramatic jewellery like the heavy bangles she wore along her arms *à la* Nancy Cunard. Rather than accompanying Yves to official functions, Loulou now went in his stead, playing the same role for him that Suzanne Luling had done for the timid Christian Dior.

Her social connections made Loulou an ideal ambassadress. The friends she had met while working at Andy Warhol's Factory gave her an *entrée* to the younger end of the Manhattan social set, and her mother, Maxime, introduced her to the fashionably arty axis around Diana Vreeland. Maxime's brother, Mark Birley, was the owner of Annabel's, the jet set's favourite London nightclub, and Loulou had an *entrée* to Hollywood thanks to her old New York flatmate, Berry Berenson, the wife of the *Psycho* star, Anthony Perkins. Back in Paris she and Thadée were at the heart of the young social scene, leading the rush to Le Palace, the new nightclub opened by Fabrice Emaer, the owner of Le Sept, in an old Montmartre music hall where Maurice Chevalier and the legendary French stripper, Mistinguett, began their careers. One of the first parties held there was hosted by the newly married Loulou and Thadée Klossowski at the end of fashion week in March 1978. Their guests were asked to come as the hostess's favourite characters, Angels and Demons, Legends and Wonders. Loulou went as a fallen angel, and Thadée as a cherub. Karl Lagerfeld pinned one of Josephine Baker's old stage costumes over his evening suit. Marina Schiano dressed as the Bloomsbury hostess, Lady Ottoline Morrell; Marie-Hélène de Rothschild as the fairy queen; and Yves Saint Laurent as himself.

Loulou was a great favourite with the models. Almost as young, and certainly as pretty as they were, she chatted in the *cabine*, and handed out restorative whiskies at the end of the day's fittings. 'We were all a little bit in love with her,' recalled Marie Helvin. 'Loulou was great fun and so stylish, the perfect muse for Yves.'[15] And she acted as a conduit between the company and the youth scene, where she was known as someone who would give a sympathetic hearing to young designers, photographers or illustrators when they came to Avenue Marceau to show their work.

'People thought of her as this glamorous social creature, but Loulou could be very kind,' said Julia Kennedy. 'One Friday night she found me in floods of tears in the office. I was supposed to be going to London for the weekend and I'd missed my flight. I'd bought one of those cheap tickets, so I couldn't switch to another plane. Loulou stopped what she was doing and tried to cheer me up. She even lent me the money to buy a new ticket. And then she said, "Don't worry about Bergé, his bark is worse than his bite." After that she often popped her head around the door of the office to make sure I was alright.'[16] Loulou confided in Andy Warhol that Yves's dark moods affected all the staff, and she felt obliged to try and cheer them up. The 'happy act' was such a strain that she drank too much, eventually developing a liver problem and was ordered by her doctor to stop drinking, which she did towards the end of 1978. After giving up alcohol Loulou still took cocaine, insisting to the sceptical Andy Warhol that she was sure it was not bad for her.[17]

Loulou's official role at the company was to play Mitza Bricard to Yves's Christian Dior, which she fulfilled by discussing the details of his designs with him and standing beside him backstage at the fashion shows draping the models with jewellery. But by the late 1970s she and Anne-Marie Muñoz played a more active role in the design of the collections, particularly the Rive Gauche ready-to-wear range with which Yves seemed increasingly disaffected.

As a young man in the 1960s Yves had positioned himself at the forefront of the *prêt-à-porter* movement and purported to despise the anachronisms of *haute couture*, but he had since become disenchanted by the new medium and nostalgic for the old rituals, seeing a Proustian analogy between the decline of the *fin de siècle* aristocrats in *À La Recherche du Temps Perdu*, and his own career as a fashion designer, beginning at the end of the old *couture* era, and the start of the new *prêt-à-porter* age. 'The theme of qualities that are disappearing, of luxury that is disappearing is very dear to me,' he said. 'In a way it is related to the theme of death – the death of an epoch – the decadence of an epoch that I was fortunate enough to know because I was of an age that permitted me to experience the slow death of one era and the birth of another.'[18]

On a practical level *haute couture* provided a better canvas for the theatrical themes and classic styles that had dominated his work since his reclusion. Once Yves's designs were inspired by changes in the society around him, such as the 1950s beatnik scene or the sight of a dynamic young woman like Nikki de Saint-Phalle in a tailored trouser suit; but by the late 1970s his life was so introspective that his inspirations came from his established repertoire of styles, or the illusory world of his imagination, from the time he spent alone poring over Marcel Proust's novels, the poetry of Guillaume Apollinaire, paintings by Velázquez and Delacroix, and images of eighteenth-century China. The workmanship of the Avenue Marceau *ateliers* and sumptuous *couture* fabrics showed them off to perfection, achieving subtleties of cut and colour that the factory-made Rive Gauche range could not replicate.

When creating *couture* Yves scrutinized the process from start to finish, worked closely with the *atelier* staff, and exercised rigorous control over the final garment by personally fitting the fabric on the models. Ready-to-wear was less intimate, as he executed the basic sketches for the designs, and discussed ideas for fabrics and trimmings with Loulou, Anne-Marie and his other assistants, but relied on factories to manufacture the clothes and, inevitably, the quality was not as high. Yves summed up the difference by telling *Time* magazine that *couture* was like being a 'sculptor who gets to work with the finest ebony', but 'that's not the case with Rive Gauche at all. I have to work with factories. I give them a sketch and have to wait twelve to fifteen days before I see the result. It's total anguish.'[19]

By the late 1970s the 'anguish' was too much and Yves disengaged from *prêt-à-porter*, progressively allowing more of the design ideas to come from his assistants, with Anne-Marie and Loulou becoming increasingly involved in planning and editing the collections. Anne-Marie Muñoz described it as 'a collaborative process, Loulou and I can contribute our ideas, but Yves takes the final decisions.'[20] In practice the level of Yves's involvement fluctuated from season to season, and at his least engaged, he left most of the editing to Anne-Marie and Loulou, making minor modifications before the show. The design studio settled into the working pattern that it was to follow throughout the 1980s and 1990s, with Yves devoting himself to *haute couture*, a process Anne-Marie likened to 'a distinguished professor at the Sorbonne giving a *cours magistral*', while she and Loulou took the themes he had defined for the previous

173

season's *couture* collection and adapted them for the Rive Gauche range.

It was a practical solution to the problem of designing four collections a year, which imposed intolerable pressure on Yves, and even conformed to *couture* tradition. Until the start of the *prêt-à-porter* shows in the early 1970s, the heads of Paris fashion houses always concentrated on *haute couture*, leaving ready-to-wear, or *confection* as it was then called, to their assistants. Some houses, notably Christian Dior, had since appointed different chief designers for *couture* and ready-to-wear, having recognized that it was difficult to expect one person to create both collections. However, Yves's initial enthusiasm for *prêt-à-porter* had produced some of the most exciting work of his career, leaving the audience with high expectations and, as his involvement lessened, some commentators felt that the standard of the Rive Gauche range was slipping.

The *couture* shows still garnered glowing reviews,[21] but after the Rive Gauche presentation for spring 1978, Hebe Dorsey noted in the *Herald Tribune* that the applause was 'a long way from the wild cheers at previous shows';[22] and six months later she dismissed the autumn line as 'terribly safe and classic'.[23] So safe, in fact, that the highlight of the event was Pierre Bergé's appearance on the catwalk before the models came out. The start of the show had been delayed for an hour because of a power failure and Pierre took out his fury on the photographers. 'He was so mad,' recalled Marie Helvin, 'that he marched up and down the catwalk and kicked all the cameras.'[24]

The discrepancy between the two collections became achingly apparent in the presentations for autumn 1979, when the Rive Gauche range attracted some of the most damning reviews of Yves's career. 'Yves Saint Laurent is on a fashion sabbatical,' wrote Hebe Dorsey. 'A designer who used to make or break fashion, he seemingly has decided to sit back and live off his old classics.' She went on to quote an anonymous American department store owner who described the collection as 'a disaster' with 'not a single new look'.[25] Yet three months later the *couture* collection for the same season was hailed as one of his greatest triumphs.

It was inspired by an exhibition that Yves had seen at the Bibliothèque Nationale of the sets and costumes designed for Diaghilev's *Ballets Russes* in the 1920s by Picasso, Matisse, Rouault and De

Chirico.[26] The models wore diamond-patterned suits inspired by Picasso's harlequin figures for the opening, and then appeared in ballerina tutus with filmy skirts flowing from velvet bodices. After a series of brightly-coloured bullfighter costumes, like those he had created for his 1976 *Carmen* collection, came an evening dress sequence inspired by Picasso's designs for the ballet, *Parade*. Yves's favourite outfit was an orange taffeta ballgown with a bouffant skirt appliquéed with abstract shapes in the *Parade* palette of orange, yellow and black. When the bride made her entrance for the finale, she was accompanied by two children dressed in harlequin suits; Paloma Picasso was so moved by Yves's interpretation of her father's work that she burst into tears in a blaze of camera flashes.

Bernadine Morris wrote in the *New York Times* that Yves Saint Laurent had 'put fashion back on the map as a serious undertaking . . . He may stir up the arguments again over whether fashion is an art. In his hands it certainly approaches it.'[27] After the show Yves told her that he was 'terrified' beforehand. 'It was a completely selfish collection. I did it to please myself. The *couture* is a dream, like opera or ballet. Ready-to-wear is for modern life. It must be worn by many women. It must be real. *Couture* is a fantasy.'[28]

The reverential reviews for the *couture* reinforced Yves's reputation for artistry, but underlined how out of synch he had become from the rest of the fashion industry. During the 1960s and early 1970s, it was his innovations which were adopted by other designers – modernizing *haute couture* and then becoming the first established designer to take *prêt-à-porter* seriously – now he had returned to *haute couture* when ready-to-wear was by far the most vibrant part of the industry.

The new generation of French designers, such as Claude Montana,[29] Thierry Mugler[30] and Jean-Paul Gaultier,[31] eschewed *couture* to concentrate on *prêt-à-porter*, which they saw as a freer, more modern medium. The audience for the Paris ready-to-wear shows expanded each season, and now easily outnumbered the *couture*,[32] as people flocked to see Gaultier's jokey version of British punk style, and Mugler's Dan Dare jumpsuits, with waspy waists and exaggerated shoulders. Kenzo drew crowds to unorthodox venues such as circuses and disused theatres, as did Karl Lagerfeld to his provocative Chloé presentations, such as the one when he sent the black American model, Pat Cleveland, along the runway wearing nothing but a shocking pink feather in her pubic hair.

Milan was emerging as an important fashion centre, with journalists and buyers going there before the Paris shows to see the work of Giorgio Armani[33] and Gianni Versace.[34] Both designers benefited from the Italian economic boom, and their work was very sellable in the United States, albeit for different reasons. Versace had a flair for flamboyant colours and dramatic prints that appealed to the flashy Latin side of American taste; while Armani's subtle, understated trouser suits and wrap skirts provided a perfect working uniform for WASPy career women. They and the other Milanese designers drew on the city's long tailoring tradition, and its proximity to the Prato woollen mills and Como silk-weavers, just as the Parisian *hauts couturiers* were fed by their cottage industry of artisanal button-makers and embroiderers.

The New York fashion scene was energized by the rise of Ralph Lauren[35] and Calvin Klein.[36] Neither matched the chic of the French designers, nor the production quality of the Italians, but they had the advantage of a huge domestic market and a close rapport with American magazines and department stores, which were hungry for homegrown talent. Both men knew the fashion business backwards, as Lauren had started his career as a tie salesman, and Klein as a design assistant in the Seventh Avenue Garment District. Ralph Lauren became known for his interpretations of the preppy look and the old-fashioned glamour of Hollywood movies, scoring a *coup* when Diane Keaton wore his baggy shirts and trousers for her Oscar-winning role in *Annie Hall*; while Calvin Klein looked like a natural successor to Halston with his simple, no frills designs and frenzied Studio 54 lifestyle.

The emergence of these new designers enabled *prêt-à-porter* to eclipse *couture* as the most exciting and creative area of fashion, and accentuated the criticism of the Rive Gauche ranges as Yves withdrew from the design process. To the new generation of fashion journalists seeing the Paris shows for the first time, the disparity between the two collections created a schizophrenic impression of Yves Saint Laurent. Sally Brampton, a fashion assistant on *Vogue* who was later to launch and edit the British edition of *Elle*, remembered being 'absolutely smitten' when she saw her first YSL *couture* show. 'It was utterly magical. As a baby on *Vogue* my job was to collect the clothes from the *couture* houses in the evening so we could shoot them at night, as they were selling them during the day. When I got them to the studio I used to try them on which, of course, you weren't supposed to do, but I couldn't resist it. They were so beautiful.'[37] Her reaction was very different when she saw the *prêt-à-porter* which she found to be '*bourgeois* and rather boring'.[38] Yet press criticism, and even growing competition from New York and Milan did not affect the commercial performance of the Rive Gauche boutiques, or Pierre's licensing deals. Meanwhile the millions of dollars streaming in from Opium's royalties elevated Yves and Pierre from the ranks of the rich to those of the super-rich.[39]

Pierre acquired a helicopter and a Lear jet for the company, and started to take flying lessons. He also sank more money into the amusing, but expensive business of running his theatre, which he renamed the Théâtre de l'Athénée-Louis Jouvet in honour of the great actor-director, and commissioned Jacques Grange to decorate a room there dedicated to Christian Bérard. He and Yves were able to bid for the very best pieces at art auctions, starting with a series of Brancusi sculptures, and then acquiring works by Picasso and Matisse for rue de Babylone. Yves, who created one of his most famous fashion collections inspired by the images in a monograph of Mondrian's paintings that his mother had given him for Christmas, treated himself to an original Mondrian, as well as a Goya portrait of Don Luis de Cistue y Martinez, a two-year-old Spanish noble-man.

In his twenties and thirties Yves's homes had owed more to the quality of his taste than to the amount of money he spent on them. The Place Vauban apartment was simply furnished with carefully chosen pieces of modernist furniture and paintings that he and Pierre were either given by friends, like Jean Cocteau, or unearthed at flea-markets. When they moved to rue de Babylone, they decorated their new home more extravagantly, but not excessively so, having bought most of the Art Deco *objets* and African art before those styles became fashionable. Dar el-Hanch was a small stone-walled villa furnished with the work of local craftsmen, and although Dar es Saada was considerably larger, it had $5 chairs on the terrace and a cut-price 1930s carpet from the *souk*. 'The last thing I wanted was a palace,' Yves told Gerry Dryansky when he was showing him around the villa. 'I'm against ultra-splendour.'[40]

Yet ultra-splendour was the perfect epithet for Yves's homes as he grew older, richer – and unhappier. The expensive additions to the rue de Babylone art collection showed the same unerring eye as his flea-market finds, but gave the apartment an eerily exquisite air. When the art critic, Barbara Rose, visited the apartment to interview him for American *Vogue*, she was struck by the 'subtlety of the mind' and 'absolute coherence of taste' that had created it, and also by the feeling of 'motionless perfection' in a place where the only noise was the birds in the garden, rather than the clamour of the traffic-choked street outside.[41] Yves's next new home was even more sumptuous: Villa Oasis, the property next to Dar es Saada which he and Pierre bought when it came up for sale in 1980, with several acres of surrounding land.

Villa Oasis was an imposing house built in the 1920s for the artist Louis Majorelle and his family, with a beautiful botanical garden in its grounds. Yves set to work with Bill Willis and Jacques Grange to restore the entire estate including the garden, which was to be open to the public, as the *Jardin Majorelle*, or *Bou Saf Saf*, leaving him and Pierre with a private area of palms, orange trees and lily ponds around the villa. Even before the restoration, Villa Oasis was one of the grandest houses in Marrakesh, with sprawling *salons* and an enchanting labyrinth of terraces, pools and shelters leading into the gardens, and across to Dar es Saada, which they were keeping on as a guest house. After the renovation work was finished it would be magnificent. Rather than foraging in the *souks* as he had for Dar es Saada and Dar el-Hanch, Yves trawled the Paris antique dealers and auction houses with Jacques Grange, eventually shipping two hundred cases of books, paintings, sculpture and furniture to Morocco. At his insistence all the books in the library were recovered in snakeskin or morocco, and a window grille was carved into an image he remembered seeing years before in a silent movie. The work took four years to complete, with a local craftsman taking nine months to paint one room, the 'red study', to the specific shade of red Yves wanted.

Even the dogs benefited from their owners' largesse. Hazel and Ficelle had bespoke beds at the rue de Babylone apartment, and special sleeping quarters in the Lear jet where they could slumber on flights to and from Marrakesh. Back in Paris, Ficelle was involved in a fight with a dog belonging to a friend of Pierre's, and Julia Kennedy was asked to send an apologetic bouquet of flowers to the victim, convalescing in an expensive canine clinic. 'My mother called from Northern Ireland that day. I think it was too much for her. "How are you darling?" "Well, I've just had Jeanne Moreau on the other line and I've been asked to send flowers to a dog!" '[42]

The Grand Old Man
1981–1983

When Pierre Bergé heard the result of the May 1981 presidential elections, he was sitting in the *salon* of Hôtel Lambert, the opulent Paris townhouse belonging to Baron Guy and Baronne Marie-Hélène de Rothschild. Thousands of Parisians were crowded on the cobblestones of nearby Place de la Bastille waiting for the outcome to flash up on a giant video screen. As soon as the news broke that François Mitterrand had been elected as the first socialist president of the Fifth Republic, the crowd erupted into jubilant cheers. Cars raced around the streets with horns blaring and *tricolore* flags draped across the bonnets, but the mood inside Hôtel Lambert was very different.

After twenty-three years in opposition, François Mitterrand had been written off as *l'éternel perdant*, the eternal loser, of French politics. This was his last crack at the presidency and he did everything he could to swing the electorate in his favour. He smartened up his suits, capped his teeth for the cameras, and hired an advertising executive, Jacques Seguela, to remould his image as a solid elder statesman - *La Force Tranquille*, or 'The Quiet Force' – on whom the French could depend in a crisis. The socialist promises of a shorter working week, longer holidays and earlier retirement were welcomed by the ecstatic crowds at Place de la Bastille, but Mitterrand's pledges to impose a 'wealth tax' on the rich and to nationalize some of France's largest companies horrified the Rothschilds' inner circle. Baron Guy not only faced the threat of higher taxes, but of losing control of the family bank. He had voted for Valéry Giscard d'Estaing, the right-wing candidate, as had most of his guests, including Pierre Bergé.

Although he enjoyed reminiscing about his radical youth, Pierre was a fifty-one-year-old millionaire, whose company had flourished under the right and stood to suffer if the new socialist government cracked down on its wealthy customers. 'I'd always voted for the left before, but in the 1981 election I voted for Valéry Giscard d'Estaing. He'd made some reforms I approved of and, at the time, I wasn't sure about Mitterrand.'[1] His doubts were reinforced by the early months of the socialist presidency when Pierre Mauroy, the new prime minister, embarked on a radical reform programme. Bergé disapproved of Mauroy's economic measures but he was swayed by some of the social initiatives, not least by the abolition of the Vichy sexuality law which had been used to crack down on homosexuality. He also made allies in the socialist camp by befriending Danielle Mitterrand, the new president's wife, who became a regular visitor at Avenue Marceau where she borrowed suits and gowns for formal occasions, and Jack Lang, the dynamic new culture minister whom he met in his role as president of the Chambre Syndicale de la Couture.

A flamboyant figure in his early forties, Jack Lang was a short wiry man, with thick black curls and an unexpectedly attractive face which would have been described as *jolie laide* had he been a woman. Everything about him exuded energy and enthusiasm, from a ready smile and perma-tanned complexion, to his blush-pink shirts and snappily tailored Mao suits. Like several other members of the Mauroy cabinet, Lang was a 'sixty-eighter', who came of political age during the May 1968 student protests and saw them as a seminal influence on his thinking. His cultural credentials were impeccable; before entering politics, he founded and ran the Nancy International Theatre Festival. Hooting with derision at the ascetic argument that socialist ideals were incompatible with a love of food, wine, fashion and the arts, Jack Lang was the archetype of what Americans call a 'limousine liberal', and one of the few government ministers to have mingled with Loulou, Thadée and the younger members of the Saint Laurent set on the Le Palace dance-floor.

As a close political ally of François Mitterrand, Lang could count on the president's support for his policies, and he had ambitious plans for his ministry, which was founded with great furore by the novelist, André Malraux, during the De Gaulle presidency, and had since slipped into obscurity. One of his aims was to raise the stature of French culture in the international arena, another was to popularize the arts in France by extending his ministry's remit into areas that had traditionally fallen outside its ambit. Fashion satisfied both criteria. It was a field where France was already acknowledged as a world leader and had huge popular appeal, or so Pierre Bergé told him at their first meeting. 'The industry had never had any support from the government in the past, so we went to see Jack Lang to put our case to him,' explained Pierre. 'He agreed with us at once and we started working together from there.'[2]

One of Pierre's chief concerns as president of the Chambre Syndicale was to protect Paris's status as the leading international fashion centre by ensuring that the press and buyers continued coming to the shows. The Paris fashion scene was so incestuous that the Chambre Syndicale had disintegrated into *guerre de dentelles*, 'lace wars', under his predecessors, and Pierre had achieved a great deal by applying the same energy and determination to his role there as he did to running Yves Saint Laurent, earning the nickname *Pierre le Panthère*, Pierre the Panther, for the Machiavellian stealth with which he imposed his will on the other members. 'He treated the Chambre Syndicale as if it was a private dictatorship, getting his way through sheer force of personality,' said one. 'Nothing got done without his say-so and all the important committees were packed with his supporters. If he disagreed with other people's opinions he shouted them down or ignored them. The rest of us didn't always like it, but Pierre Bergé was what the industry needed. He got things done.'

In the early 1970s Pierre's main achievement was to force the Chambre Syndicale to embrace *prêt-à-porter*, which it had done with great success, ensuring that the city became the main forum for ready-to-wear, as well as for *haute couture*.[3] A decade later the rise of Giorgio Armani and Gianni Versace in Milan, Calvin Klein and Ralph Lauren in New York, posed a new threat to Paris's prominence, and Pierre was anxious to find a more attractive venue for the *prêt-à-porter* shows, which at present were scattered across the city from Porte de Versailles on the outskirts, to the lavatorial Forum des Halles shopping centre. He hoped to secure a central location, preferably a prestigious one, where the designers could show each season, and enlisted Jack Lang's help to find it. During fashion week that October, the Chambre Syndicale announced that the culture ministry had agreed that future *prêt-à-porter* presentations would be held in tents erected within the *Cour Carrée*, the sumptuous sandstone court-yard in the eastern wing of the Louvre Museum.

Jack Lang and his wife, Monique, were invited to join Pierre and his friends, even the conservative Rothschilds, in his box at the Opéra Garnier and for his 'Musical Mondays' at the Théâtre de l'Athénée-Louis Jouvet. Another addition to his entourage was Madison Cox, a handsome young American landscape gardener whom he had befriended. Life at rue de Babylone had become increasingly difficult as Yves's depressions deepened and his drug use spiralled out of control. 'I think Pierre had a beastly time with Yves for some years,' said a friend of both men. 'He'd tried to talk some sense into him. But it can't be easy living with someone who's trying to destroy himself, particularly if you love him as deeply as Pierre does Yves. He'd done everything he could to help him but it didn't work. Finally he gave up.'

Keeping 55 rue de Babylone as his official address, Pierre took an apartment in Hôtel Lutétia on nearby Place Le Corbusier. Despite the change in their domestic arrangements, his professional relationship with Yves continued as before. 'By then they were so welded together that they couldn't have broken up their business partnership even if they'd wanted to,' said another friend. 'It's a mutual dependence. Pierre protects Yves and takes care of him, but he understands that the business is really all down to him sitting there with his pencil and paper. Yves is his golden goose and he knows it. The company would be nothing without him. And then there's the emotional side of things. Yves Saint Laurent is the love of Pierre Bergé's life. That's the sort of thing you never get over, however much the other person changes.'

Sometimes things went smoothly between them, at other times the two men barely seemed able to stand being in the same room. On good days they lunched together at rue de Babylone and, even when Pierre had virtually taken up residence at the Lutétia, they still spoke on the telephone several times each evening. Pierre continued to take care of their financial affairs and kept a watchful eye on Yves, banning him from driving his Volkswagen convertible on the grounds that he would be safer with a chauffeur. Yves's haphazard driving and blithe disregard for traffic regulations were standing jokes among his friends, who had known it was only a matter of time before Pierre ordered him off the road. 'Pierre could be very tender with Yves,' recalled Marie Helvin. 'He'd sometimes come up during the *couture* fittings and put his hand on Yves shoulder saying "Bravo!". Yves always looked really pleased. He led such a strange life surrounded by people telling him he was wonderful, but he's too intelligent not to have realized that they weren't all being sincere. It must have been reassuring for him to have someone he could trust.'[4]

By then Yves's public appearances were restricted to dutiful, but doleful strides along the catwalk at the end of each show and at special events such as the launch of Kouros, the new YSL men's fragrance, at the Opéra Comique. The official highlight of that evening was a performance by Rudolf Nureyev, and the unofficial one was the moment when the host, Yves, thanked Nureyev for his performance by kissing him on the mouth, rather than a polite peck on the cheek, in front of twelve hundred guests.[5]

Official statements from the fashion house painted a reassuring picture of Yves's condition, admitting that there had been problems in the past and insisting he was getting better; but if anything he was worse, having developed a cortisone imbalance after being prescribed the drug by his doctor as part of a routine course of treatment. Cortisone is the hormone that wakes up the body and gets it ready for action. If the natural cycle is disrupted, the body sometimes requires additional supplies to achieve the customary 'wake up' effect. Yves developed this problem after his treatment, but the extra doses of cortisone had unfortunate side effects. He piled on weight, particularly on his head and chest, his skin puffing out around his face.

When in Paris Yves visited a psychoanalyst five times a week, but neither those sessions, nor his occasional 'rest cures' in the American Hospital, seemed to curb his addictions. Grace Mirabella, editor-in-chief of American *Vogue*, saw Yves every three months when she returned to Paris for the collections and noted in her memoirs how as the years went by 'you saw the signs that substance abuse was destroying Yves Saint Laurent. If you caught him in his studio at an off-hour when he wasn't expecting you, you often found a rather lost-looking man with a bottle and a glass in his hand, looking like someone who couldn't remember any more how or where he'd started.'[6] Pierre was so concerned that he hired a couple of doctors to be on call during the fashion shows. The doctors stood among the *mêlée* of models, hair-stylists and make-up artists in the backstage area, just in case they were needed.

Now in his early forties, Yves behaved as though he was a senile old man whose active life was far behind him. Having looked and dressed younger than his age in his twenties and thirties, he seemed much older after his fortieth birthday. His physical appearance changed, partly because of his drinking and the weight he gained from the cortisone doses, but the effect was accentuated by the staid business suits he wore and his habit of referring to himself as an elderly person, reminiscing about his youth as though it was decades, rather than years ago. Karl Lagerfeld blamed Pierre Bergé and the rest of the Saint Laurent set. 'I think back twenty years and remember his charm and his laugh,' he told *Time* magazine. 'That entourage has managed to convince him that he's an old man now.'[7] The reality was more complex. Yves had not simply slipped from youth into his dotage, but seemed to have decided to miss out on middle age altogether. It was as though he could not bear to accept the responsibilities of adulthood, and having lost his youth, had assumed another role in which he would need to be looked after, that of a helpless elderly man.

'Yves is a child. It's one of the things that makes him so special and so enchanting,' said an old friend. 'For as long as I can remember he's behaved in the slightly helpless way of a lovable little boy who wants someone to mother him. It's very appealing, but sometimes he goes too far. I remember one time when he'd fallen over when he was drunk and really hurt himself, broken his arm or something. He looked at me with those big blue eyes and said: "You know I really didn't realize I was drinking so very much." Well! I thought, "If you don't, Yves, you're the only one who doesn't."'

His constant companion was Moujik, a black and white French bulldog he was given to replace his little chihuahua, Hazel, after her death. Dogs had always been part of Yves's life starting with

Bobinette, the Mathieu-Saint-Laurents' family pet during his boy-hood, and Zou Zou, the mongrel he found straying on the back streets of Oran. Yves doted on both of them, as he did on Zou Zou's puppy, Églantine, and Hazel, but his affection for Moujik seemed particularly intense. The dog went everywhere with him, even to work at his Avenue Marceau studio, where they were now chauffeured each day in the company Peugeot. Whereas the staff were fond of sweet-tempered Hazel, Moujik had a snappy nature that made him less popular with everyone, except his master. Marie Helvin and the other models loathed him. 'You'd be standing there trying to look beautiful in a wonderful dress and that dog would be slobbering all over the skirt, or scratching its paws on your legs. Sometimes it could be quite fierce, but none of us dared give it a little kick because we knew how much Yves loved it.'[8]

Yves settled into a new routine of spending most of his time in Marrakesh, rather than Paris, leaving for Morocco with Moujik in the Lear jet as soon as the fashion shows were over, and staying on at Dar es Saada until Pierre called him back to work on the next collection. He told Le Monde that he felt 'at home' in his native North Africa and dreaded the day that he had to return to France.[9] The climate suited him, and he felt less conspicuous there than in Europe. Marrakesh had become more commercialized since he discovered it in the 1960s, despite Pierre's efforts to block hotels and tourist developments by haranguing the authorities, but Yves still felt able to stroll around the souks, and to dine at the Hôtel Mamounia restaurant with Bill Willis, Boule de Breteuil or Fernando Sanchez, who had taken over Dar el-Hanch. Sometimes Yves invited them to eat with him at Dar es Saada, when he insisted on being served his favourite dish, a plate of vegetables with Uncle Ben's Rice, flown in specially from Paris. In the evenings Bill Willis often hosted parties at his villa, where guests observed Yves flirting brazenly with Arab boys.

For years Yves had longed for a rural retreat in France, ideally an estate in the area of Normandy where Marcel Proust had spent his summers. In 1983 he and Pierre found one in Château Gabriel, a late-nineteenth-century mansion near the village of Bénerville, which was mentioned in À La Recherche du Temps Perdu as a station on the route of the 'Little Train' that collected members of the Verdurin set on the journey between Cabourg and Trouville. Proust had visited the village to see his actress friend, Louisa Mornand, and met his future publisher, Gaston Gallimard, for the first time at Château Gabriel. Yves asked Jacques Grange to restore the house to the *Belle Époque* style of Marcel Proust's heyday.

Belle Époque furniture was so scarce that it cost even more than fine eighteenth-century pieces, but Jacques Grange was given *carte blanche* to comb the Paris antique dealers and auction rooms to assemble a collection for Château Gabriel. He bought bundles of original nineteenth-century fabric from Comoglio, a dealer on rue Jacob, and had other fabrics woven in authentic designs to achieve the same subdued sumptuousness. Some of the decorative details were dreamt up by him and Yves as tributes to members of Proust's circle. The *jardin d'hiver*, or winter garden, was a conservatory filled with palms, ferns and amaryllis like the one belonging to Princesse Mathilde Bonaparte, a favourite hostess of Proust's; and a pair of tall Chinese pottery plinths stood in the dining room, in homage to Boni de Castellane, a friend of the writer's who collected esoteric pieces of Ming. After leafing through a monograph of the work of Claude Monet, the model for Proust's fictional artist, Elstir, Yves commissioned Paul Meriguet, a theatrical set painter, to create a frieze inspired by Monet's *Waterlilies* for the walls in the reception rooms. Jacques Grange gave Yves a set of Gothic chairs for the billiard room which were bequeathed to him by Marie-Laure de Noailles, the society hostess he befriended in the 1960s and whose mother, Laure de Chevigné, was Proust's model for the Duchesse de Guermantes.

The bedrooms were named after, and modelled on, characters from *À La Recherche* who resembled various members of the Saint-Laurent set. Yves's suite bore the name of Charles Swann, who charmed his way into the gilded circle of the Faubourg Saint-Germain. Above the door to Pierre's room was a plaque emblazoned Baron Palamède de Charlus, the odious aristocrat whose sexual debauches are catalogued in *Sodomme et Gomorrhe*. Loulou and Thadée Klossowski were given the room named for the Verdurins, who begin the novels as vulgar social climbers and end them with Madame Verdurin perched at the peak of Paris society as Princesse de Guermantes. Anne-Marie Muñoz was cast as Albertine, Swann's daughter, and her husband, José, as Elstir the painter. Betty Catroux was assigned the role of

Madeleine Lemaire, the inspiration for the character of Madame Verdurin, and Charlotte Aillaud, a Parisian socialite whom Yves had befriended, that of Oriane de Guermantes.

Yves's idea was to create a house which was so faithful to the spirit of Proust's era that if Marcel Proust himself happened to drop by he would have felt perfectly at home there. Although as the art critic, John Richardson, pointed out, Château Gabriel was so sumptuous and the collection amassed by Jacques Grange so exquisite that 'it would put the contents of the Bénerville villas frequented by Proust to shame'; Pierre's 'Napoleonic supervision' ensured that the house was 'more lavishly and efficiently run than most stately homes. The chef is one of the best left in private service, the butler and Moroccan *valet* are incomparably *stylé*; and gardeners, estate workers and grooms perform their duties to pre-phylloxeral perfection.'[10] When Yves and Pierre visited Château Gabriel together, Pierre piloted them there in the company helicopter and during their visits they would tour the grounds in a Proustian pony and trap.

As Yves withdrew into neurasthenic seclusion, the members of the Saint Laurent set were drifting apart: Pierre was engrossed in the Théâtre de l'Athénée-Louis Jouvet and his new political friends, and Loulou by married life with Thadée. Fernando Sanchez spent more time in New York than Paris, as did Paloma Picasso since her marriage to the Argentinian playwright, Rafael Lopez Cambil. Betty and François Catroux had two little girls, one of whom, Maxime, named after Loulou's mother, was Yves's god-daughter. The last link with their heady clubbing era disappeared in 1983 when Fabrice Emaer, the owner of Le Sept and Le Palace, died of cancer. 'Le Palace was the last of the nightclubs for us,' recalled Betty. 'After that it stopped. We were older. People split up. Illness. Problems. All the bad things seemed to happen at once.'[11]

They still rallied round for special occasions such as the gala Pierre organized at the Paris Lido in January 1982 to celebrate the company's twentieth anniversary. Bewigged footmen in eighteenth-century costumes served champagne and *hors d'oeuvres* to over a thousand guests, while Yves cut a towering birthday cake. Diana Vreeland flew in from New York to present him with a gilded statuette as a special 'International Award from the Council of Fashion Designers of America'. Clutching his prize, Yves posed with Catherine Deneuve for the paparazzi, as he had fifteen years before at the opening of the Rive Gauche boutique on rue de Tournon.

The Avenue Marceau press office secretly produced a commemorative magazine, 'Bravo Yves', for him, explaining the presence of the journalists and photographers who swamped the *couture* house as a team from 'an American magazine'. The entire staff of Avenue Marceau posed for a group portrait, and the seventeen employees who had worked there since the first Hôtel Forain show were photographed standing behind Pierre Bergé's desk under one of Andy Warhol's portraits of Yves. Diana Vreeland wrote a prologue, and Rudolf Nureyev, Helmut Newton, Alexander Liberman and Anthony Burgess paid tribute to Yves's talent. John Fairchild ended his contribution on a poignant note. 'The world has been enjoying him now for twenty years. What a pity Yves Saint Laurent does not enjoy what he's given to all of us.'[12]

That season Hebe Dorsey of the *Herald Tribune* hailed Yves as 'the eternal winner, the most French of all French designers, with the innate tact, restraint and sense of proportion that is known, for lack of a better word as style.'[13] After Chanel's death in 1971, Yves had rebelled against being cast as the 'Grand Old Man' of French fashion by creating his most controversial collection, the iconoclastic '1940s Look', but now he tacitly accepted the role by reworking the same classic styles – the *smokings*, safari jackets, peasant smocks, simple sweaters and pants – season after season.

By sticking to a stable repertoire, his 'heavy artillery', as he called it, Yves could refine familiar forms such as his safari jackets, which he reintroduced in 1982 in heavier gabardine with longer peplums.[14] And rather than distracting his audience with novelties, he focused attention on to the formal qualities of his work: the precision of the cut, masterful mixes of colour and unerring sense of proportion. Yves told Joan Juliet Buck of American *Vogue* that in recent years he had grown surer of his judgement, rarely starting sketches without finishing them, or rejecting them as he used to do. His sketching had improved, and the *atelier* staff, many of whom had worked with him for twenty years, were so familiar with his drawings that they could read them 'like a road map'.[15]

One of the keys to Yves's commercial success was that he created clothes which women enjoyed wearing for themselves. There was no sign of the misogyny that crept into the collections of other male designers, nor did he dress his clients like sex objects. Yves loved the traditional trappings of femininity – black laces, translucent silk chiffons and sheer black stockings – but he had no truck with bland, babeish beauty, once saying that women only became truly attractive as they aged and their characters showed in their faces. He adored the androgynous look of caffeine-thin figures such as Zizi, Loulou and Betty, who stayed whippet-slim in her forties by exercising at a Montmartre dance class each morning. Marie Helvin remembered his horror when, towards the end of her modelling career in the mid-1980s, she decided to gain a little weight and make her figure curvier. 'Yves was horrified! He couldn't believe it. He pointed at my breasts and said "What are those?"'[16] Yves saw his classics as a basic selection of clothes which would give women the same sense of confidence and continuity that men derived from their established repertoire of shirts, suits and ties.

Like most people who combine critical acclaim with commercial success, Yves's timing was impeccable. At its simplest he had the good fortune to be Christian Dior's ablest assistant at the time of his death, but before then he was fortunate to have joined Dior at a time when Christian Dior was wearying of his work and eager to draw on someone else's ideas. Yves had set up his own *couture* house in the early 1960s when there was a thirst for new talent in the fashion field and his radical designs were more marketable than they had been a few years before when he was at Dior. His most innovative period as a designer, in his late twenties and early thirties, coincided with the experimentation of the hippy era, and now, with his classics, he had become the 'Grand Old Man' at a time when the fashion scene needed authority.

The London designers, Vivienne Westwood and Rifat Ozbek, were picking up on the theatrical styles of New Romantic bands, such as Human League and Culture Club. Jean-Paul Gaultier was playing with his jokey post-punk designs in Paris, and Azzedine Alaïa had started showing his comic-book versions of little black dresses with synched-in bodices and thigh-skimmingly short skirts.'[17] The new wave of Japanese designers, Rei Kawakubo, the woman behind Comme des Garçons,[18] and Yohji Yamamoto,[19] were presenting irregularly-shaped clothes in a funereal palette of blacks and greys.

Their work bore a superficial resemblance to traditional fishermen's clothes and military uniforms, but the dominant themes were abstract concepts of shape and movement. When Kawakubo and Yamamoto first showed in Paris, their clothes were incomprehensible to the Western press; but by 1983 the fashion week crowds outside the *Cour Carrée* tents had adopted a new uniform of shapeless black and grey Japanese shrouds.

Yves's classicism lent stability to the febrile fashion scene, and struck a chord with the conservative climate of the early 1980s. The dissolute disco era came to an end when AIDS cast a pall over the social scene. The alarm had been raised in September 1979 when Dr Linda Laubenstein, a blood specialist at New York University, diagnosed a male patient as having Kaposi's sarcoma, a rare form of skin cancer, and a fortnight later was told of an identical case at a nearby hospital, but AIDS was not officially identified as a medical condition until February 1983 when Professor Luc Montagnier of the Institut Pasteur in Paris announced the discovery of a new virus that killed certain cells in the body's immune system. The *New York Times* ran its first front-page story on AIDS that summer and, as the death toll rose, governments unfurled 'Safe Sex' campaigns to encourage people to use condoms, while the infamous bath houses closed down.

Politics was also becoming more conservative. Ronald Reagan's Republican administration embarked on a radical programme of tax cuts and financial deregulation in the United States, as did Margaret Thatcher's right-wing government in Britain. Even socialist France swung to the centre when François Mitterrand halted Pierre Mauroy's reforms with a 1983 cabinet reshuffle that paved the way for the appointment of Laurent Fabius, the son of a wealthy Parisian antiques dealer, as prime minister. The Western economies returned to growth, having finally emerged from the recession and hyper-inflation that started with the mid-1970s oil shocks. Stock markets were rising, as were property prices, and consumers felt confident about spending money again, particularly as the abolition of credit controls in many countries enabled them to do so by running up credit and debts.

Once a symbol of subversion, Yves's *smokings* were adopted as totems of wealth by the beneficiaries of Ronald Reagan and Margaret

Thatcher's tax cuts, and Rive Gauche's sales soared, as did those of the YSL licensed lines.[20] Determined to replicate Yves Saint Laurent's financial success, Alain Wertheimer, the young owner of Chanel, was trying to revitalize that company. The grandson of Pierre Wertheimer, who manufactured No. 5 for Coco Chanel and bought the *couture* house from her, he had taken over from his father in 1974, when he was twenty-five and the business was in the doldrums. Having spent his first few years trying to restore Chanel No. 5's prestige by hauling it out of the discount stores,[21] Wertheimer then sought a new designer for the fashion house. Rebuffed by Yves, he courted Karl Lagerfeld who eventually agreed to sever his contract with Chloé and become Chanel's chief designer for an annual salary of $1 million.

Even as a lowly design assistant 'Kaiser Karl', as *Women's Wear Daily* called him, enjoyed a certain stature on the Paris social scene, largely because of his family's wealth. Lagerfeld had driven to Balmain in the 1950s in a Jaguar saloon, and during his early years at Chloé he lived in the expensive Left Bank apartment where Andy Warhol shot *L'Amour*. The clues for what he intended to do with the Chanel collection lay in his new Monte Carlo apartment, filled with furniture by Memphis, a group of young designers working with Ettore Sottsas in Milan. They applied the post-modernist theories, then popular in architecture, to furniture by adding neoclassical columns and pillars to chairs and tables made from modern materials in candy floss colours, and Lagerfeld planned to adopt the same irreverent approach to Coco Chanel's classic clothes for his debut *couture* presentation on 25 January 1983. After watching Yves's star soar above his, from the time he was beaten into second place in the 1954 Wool competition, Karl Lagerfeld was finally in a position to compete against Yves Saint Laurent, with the Wertheimers' money and the grand old name of Chanel behind him.

For the time being 'Kaiser Karl' seemed a distant threat on Avenue Marceau. A few days after the Chanel show, Yves ended his *couture* collection with Mounia, his favourite model of the moment, coming on stage in a dress of pink and black feathers carrying a giant bottle of Paris, the new YSL perfume. Paris reflected the classical drift of Yves's designs, with the gently floral smell of an old-fashioned French fragrance, and an impeccably elegant advertising image of a woman in a tailored suit with white collar and cuffs, standing in front of the misty silhouette of the Eiffel Tower, clutching a bouquet of pale pink roses.

When Yves discussed the advertisement with Maïmé Arnodin and Denise Fayolle, he told them that it had to include roses and the Eiffel Tower. 'When he said the Eiffel Tower we thought "Oh no! It'll be too touristy, like a postcard!",' recalled Arnodin. 'But he was right.'[22] After completing the commercial they showed it to Yves for his approval, but afterwards he was so quiet that the two women knew something was wrong. 'Yves telephoned the next day to say that when the model turned round he'd seen a zip,' said Arnodin. 'We looked and the zip did show, only for a second, and no one else had spotted it, but we had to shoot the whole film again.'[23] Helped by a flurry of publicity when the Paris City Council objected to the name, Paris joined Opium among the top ten best-selling scents.

The introduction of Paris was a prelude to one of Pierre Bergé's most ambitious projects, a retrospective of Yves's work at the Costume Institute of the Metropolitan Museum of Art in New York with which he intended to seal Yves Saint Laurent's reputation as the world's greatest fashion designer. It would be the first show at the Metropolitan devoted to a living artist or designer, and was the brainchild of Diana Vreeland, who had become a consultant to the Costume Institute after leaving American *Vogue*. Her previous exhibitions dealt with historical subjects, such as *The Eighteenth-Century Woman* in 1981 and *La Belle Époque* the following year, and the Saint Laurent retrospective would be her first attempt at tackling a contemporary theme. 'Why Yves Saint Laurent?' she wrote in the catalogue. 'Because he is a genius, because he knows everything about women.'[24]

Vreeland was born Diana Dalziel in Paris at the turn of the century (she successfully avoided specifying the year) to an American mother and a Scottish father who led the leisurely lives of the idle rich. Her family fled to the States during World War I and in 1922, two years after coming out, she married a wealthy banker, T. Reed Vreeland. When Carmel Snow spotted Diana Vreeland dancing in Chanel white lace at the St Regis Roof in 1937, she invited her to contribute a 'Why don't you . . .' column to *Harper's Bazaar* which included such eminently caricaturable tips as 'Why don't you put all your dogs in bright yellow collars and leads like all the dogs in Paris?' and 'Why don't you have a furry elk-hide trunk for the back of your car?' Vreeland eventually became *Bazaar*'s fashion editor, and stayed there until she joined *Vogue* in 1962. A prepossessing figure with black lacquered hair, heavy rouge and a daily uniform of black turtleneck and pants, she was described by Cecil Beaton as looking like 'an elegant crane picking its way out of the swamp'.[25] Presiding over the New York fashion scene from a Park Avenue apartment designed for her by the Hollywood decorator, Billy Baldwin, Vreeland decamped to Paris for the collections each season to hold court in her favourite suite at the Hôtel de Crillon.

Yves was one of Diana Vreeland's favourite designers, whom she had championed from her earliest days at *Vogue*. Even at his most melancholic, he could usually be coaxed into lunching with her at rue de Babylone during fashion week and she had lobbied hard on his behalf to persuade the Metropolitan Museum to stage the retrospective. 'It was absolutely her idea,' said Katell le Bourhis, the French fashion historian who was one of Vreeland's assistants for the show. 'She wanted to make the Costume Institute contemporary and Saint Laurent was for her the only living designer whose work could have been showcased. Who else could it have been? She had a tremendous admiration for his talent and she understood that he would cast a long shadow in fashion history. She also had a great affection for him. She always saw him as the twenty-one-year-old boy on the balcony at Dior. They wrote letters to each other, really lovely letters. But she wasn't the type of women who talked about her emotions in public. She'd have seen that as "cute". And "cute" was a word which Diana Vreeland never allowed.'[26]

Seriously ill in 1983, Vreeland organized the exhibition from her apartment, arriving at the museum late in the afternoon and returning home each evening with her assistants to work into the night. They assembled one hundred and fifty of Yves's original designs, starting with a 'Trapeze' dress from his first Christian Dior collection. The clothes were to be displayed thematically, with trouser suits in one room and the oriental designs in another, alongside some of the paintings that had influenced Yves including works by Albers, Mondrian, Matisse and Warhol from his personal collection at rue de Babylone. Diana Vreeland lent a couple of her own vintage YSL outfits to the exhibition, as did Loulou de la Falaise and Paloma Picasso. Other pieces were borrowed from Lauren Bacall, Marella Agnelli, Princess Lee Radziwill, and Christian Dior, which allowed the museum to select forty outfits from its archives.

On the day of the opening, 5 December 1983, a blue banner emblazoned 'Yves Saint Laurent, 25 Years of Design' fluttered outside the Metropolitan Museum. Tickets for the opening gala, a dinner for eight hundred at $500 each, had sold out months before. Jacques Grange flew over from Paris to decorate the museum for the night. Filling the galleries with flowers, he garlanded gold leaves around the columns of the Pool Room and draped the tables with silks in shades of pink, red and orange woven specially for the occasion by Abraham, the Swiss silk-weaver which supplied the *couture* house.

At half-past-seven the guests filed into the Temple of Dendur, where they were to have drinks before dinner. Yves arrived hand-in-hand with Diana Vreeland, who was clad in one of his jewelled sweaters over a narrow skirt. Henry Kissinger came with his wife, Nancy, who wore a YSL tunic. Marie-Hélène de Rothschild was dressed in black velvet, and Olimpia, one of the younger Rothschilds, in white lace. Catherine Deneuve wore panne velvet, and Paloma Picasso was resplendent in black *lamé*. The guests were summoned to dinner by trumpets, and settled into their seats at the silk-covered tables to tuck into a formal French menu of scallops, followed by fillet of beef wrapped in veal, then cheeses and a rich chocolate cake. After dinner, they were joined by another two and a half thousand people who had bought $100 tickets to wander around the exhibition and dance to a jazz band in the Temple of Dendur.

It was a splendid evening, if somewhat more subdued than the wildly glamorous Opium party on the *Peking* five years ago. Yves's devotees at the *New York Times* and American *Vogue* painted him as a dashing French designer sweeping into the Metropolitan Museum with Diana Vreeland on his arm, but the objective eye of *Time* magazine presented a mournful picture of an accomplished, but 'painfully isolated' man.[27] William Blaylock, its Paris correspondent, described Yves's daily visits to his psychotherapist and the 'regimen of *calmant* pills which he unwisely chases down with alcohol on occasion'. Yves told him that in recent years 'my solitude has become so dominating, so much a part of me that I am incapable of loving or being loved', an observation that Blaylock regarded as a 'sad confession of a rich, well-beloved man in the prime of life'.[28] A few days earlier a bewildered Yves was seen walking uncertainly into the Costume Institute, where Pierre Bergé and Diana Vreeland were overseeing the installation of the show. A security guard stopped him asking for some form of identification, and Yves Saint Laurent meekly signed himself in to see a retrospective of his own career.[29]

The Gauche Caviare
1984–1986

Given Yves's melancholic state of mind he was probably in no mood to appreciate the irony, but at the very moment when he was celebrating the summit of his achievements with the opening of a retrospective at the Metropolitan Museum, his old employers at Christian Dior hit the nadir of their fortunes. Marcel Boussac's business empire had crumbled in the 1960s and 1970s, when his textile mills and clothing factories lost their captive markets in the old French colonies, and in 1978 the 'King of Cotton' went bust. His company was rescued by the Willot brothers, a pair of industrialists from northern France, only for their own business, Agache-Willot, to collapse three years later. The government kept the company afloat to protect the jobs of its thirty thousand employees, and prepared to auction it off to the highest bidder.

By then Dior was a carcass of the company that abandoned Yves to the army in 1960. Marcel Boussac had sold its perfumes to Moët-Hennessy, the champagne and cognac company, and all that remained of the old Christian Dior was the fashion house and its licensing rights, which Jacques Rouët had distributed so liberally that the company was known in the *couture* trade as the 'General Motors of Fashion'. Marc Bohan still had a faithful band of *couture* clients, including Princess Caroline of Monaco and Christina Onassis, whose bill usually came to $500,000 a year, but Christian Dior's reputation as a fashion force had fallen steadily since Yves's departure. Nonetheless it was still one of the world's best-known brand names, which was enough to interest Bernard Arnault, a young businessman who had recently returned to France after a few years living and working in the United States.

A slight man with fine dark hair and even, rather colourless features that gave him the same aloof air as the subdued greys and browns of his suits, Arnault was born in Roubaix in 1949, the son of a successful builder. After going to school in Lille, he graduated in mathematics from the prestigious École Polytechnique before marrying Anne Dewavrin, who, like him, came from a wealthy northern business family.[1] When François Mitterrand was elected president in 1981, the conservative Arnault left France with Anne and their two young children, Delphine and Antoine, for a new life in North America. After three years of building condos in Florida, he was persuaded that the socialists were not as inimical to business as he had feared, and brought his family back to France where he searched for new investments.

Agache looked like an excellent opportunity, particularly as it was bound to be sold cheaply. The problem was that the French government, shaken by the Willot brothers' demise and reluctant to risk more job losses in the depressed areas around the Boussac textile mills, needed to be confident that whoever bought the company would be able to keep it going. A thirty-five-year-old, with no experience of running a business of Agache's size, did not look like a strong contender to the Parisian bankers and bureaucrats who were orchestrating the sale, but Arnault had the advantage of family connections that gave him an *entrée* to the Willots' circle. His wife, Anne, was distantly related to them, and his legal adviser, Pierre Godé, was friendly with the brothers' lawyer. He also secured the support of Lazard Frères, one of France's most powerful investment banks, an institution so sure of itself that it does not even have a name plate outside its Paris headquarters on Boulevard Haussmann. While living in the States, Arnault had befriended François Polge de Combret, a fellow-expatriate working in the bank's New York office,[2] who subsequently introduced him to Antoine Bernheim, a senior partner of Lazard Frères in Paris and a powerful figure in banking circles.[3]

One of the few influential French financiers with first-hand business experience, having worked for Alain Wertheimer's grandfather at the Chanel cosmetics company before becoming a banker, Bernheim was impressed by Bernard Arnault and his courteous, thoughtful manner. Lazard had attained its powerful position in banking because of the close links between its senior partners and the industrialists who orchestrate take-over deals, but investment banking was changing and by the mid-1980s it faced fierce competition from aggressive American financial groups such as Goldman Sachs and Morgan Stanley, and the new take-over specialists, Drexel Burnham Lambert and Kohlberg Kravis Roberts. Still a force in New York and London financial circles, Lazard's powerhouse was Paris, and if it was to keep the American banks at bay, it needed to nurture new French clients whom it could advise on their expansion into other countries. The task of finding them was complicated by the idiosyncratic structure of French industry, whereby most large companies were controlled by the government or by their founding families. Antoine Bernheim was anxious to find young entrepreneurs with whom Lazard could build long-term relationships and the ambitious, intelligent Bernard Arnault was a promising prospect.

Bernheim was particularly impressed by the apparent ease with which Arnault, through Pierre Godé, arranged a meeting with the Willots and secured their support for his bid. With Lazard Frères and the brothers behind him, Bernard Arnault looked like a credible candidate in the Agache auction. He raised 310 million francs from an investment consortium assembled by Lazard and another 90 million francs from his family. His offer was accepted and, once the bid was completed, Antoine Bernheim helped to find buyers for the businesses that did not interest him in order to concentrate on the ones which did – including Christian Dior. Dilapidated though Dior was at the time, Bernheim was well aware of its commercial potential thanks to his experience of working with the Wertheimers, and all Bernard Arnault needed to do was look around him to see how much money could be made in the luxury industry.

Japan was becoming a goldmine for Western luxury companies as its economy boomed and the yen soared against other foreign currencies. Brand names have greater significance in Japan's rigidly consensual society than in the West, and as taste became increasingly Westernized from the early 1960s, when the Yves Saint Laurent *couture salon* opened in Tokyo, the Japanese bought European status at Seibu-Saison symbols, such as YSL silk ties and Chanel's quilted bags, on a massive scale. Property prices were so high that the Japanese tended to spend less money in their homes and more on their appearance, than their Western counterparts, creating a larger customer base for the luxury industry.

New consumers were also moving into the luxury market in the West, having discovered that they could afford to treat themselves to expensive clothes and trinkets, because of tax cuts, stock market speculation or profits from property deals. These people had all the insecurities of any upwardly mobile social group; they not only wanted to spend money, but to be seen to be spending it, and the totems of old money, bearing the names of the artisans who made bespoke products for the aristocracy, gave them the reassurance they needed.

The chief beneficiaries were the old-established French firms which, like Chanel, were taken in hand by new management in the 1970s. One was Hermès, which dated back to 1837 when Thierry Hermès set up a harness workshop in Paris, and was now enjoying a renaissance under his great-great-grandson, Jean-Louis Dumas, a *Sciences Po'* graduate who was sent to learn about American marketing techniques by training as a buyer at Bloomingdale's in New York, where he befriended Richard Salomon.[4] Another was Louis Vuitton, the luxury luggage company founded in 1854 by a miller's son from the Jura mountains who made trunks for the Empress Eugénie and her ladies-in-waiting. Vuitton acquired a new chairman in 1977 with the arrival of Henry Racamier, a sixty-five-year-old steel tycoon whose wife, Odile, was a Vuitton heiress.[5] Like Jean-Louis Dumas at Hermès, he modernized the business by opening new shops, moving into new international markets and introducing cheaper products, notably soft travel bags made from waterproof canvas emblazoned with the company's distinctive LV initials.[6]

One of the most dynamic French luxury firms was Cartier, which traced its roots to the 1880s when Louis Cartier opened a jeweller's on rue de la Paix. The architect of its expansion was Alain-Dominique Perrin, who had a different trajectory to the clubbably patrician Jean-Louis Dumas and Henry Racamier. A businessman's son from Nantes, Perrin was a thickset man with a vigorous manner, who went to business school, rather than university, and worked his way up the ranks after joining Cartier in his early twenties.[7] His *coup* was the introduction in 1972 of Les Must de Cartier, a new range of inexpensive, factory-produced versions of Cartier's handmade watches which he positioned for self-made men and women like himself; 'for the guy on his way up, we sell him a $600 watch, and when he hits forty and starts going out socially, we sell him a $5,000 watch.'[8]

Just as the older *hauts couturiers* had opposed the development of *prêt-à-porter*, Les Must caused a furore among the snootier Parisian jewellers. 'For years I was the *bête noire* of the industry,' recalled Perrin. 'Whenever I picked up a trade magazine someone was accusing me of devaluing the prestige of the Cartier brand or bringing the industry into disrepute. They treated me like a monster.'[9] By the mid-1980s the new range was generating sales of $250 million a year and *Business Week* calculated that a Les Must watch, which retailed at $600, cost just $125 to manufacture at one of Cartier's sub-contractors in Switzerland. Given that Cartier owned shares in many of its suppliers, the company probably also made a profit on the $125.[10] 'Suddenly everybody recognized that Les Must was a success. It became a case study for MBA students. I was someone in the industry and the business went crazy.'[11] Perrin became president of Cartier International and bought a Rolls-Royce and a fourteenth-century château where he spent his weekends with his third wife, Marie-Thérèse, and their five children.

He wanted to expand Cartier by taking it into the market niche beneath Les Must, but was wary of weakening the brand name as Gucci, the Florentine leather firm had done when it fell prey to family feuds in the 1970s and acquired a tacky Eurotrash image. Cartier had already made one blunder by launching a range of cheap electro-plated jewellery in the late 1970s. 'It was rubbish,' acknowledged Perrin, 'and we got rid of it.'[12] Rather than risk a repetition, he decided to diversify under different brand names, and in 1983 Cartier acquired the licensing rights to produce men's watches for Enzo Ferrari, the Italian sports car company, and women's watches for Yves Saint Laurent.

The Yves Saint Laurent watches, which Cartier intended to sell for $250, against $500 for Ferrari and $600 for Les Must, were the latest addition to the long list of licensing contracts that Pierre Bergé had signed in the decade since he and Yves took over the YSL licensing rights from Squibb. Licensing was a lucrative business, as the licensee paid for manufacturing and marketing, and Yves Saint Laurent's investment was so low that it made substantial profits on its royalties of between five and ten per cent of the product's wholesale price.[13]

One school of thought in the fashion industry was still sceptical about licensing, but Pierre took a more aggressive stance, being determined to turn Yves Saint Laurent into an international brand name. When he clinched the Cartier deal in 1983, Pierre had already sold the rights to nearly two hundred YSL products including shirts, sunglasses, hosiery, handkerchieves, handbags, and even cigarettes; thereby ensuring that Yves Saint Laurent had a significance to people who had little interest in Yves or his work, but associated his name, and the spindly YSL logo designed by Cassandre in 1961, with vague notions of French elegance and luxury, just like Chanel and Christian Dior. By then the company was already making tens of millions of dollars a year from licensing, and the Yves Saint Laurent name was so well known that when luxury sales took off in the mid-1980s, it was able to take full advantage of the market's expansion.

While the 1960s boom had been fuelled by growth and optimism, the conspicuous consumption of the 1980s had a cynical edge, the product of a *fin de siècle* society that had turned its back on the ideals of May 1968 and was learning to live with AIDS, unemployment, drug abuse and homelessness. The extremes of the era were captured in the films of the new French directors, the beneficiaries of Jack Lang's generous arts subsidies, such as Jean-Jacques Beineix's *Diva* and Luc Besson's *Subway*, which juxtaposed the glittering lives of the rich with the nihilism of the urban underclass. The art pendulum swung away from the socially-purposeful work of the 1970s to the brash images of Julian Schnabel, Francesco Clemente and David Salle, photogenic figures who displayed a Warholesque appetite for socializing, looking and acting like rock stars rather than old-fashioned painters. Hot fashion photographers, Herb Ritts and Bruce Weber, shot all-American models like Patti Hansen, Rene Russo and Janice Dickinson. Pop music became slicker and stylized under MTV's influence. Air-brushed images of videogenic stars – Madonna and Prince – were blasted all over the world by satellite. Terrestrial television was stuffed with glossy shots of the machinating multimillionaires in the American soap operas, *Dallas* and *Dynasty*.

The most successful new perfumes reflected that ethos, either by conveying conventional images of luxury, like Yves Saint Laurent's Paris and Estée Lauder's Beautiful,[14] or the intensity of the era, such as Obsession by Calvin Klein,[15] Christian Dior's Poison[16] and the unashamedly glitzy Giorgio of Beverly Hills.[17] By 1985 Alain Wertheimer was ready to cash in on Karl Lagerfeld's success with the Chanel collections by introducing a new Chanel scent, Coco.[18] Lagerfeld's mini-skirted versions of Coco Chanel's classic crêpe suits infuriated fashion purists (one of whom described him as 'stomping in his jackboots through rue Cambon') but were perfect for the *ingénus* luxury shoppers who loved the very visible double Cs on the gilded buttons. When Lagerfeld's contract came up for renewal in 1985, he reportedly demanded that his fee be raised from $1 million a year to $1 million for each collection. Alain Wertheimer refused, until Lagerfeld forewent his customary catwalk appearance at the end of the October show. Chanel issued a public denial that Lagerfeld had quit, and privately agreed to his demands.[19]

Chanel's success redoubled Bernard Arnault's determination to revitalize the Christian Dior collections, as Karl Lagerfeld had done for Alain Wertheimer. Yet Chanel was not the only fashion label to be flourishing: Giorgio Armani's self-effacing suits were adopted as the unofficial uniform of the new army of 'yuppies', the young urban professionals who were drawing high salaries at banks, brokerage houses and advertising agencies; as were Gianni Versace's gaudy silks and leather for parvenu pop stars. Even young designers were thriving as the children of the postwar baby-boomers were entering their twenties and creating a fertile market for new designers – John Galliano in London, Romeo Gigli in Milan, and Sybilla, a young Spaniard who set up a design studio in Madrid after working as one of Yves's assistants in Paris.

The emergence of young, energetic designers with new ideas made fashion seem more exciting to the media, and magazines published lengthy profiles of designers and their lifestyles. Ralph Lauren and Calvin Klein acted out their Bronx-boy fantasies for *Vogue*'s photographers: Lauren riding around his Colorado ranch, and Klein lounging in his Manhattan penthouse where the walls dripped with $2.5 million of Georgia O'Keeffe paintings. Giorgio Armani and Gianni

Versace were snapped sniping at one another from their Milan *palazzi*. Karl Lagerfeld always seemed to have a soundbite for *Women's Wear Daily*, generally to the detriment of one of his rivals, and appeared in features on everything from his greying ponytail and penchant for eighteenth-century dress, to the Memphis boxing ring in his Monte Carlo apartment and manicured lawns of his Brittany estate.

When *Vanity Fair* published a piece on the '*couture* courts' of Paris in March 1986, it highlighted three designers. Karl Lagerfeld was described as the 'polished Dark Prince, whose public image is a studied version of the grand sophisticate', Azzedine Alaïa as the 'conquistador' living and working in 'the frenzied set of a lively fashion comedy'; and Yves Saint Laurent as the '*Roi du Soleil*', or 'Sun King', who 'like an ayatollah . . . appears in public only for official occasions'. 'Today only the profane, and downright heretical, would question Saint Yves's stature,' wrote Javier Arroyuelo, a close friend of Paloma Picasso and Rafael Lopez Sanchez. 'You don't dismiss Notre Dame cathedral – even if monuments bore you to tears.'[20]

'Saint Yves' was a monument in the fashion world. When the British writer Nicholas Coleridge was researching his book, *The Fashion Conspiracy*, in the mid-1980s he found that Yves was much discussed, but rarely seen by his competitors. 'Rival *couturiers* will talk about him for several hours on end, but when you ask "When did you last talk to Saint Laurent?" they admit it is not for two or three years.'[21] Other designers shied away from the limelight. Rei Kawakubo of Comme des Garçons was notorious for giving monosyllabic answers to journalists' questions, but she agreed to occasional interviews, as did the enigmatic Giorgio Armani, yet Yves Saint Laurent was virtually inaccessible. From time to time *Vogue* or *Elle* was permitted to photograph one of his homes, although Yves himself, as Clara Saint and Gabrielle Buchaert endlessly explained, was not available for interview.

Once the hippest ticket in Paris, the Saint Laurent shows seemed quaintly antiquated beside Thierry Mugler's extravaganza at the Zenith sports stadium where six thousand people watched the pregnant model, Pat Cleveland, being lowered from the ceiling dressed as an angel, and the Chanel presentations where Karl Lagerfeld's star model, Inès de la Fressange, the daughter of a titled French stockbroker, demolished the rituals of modelling as successfully as he did

Coco Chanel's clothes, by lolloping along the catwalk with her dog on a (Chanel) lead, and stopping to chat with friends in the audience.

The press still turned out *en masse* for the Saint Laurent presentations: partly out of respect for Yves's achievements, and partly because, by then, the company spent so much money on advertising that fashion magazines had no choice but to field a posse of reporters. There was also still a sentimental hope among the older journalists that Yves might surprise them again. But even loyalists like Janie Samet of *Le Figaro*, Bernadine Morris of the *New York Times* or Nina Hyde of the *Washington Post*, were becoming more restrained in their praise, particularly about Rive Gauche, where the studio was still churning out *prêt-à-porter* copies of his *haute couture* classics.[22] Hebe Dorsey of the *Herald Tribune* reflected the consensus by reviewing the March 1984 ready-to-wear show under the headline 'Saint Laurent shows lack of Sparkle'. 'The strictly-about-Yves story looked as though the designer had not recovered from his New York triumph. Trouble is, between the New York retrospective and the forthcoming one at the Paris Museum of Costume, Saint Laurent is in serious danger of becoming an institution.'[23]

An institution was exactly what Pierre Bergé wanted. Firm friends with Jack Lang,[24] he was intent on using his newfound political influence for the benefit of the Chambre Syndicale's members in general, and Yves Saint Laurent in particular. Pierre relished the reflected glory of mixing with one of the most powerful members of the cabinet and he enjoyed the culture minister's company. As for Jack Lang, he looked forward to his trips in the corporate helicopter, or Lear jet, to the opulent outposts of the YSL empire; and he needed the support of wealthy, well-connected men like Pierre Bergé at a time when he was under fire from the right for policies such as bringing an old-fashioned French fairground into the Tuileries Gardens, and proposing to found a graffiti museum when a set of sculptures was defaced by vandals.

Through his friendship with Lang, Pierre was becoming closer to François Mitterrand. 'We'd met a couple of times since he'd become president, but we had our first *real* meeting in 1984. It was then that we became friends.'[25] By a '*real* meeting', Pierre meant one of the long cerebral conversations that he and the president enjoyed. The two men had a great deal in common: both came from provincial *bourgeois* backgrounds; Mitterrand was born at Jarnac in the rural Charente region where his father was an agent for the Paris-Orléans railway, and loved literature, sharing a fondness for esoteric French poets.[26] Pierre was flattered by the prospect of intimacy with someone as powerful as Mitterrand, and the president, like his culture minister, needed allies in the business world. 'Pierre Bergé isn't typical of Mitterrand's friends,' observed Franz-Olivier Giesbert, editor-in-chief of *Le Figaro*, who wrote an influential biography of the socialist president. 'Bergé is interested in politics but he isn't a professional politician and most of Mitterrand's friends are. But he's a lively man with a strong sense of culture and François Mitterrand has always been attracted to people like that.'[27] *Le Canard Enchaîné*, the satirical magazine which was the French equivalent of *Private Eye* in Britain or *Spy* in the States, marked Pierre's ascent to the president's inner circle, and parodied his sybaritic lifestyle, by nicknaming him *Don Magnifico*.

Pierre Bergé was now known as a bastion of what the French press called *la gauche caviare*, the 'caviar left', or 'champagne socialists' as they are called in Britain. When Harlem Désir, the political activist, set about raising funds for SOS Racisme, the anti-racist organization he founded in 1984, someone suggested he contact Pierre Bergé. 'They said he was likely to be sympathetic – and he was,' recalled Désir. 'We went to see him and it was obvious that he was genuinely committed to our cause. He made a fairly large donation then and promised to carry on supporting us.'[28] Pierre also baled out *Globe*, a struggling magazine launched by a group of writers associated with Bernard-Henri Lévy, a member of the *nouveau philosophe* school of anti-Marxists, whose Byronesque looks and penchant for posing for photographs with his white shirt unbuttoned down to his waist, had made him the pet intellectual of the press and a regular dinner guest of Guy and Marie-Hélène de Rothschild. Lévy suggested that Pierre might like to invest in *Globe* and the editor, Georges-Marc Benamou, invited him to contribute a regular column. Pierre filled it with fierce attacks on anyone he disliked – Jacques Chirac, the right-wing mayor of Paris and one of François Mitterrand's chief critics, was a prime target – and fulsome tributes to friends.

It is a testimony of Pierre Bergé's political prominence that when he tried to buy Ledoyen, an old-established Paris restaurant on the

Champs-Élysées near the president's residence, his bid was blocked by Paris City Council. The authorities claimed that there had been a technical hitch, but Pierre and his friends were convinced that Jacques Chirac had intervened personally, picking on *Don Magnifico* as a way of getting at François Mitterrand. Undeterred, Pierre rose to his new nickname by making the munificent gesture of 'selling' the expensively renovated Théâtre de l'Athénée-Louis Jouvet to Jack Lang's culture ministry for a token franc. Even after the sale he took a proprietorial pride in the theatre, continuing to organize his 'Musical Mondays' and pinning a poster of the current season's repertoire on the wall of the Avenue Marceau secretariat.

For his part Jack Lang was honouring his promise to support Pierre's efforts at the Chambre Syndicale. The rationale for his policies as culture minister was to use a combination of public and private sector funding to foster a climate in which the arts could flourish, thereby eventually expanding the economy. Jack Lang's argument was difficult, though not impossible, to prove when applied to film subsidies and museum renovation schemes, but relatively easy in an area such as fashion, where there was a direct link between his ministry's initiatives and the industry's economic performance. Fashion and cosmetics were two of France's largest sources of exports, employing hundreds of thousands of people, and the packed tents in the *Cour Carrée* not only provided a showcase for those industries, but benefited other parts of the economy by perpetuating France's international image as the apogee of chic.

In the three years since Jack Lang allowed the Chambre Syndicale to colonize the *Cour Carrée* for fashion week, the number of journalists registering to see the shows had risen by 600, to over 1,600,[29] and the turnover of the *couturiers*, including their income from *prêt-à-porter* and accessories, had doubled from 1.22 billion francs to 2.46 billion francs. Spurred by their success Lang promised to support the plan to found an Institut de la Mode, intended to train young managers for the fashion industry, and agreed to finance a new fashion museum in a westerly wing of the Louvre. He also helped Pierre to persuade François Mitterrand to host a reception for the Paris fashion designers at the Élysée Palace during the October 1984 ready-to-wear shows. Pierre stood beside the president in the reception line and introduced him to the designers as they arrived. Yves was escorted by Catherine

Deneuve, and one of Jean-Paul Gaultier's business partners, Francis Menuge, appeared in a sarong skirt, describing it to the amused Mitterrand as 'an expression of equality of the sexes'.[30]

All the Chambre Syndicale members benefited from these initiatives for which Pierre received most of the credit in his official role as president, and his unofficial role as a friend of Jack Lang and François Mitterrand. However, as his critics pointed out, the French government's newfound enthusiasm was frequently as helpful to Yves Saint Laurent, and to Pierre's efforts to establish Yves as a fashion legend, as it was to the rest of the industry. Honour after honour was heaped on Yves. He was made a Chevalier of the Légion d'Honneur, one of the most prestigious awards given by the French government, at a ceremony in 1985 for which Charles Mathieu-Saint-Laurent made a rare trip from Monte Carlo to Paris. When Jack Lang hosted the French fashion 'Oscars' that autumn, the prize for 'best designer' went to Azzedine Alaïa, 'best collection' to Claude Montana and 'best foreign designer' to Issey Miyake. There were also two special awards for 'contributions to fashion history', one of which went to Yves Saint Laurent. The other, much as Pierre Bergé must have disliked it, was given to Pierre Cardin.

When Mikhail Gorbachev, the Soviet president, paid a state visit to Paris in October 1985 his wife, Raisa, visited two fashion houses: Yves Saint Laurent and Pierre Cardin. Saint Laurent was originally designated as her first visit but Cardin kicked up such a fuss – having recently signed agreements to sell perfumes and cosmetics to the Soviet Union, and to buy cigars and caviar there for his Paris restaurant – that Mrs Gorbachev went to see him first. Yves was photographed kissing her hand as she was ushered into the Avenue Marceau *salon* for a private presentation. At the end of the show, he gave her a bottle of Paris and, at her request, a bottle of Opium too.[31]

Pierre used his political contacts to arrange for the Yves Saint Laurent retrospective to be shipped around the world to Beijing, Moscow, Sydney and finally to the new fashion museum in Paris. After New York, where a million people had visited the exhibition, the first port of call was the Palace of Fine Art in Beijing and the exhibits were sent there by cargo plane, which also carried three of Diana Vreeland's assistants at the Costume Institute, including Katell Le Bourhis. Too ill to travel to China, Vreeland stayed behind in

Manhattan, leaving her assistants to organize the show with a group of students from Beijing University. None of the students had any experience of exhibition organization, and the facilities at the Palace of Fine Art were primitive at best. The New York team had to ask for most things they needed to be specially made in China. 'There were some disasters,' recalled Le Bourhis. 'They made the spotlights to our instructions but screwed the bulbs in too tightly. When they switched them on – bang! The whole ceiling set on fire.'[32]

At the time the Chinese authorities were adopting more liberal social and economic policies in the wake of the Cultural Revolution, which included encouraging people to wear Western dress rather than indistinguishable blue Mao suits, and the YSL retrospective was part of their efforts to speed up that process.[33] The exhibition opened with an official reception at the Palace of Fine Arts to which the student helpers were invited, together with politicians, bureaucrats and textile workers. Yves escorted Li Zhao, the wife of the Communist Party leader, Hu Yaobang, around the show, accompanied by Bian Tao, whose husband, Wan Li, was senior deputy leader. Some guests admitted to being stupefied by the exhibits. Wang Meng, the head of the Chinese Writers Association, told an American reporter that the clothes were too 'sexy' for Chinese taste, and a textile factory manager, An Jing, confessed that he was not sure how they should be worn.[34] But by the time the museum opened to the public the following day, hundreds of people were queuing outside. 'There were long, long lines,' said Katell Le Bourhis. 'I wasn't sure whether people would come, whether they'd even know who Yves Saint Laurent was. But they did. I even saw men in uniforms sketching inside the exhibition.'[35] Over the next two months some six hundred thousand people trooped through the Beijing Palace of Fine Arts to see the smokings, the Ballets Russes dresses, the velvet and satin Parade ballgowns and Yves Saint Laurent's other designs.

The Chinese trip seemed to lift Yves's spirits, taking him into a fascinating foreign culture where he could see more of the traditional Asian art that he loved. At the end of their stay, he and his party went to a department store to look for souvenirs to take back to Paris. 'Most of the stuff was horrible touristy rubbish,' recalled Katell Le Bourhis. 'But Saint Laurent found these little wicker baskets in animal shapes. They cost nothing, but they were beautiful pieces of handwork, everything the Chinese do best. We all loved the baskets and he was in rapture, staring and staring at them. Over on the other side of the store was an American tourist, one of those over-weight Texans in a plaid shirt, polyester trousers and a belt with a big buckle. The buckle might have had a cow on it, but it didn't, it said YSL. The Texan was smiling at Saint Laurent from the other side of the store, swaying to and fro, pointing at the buckle.' Le Bourhis and her colleagues rushed up, hoping to divert his attention away from Yves. 'We went up to him. "Hello. Hello." Saint Laurent just stayed where he was staring at his beautiful wicker baskets.'[36]

Bulls and Bears
1986–1988

For years Pierre Bergé, the reluctant businessman and frustrated man of letters, had enjoyed boasting that he had never met an investment banker: but that was about to change. Squibb had told him that it planned to sell Charles of the Ritz, including the Yves Saint Laurent perfumes, and, loth to see the business slip into the hands of another parent company, Pierre hoped that he and Yves might buy it. The hitch was the price. Squibb intended to sell Charles of the Ritz for at least $600 million – well out of their league.

Like many other American companies, Squibb was paranoid about falling prey to a hostile take-over bid. Shares prices were soaring, entrepreneurs were becoming 'paper millionaires' by taking their companies public, and companies were using cunning new financial instruments, such as junk bonds, to stage more ambitious acquisitions than they could have afforded with old-fashioned bank loans. The once-obscure world of the financial markets suddenly seemed glamorous to the public, as optimistic 'bulls' and pessimistic 'bears' appeared as cartoon characters in the newspapers. The New York stock market slipped into a vicious cycle whereby any company which was not actively contemplating a take-over was seen as so staid that it risked being bid for by another.

Anxious to spruce up its stock market image, Squibb had decided to concentrate on health care, by far the biggest part of its business, and looked for buyers for its other interests. Charles of the Ritz, which included Gianni Versace's perfumes and a dozen or so other brands, as well as the Yves Saint Laurent scents, was an obvious candidate for sale, and the company told Pierre that it was looking for a buyer. Yves and Pierre had few complaints with Squibb on the financial front, having made tens of millions of dollars in royalties from Opium and Paris; but the relationship had never been easy and Pierre had regular rows with the Americans, not least with Bob Miller, whom Squibb put in charge of the YSL perfumes when it acquired them in 1972. A financier by training, Miller had little in common with Pierre Bergé. 'We didn't get on,' acknowledged the latter. 'Bob Miller was a nice man, but I didn't think he was the right person to be running our business.'[1]

Problems also arose because of Yves's right of veto over new products and their advertising. 'It wasn't always easy,' said Maïmé Arnodin. 'The Squibb people insisted that we showed our ideas to them first, before the Saint Laurent people saw them. But Yves had his veto, so then we'd have to show everything to him.'[2] Sometimes the need to consult so many different people led to delays, and Squibb's executives were infuriated by some of Yves's demands. His insouciant attitude to the controversy over Opium's launch still rankled, and Yves's perfectionism, such as the insistence that they reshoot the entire Paris commercial because he had spotted a stray zip, often turned out to be expensive, with Squibb invariably paying the bill.

The last thing Pierre Bergé wanted was to have to deal with another Bob Miller or, worse still, with a new parent company which unlike Squibb would not invest in the business. He had seen what had happened to Halston, whose company had been sold five times in the last five years, ending up with Ronald Perelman, the American financier who had taken over Revlon. Having signed away the rights to his name, Halston was powerless to stop the new owners from licensing it to shoddy products, and was eventually dropped as chief designer of his own company.[3]

Realizing that Halston's fate could befall other fashion designers, even Yves Saint Laurent, Pierre strengthened his resolve to buy the perfumes. He approached the big French banks, asking for loans, but they turned him down flat. Merger mania had spread across the Atlantic to Britain, but not yet to France and the Paris Bourse was still awaiting the 'Big Bang' which had revolutionized the London stock exchange. Some French family firms had broken with tradition by going public, including Louis Vuitton which staged a successful flotation followed by an $850 million bid for the Veuve Clicquot champagne company. But the banks were understandably wary of backing a privately-owned fashion house in a $600 million transatlantic deal, particularly as it would be its first acquisition.

Having drawn a blank with the banks, Pierre looked for help from other investors. His most intriguing prospect was Carlo de Benedetti, the Italian industrialist whose French company, Cerus, had participated in Pierre's unsuccessful bid to buy Ledoyen, the Champs-Élysées restaurant. The *bête noire* of the *salotto buono*, the old boy network that dominated Italian industry, Carlo de Benedetti came from a wealthy Jewish family in Turin and turned his father's firm into one of Italy's fastest growing companies before selling it to Fiat, the motor group controlled by the Agnelli dynasty. He then invested in Olivetti, a loss-making typewriter manufacturer, and having restored it to profit, made other acquisitions. By the mid-1980s Carlo de Benedetti was lionized by the Italian newspapers, at least those not owned by the Agnellis, as a handsome, dynamic young businessman who was shaking up the *salotto buono*.

De Benedetti invested in Cerus, hoping to use it as a vehicle to expand into France. The Ledoyen bid was one of its earliest efforts, and after that failed Cerus moved on to other deals, but its directors stayed in contact with Pierre Bergé, and when a new chief executive joined in 1986, he was introduced to the YSL chairman. 'As soon as I met Alain Minc, I knew we could do business with him,' said Pierre. 'It was obvious.'[4]

The clever son of a Jewish dentist, Alain Minc acquired the requisite credentials to join the French equivalent of the *salotto buono* by attending one of the plusher Parisian *lycées*, followed by stints at *Sciences Po*' and the élite École Nationale de l'Administration where he graduated top of his year. After a few years in the civil service, he moved into industry and made his name when, as a young executive at Saint-Gobain, he orchestrated an expensive and ultimately unsuccessful bid for Compagnie Générale des Eaux, another bastion of Gallic industry. Minc also found time to write and, by the time he joined Cerus, at thirty-seven, he had already published four lengthy essays on economic theory – all critical and commercial successes.

When he met Pierre Bergé, Minc and his economist wife, Sophie, were members of the *gauche caviar* crowd that included Bernard-Henri Lévy, the Rothschilds' *salon* philosopher; Jacques Attali, who was chief adviser to François Mitterrand; and Franz-Olivier Giesbert, the president's biographer who was then editor-in-chief of *Le Nouvel Observateur* and soon to become editor of *Le Figaro*. Impeccably read with a wide frame of reference, Alain Minc was as opinionated as Pierre, veering in conversation from soaring superlatives to describe anything he liked, to a damning *'complètement nul'* for anything he disliked.

There were two schools of thought on Alain Minc in French financial circles: one saw him as a brilliant, almost visionary business-man; the other as a loose cannon whose wild ideas had almost crippled Saint-Gobain. 'He was very smooth and quick-witted, obviously highly intelligent, but a bit of a shark,' said one observer who enjoyed Minc's company, but took a sceptical view of his professional achieve-ments. 'He was always telling the press, and anyone else who would listen, what a genius he was. His deals were clever and incredibly complicated, but there was usually a reason to be slightly suspicious of them and no one ever knew who was really pulling the strings at Cerus – Alain Minc or Carlo de Benedetti.'

It was not a question that seemed to concern Pierre Bergé. Charmed by Minc's intellect and dazzled by his apparent mastery of 1980s financial tricks, Pierre was convinced that he had found an invaluable ally and adviser for Yves Saint Laurent. He liked the idea of the company throwing in its lot with two charismatic outsiders who had the chutzpah to take on the establishment and looked as though they would win. And Alain Minc swiftly proved his useful-ness, by explaining how Carlo de Benedetti's contacts could arrange loans to buy back the perfumes, and how they could then pay off those debts by finding buyers for the unwanted parts of Charles of the Ritz, as Bernard Arnault had done at Agache, and floating Yves Saint Laurent on the stock market, like Louis Vuitton, possibly turning it into a conglomerate by buying other luxury businesses. Pierre flew to Italy for a meeting with Carlo de Benedetti, who made the same positive impression on him as Alain Minc had done.

On 6 November 1986 Pierre Bergé announced that Carlo de Bene-detti was buying a twenty-five per cent stake in Yves Saint Laurent for $38 million, telling the *New York Times* that the deal was intended

Catherine Deneuve and Yves at the opening of the first Rive Gauche boutique at rue de Tournon on 26 September 1966. She bought a coat, a dress, a trouser suit and three suede mini-skirts, and the shop sold $24,000 of clothes by four o'clock that afternoon.

The 'scandalous' see-through dress of 1968.

A 1971 version of the classic YSL *smoking*.

One of the Bakst-inspired outfits designed for 1977.

(Left) Betty Catroux,
Yves and Loulou de la
Falaise, all in YSL safari
suits, at Rive Gauche's
London opening in 1969.

(Below) Betty with her
'best friend' at Place
Vauban in 1972.

(*Above*) Mick and
Bianca Jagger marry
in 1971, both in YSL.
(*Right*) Paul and
Talitha Getty at their
Marrakesh palace.

(*Right*) The hippy *de
luxe* with Loulou in
Paris, and Hazel, his
chihuaha, tucked
under his arm.

(Above) In the salon of 55 rue de Babylone. (Left) Rudolf Nureyev embracing Yves. (Below) Yves alone in Paris, without his 'Byzantine court' for once.

(Clockwise) In the Avenue Marceau studio; Loulou and Thadée Klossowski welcome Yves to their 'Angels and Demons' party at Le Palace, 1978; Halston, Loulou, Potassa, Yves and Nan Kempner at Studio 54, after the Opium launch.

The advertisements that Yves Saint Laurent has created have been as influential – and as innovative – in advertising and marketing, as his *couture* collections in fashion.

When Yves arrived at Jeanloup Sieff's studio he asked to be photographed nude as he 'wanted to create a scandal'. 'It was all Yves's idea,' said Sieff. The ad caused an enormous scandal as its subject had hoped. Despite a ban by some magazines, it became a gay icon of the 1970s.

Whenever he could Yves stole away from his duties at YSL to his opulent houses in Marrakesh, where the warm climate reminded him of Algeria and he felt able to walk discreetly around the *medina*, free from the intrusions that so distressed him in Paris.

to help YSL 'move on to a faster track',[5] and barely bothering to disguise the fact that it was a prelude to the acquisition of Charles of the Ritz. The details of that transaction were announced two weeks later. There had been competitive bids from Avon, Revlon and the Japanese cosmetics giant, Shiseido, but Yves Saint Laurent had agreed terms to buy Charles of the Ritz from Squibb for $630 million. It was financing the deal with a $465 million loan package arranged by Crédit Suisse First Boston, one of the investment banks that often advised Carlo de Benedetti.

Business Week magazine billed the acquisition as 'the mix of glamour and business that Paris loves'.[6] Carlo de Benedetti was praised by the French financial press for having spotted the financial potential of France's greatest living fashion designer, and even Pierre Bergé found himself fêted on the financial pages. 'Carlo de Benedetti got a lot of the credit, probably because of his publicity machine,' commented George Graham, who covered the transaction as Paris correspondent of the *Financial Times*. 'He was quite a hero in the French business pages. There were all these articles about how French banks had turned their backs on the deal and it took an Italian financial genius to pull it off. Pierre Bergé hadn't really emerged in the business world until then. People admired him for what he'd achieved at Yves Saint Laurent and realized that he'd created more than a *couture* house by licensing everything down to cigarettes, but before that he hadn't been seen as a major financial figure.'[7]

For the first time Yves Saint Laurent was analysed as a financial force. The small but prestigious fashion house that Yves Saint Laurent and Pierre Bergé had bought from Squibb for $1.1 million in 1972 had since become an enormous international business. The hundreds of products bearing the YSL brand name generated sales of $1.2 billion in 1985, the year before the Charles of the Ritz acquisition,[8] and their royalties enabled the company to make net profits of $8.4 million on turnover of $40 million.[9] Yves Saint Laurent had now taken over a company with annual sales of $432 million, two thirds of which came from its own brands, and Pierre Bergé hinted at the possibility of making further acquisitions, citing Louis Vuitton's bid for Veuve Clicquot as a precedent for what they might do in the future. 'We're in another game now,' he told the *Wall Street Journal*. 'We will have the power to add other designers, or other brands perhaps a little bit down in the dumps.'[10] But first he had a more mundane task to perform: ending his squabbles with Bob Miller. 'As soon as we took control of the perfumes – he went.'[11]

Yves Saint Laurent had no problem in finding a buyer for the unwanted Charles of the Ritz brands, as so many companies were anxious to invest in the buoyant luxury business. Revlon bought those brands for $150 million, and Avon, another disappointed bidder for Charles of the Ritz, paid $165 million for Giorgio of Beverly Hills. Investcorp, a Bahrain investment bank, took over Tiffany, the famous New York jeweller, and commenced negotiations to buy a stake in Gucci from the bickering Gucci clan.[12] L'Oréal, the French cosmetics company, acquired the rights to Ralph Lauren's and Giorgio Armani's scents; but more important Henry Racamier started talks to merge Louis Vuitton with Moët-Hennessy, the cognac and champagne company which owned the Christian Dior fragrances.

The news of their alliance was a blow to Bernard Arnault who had hoped to persuade Alain Chevalier, the Moët-Hennessy chairman, to sell the Dior perfumes to him so he could reunite them with the fashion house as Pierre Bergé had done at Yves Saint Laurent. Arnault's early days at Dior had not been easy, as his aloof manner did not endear him to the staff, who leaked stories to the press claiming that he had reserved a lift for his private use, and banned them from walking along the corridor beside his office in case the noise disturbed him.[13] The tension had erupted into a clash between Arnault and Jacques Rouët who, after running the company for nearly forty years, resented having to defer to a younger man. Rouët resigned, and Arnault then tried to rationalize the labyrinth of licences he had negotiated, and searched for a new designer who, he hoped, would have the same effect on Christian Dior's reputation as Karl Lagerfeld had on Chanel's. By autumn 1986 he thought he had found the right one in Christian Lacroix.

Born in 1951, the son of an Arles businessman, Lacroix studied art history at the Sorbonne before becoming a design assistant at Hermès and then chief designer at Jean Patou, one of the older *couture* houses which was better known for Joy, the famous perfume, than for fashion. The hallmarks of Lacroix's style were his vibrant palette and the playfulness with which he reinterpreted historical forms, such as bustles and petticoats, into contemporary clothes. His own appearance had a quaintly nostalgic air, with straight black hair slicked back on his head like a 1950s *mondain* and beautifully tailored suits with a conventional cut in unconventionally vivid colours. Lacroix's pretty *pouf* skirts and frivolous bubble dresses were perfect for the exuberant mood of the mid-1980s. Striking a chord with the visual puns in Jeff Koons's sculpture, Philippe Starck's furniture and Frank Gehry's architecture, they added a sense of fun to Paris fashion after the asceticism of the Japanese designers, Karl Lagerfeld's cynicism and Yves Saint Laurent's joyless perfectionism.[14] In January 1986 his talent was recognized by his peers, and he was awarded the *Dé d'Or*, or Golden Thimble, for creating the best *haute couture* collection of the season.

Christian Lacroix had a slight acquaintance with Pierre Bergé, having asked his advice about pursuing a career in theatrical design when he left the Sorbonne, and often voiced his admiration for Yves Saint Laurent in press interviews. After his *Dé d'Or* triumph he received an invitation to the next YSL *couture* show in July, which he was about to accept until it was explained to him 'very delicately and very politely' that it would not be proper to attend unless it would be the only other *couture* show he saw that season. 'Well! At that time I was very friendly with Inès de la Fressange and she had invited me to Chanel. I'd already accepted and I couldn't take it back. So, although I'd have loved to have gone, I had to say "no" to Saint Laurent.'[15]

Towards the end of that year Bernard Arnault invited Lacroix and Jean-Jacques Picart, his friend and colleague at Patou, to lunch. They met in the restaurant of the Hôtel Bristol on rue Faubourg Saint-Honoré, and Arnault offered Lacroix the position of Christian Dior's ready-to-wear designer. The answer was 'no'. Lacroix explained that he might be willing to leave Patou, but only if it was to open his own *couture* house. A few weeks later Arnault arranged another meeting and agreed to set him up in business as a *couturier*. Bernard Arnault had every reason to believe that his new protégé would be successful. He had heard flattering reports of Lacroix's collections from his fashion contacts and read complimentary articles about him in the press: but he was promising to invest $7.5 million in Christian Lacroix's new *haute couture* house without having seen one of his Jean Patou shows.[16]

Christian Lacroix would be the first new *haute couture* house to open in Paris for nearly twenty years. The timing seemed propitious as, after years of decline, *couture* sales were increasing again.[17] The Asian billionaires and oil-rich Arabs who had started buying *couture* in the late 1970s continued to do so, as did the wives and mistresses of Latin American drug-lords, but the chief catalyst for the revival was the arrival of a new set of *nouveau riche* American socialites at the Paris shows. These were the photogenic wives of Wall Street warriors such as Susan Gutfreund, a former air hostess who had married the chairman of Salomon Brothers, and Ivana Trump, the wife of Donald Trump, the New York property magnate, who joined the older generation of American clients, like Nan Kempner, in the front rows of the *couture* shows. In his book, *The Fashion Conspiracy*, Nicholas Coleridge estimated that a typical member of what *Women's Wear Daily* called the 'Shiny Set' spent around $367,500 on her wardrobe each year, including six *couture* dresses a season – at $10,000 each for winter and $7,000 for summer – up to $500 on sunglasses, and as much as $6,000 on shoes.[18]

The new *couture* crowd needed a champion, just as their predecessors did when Christian Dior emerged in the late 1940s and Yves Saint Laurent in the early 1960s, but none of the existing designers fitted the bill. Jean-Paul Gaultier was the hit of the *prêt-à-porter* presentations, and the darling of pop stars such as Madonna, but his clothes were too funky for the Shiny Set, just as Giorgio Armani's were too businesslike, Romeo Gigli's too bohemian, and Karl Lagerfeld's a little *too* knowing.[19] As for Yves Saint Laurent, he had sealed himself off from the world at Villa Oasis and Château Gabriel with only Moujik for company. In a portrait taken of him at that time by Horst, the German photographer, Yves poses in full evening dress on a brocade sofa in the Château Gabriel *salon*, with a pink rose wilting from his buttonhole, looking as much a vestige of the *Belle Époque* as the *faux* Monet friezes and the chandelier dripping from the ceiling. It struck a mournful contrast to the photograph Horst took of him as a vigorous young *couturier* at Christian Dior nearly thirty years before. Even the virtuoso *couture* collection Yves designed for spring 1987, the season before Christian Lacroix's debut, was not enough to excite the press. 'Nothing like a nice surprise!' reported Hebe Dorsey in the *Herald Tribune*, adding, 'Saint Laurent has said and done practically everything; all he has to do now is say it again, in his own pure, perfected hand. But Lacroix is the future.'[20]

Bernard Arnault invested heavily to help his protégé fulfil that promise. The new *couture* house was to be based in a pretty *hôtel particulier* with a tranquil garden on rue Faubourg Saint-Honoré, a few streets away from Chanel and opposite the Hôtel Bristol where Lacroix and Picart held their first meeting with Arnault. The *hôtel* was redecorated in Lacroix's favourite shades of fiery pink and orange with dramatic black detailing by the fashionable decorators, Elisabeth Garouste and Mattia Bonetti. The charming, slightly bashful *couturier* made an appealing interviewee, and fashion magazines were filled with articles on his *haute bohème* life with his chic Parisienne girl-friend, Françoise Roesenstiehl, and the gregarious Jean-Jacques Picart. Under the Chambre Syndicale rules, Lacroix needed two *par-rains*, 'godfathers', to sponsor his application for registration as an *haut couturier*. Bernard Arnault would be one, and he asked Pierre Bergé to be the other as 'he was one of the first people to help me when I was young'.[21] Pierre accepted the invitation, even going to the trouble of tracking down a former Avenue Marceau employee, who was taken on as the head of Christian Lacroix's tailoring *atelier*.

On the morning of 26 July 1987, the ballroom of the Hôtel Intercontinental on rue de Castiglione was packed for the presentation of Christian Lacroix's first *couture* collection. There were to be two shows that day: Bernard Arnault sat in the seat of honour in the front row at the centre of the catwalk for the first; and Pierre Bergé would be there for the second. The press officers discreetly let it be known that Madonna had telephoned to request a private presen-tation. The collection was inspired by the Camargue, the bleakly beautiful region of southern France where Lacroix spent his child-hood, and included *pouf* skirts and bubble dresses in vibrant silks and satins with magnificent hand-woven laces. When Christian Lacroix took his bow, the audience treated him to the tearful ovation usually reserved for Yves's greatest triumphs, bombarding the young *couturier* with the gaudy carnations that had thoughtfully been left on their seats. Hebe Dorsey described the event as 'a new chapter of fashion history' on the front page of the next day's *Herald Tribune*,[22] and *Women's Wear Daily*'s headline read: 'For Lacroix, a Triumph, for Couture, a Future'.[23]

When Christian Lacroix returned to his *couture* house at the end of the day, he went out into the garden to sit quietly for a while. His thoughts were interrupted by the arrival of a huge bouquet of flowers: the first, and probably the loveliest of dozens of congratulatory bouquets which were to be delivered over the next few hours. 'It was from Monsieur Bergé and Monsieur Saint Laurent. They were wonderful flowers, really sumptuous, and the letter they sent was more than merely polite. It was beautifully written, really charming. I was very moved.'[24]

Behind their gracious façade Pierre Bergé and Yves Saint Laurent were incensed, not with Christian Lacroix, but with the press, whom they suspected of deserting Yves in favour of the new *couturier*.[25] The butt of their wrath was *Women's Wear Daily* which, delighted to discover an exciting new talent, had run scores of favourable stories on Lacroix before his debut.[26] Like all self-absorbed people Yves and Pierre found it easier to believe that *Women's Wear* had decided to praise Lacroix in order to wound them, rather than because the editors genuinely admired his work. Pierre described John Fairchild as a 'megalomaniac' who was championing Lacroix 'to destroy Saint Laurent' and banned him from attending the YSL show.[27] Christian Lacroix sensibly said nothing. 'It was a *guerre de dentelles* (a lace war),' he said. 'But it was between them and had nothing to do with me, so I tried to ignore it.'[28]

A few months later Lacroix met Yves Saint Laurent for the first time at the *Bal des Fées*, a coming-out ball given by Guy and Marie-Hélène de Rothschild for their niece, Vanessa, at Hôtel Lambert. It was Yves's first appearance at a society event since the gala opening of his retrospective at the Metropolitan Museum in New York four years before. The *hôtel* was decorated like a fairy's lair in white, gold and silver, with the guests walking into the Rothschilds' quarters through an *Alice in Wonderland* looking-glass to be greeted by dancers from the *corps* of the Ballet de Paris dressed as Lewis Carroll's white rabbits, who were 'on loan' for the night from Rudolf Nureyev, artistic director of the ballet.

When Christian Lacroix passed through the looking-glass, he saw Yves standing in front of him in a corridor. 'Someone introduced us and he was very, very pleasant. He said – and I'll never forget it – "The most important thing is to last." Well! He'd been my idol for years and I was so awed at actually meeting him that I couldn't think what to say. Later that evening he came to sit at my table, presumably to continue our conversation. I was still dumbstruck, and he rarely says very much. Everyone was talking around us. But I was so intimidated that I couldn't say a thing. He must have thought I was an idiot.'[29]

For the first time Yves faced the threat of a rival who appeared capable of competing against him on equal terms. So far his closest competitor had been Karl Lagerfeld, but as the fashion journalist, Christa Worthington, once said: to the French Yves Saint Laurent was 'a god', but Lagerfeld would only ever be 'a German'.[30] And, despite his commercial success at Chanel, Lagerfeld had never broken out of the fashion ghetto by achieving the accepted benchmarks of 'fame', a *Time* cover story or articles on the front page of the *New York Times*, as Yves and, now, Christian Lacroix had done. Lacroix also had tremendous talent, charisma and the financial backing of Bernard Arnault; but he lacked one essential ingredient for success – good timing.

Three months after his debut, the New York stock market crashed on 'Black Friday', 23 October 1987. Christian Lacroix flew to New York that weekend to prepare for a special presentation of his *couture* collection at a charity gala on Wednesday, 28 October. 'We held the show in the Wall Street district,' he recalled. 'It was terrible. There had been three suicides already that day. No one was in the mood for Parisian frivolity.'[31]

Bernard Arnault regarded 'Black Friday' as a temporary setback, and continued to pump money into his new investment, and the other heads of the French luxury groups took the same optimistic view. Pierre Bergé's chief concern was how the stock market crash would affect his plans to pay off the Charles of the Ritz loans.[32] Originally he and Alain Minc had planned to float a tranche of Yves Saint Laurent shares on the Paris stock market that December, and to raise more money a few months later by arranging a private placing of shares among a group of 'friendly' institutional investors. After 'Black Friday' they put both projects on ice until the stock market recovered, quickly they hoped, and they could sell the shares at a higher price.

Pierre flung himself back into politics by helping his *'gauche caviare'* friends to prepare for the French presidential and parliamentary elections in spring 1988. Having made a substantial contribution to the socialist campaign fund, he put the Yves Saint Laurent helicopter and Lear jet at François Mitterrand's disposal during the elections, and accompanied him on the hustings. Pierre then sent a letter on YSL-headed paper to the heads of five thousand French companies urging them to vote for François Mitterrand. Jacques Calvet, the conservative chairman of Peugeot, the car company, retaliated by sending a sternly-worded memo to his workforce forbidding them to shop at Yves Saint Laurent.

The socialists swept the board in both elections; the moderate Michel Rocard was appointed prime minister and Jack Lang returned to the culture ministry. The successfully re-elected President Mitterrand was eager to show his gratitude for his friend's help during the campaign, and on 31 August 1988, Pierre Bergé was named president of the Opéra de Paris. His new fiefdom included the grandiose Opéra Garnier, where he and Yves had gone to hear Maria Callas sing in the 1950s, the smaller Opéra Comique on rue Favart, and a new 'People's Opera' under construction at Place de la Bastille as one of the *Grands Projets* commissioned by François Mitterrand and Jack Lang to commemorate the two-hundredth anniversary of the French Revolution on 14 July 1989. The Opéra de Paris was one of Europe's most prestigious arts institutions, which boasted Daniel Barenboim, the distinguished conductor as artistic director of opera, and Rudolf Nureyev in the same role for ballet. Ominously it was also haunted by a tangled history of financial problems and trade union conflict.

The Mitterrand camp presented Pierre to the press as a successful businessman who, buoyed by his experience of running the Théâtre de l'Athénée-Louis Jouvet, was admirably equipped to open the new opera house on schedule, and to tackle the problems of the old one.[33] The Paris arts world took a more cynical view, suspecting that Pierre's appointment had more to do with his friendship with François Mitterrand than his merits as an arts administrator. 'By then Pierre Bergé was very close to François Mitterrand,' commented Franz-Olivier Giesbert. 'There was a bit of controversy when he was appointed. But it wasn't considered unusual for someone so close to the president to take such a post, so there wasn't any great scandal.'[34]

After thirty years of living in Yves's shadow, Pierre Bergé had found a role which was arguably more prestigious, if rather less lucrative, than running Yves Saint Laurent. Despite his not inconsiderable achievements as a businessman, he was still seen primarily as Yves's boyfriend and business partner. It was Pierre who had buried himself in the financial affairs he claimed to despise, only to see the staff beam with deferential smiles for '*le patron*' when Yves stumbled in for one of his increasingly infrequent appearances at Avenue Marceau. As for Yves, he had made it achingly apparent through his illnesses, addictions and depressions that he expected Pierre to be on call twenty-four hours a day. As Betty Catroux said, she and Yves were cast in the roles of the 'naughty children', with Pierre and her husband, François, as their 'parents'.[35] Until then Pierre had seemed content to play that part, but now he had found a new domain in the Opéra de Paris, where he would be '*le patron*', leaving him, inevitably, with less time to attend to the needs of Yves Saint Laurent.

For Yves, that realization might have been easier to bear had he not lost his real father, the one whom Pierre Bergé had so efficiently supplanted, shortly after the news of the Opéra appointment, when Charles Mathieu-Saint-Laurent died in Monaco after a long respiratory illness. His death was not unexpected; Charles was seventy-nine with a history of lung problems, having smoked heavily throughout his adult life. Like his son, he was rarely photographed without a cigarette clasped between his fingers.

Never as close to Charles as he was to his mother, Yves nonetheless had fond memories of the kindly, dignified man who had done his best to help a son who, by the conservative standards of the Mathieu-Saint-Laurents' circle, cannot have been an easy child. Unfailingly generous in his praise of Yves, he seemed to delight in his success, and when Andy Warhol visited Monte Carlo for a film première, he and his clique received a warm welcome from Charles on their arrival at the Rive Gauche boutique. After a couple of days mixing with Princess Grace, Prince Rainier, Paulette Goddard, Aristotle Onassis and Elizabeth Taylor, Warhol was asked who was the most exciting person he had met during his stay and replied 'Yves Saint Laurent's dad'.[36]

During Yves's reclusion, he had continued to see Lucienne, but not his father, and their last meeting had been in March 1985 when Charles made a special trip to Paris from Monaco to attend the ceremony for Yves's investiture as a Chevalier of the Légion d'Honneur. Pierre Bergé took a photograph of the Mathieu-Saint-Laurent family at rue de Babylone, all apparently in good humour, with Brigitte and Michèle giggling as their septuagenarian father sat astride one of Claude Lalanne's 'sheep', his hand resting gently on Lucienne's arm as, typically, she gazed adoringly up at Yves. Years later Yves told the French writer, Laurence Benaïm, that he had finally broached the subject of his homosexuality with Charles that day. 'I don't know why, but I found myself alone with him and burst into tears. And I said: *"Papa, you know what I am. Perhaps you would rather have had a real boy who could have continued your name."* He said: *"It doesn't matter, mon chéri."* '[37]

Yves did not see his father again, although he must have been told by Lucienne that Charles was seriously ill, and it would have only taken a few hours to fly to Monaco from Paris or Bénerville in the Lear jet. After Charles's death he travelled to Monaco to attend the funeral with his mother and sisters. During the ceremony the fifty-two-year-old Yves's grief seemed uncontrollable, as he broke down in the church, sobbing hysterically and screaming *'Papa'*.

The Battleground
1988–1989

Only three years earlier Bernard Arnault had been dismissed as too young and inexperienced to win the Agache auction; but by 1988 he was lauded by the press as France's most promising industrialist, the visionary backer of Christian Lacroix, and when Henry Racamier started looking for allies in the boardroom battle that followed the merger between Louis Vuitton and Moët-Hennessy, he looked like an attractive candidate.

The merger had created the world's largest luxury goods group with an impressive array of products including Louis Vuitton luggage, Christian Dior perfumes and a quarter of the entire champagne industry. But Henry Racamier and Alain Chevalier, the Moët chairman, had very different views of how the new company should be run, and the state of their relationship was probably best summed up by the name they gave it: LVMH: Moët-Hennessy Louis Vuitton. They had not even managed to agree whose name should go first.

A spruce figure in his mid-fifties, Alain Chevalier was highly regarded in corporate circles for the finesse with which he had merged a string of family-owned French champagne and cognac houses into Moët-Hennessy,[1] a process that involved a number of complex transactions as the shares of the old family firms had been parcelled out among various heirs through the generations. 'Alain Chevalier was the golden boy of French business,' recalled George Graham of the *Financial Times*. 'He'd achieved a lot. He was a very able financial man and he was billed by the business magazines as the technocrat who was going to modernize French industry.'[2]

Henry Racamier had some characteristics of a modernizer, having turned Louis Vuitton into a publicly quoted company and taken over the Veuve Clicquot champagne house, but in other respects he behaved like an old-fashioned *grand patron*, running his business with patriarchal panache. A tall man with owlish spectacles and the courtly manner one might expect to find in the owner of a provincial château, he enjoyed an engagingly eccentric reputation for racing around Paris on the Métro one day, then flying to New York and back on Concorde the next.[3] 'Everyone took their hats off to Racamier for what he'd achieved at Vuitton,' observed George Graham. 'He wasn't such a high profile figure in business circles as Chevalier but he had a certain *éclat*. Vuitton had always done very good parties at Longchamp and Racamier was often in the society pages for this or that.'[4] After the merger with Moët-Hennessy, it was generally expected, not least by Alain Chevalier, that Henry Racamier, then in his early seventies, would step aside into a well-deserved retirement; but it soon became clear that Racamier had other ideas.

The new LVMH group had made some progress since the merger in 1987, notably by buying Hubert de Givenchy's *couture* house, but after months of friction with Racamier, Alain Chevalier appealed to Guinness, the British drinks group which held a large block of LVMH shares, asking for its help in his struggle against the Vuitton chairman. Henry Racamier searched for an ally of his own and, after making tentative, but unsuccessful approaches to Pierre Bergé at Yves Saint Laurent and Jean-Louis Dumas at Hermès, he turned to Bernard Arnault. At thirty-nine, Arnault was younger and less experienced than Alain Chevalier, and promised to be more malleable. Henry Racamier was impressed by his attentive manner, just as Antoine Bernheim and the Willot brothers had been, and in June 1988 he agreed to allow the Arnault family to acquire up to thirty per cent of LVMH, convinced that they would side with him against Alain Chevalier and Guinness to help the Vuittons win control of the company. It was a judgement that he later admitted was 'a mistake'.[5]

Bernard Arnault began buying LVMH shares that summer, and by the end of September he controlled such a large stake in the company that his father, Jean, was appointed chairman of the LVMH supervisory board. So far he had been buying shares with the company's knowledge, but on 5 January 1989 he staged a 'dawn raid' on LVMH, instructing his stockbrokers to buy a large block of shares when the market opened for trading. Thirty-six hours later Arnault owned another eight per cent of the stock. Alain Chevalier resigned as chairman at a board meeting on 12 January and Bernard Arnault was appointed his successor the following day. Having disposed of Chevalier, Arnault turned his attention to a new target. At the next board meeting his lawyer tabled a proposal that all LVMH directors should be forced to retire at the age of seventy. Henry Racamier was seventy-four years old.

The battle for LVMH had begun. Bernard Arnault, Alain Chevalier and Henry Racamier assembled teams of investment bankers, corporate lawyers, public relations consultants, even private detectives to fight for control of the company. 'It was all-consuming in Paris at the time because everybody was taking sides,' recalled George Graham. 'The Paris financial world was still fairly small. There weren't that many advisers to go round and there were so many different factions that it seemed as though everyone was involved somewhere or another. There was the Henry Racamier party, the Bernard Arnault party, the Alain Chevalier party, and then the families of the drinks companies had people advising them, with lawyers on all sides. There was also lots of symbolism. The so-called old money of the Vuittons versus the new money of Arnault. The technocratic Chevalier versus the family-run businesses. There had never been a fully fledged take-over battle like this in France so the rules weren't clear and they got a lot less clear as things went along.'[6]

The *leitmotif* of any take-over bid is that each faction tries to convince the shareholders that they are better equipped to manage the business than their rivals and that, by pledging their shares to them, the investors will eventually make more money. The civilized side of a bid battle is that it forces the protagonists to articulate their management philosophies, by explaining what they intend to do to improve the company's performance. The less civilized side is that the business arguments are often accompanied by attacks on the competence, or integrity, of the opposing faction. The bullish stock markets of the mid-1980s had triggered some bruising battles in

Britain and the States, including Guinness's fight for control of the Distillers' drinks group, which ended with the imprisonment of the Guinness chairman, and Ronald Perelman's bruising, but successful assault on Revlon. The French take-over scene had been rather tame in comparison – until then.

The battle of LVMH was conducted in a gloves-off Anglo-Saxon style with writs and counter-writs flying around, shouting matches at shareholders' meetings and accusations of dubious dealings from both camps. 'The jugular stuff started early on,' recalled Graham. 'They had private detectives digging up dirt on both sides, which wasn't entirely unheard-of in Paris at the time, but rather unusual. Henry Racamier was more directly aggressive, the Arnault camp acted more stealthily. You'd sometimes be told something derogatory about one side by someone who wasn't apparently connected with the fight only to wonder why they'd told you that and which side they were on. You could never really quite work out who was working for whom.'[7] Slowly, but surely, Bernard Arnault crept ahead of his opponents, and Henry Racamier, the man who had revitalized Louis Vuitton, and Alain Chevalier, the 'golden boy of French business', were defeated.

The drama at LVMH, coupled with the glamour of the products – Christian Dior perfumes, Dom Pérignon champagne, and Christian Lacroix's *couture* – turned the media spotlight on to the luxury market and brought more investors into the industry. There was no shortage of investment opportunities, largely because of the tensions within the old family firms. Investcorp concluded negotiations to acquire a fifty per cent stake in Gucci when Maurizio Gucci, one of the heirs, forced his feuding cousins to sell their shares.[8] It then invested in Chaumet, an old-established Paris jeweller which came up for sale after its owners, the Chaumet brothers, were jailed for fraud. L'Oréal acquired the remnants of Helena Rubinstein's beauty empire, and Unilever, the consumer products giant, spent nearly $2 billion in one month during summer 1989 on buying Rimmel, Fabergé and Elizabeth Arden, which owned Calvin Klein Cosmetics and Elizabeth Taylor's Passion. The losers in the LVMH battle found no difficulty in persuading investors to back their new ventures. Alain Chevalier took control of Pierre Balmain, with the help of Midland Bank, and Henry Racamier raised capital to create a new luxury conglomerate,

Orcofi, which launched a chain of boutiques for Inès de la Fressange, after Karl Lagerfeld fired her from Chanel, and then joined forces with L'Oréal to buy Jeanne Lanvin's old fashion house.

These investors hoped to revitalize their acquisitions by injecting fresh capital and modern management techniques as Pierre Bergé and Carlo de Benedetti had done at Yves Saint Laurent. Their theory was that a grand old luxury name could be turned into an international brand, just like Heinz in food or Persil in soap powder, but that the luxury product would be more profitable as it sold for a higher price, and even more profitable if a number of them were owned by the same company which could then exploit economies of scale to drive down manufacturing and marketing costs while having more clout in negotiations with department stores and duty-free shops.

At first the new investors were seen as a welcome source of capital, not least by the old owners of the old luxury houses, such as the squabbling Gucci cousins, who could make money by selling their shares. But the battle for control of LVMH and Bernard Arnault's new régime at Christian Dior offered an insight into the harsher side of life under the new investors. Jacques Rouët's departure from Dior was followed by that of Frédéric Castet, its veteran fur designer,[9] and then by the announcement that Marc Bohan was to be replaced as chief designer by Gianfranco Ferre. Bohan complained that after twenty-nine years he had been 'thrown out as abruptly and brutally as an incompetent valet' and the Paris fashion community rallied behind him, having conveniently forgotten the ill-feeling thirty years before when he had taken Yves Saint Laurent's place at Dior. Karl Lagerfeld told the press that he would 'rather be a beggar on the streets than work for Bernard Arnault'.

If a French industrialist were asked to list the qualities that they admired in their peers, 'creativity' would almost certainly be among them. The tradition of family ownership in French industry with its paternalistic *grands patrons* created a climate where company chairmen were expected to display originality and imagination in the way they developed their businesses. Pierre Bergé was admired for the skill with which he had turned the fragile brilliance of Yves Saint Laurent into a commercial concern, and Jean-Louis Dumas for his flair in modernizing Hermès while guarding its artisanal heritage. By backing Christian Lacroix, Bernard Arnault had appeared to be dem-onstrating similar panache, but it soon became clear that he saw the new *couture* house purely as an investment opportunity, an attitude which would have been perfectly acceptable, even admirable, in North America or Britain, but not in France.

Arnault's manner also jarred. The culture of the French corporate scene is epitomized by the etiquette of the business lunch, whereby it is deemed acceptable to talk about anything for the first few courses – politics, fashion, architecture, the sexual proclivities of a cabinet minister – except for business, which should only be raised *après le fromage*, after the cheese course – in other words during the few minutes it takes to eat dessert. Hence it is considered an asset for successful businessmen to be good conversationalists. One reason why Pierre Bergé and Alain-Dominique Perrin got on so well was a mutual passion for contemporary art, which they discussed at length before dealing with the minutiae of their licensing arrangements. Bernard Arnault appeared to have little interest in such niceties. Shortly after his arrival at Dior an executive suggested they meet for lunch, and Arnault was said to have replied 'What for?'. None of his rivals doubted his intelligence, but Arnault's chilly manner won him few friends in the luxury industry accustomed to a cordial greeting from Henry Racamier at Louis Vuitton's dinners, and to being welcomed by Jean-Louis Dumas to Hermès's annual party at the Prix de Diane horse race, the French equivalent to Ladies Day at Royal Ascot, where the prettiest Parisian socialites competed to see who was wearing the most outlandish hat. 'He doesn't fit into this industry,' complained the head of a rival French luxury group. 'The rest of us get on well together. We're competitive when it comes to business, but afterwards we're friends. Jean-Louis Dumas is a clever, amusing man, who anyone would be happy to mix with. Bernard Arnault's a cash machine.'

As a 'cash machine' Arnault was remarkably efficient, and his success struck a nerve among his competitors. The other heads of France's luxury groups had reached the top by transforming the fortunes of family firms, as Jean-Louis Dumas had done at Hermès and Alain Wertheimer at Chanel, working their way up the ranks like Alain-Dominique Perrin at Cartier, or building the business from nothing as Pierre Bergé did at Yves Saint Laurent: whereas

Bernard Arnault, now known as the 'wolf in cashmere clothing', seemed to have got there thanks to a lucky punt in a take-over bid. 'Everyone in Paris was freaked out by what was happening at LVMH,' commented one observer. 'Here was this upstart, Bernard Arnault, waltzing in and taking control of the company. All the others knew that if it had happened there, it could happen to them.'

The turmoil at Christian Dior, and the enforced exits of Henry Racamier and Alain Chevalier from LVMH, redoubled Pierre Bergé's determination to prevent a predator like Bernard Arnault from preying on Yves Saint Laurent, particularly as he had only just broken free from Squibb less than three years before into what seemed a more satisfactory arrangement with Carlo de Benedetti and Alain Minc, and was now engrossed in integrating the cosmetics company with the fashion house. Some of his peers might have baulked at the challenge of adding the large and complex beauty business to his existing responsibilities at Avenue Marceau, but Pierre seemed to thrive on it.

His office still had the deceptively amateurish air of a rather splendid study with a Warhol portrait of Yves above his desk, auction catalogues and artist monographs heaped on low tables, and *objets* from his travels cluttering up the shelves alongside framed photographs of Jean Cocteau, Andy Warhol, Louis Aragon, Rudolf Nureyev and his new friend, François Mitterrand. After Bob Miller's departure Pierre put Chantal Roos, a former Air France stewardess who had proved herself to be an astute, imaginative manager as head of international marketing, in charge of the perfumes, and his closest aides were two men in their thirties who had worked with him for several years. His finance director, Jean-Francis Bretelle, was a wiry, boyish-looking figure with an intense air who was offered a job by Pierre in 1976 when, as a young accountant, he was sent by his firm to audit the YSL accounts. The company secretary, Christophe Girard, arrived a few years later having met the YSL chairman as a student in Tokyo when he was teaching English to the staff at the Rive Gauche boutique. 'He told me to call him when I got back to Paris, but I assumed he was just being polite, so didn't do anything about it. One day I came to the *couture* house to take Loulou out to lunch and bumped into him. He said: "Why didn't you call me?" Almost as if he was annoyed.'[10] An affable man with a relaxed charm, Girard was adept at smoothing things over after Pierre's outbursts. 'Christophe's great at playing good cop to Pierre's bad cop,' said a fellow employee. 'He's terribly charming, very easy-going and can always think of something pleasant to say.'

With their help the company had made a smooth transition after the acquisition of Charles of the Ritz. Opium and Paris were still selling well, as was Jazz, the new men's scent they launched in March 1988 with an advertising campaign shot by the French fashion photographer, Jean-Baptiste Mondino. The next logical step was to resurrect the plan to reduce the company's debts, and to allow Carlo de Benedetti to cash in part of his investment, by staging a stock market flotation.

When Pierre negotiated the original deal to buy Charles of the Ritz in November 1986, he took on a $465 million loan, which Alain Minc assured him they would soon be able to reduce by raising capital through disposals and a flotation. At the time his argument was perfectly plausible, but after 'Black Friday' share prices fell so sharply that in order to raise the necessary amount of money, Yves and Pierre would have to sell so many shares that their stake in the company might fall below fifty per cent. Reluctant to risk opening the door to a predator, Pierre had agreed to postpone the flotation, but as the months went by the pressure to reduce the debts mounted. Even after selling the Charles of the Ritz brands to Revlon, Yves Saint Laurent was left with debts of over $400 million at the end of 1988, costing nearly $40 million in interest that year, a hefty chunk of its $66 million operating profits.[11] Pierre needed to raise money to pay off the loans, but the spectacle of Bernard Arnault's régime at LVMH and Christian Dior made him even warier of losing control of the company.

Alain Minc came up with a solution. They could still go public but only after turning Yves Saint Laurent into a *société en commandite par actions*, an obscure French device whereby the power to control the company would be vested in a special category of share, owned by Yves and Pierre. This meant that other investors could trade their shares on the stock market as usual, but even if Yves's and Pierre's holding was reduced to less than fifty per cent, they could use their *commandite* shares to block a hostile bid. The *commandite* was an archaic device that financial modernists like Minc usually despised, and some companies had been criticized for implementing it. The prospect of a take-over bid invariably inflates a company's share price, so if it becomes bid-proof the shares are automatically worth less. Compagnie Générale des Eaux, the industrial conglomerate that Alain Minc had encouraged Saint-Gobain to bid for, was attacked for restructuring itself as a *société en commandite par actions* two years after going public; but Minc advised Pierre that the *commandite* should not pose problems as long as they introduced it before the flotation and told prospective investors about it. Pierre agreed and arrangements were made to put the *commandite* in place.[12] In December 1988, he announced that Yves Saint Laurent intended to stage a private placing the following spring, and that by the end of that year the company would be floated on the Paris stock market.[13]

The omens for the flotation were encouraging. Despite the stock market crash, sales of luxury products were still robust, if a little less so than before. The 'paper millionaires' in London and New York were not spending quite as freely as three or four years ago, but business was brisk in the Gulf states, and sales in Asia were soaring. So many Japanese tourists tried to squeeze into the Chanel boutique on rue Cambon that the company was forced to 'ration' its classic quilted bags to two per person. Unabashed, the Japanese lurked outside and bribed passing Parisians to go in and buy a couple of extra bags for them. Louis Vuitton found that the Japanese were buying four or five of its LV initialled bags at a time because they preferred the leather to be pale and new, rather than with the aged dark patina that its European customers coveted. Yves Saint Laurent, like other luxury companies, was faring well financially. The bankers and brokers advising Pierre assured him that he would have an impressive set of figures to present to investors when the time came for the flotation.

The only cloud on the horizon was Yves, whose condition had deteriorated so much that the physical effects of his depressions and dependencies were impossible to hide. A nagging prostate problem caused his weight to fluctuate wildly, and his speech was slurred as he seemed unable to control his mouth muscles. For years Yves's health had been a source of speculation on the Paris fashion scene, which had him suffering from every conceivable illness from terminal cancer to the rumour-mongers' current favourite, AIDS. The toll of

AIDS casualties in the fashion industry was mounting, and rumours were rife as to who would be the next victim. The New York fashion industry had already lost two of its brightest young designers in Perry Ellis and Willi Smith. Yves's groggy progress along the runway each season fuelled suspicions that he would be the next to go.

'The speculation about his health was really tasteless, but he did look dreadful,' recalled Paula Reed, who attended the collections each season as fashion director of the *Sunday Times*. 'Sometimes you'd see him stagger to the end of the catwalk and just wish that the poor man could retire. There was one awful season when he couldn't walk properly and got along by gripping on to the models. One of them kissed him and left the imprint of her lipstick on his face. He kissed the other models but smeared them with his mouth so the lipstick rubbed off on their faces. It was macabre – like something out of Edgar Allan Poe. Catherine Deneuve stood up and gripped him firmly, leading him backstage again.'[14]

Speculation about Yves's condition, coupled with the surge of interest in the company's financial affairs after the flotation announcement, prompted the *Wall Street Journal* to send Philip Revzin, its Paris correspondent, to the March 1989 *prêt-à-porter* show. He then collaborated with Teri Agins, who covered the fashion industry for the paper in New York, on an article about what would happen to the Paris, Milan and New York fashion houses after the deaths of the designers who founded them. It was published on the front page of the paper on 7 April 1989 entitled, 'Saint Laurent Remains Idol of French Fashion But He Isn't Immortal', and described the fifty-two-year-old Yves as looking 'terrible . . . He limps and stands hunched over. His lips tremble as he struggles to greet friends.'[15]

A few days later Liz Smith, the gossip columnist of the *New York Post*, picked up on the story in her column under the headline 'Spooky News About King of Couture', claiming that the *Wall Street Journal* had speculated openly that Yves Saint Laurent had AIDS.[16] The Avenue Marceau switchboard was flooded with calls as reporters, suppliers and customers demanded to know whether the rumour was true.[17] Pierre Bergé was forced to issue an official denial, and the *New York Post* published a correction. It was like an eerie repetition of the stories of Yves's 'death' that had haunted him in the spring of 1977; then he had been deeply wounded at being sullied by such macabre speculation, but this time he barely seemed to notice.

Despite the 'AIDS scare' the preparations for the private placing and stock market flotation proceeded smoothly, so smoothly that the company would be ready to go public six months earlier than planned, in summer 1989. The private placing was also brought forward, and arrangements made to raise $180 million by selling shares to a carefully chosen group of investors, with most of the stock going to Cartier which, after the flotation, would own six per cent of Yves Saint Laurent. 'We didn't know Carlo de Benedetti at all, but we had a long relationship with Yves Saint Laurent and Pierre Bergé through our licensing arrangement,' explained Alain-Dominique Perrin. 'It had been a good business for us, so we decided to strengthen the relationship.'[18]

On 28 June 1989 Pierre Bergé called a press conference to announce the details of the flotation. Most French companies held such events in conference rooms at their corporate headquarters, or in grand Parisian hotels such as the Crillon or Bristol. Predictably Pierre Bergé plumped for a more spectacular venue in the futuristic setting of the gigantic glass Pyramid in the heart of the Louvre, designed by I. M. Pei, the Chinese-American architect. Protruding from the sandstone flags of the magnificent *Cour Napoléon*, the Pyramid was one of the most controversial of François Mitterrand's *Grands Projets*, with escalators leading down from the glazed entrance into an elegant reception area from which the museum's visitors filed through to the galleries.

Each of the journalists and stock market analysts who attended the press conference was given one of Yves's theatrical sketches as a memento, as well as the conventional prospectus explaining the financial details.[19] Yves was nowhere to be seen, but Pierre Bergé took centre-stage, describing the structure of the company and answering questions. 'He came over very well,' recalled George Graham of the *Financial Times*. 'Whereas someone like Bernard Arnault was seen as sticking to the financial issues, it was clear that Bergé was an efficient manager but he also had a certain amount of credibility on the creative side.'[20]

Yves Saint Laurent's share price was fixed at 853 francs, or $12.80, which would value the company at $500 million after it went public. The criterion that investors use to gauge the value of a company is called a 'multiple', which is calculated by dividing the share price by the profit expected to be made for each share the following year. The higher the multiple, the more favourable the stock market's view of a company's prospects. At that time a typical multiple for the companies quoted on the Paris stock market was ten or eleven times; Yves Saint Laurent's shares were relatively expensive at fifteen times, but the bankers and brokers advising Pierre were confident that the company merited such a high price because of its strong past performance and the prestige of the brand name.[21] Even the existence of the *commandite* did not seem to pose a problem: investors appeared to accept the argument that it was a necessary defensive measure to shelter the legendary Yves Saint Laurent from the rigours of corporate life.[22]

On the day after the press conference, Pierre Bergé issued a media statement: Yves Saint Laurent was cutting off all commercial links with China in protest at the treatment of the student demonstrators at Tiananmen Square in Beijing, many of whom had been killed or injured by government troops. Pierre announced that in protest, he was resigning the post of special adviser to the Chinese government on the cultural and textile industries, which he had been given after the 1985 retrospective, and that the company would cease supplies of perfumes to the newly opened YSL counter at the Friendship Stores in Beijing. He also called a halt to plans to build a cosmetics factory in China and declared that the old Rive Gauche boutique on rue de Tournon would be used to provide emergency accommodation for Chinese political refugees streaming into Paris. Yves Saint Laurent might be about to become a publicly quoted company but Pierre Bergé, the man who had written to French industrialists urging them to vote socialist in the 1988 presidential elections, clearly saw no reason to change the way he ran the business.

By 6 July, the day when Yves Saint Laurent was due to go public, its stockbrokers had received applications to buy 103 million shares, over 250 times more than the 400,000 shares which were available.[23] Under the French stock market rules, if an issue attracted applications for over 120 times the number of shares available, it had to be withdrawn and re-presented to the market, generally at a higher price. Pierre and his advisers decided to re-present the issue a few days later at the same price, but asked applicants to pay in advance for their shares, a ruse designed to weed out the 'stags', or speculators who applied for shares in popular new issues hoping to sell them afterwards at a profit. Asking for advance payment generally limited the number of applications to the people who genuinely wanted to invest in the company; but Yves Saint Laurent's shares were so sought-after that even when prospective investors were asked to pay up front, it attracted applications for 10.75 million shares, twenty-seven times more than the number on offer.[24]

Yves Saint Laurent had become the first French fashion house ever to be quoted on the stock market, and the flotation was a resounding success. Sales and profits were rising reassuringly, as was the share price.[25] Pierre's audacious bid to buy back the perfumes seemed to have paid off. Carlo de Benedetti had pocketed a handsome profit on his investment, and the YSL group was well on the way towards repaying its debts.[26] And finally, the company was safe, thanks to Alain Minc's *société en commandite par actions* device, which would enable Pierre Bergé to keep Bernard Arnault and any other 'wolves in cashmere clothing' at bay.

It was a considerable *coup* for Pierre Bergé, and all the more impressive as he had orchestrated the flotation at a time when his new post as president of the Opéra de Paris was demanding a great deal of his time and attention. His priority at the Opéra was to ensure that the Bastille opera house was ready for its official opening by President Mitterrand at a gala on 13 July 1989, the night before the celebration of the bicentenary of the French Revolution, and for its first full operatic production, a performance of Mozart's *Don Giovanni*, conducted by Daniel Barenboim, the Opéra's artistic director, in January the following year.

Even before Pierre's arrival the Bastille project had been plagued by problems, starting with the choice of architect. Architects were invited to bid for the commission in an open competition, as they were for all the *Grands Projets*, but the Bastille selection committee reportedly chose a set of plans as the winner thinking they were the work of the distinguished American architect, Richard Meier, only to discover that they belonged to the relatively inexperienced Brazilian, Carlos Ott. 'That's what people say, but who knows whether it's true?' observed Pierre. 'All I know is that when I arrived there, it was nothing but a hole in the ground.'[27] By the beginning of 1989 he had harangued the builders into making up for some lost time, but with less than six months to go before the opening gala, construction was still running behind schedule and the project threatened to exceed its $400 million budget.

There were also problems on the administrative front. Pierre arrived at the Opéra with a doughty reputation at Yves Saint Laurent and the Chambre Syndicale, so it came as no surprise to the staff when heads started rolling. The administrative director and technical director were among the first to go, then he clashed with Daniel Barenboim, the famous conductor whose appointment as artistic and musical director of the Opéra de Paris had been seen as a *coup* to put the Bastille on a par with La Scala in Milan and the Metropolitan Opera in New York. Barenboim was hired by François Léotard, the centre-right culture minister who took over from Jack Lang during the *cohabitation* government of 1986 to 1988 when the socialists were out of power, and he was lured to Paris with a four-year contract which included $1 million a year in salary and conducting fees. Anxious to cut the Opéra's overheads, Pierre asked him to accept a reduction in pay to $650,000 a year, and either to relinquish responsibility for artistic direction, or curtail his contract from four to two years. He refused and on Friday, 13 January 1989, Pierre Bergé released a statement saying that Daniel Barenboim was no longer the artistic director of the Opéra de Bastille.

He had fired one of the most powerful and well-connected men in classical music, and neither Daniel Barenboim, nor his friends, intended to cede control of the Opéra de Bastille to him without a fight. Barenboim opened fire in the press accusing Bergé of 'bad faith' and 'incompetence'.[28] He then appealed for support to François Mitterrand and Jack Lang, hinting to the media that he was being treated as a political scapegoat: hired by the right, and fired by the left. Pierre Boulez, the prominent French conductor who was a close friend of Barenboim's, resigned his seat on the board in protest and persuaded ten of the world's most famous musicians and singers to sign a petition to President Mitterrand threatening *not* to work at the Bastille under Pierre Bergé. The French press hinted, but never proved, that the signatories included Jessye Norman, Montserrat Caballé, Riccardo Muti and Placido Domingo. Pierre retaliated by leaking the details of Barenboim's $1 million contract to the newspapers. Years later Pierre Boulez, still bitter about the affair, told the *New Yorker* that Bergé was out of his depth. 'The political people kept telling us he knew something. They said: "But he was in charge of the Musical Mondays at the Athénée." What he did was engage singers. That's easy: I call, I pay, you come. Musically he had no idea.'[29]

Not only did Pierre have 'a hole in the ground' to fill at Place de la Bastille, he had to find a new artistic and musical director, no easy task given that half the obvious candidates were boycotting the Opéra de Paris, and the other half were too frightened to take the post for fear of offending Daniel Barenboim. After months of rejections he finally found someone willing to accept in Myung-Whun Chung, a thirty-six-year-old South Korean conductor, who was a rising star in American music circles, but virtually unknown in France.[30] Chung met Pierre in March when he flew to Paris to discuss the possibility of conducting Verdi's *Don Carlos*, which had been hastily rescheduled as the opening production in place of Barenboim's version of *Don Giovanni*. To his astonishment, after a brief discussion about the arrangements for *Don Carlos*, Pierre Bergé offered him the position of musical director.

Such an impetuous gesture was completely in character for Pierre, who was as doctrinaire and decisive in his handling of the Opéra as in his management of the fashion house. The pragmatist in him knew that the Barenboim clique had destroyed his chances of persuading an established conductor to take over the Bastille, and that the sensible solution was to find someone young, promising and so hungry for success that they were willing to take a gamble. That scenario also touched the sentimental side of Pierre's nature, as he still liked to see himself as a nurturer of new talent, whether it was Yves Saint Laurent in fashion or Myung-Whun Chung in music.

The situation was less straightforward for Chung. With less than four months to go before the official opening, and ten months before the first operatic production, all the Opéra de Bastille consisted of was an unfinished building with an inadequate administrative staff and depleted orchestra. Some of the most famous names in opera had cancelled their contracts and were threatening to boycott, with the result that not a single singer was contracted to perform there. 'My closest friends, even my family members, said I shouldn't even be talking to them about the opening production,' recalled Chung. 'Just don't get involved with this crazy mess. Why would you want to do that?'[31] It was a gamble, but Chung took it. One commentator likened his appointment to 'taking command of the Titanic after it hit the iceberg'.[32]

Pierre's impetuosity paid off. The conscientious and quietly charming Chung won the respect of the Opéra orchestra, and rustled up an impressive list of singers for the official opening of the Bastille on 13 July 1989, while Pierre Bergé harried the construction crews into completing the building in time. The American *diva*, Jessye Norman, agreed to honour her promise to sing the *Marseillaise* at the finale of the following day's triumphal procession along the Avenue des Champs-Élysées, which was to be the highlight of the bicentennial celebration, although she, like other stars, was still boycotting the Bastille.

The Opéra erupted again in early autumn when Pierre clashed with Rudolf Nureyev. A row had been brewing for some months, with Pierre complaining that Nureyev did not spend enough time attending to his duties as artistic director of the Ballet de Paris. The conflict came to a head when Nureyev signed a lucrative two-year contract to perform in a travelling production of *The King and I*. The old Opéra management had allowed him to slope off on other projects, but Pierre called his bluff, and after weeks of mutual abuse in the press he announced that Rudolf Nureyev was relinquishing his responsibilities as artistic director and would become 'chief choreographer'. Pierre had taken on a man who was as powerful and respected in his sphere as Daniel Barenboim was in his; but this time his opponent was someone he had known intimately and, by all accounts, liked and admired, since 1961 when they met during Nureyev's first trip to Paris with the Kirov Ballet before his defection to the West. He even had a photograph of him in his office.

Temperamental though Nureyev could be, he had achieved a great deal at the Ballet de Paris: overhauling the antiquated company, modernizing the repertoire and nurturing new stars, including the brilliant young ballerina, Sylvie Guillem. 'It was thanks to him,' said Alan Robertson, the British dance critic, 'that the Ballet de Paris became a world class company again.'[33] To make matters worse, at the time of his dismissal Rudolf Nureyev was HIV positive, something Pierre Bergé must have known as his condition had been diagnosed five years before and was, by then, an open secret among balletomanes. While some prominent homosexuals still refused to publicly acknowledge their sexuality, Pierre had always been admirably honest about his. He played a prominent part in France's AIDS campaign long before it became a fashionable cause, and founded an AIDS charity of his own, ARCAT-SIDA, which made his high-handed treatment of Rudolf Nureyev seem all the more surprising.

It seems too simplistic to assume that Pierre was wreaking revenge on Nureyev for his intimacy with Yves in the 1970s. Even if they did not actually have a sexual relationship, the two men were openly flirtatious, often in front of Pierre, which he must have found hurtful as well as humiliating. But such flirtations, even when publicly conducted, were perfectly acceptable in their circle and Pierre was too astute to attack Nureyev out of sexual pique, particularly when his credibility as the president of the Opéra de Paris was at stake. His behaviour looked more like a manifestation of power, a blatant demonstration that Pierre Bergé was now too important a figure to allow personal considerations to affect his treatment of anyone, even an old friend like Rudolf Nureyev.

Other friends of Nureyev's were outraged on his behalf, not least Guy and Marie-Hélène de Rothschild. Staunch conservatives, they had been none too pleased at Pierre Bergé's drift into the Mitterrand camp, and relations with him had already cooled because of it. They were also deeply attached to Rudolf Nureyev, whom Marie-Hélène often invited to spend Christmas with them at their estate, Château de Ferrières. The Rothschilds closed ranks with Nureyev against Pierre, who found himself frozen out by the couple whose friendship had once been so important to him.

These days he had other preoccupations. There was his friendship with the president, with their Sunday lunches at L'Assiette or another favourite Paris restaurant, and weekends at the Mitterrands' rural retreat in Les Landes. And there were Pierre's responsibilities at SOS Racisme. 'He was always very involved, very interested in whatever we were doing,' recalled Harlem Désir. 'Whenever we needed money for a special event like a concert, Yves Saint Laurent gave much more than any other company. Its donations were in a different league to the rest. When we had our annual dinner for our *parrains* (chief supporters), Pierre Bergé was always there, usually with the President of the Republic.'[34] In addition Pierre had his Chambre Syndicale duties to attend to, and the dozen or so boards he sat on, including the Cartier contemporary art foundation and France-Liberté, a human rights charity associated with the first lady, Danielle Mitterrand.

Pierre Bergé, the man who once said he devoted 'twenty-six hours a day' to looking after Yves Saint Laurent,[35] still saw his charge most days when they were in Paris and spoke to him on the phone even if they were not, but it was not the all-consuming commitment he had given him before. 'When you meet, when you work with someone like Yves, it's a full-time job,' he told the *New Yorker*. 'For years and years I had to support Yves. Support him in the French sense and the English sense. *Voilà!* I had given all my energy to him and all of a sudden I gave a little bit to Mitterrand, I gave a little bit to Harlem Désir, I gave a little bit to the Opéra. All that I took from him.'[36]

After years of self-imposed seclusion, there was no one with whom Yves could replace Pierre and the other friends who were slipping away. By then his circle had shrunk to a handful of intimates, whom he preferred to see one at a time, finding even small groups too much of a strain, and the peripheral figures who had once hung out on the fringes of his circle, like Jeanloup Sieff, had not seen or spoken to him for years. There were still bonds between individual members of the old Saint Laurent set, such as Clara and Paloma, but Pierre had fallen out with Nureyev and the Rothschilds; and Loulou and Thadée were absorbed by life with their daughter, Anna. Rudolf Nureyev was now very ill, and Andy Warhol had died in 1987, after completing one of his final commissions, a series of silkscreen portraits of Yves's beloved Moujik.

Professionally, as well as personally, Yves seemed painfully isolated. His repertoire of classics had passed muster in the mid-1980s, but seemed hopelessly out of synch with the softer, more introspective mood of the end of the decade. The Berlin Wall fell in 1989, paving the way for the reunification of Germany, and the collapse of the old communist régimes that had dominated Eastern Europe since World War II. Just as Mao-tse Tung's Cultural Revolution had heralded the end of the giddy early 1960s, and the start of the reflective hippy era, so the fall of the Berlin Wall signified a similar shift in values at the end of the 1980s.

The art world swung away from the stylized work of Julian Schnabel and Jeff Koons towards less marketable media, such as installation art, and fringe shows like *Freeze*, an exhibition organized by the young British painter, Damien Hirst, in a disused industrial space in London's Docklands. The latest European youth craze was 'raves', impromptu parties held in disused warehouses or open fields, where thousands of people danced to the repetitive beat of computer-generated dance music into the early hours of the morning, spurred on by the artificial energy of the hip new drug, Ecstasy. Ravers wore whatever was easiest to dance in – T-shirts, track pants, trainers and ballcaps – which made the clothes on the Paris runways look staid, stiff and outdated; as did the sportswear and gold chains of the rap and hip-hop stars who were the new youth cult figures in the United States. 'Fashion today is on the cusp of change,' wrote Suzy Menkes, the British journalist who had succeeded Hebe Dorsey as fashion editor of the *International Herald Tribune*, on the eve of the autumn 1989 ready-to-wear collections. 'The hard-edged, mannish silhouette is in retreat. But no one is quite sure what will replace it.'[37]

One suggestion came from Romeo Gigli, the soulful Italian designer who showed his artisanal velvets and raw silks in Paris to wild applause that season.[38] Another was the all-white collection unveiled by the Turkish-born designer, Rifat Ozbek, inspired by the fad for 'New Age' chants and crystals. Helmut Lang, an Austrian designer who had started showing in Paris, favoured a lean, almost futuristic form of tailoring. The young Belgian designers, Martin Margiela and Ann Demeulemeester, proposed a stronger antidote to 1980s excess in their deliberately downbeat collections of rough-hewn garments with raw edges, fraying seams and dangling threads that the press described as fashion's equivalent to the deconstructivist architecture of Rem Koolhaus and Coop Himmelblau, calling it '*la nouvelle pauvreté*', or the 'new poverty' look.

Other designers were at least trying to reflect the changing climate, but Yves Saint Laurent stuck stubbornly to the same course. In the good seasons when he was engaged by his *couture* work, even his least appropriate designs were flawless in taste and technique, such as the $100,000 beaded jackets emblazoned with images of Van Gogh's

Sunflowers and *Irises* that he unveiled, apparently without a hint of irony, in the *couture* show that followed 'Black Friday'. At a recent *couture* show Yves had delighted his audience by presenting two dozen different versions of his classic black *smoking*, each with satin lapels, but distinctive details. However, his detractors saw such self-referential exercises as inexcusable self-indulgence, and the reviews of the Rive Gauche range remained unenthused until the October 1989 show when they were openly hostile. An embarrassed silence fell on the audience as a series of the see-through blouses that had caused a sensation when Yves first designed them, so much more successfully in 1968, appeared on the runway. 'What did it mean?' speculated Suzy Menkes in the *Herald Tribune*, suggesting that 'someone else' was responsible for them. 'It was as though Saint Laurent was determined to prove that he was alive and kicking against the staid image his ready-to-wear has been projecting in recent years. It made a patchy show.'[39] Her report was published on the front page of the newspaper, where reviews of Yves's past triumphs had often appeared, but this time it was there because the collection was so weak.

The audience was as appalled by Yves's physical appearance as by the clothes. They had become accustomed to seeing him stumbling groggily along the catwalk, but that season he seemed in particularly poor shape. The Paris gossips openly speculated not on whether, but *when* Pierre Bergé would name a *dauphin*, a crown prince to take over from him. 'It was heartbreaking to see Yves at that time,' said a friend who had known him since his Dior days. 'He seemed so sad and so lonely, staggering around as though he was in a daze. He didn't seem able to focus on anything. There was nothing left of the handsome young man he used to be. He looked like a blown-out shell of his old self, and it was obvious he was suffering horribly, mentally and physically.'

Diamonds and Spades
1990–1991

When he mounted the runway at the end of his next show in January 1990, Yves looked like a new man, slimmer and smiling, with a hint of his old vigour. He had stopped drinking that winter, shedding a stone in excess weight and losing some of the ungainly puffiness around his face. The competition was stiff that season. Christian Lacroix staged a jolly variety show at the Opéra Comique with Sylvie Guillem and a troupe of dancing bears to launch his perfume, C'est La Vie!. Karl Lagerfeld drew praise for his Chanel show, where he paired long jackets with wispy skirts in silk chiffon as an expensive, but exquisite take on *la nouvelle pauvreté*. Chanel also hit the headlines when Lagerfeld unveiled the Bardotesque blonde model, Claudia Schiffer, whom he had chosen as his new 'star' in place of Inès de la Fressange.

It was a vintage *couture* week, but the Saint Laurent show topped them all. Yves had created a collection of the rigorously elegant clothes at which he excelled and that his devoted *femmes d'un certain âge* loved to wear. The women in the audience clapped and cheered, smiling appreciatively, as they recognized his *homages* to the writers, painters, singers, actresses and socialites who had inspired his work over the years. Some of the designs evoked memories of past collections. The slinky black sequined slip inspired by the beaming Zizi Jeanmaire was reminiscent of the daring mini-dresses Yves had presented in the 1960s; and Coco Chanel's snappy navy-blue suit harked back to his first public tribute to her, and to Arthur Penn's *Bonnie and Clyde*, in the collection of little black dresses and suits he had shown in 1967 when Chanel was still alive. At the end of the show Pierre Bergé did not need to coax him out on to the runway as he had in recent seasons; this time Yves bounded out happily to acknowledge the applause, before Catherine Deneuve, Betty Catroux, Nan Kempner and the other *fidèles* dashed backstage to embrace him. 'Not for ten years has he sent out such a collection,' pronounced Suzy Menkes on the front page of the next day's *Herald Tribune*, 'breathtaking in its variety, pure in its conception, whimsical in its fantasy, lyrical in its colouring.'[1]

Cheered by the compliments for his work, Yves hosted an impromptu party at rue de Babylone that night, the first time for years that he had entertained on the evening after a show. But in the early hours of the morning he was shaken awake by a fire in his bedroom. The *valets de chambre* came to his aid, and swiftly extinguished the blaze, which turned out to have been caused by a minor electricity fault. Yves was helicoptered to Normandy, to spend a few days of seclusion at Château Gabriel, and as his condition was little better when he arrived back in Paris, off he went again, this time to Villa Oasis in Marrakesh. There had been black bouts for Yves before, but this one was worse. After years of illness and despondency, his spirit was shattered and his insecurities so acute that the accident at rue de Babylone rekindled his old anxieties. At fifty-three Yves Saint Laurent, praised throughout his adult life as one of the most brilliant men of his generation, was trapped in a masochistic cycle of addiction and depressive fantasies, and fearful of being abandoned by Pierre Bergé, on whom he had depended for thirty years.

When the servants at Villa Oasis sent reports of Yves's conduct back to Pierre in Paris, they made alarming reading. Yves had locked himself in a room of Villa Oasis, where he was downing two bottles of whisky a day and refusing to eat, flinging himself into a fury at the suggestion that it was time to return to Paris to work on the Rive Gauche collection due to be shown on 21 March. As the show drew closer, the reports grew more alarming, and Yves still refused to return.

Someone needed to be sent over to Morocco to bring him back, but Pierre Bergé was too busy. The Opéra de Bastille was preparing for its first full production, Myung-Whun Chung's version of Hector

Berlioz's *Les Troyens* on 17 March 1990. The new opera house was nearly ready, but still dogged by problems, and there were various organizational difficulties and technical hitches to be tackled before the opening. Pierre decided that he should stay in Paris and asked Brigitte, Yves's youngest sister, to fly out to Marrakesh and remonstrate with him.

When Brigitte arrived, she found Yves in a dreadful state, unshaven and unkempt, having hacked his hair off in a rage. It was inconceivable that he could be patched together in time for the Rive Gauche show on 21 March so she and the servants bundled him into the Lear jet. When they landed in Paris, Yves and his party were rushed through the high security area of the airport, using the closed corridors generally reserved for dangerous criminals or the critically ill, to make sure that no one would see him. Yves Saint Laurent was taken to the American Hospital in Neuilly-sur-Seine, the scene of so many of his 'rest cures', on Saturday, 17 March 1990. After examining him Dr Michel Prendeville told Pierre Bergé that it would be impossible to release Yves in time for the show that Wednesday, as he needed to be confined to hospital for several weeks, perhaps for a couple of months.

A few hours after Yves's admission, Pierre Bergé settled in his seat to watch the curtain rise at the Opéra de Bastille for the opening act of Chung's *Les Troyens*. It was a poignant choice for the Bastille's opening night. One of the finest nineteenth-century French operas, *Les Troyens* tells the story of Aeneas's flight from the fallen city of Troy and his ill-starred love for Dido, Queen of Carthage. Torn between devotion to Dido and his duty to appease the gods by rebuilding a new empire in place of the Trojan dynasty, Aeneas abandons Dido and, in despair, she kills herself. This was to be the first time that the opera was performed in its entirety in Paris and the Bastille auditorium was filled to capacity. There were a few technical hitches during the performance – a lift broke down and a wayward piece of scenery hit the stage, nearly injuring a singer – but the music was wonderful and Chung's conducting a delight. *Les Troyens* was a triumph: for Myung-Whun Chung, the hastily assembled company of the Opéra de Bastille, and for Pierre Bergé.

Two days later, Pierre Bergé arrived in his office at Avenue Marceau to pore over the glowing reviews of *Les Troyens*[2] and prepared to issue a press release saying that Yves would not be attending the Rive Gauche show that Wednesday as he was suffering from 'overwhelming nervous exhaustion'. The YSL share price fell by 20 francs to 1040 francs the next day.

The official explanation from the company was that Yves had finished his sketches for that season's collection before his collapse, leaving Anne-Marie and Loulou to prepare the final designs from his outlines. In reality, they and the other assistants had assembled the preliminary designs as usual, put them into production and pulled together the outfits for the show without going through the formality of consulting Yves about the finished collection. The presentation was a lacklustre affair. Lucienne, who had not yet been allowed to see her son in hospital, sat in the front row as usual, flanked by Michèle and Brigitte, but there was a disquieting number of empty seats, and for the finale there was a trickle of polite applause rather than the customary standing ovation. It was, as Suzy Menkes noted in the *International Herald Tribune*, 'a sad affair' that brought fashion week to a close 'not with a bang, but a whimper'.[3]

Yves Saint Laurent stayed in hospital for three weeks. For the first few days he was forcibly confined to his room; he then agreed to stay and complete the course of treatment. Conditions in the American Hospital were very different to those at Val-de-Grâce, the mental institution where he was placed by the army thirty years before. Architecturally it was undistinguished, a typical postwar medical complex with a motley assortment of annexes and extensions tacked on to the main building; but the rooms were comfortably furnished, and the windows looked out across trees and lawns into the leafy suburb of Neuilly-sur-Seine. The staff were well trained, pleasant and polite; many of them had dealt with Yves before, as he had paid numerous visits to the American Hospital over the years for various attempts at detoxification.

Sometimes those treatments had worked for a while, at other times not at all, but Yves always slipped back into his spiral of addiction and suicidal fantasies, his favourite being weighing himself down with a heavy bronze sculpture and plunging into the River Seine. This time seemed to be different. When he was bundled into hospital Yves was in a dreadful state, mentally bruised, and physically drained by the huge quantity of alcohol he had drunk; as the treatment took effect, he was prey to violent nightmares and terrifying hallucinations. 'I felt horrible emotions during the cure,' Yves told the American writer, Edmund White, 'and that frightened me.'[4]

After his discharge Yves appeared to have aged ten years. The weight he lost during the winter piled back on, and his face puffed out around the jowls again. His hair, freshly grown after he had hacked it off in Marrakesh, was tinted a tangibly artificial shade of auburn; and his once mellifluous voice crackled like an old man's. Often he appeared to be in physical pain. The left side of his body looked stiff and rigid. Yves seemed to have difficulty controlling his left arm, clawing his hand and holding it guardedly behind his back with the right one. His walk was unsteady, as though he were afraid of falling over. From time to time his face twitched, and his mouth muscles were so weak that he sometimes seemed to have difficulty speaking.

A prominent television journalist who had known Yves for many years filmed an interview with him a few months after he came out of hospital, and later edited swathes of footage from the finished film. 'It was clear that sometimes he was suffering physically. He couldn't control his facial muscles. It wasn't very pleasant to watch and I didn't want him to be shown like that on television. That might make me a bad journalist in a way, but I didn't want people to see that side of him. Afterwards I sat with the editor and said "Cut there, there and there." I took out all the footage where he looked bad. We've still got the film. When he dies I might make a documentary about his life and explain how ill he was so people can see how badly he was suffering, but until then those clips will stay in the archive.'

After the Marrakesh crisis Yves was watched more closely than in the past. The servants, chauffeurs and bodyguards who looked after him reported back to Pierre about where he went and what he did. Once the doctors charged with looking after him were tucked discreetly backstage during the fashion shows, under instructions to emerge only if they were needed, but now his retinue was ever-present, and Pierre treated Yves as though he were a helpless infant: snapping instructions to the bodyguards, or deputing a trusted employee, such as Christophe Girard, to look after him at official events. 'Saint Laurent didn't seem to have a mind of his own,' said someone who worked with them after Yves's hospitalization. 'Pierre Bergé told him what to do, even where to stand. He'd tell the bodyguards where to move him and then gesture for them to take him to another place. Saint Laurent did what he was told. He didn't seem particularly unhappy about it. He seemed so out of it, that it was impossible to tell whether he felt anything at all.'

Yves was spotted dining out in Paris with Jacques Grange and Betty Catroux a couple of times that summer, but otherwise stayed out of sight. After years of seclusion his public appearances were so rare that a report of him dining at the Ritz-Espadon made an item for *Women's Wear Daily*'s gossip column. He looked pale and shaken at his *couture* show that July, still showing the strain of his breakdown. The audience gave him the usual standing ovation, but more out of sympathy than admiration, and the show received tepid reviews,[5] as did his efforts the following season which Suzy Menkes of the *Herald Tribune* likened to 'a downmarket travel brochure'.[6]

Whether the collections were good or bad had almost become irrelevant. Even *les fidèles*, the women who loyally applauded Yves from their front-row seats, had abandoned hope of Yves resurrecting his old role as an innovator. Betty Catroux talked tactfully of the distinction between Yves's recent work and the time when they were young and 'he was still interested',[7] but she and her fellow *fidèles* had grown middle-aged with Yves and preferred his classics to the old show-stopping innovations. 'I remember reading an article in *Newsweek* that said something like "Yves is greying with his clients . . .",' said Marie-José Lepicard, who had followed his career since she was a junior on Paris *Vogue* in the 1950s and was now one of France's most influential fashion commentators as the fashion correspondent of the France 2 television channel. 'Well I'm greying too. The style of my generation of French women is Yves Saint Laurent. I can't imagine wearing anything else. Sometimes I think I'll live and die in the style of Saint Laurent.'[8]

For her and the other fashion journalists in their fifties and sixties who had followed him throughout his career, even Yves's physical deterioration added to his allure. 'There's a great tenderness towards him because he has given us so much,' said Janie Samet, fashion editor of *Le Figaro*. 'He is so fragile, so delicate, like a frail beautiful butterfly. His ill-health adds to his stature, making him even more precious because we are all frightened of losing him.'[9] But the new *grandes dames* of fashion journalism, such as Suzy Menkes of the *Herald Tribune* and Anna Wintour of American *Vogue*, were women in their forties who, having started their careers when Yves Saint Laurent was already established as the world's greatest fashion designer, were emotionally engaged with their own discoveries. Menkes, who tapped her columns into a laptop computer from the front row of the shows, championed Christian Lacroix, while Wintour was a devotee of Karl Lagerfeld at Chanel, as was Liz Tilberis, her opposite number at British *Vogue*.

The next generation of fashion writers and assistants in their twenties and thirties were too young to have seen Yves's early *coups*, and all they knew of Yves himself was the bleary, bloated figure who hauled himself uncertainly along the catwalk each season after presenting collections which, at their best, seemed staid and, at their worst, verged on vulgarity. Some newspapers, less constrained by the demands of their advertising departments than magazines, dropped the Saint Laurent show from their Paris fashion week reports as it was no longer deemed indispensable for an overview of the coming season's trends, and if Yves's work was mentioned, the comments were often critical. 'As usual the audience gave Saint Laurent a standing ovation,' wrote Cathy Horyn of the *Washington Post* after another uninspired show. 'But was it for the past, or the present?'[10]

For once Pierre Bergé had more pressing concerns than Yves's reviews. Carlo de Benedetti had told him that, reluctantly, he was selling his 14.9 per cent stake in Yves Saint Laurent. The reason for the sale was Cerus's ill-fated attempt in 1988 to take over Société Générale de Belgique, a rambling conglomerate which was one of Belgium's largest companies. The bid had the hallmarks of Alain Minc and Carlo de Benedetti's swashbuckling style, starting with a stock market raid, and continuing with fierce attacks on the Belgian group's management. Until then Générale, one of the oldest and best-connected companies in Europe, was regarded as bid-proof, or at least it was in the days when financial affairs were conducted in a gentlemanly manner. The idea of Carlo de Benedetti and Alain Minc taking it over seemed little short of heresy to Europe's corporate establishment, which promptly closed ranks against them. Suez, the old-established French conglomerate whose chairman Renaud de la Genière was a former governor of the Banque de France, mounted a counter-bid against Cerus, and Générale's other shareholders took sides, mainly Suez's side.[11]

After months of machinations Suez finally won control, leaving Cerus with a useless seat on the Société Générale de Belgique board, together with a fifteen per cent shareholding which was rapidly losing value because of the steady decline in the share price, and debts of almost $1 billion. By spring 1990 Carlo de Benedetti's fortunes were so low that the *Economist* published an article entitled 'Can Carlo come back?'[12] Six months later the magazine wondered whether Alain Minc's career could survive the Générale de Belgique debacle in an article entitled *La Grande Désillusion*, a pun on *La Grande Illusion*, the title of one of Minc's books.[13]

Desperate to reduce Cerus's $1 billion debts, Alain Minc had no choice but to sell assets, including its shares in Yves Saint Laurent. The news was a blow to Pierre who had genuinely enjoyed working with Minc and De Benedetti, and was proud of the aplomb with which they had bought back the perfumes. It seemed particularly harsh that Cerus should have to sell at a time when the business was doing so well and was back on course financially after the flotation. Now, thanks to the ill-fated Société Générale de Belgique bid, their carefully-laid plans for the future were in shreds. 'They'd dreamt up the most incredible wheeze with De Benedetti's help – and very nearly pulled it off,' said one observer. 'It was brilliant. They bought the perfumes, plus they kept control of the company. They almost got away with it. They probably would have done if Carlo de Benedetti hadn't messed up in Belgium.'

Years later Pierre Bergé seemed to bear no ill will against Carlo de Benedetti, indeed he was still grateful to him for his help with the Charles of the Ritz deal. 'He did us an incredible service in helping us buy the perfumes. I could never have done it without him.'[14] But it was proving more difficult than he expected to find a buyer for Cerus's shares. Pierre had hoped that Cartier would step into the breach, but Alain-Dominique Perrin turned him down. 'We'd had a successful relationship with Yves Saint Laurent, but fashion wasn't our business. We've never wanted to get too heavily involved in it.'[15] Other likely buyers were dishearteningly hard to find and the situation became even worse after 2 August 1990 when the Iraqi leader, Saddam Hussein, declared war on Kuwait.

The Gulf War was disastrous for the luxury industry. Air travel ground to a halt in the West for fear of Arab terrorist attacks, cutting off an important source of duty-free sales. France, with its large population of North African *émigrés*, was a prime terrorist target and the Paris police received over one hundred bomb threats a day. The fighting escalated in January when the United States and its allies sent troops into Kuwait to repulse the Iraqis. *Couture* week was a wash-out. The Manhattan socialites, who usually Concorded over for a spot of self-indulgent shopping, stayed at home in the States for safety; even the models were too frightened to fly to Paris for a few days of very well-paid work. By the time the conflict ended in March, Yves Saint Laurent, like its competitors, had lost a significant chunk of the year's sales. Pierre Bergé prepared to warn shareholders that the Gulf War would have a negative effect on the company's performance in 1991 when he announced its 1990 financial results in April.[16]

Yves Saint Laurent's share price had fallen steadily during the Gulf War and with no buyer in sight for the Cerus stake, Carlo de Benedetti needed to act swiftly. Shortly after *couture* week he told Pierre that unless they found a purchaser within the next few weeks, he would have to auction off his shares. Pierre panicked. If the shares were auctioned they could fall into the unfriendly hands of someone like Bernard Arnault, and Yves Saint Laurent might then face the same pressures as Christian Dior and LVMH. In theory the *société en commandite* mechanism meant that whoever bought the stake would not be able to take over the company without his and Yves's consent, but even so a troublesome investor could make their lives intolerable, by challenging Pierre's decisions and attempting to erode his authority. Convinced that all he needed was a little more time to find a friendly buyer once trading conditions improved, Pierre decided that he and Yves would buy Cerus's shares as a short-term solution. 'I didn't want to buy the stake. We didn't need any more shares. We already had control of the company. But at the time, after the crash, it was very difficult. There weren't any buyers around.'[17]

Over the years Yves and Pierre had earned tens of millions of dollars, but they lived the surreally extravagant lives of the super-rich. They owned two houses in Marrakesh, Villa Oasis and the Dar es

Saada guest house, a château in Normandy and a New York pent-house. Back in Paris, Yves spent most of his time in the rue de Babylone duplex, while Pierre, although still resident at the Hôtel Lutétia, was renovating an apartment on nearby rue Bonaparte. The latest addition to their properties was the stone-built house he had bought in the pretty Provençal village of Saint-Rémy, where Princess Caroline of Monaco and Jacques Grange already owned rural retreats. All these properties were fully staffed and impeccably maintained: as were the cars, the helicopter and the Lear jet. The cost of sealing Yves off from the world in neurasthenic retreat was colossal; then there were his whims, such as the sumptuous jewels he liked to give his mother, and having special supplies of his favourite Uncle Ben's Rice flown out from France to Morocco. *Don Magnifico* lived in similarly sumptuous style, insisting on the best tables in the most prestigious Parisian restaurants, and bidding high in the auction rooms. Even their pets were expensive, particularly Moujik, who at one time had a nanny to attend to his needs. Over the years they had made financial provision for various friends and employees, as well as for Yves's relatives. Loulou's mother, Maxime de la Falaise, was given an annual pension, and Pierre still paid occasional hospital bills and other expenses for loyal members of staff, as well as for Loulou's rest cures.

Their princely lifestyle left them with relatively little spare capital, which meant that Pierre would have to borrow most of the money they needed to meet Carlo de Benedetti's terms. Cerus was asking for 950 francs for each share in its 14.9 per cent stake, well above the 853 francs the public had paid for their shares when the company joined the stock market eighteen months before, and a level that the shares had not reached since the previous August at the start of the Gulf War. On 1 April 1991 the shares traded at 797 francs, nearly sixteen per cent less than Carlo de Benedetti was demanding.

Pierre arranged bank loans for 545 million francs, or $99 million, borrowing most of the money from Neuflize Schlumberger Mallet, a small investment bank. As he needed the money at short notice, and expected to be able to repay it fairly swiftly, the loans were structured on a short-term basis at a relatively high rate of interest with provision for the banks to demand the repayment of part of the capital under certain circumstances. The deal with Carlo de

Benedetti was concluded in April 1991 just in time to avoid an auction, but too late to save Alain Minc who resigned from Cerus a few weeks before. Having already dealt a devastating blow to Carlo de Benedetti's reputation and crippled Cerus with debt, the Générale de Belgique bid had cost Alain Minc his job as well as lumbering Yves Saint Laurent and Pierre Bergé with shares they did not need in a company they already controlled, and huge personal loans.

Once the Gulf War was over, Pierre was certain the luxury market would revive and he would be able to find an empathetic buyer; instead sales remained sluggish as the economic recession deepened in the United States and United Kingdom. The 'yuppie' bankers, brokers and advertising executives who had spent their high salaries on expensive clothes and cosmetics now faced the threat of redundancy; even those who had managed to cling to their jobs were too nervous about the future to risk running up credit-card debts as they had done so blithely a few years before. The key economic influence over consumer spending is the level of 'real interest rates', that is the difference between interest rates and inflation. If the former are low and the latter high, as was the case during the 1970s oil shocks, consumers tend to continue spending money, because there is little to be gained by saving it, particularly at a time when prices are rising rapidly. But if the relationship is reversed, as it was in the early 1990s, and interest rates are higher than inflation, there is more incentive to save money and less to spend it.

Soaring 'real interest rates' affected every area of the economy, but the fashion and beauty markets were also destabilized by the financial difficulties of their largest customers, the North American department store chains, many of which were burdened by leveraged buy-out debt. Bonwit Teller and B. Altman filed for bankruptcy protection, and Robert Campeau, the Canadian tycoon who had bought a string of stores in the States during the 1980s, sold Brooks Brothers and I. Magnin, and then put Bloomingdale's up for sale. Fashion and cosmetics companies faced a difficult choice between refusing to supply goods to stores unless they were paid in cash on delivery, or running the risk of incurring bad debts, and losing their merchandise, if the retailers went bust.

At the same time as sales were slowing, the cost of running a company like Yves Saint Laurent was escalating, not least in perfumes, which for years had been one of the most profitable parts of the business. The companies that had expanded their beauty interests during the 1980s – Unilever, LVMH and L'Oréal – were introducing new scents to recoup their investment, presenting them in a softer, more subdued style than the glitzy fragrances that had sold so well in the 1980s.[18] Calvin Klein followed Obsession with Eternity and then Escape, and Christian Dior's successor to Poison went by the naturalistic name of Dune. However, these 'gentle' scents were marketed much more aggressively and expensively than their predecessors. Unilever spent $40 million on launching Calvin Klein's Escape in North America, and L'Oréal spent a similar sum on introducing Trésor de Lancôme. LVMH picked up a bill for $1 million after throwing a party for eleven hundred people at Château de Vaux-le-Vicomte near Paris to mark Dune's debut.

So many heavily promoted new perfumes were coming out that the market was crowded, and the risk of failure rose. Only one out of every ten new scents would still be on sale in two years, and an expensive advertising campaign could not guarantee success, as LVMH discovered when, after spending $30 million on Christian Lacroix's C'est La Vie!, its sales still fell below target.[19] Even successful fragrances did not stay in the best-seller lists for as long as they used to; by the early 1990s Opium, Paris, Beautiful and Giorgio were still in the top ten, but other epic 1980s launches such as Coco, Obsession and Poison had been squeezed out by new products. Manufacturers were trapped in a vicious cycle of having to spend more money to attract attention to their new perfumes, and then yet more to hold on to it. L'Oréal and Unilever had the financial strength to bankroll these lavish launches, but small companies, such as Yves Saint Laurent, did not. Ideally Pierre Bergé would have liked to introduce a new YSL women's scent at that time, but the investment required was too high and, as he was already aware, the casinoesque finances of the beauty business were making it even harder for him to find a buyer for Carlo de Benedetti's old shares.

Meanwhile the cost of operating a fashion house was rising, chiefly because of the growing expense of staging a fashion show. Every aspect of the shows seemed costlier: from the florists' bills for filling the Louvre tents and the hotel rooms of influential editors, to the fees for hiring fashionable make-up artists, such as Kevyn Aucoin and François Nars, or star hairdressers, like Julien d'Ys. But the chief culprits were the supermodels, *les tops* as the French called them, the handful of supremely successful models who commanded more media attention – and considerably more money – than their predecessors. *Time* magazine signalled their ascent in September 1991 with a cover feature analysing the 'Supermodel' phenomenon, in which it calculated that a handful of models – Naomi Campbell, Cindy Crawford, Linda Evangelista, Claudia Schiffer and Christy Turlington – were being paid $15,000 to $25,000 for advertising assignments, compared with $5,000 for models of the same status ten years ago.[20]

The supermodels were no brighter or more beautiful than their predecessors in the 1960s, 1970s or 1980s; but they attracted more personal publicity. At a time when Hollywood starlets, like Julia Roberts and Juliette Lewis, were snarling at the paparazzi in grungy clothes with unkempt hair, supermodels supplied a sorely needed source of glamour by looking drop-dead gorgeous in their Chanel freebies. Linda Evangelista hit the headlines with her constantly changing hair colour; Cindy Crawford with her multi-million-dollar advertising contracts; and Naomi Campbell with an army of admirers, including the boxer, Mike Tyson, and the actor, Robert De Niro. And as their fame grew, so did their fees. Linda Evangelista was once quoted (out of context, or so she claimed) as saying that she 'wouldn't get out of bed for less than $10,000 a day'. Sometimes she did work for less, such as the days when she posed for Steven Meisel or Patrick Demarchelier for the cover of *Vogue* for a token $300, or appeared in the show of a favourite designer, such as Helmut Lang, in exchange for free clothes, but Lanvin reportedly paid her $20,000 to appear in a single show.

Supermodels were a boon and a bane for the designers. At a time when fashion was floundering around in search of new directions, the clothes often seemed less interesting to the press and the public than the photogenic women who wore them on the catwalk. The photographic *corps* at Paris fashion week expanded as the paparazzi discovered that the best place to snap supermodels *en masse* was slipping in and out of the changing rooms at the back of the Louvre tents. By paying Christy Turlington or Naomi Campbell to appear in their shows, designers could be sure that their clothes would be featured in the next day's newspapers at a time when they sorely needed the 'free' publicity and might not otherwise have got it. The flipside was that all the designers, with the exception of the fortunate few like Helmut Lang, had to pay more for their models. *Women's Wear Daily* reported that the going rate for Linda Evangelista, Cindy Crawford and Naomi Campbell to appear in a show was $6,000 in autumn 1991, while Claudia Schiffer's was $7,500. The magazine totted up the average cost of a catwalk show at $169,910: including $5,085 for invitations, $34,240 for press kits and $50,845 for the models.[21] Gianni Versace paid at least three times as much for the extravaganza in which each of the supermodels in George Michael's *Freedom* video earned $10,000 for striding down the runway with him lipsynching the lyrics.

The fashion industry was polarized between the established houses, which were willing to pay the supermodels' spiralling fees to secure the press coverage they needed to stay in business, and *avant garde* designers such as Martin Margiela and Ann Demeulemeester, who staged their shows in off-beat locations – disused Métro stations or industrial spaces and once, in Margiela's case, the Salvation Army headquarters designed by Le Corbusier – often using friends as models. Yet Yves Saint Laurent carried on in the same idiosyncratic way, whatever was happening to its competitors.

Sometimes the company used supermodels in its shows, but only if Yves happened to like their look that season. Naomi Campbell occasionally won his approval, but not Cindy Crawford, Claudia Schiffer, or even Linda Evangelista, although one of her first big advertising assignments was as the 'face' of Opium in the 1980s. Each season Yves told Loulou or Nicole, a house *mannequin* from the 1970s who now ran the *cabine*, if he had any particular favourites, such as Lucie de la Falaise, Loulou's angelically pretty niece, and the other models were chosen from the hundreds of prospects sent by their agencies to casting sessions held at the start of fashion week. Nicole picked a short-list of a couple of dozen models at the castings who she thought Yves might like and they were then summoned to Avenue Marceau so he could make the final choice.

It could be a chastening experience for those who were rejected. Eleanora Cuinetti, a Canadian model, got through the Saint Laurent casting sessions one season and was called in to the *couture* house for Yves's inspection. 'Just when I was about to go in and see him,

Nicole said, "Your lipstick's crooked." That made me feel really great. And then I was told to try on a paisley wool dress with a drawstring skirt. Well, I don't have the smallest hips, and I knew it would make them look even bigger than they were. Yves Saint Laurent just took one look at me, and waved his hand in disgust as though to say "Just take her away." I was out of there so fast. They ripped that dress off, and showed me the door. As a model you try not to take these things personally but it's impossible not to. I felt *so* crushed.'[22]

Any models whom Yves deemed acceptable were whisked away by Nicole, to be told what was expected of them. For the *couture*, they still attended personal fittings with Yves in his Avenue Marceau studio, with Moujik snarling at them from among the fabrics, while for ready-to-wear the models were assigned outfits from the racks of neatly-numbered clothes waiting in readiness at Rive Gauche's headquarters on Avenue Georges V; and before each show they were summoned to a dress rehearsal. At Chanel or Versace, rehearsals could be fun, with models swapping jokes and dancing along the runway to blaring rap music; but at Yves Saint Laurent, they were told precisely how to walk and what expression to wear by the imperious Pierre Bergé, while the selection of operatic arias or old French songs he had chosen for that season's soundtrack crackled in the background.

Other houses were equally cavalier when it came to dispatching invitations, often sending them out without asking for formal replies and assuming that any empty seats would be filled by the students and freelance journalists who always seemed to sneak past the security guards. At Yves Saint Laurent nothing was left to chance; Gabrielle Buchaert and her assistants telephoned each of the hundreds of people invited to the *couture* show to check that they would be attending, and wrote out the name cards by hand, before tying them on to the seats with ribbons. The final ritual was the arrival of the bejewelled heart that had been Yves's lucky totem since his debut at Hôtel Forain in 1961, which was now locked away in a secret hiding-place at rue de Babylone until it was chauffeured over to the Hôtel Intercontinental for him to pin it on his favourite outfit of the season.

Once the spectators had taken their seats Pierre Bergé strode purposefully along the runway, peering into the auditorium to check that everyone had arrived. He then slipped backstage and, by brusquely swinging his arm as if conducting from the Opéra de Bastille orchestra pit, signalled to the first model to start. Loulou flitted around, making sure that the hairdressers and make-up artists were on cue, and that the outfits were properly accessorized with the elaborate jewellery she had designed, while Pierre ensured that the models stuck to the correct running order. At one *couture* show the audience could hear Pierre haranguing the woman who was reading out the numbers of the outfits, angrily accusing her of muddling them up.

In the old days it had been Yves, not Pierre, who stood soldier-style beside the entrance to the catwalk, making sure that each model was ready to go on, but now he stepped aside, apparently lost in a world of his own. One season a BBC camera crew filmed backstage at the *couture* show, and after catching Yves grumbling 'Why aren't they clapping?' at the audience that had unfailingly treated him to standing ovations year after year, it captured him picking up a huge can of hairspray and squirting it round and round his head, oblivious to the scores of people working frantically around him.[23] Minutes before the finale Lucie de la Falaise, his favourite 'bride' of the early 1990s, would be sent to collect him, and after tucking her arm daintily into his, she chaperoned Yves along the runway, just as her aunt had told her to.

After the shows, the bejewelled heart was chauffeured safely back to its rue de Babylone hiding-place and Yves generally flew off to Villa Oasis or, if it was the summer, to Château Gabriel, as Marrakesh in August was too hot for Moujik's taste. One example of each of Yves's *haute couture* designs was squirrelled away to be preserved in the company archive in readiness for the Yves Saint Laurent museum that Pierre Bergé intended to open one day. The press officers then responded to requests for pieces from the collections from newspapers, magazines and television programmes. While other fashion houses sent the specified items, leaving it to the fashion editors to accessorize them, Yves Saint Laurent dispatched complete outfits, with shoes, belts and jewellery, tucked creaselessly between folds of tissue paper in pristine boxes.

When Lindy Woodhead's public relations firm was hired to represent Rive Gauche in London, she was given meticulous instructions by Clara Saint. 'Everything had to be absolutely correct. If you sent flowers, it was always the most beautiful roses and only from certain florists. If we asked for an outfit to be sent over for a magazine to be delivered on Thursday, it was always there that day, beautifully wrapped. The company reminded me of a very grand stately home with Yves Saint Laurent as the master, and Pierre Bergé as the butler bossing about the staff.'[24]

For years Clara Saint and Gabrielle Buchaert had politely declined requests for interviews with Yves, but on the eve of the July 1991 *couture* show he broke his silence by talking at length to Franz-Olivier Giesbert, editor-in-chief of *Le Figaro*, and the fashion editor, Janie Samet. Headlined 'Yves Saint Laurent: "I was born with a nervous breakdown"', the interview was published in two parts on consecutive days and included Yves's descriptions of his struggle against drink and drug abuse, the 'psychological torture' of his schooldays and his homosexuality.[25] French privacy laws are extremely strict and although Yves's addictions and gender preferences were common knowledge in Paris, the press had not preyed on them, partly from fear of the litigious Pierre Bergé, but also out of respect for Yves's achievements. In past interviews Yves had alluded to his illness and depressions, but this was the first time he had spoken publicly about them and his sexuality, and the *Le Figaro* articles were syndicated to newspapers and magazines all over the world. Although Janie Samet had known Yves for many years, it was his first encounter with Franz-Olivier Giesbert, who found him 'absolutely intriguing. He came across as a highly intelligent man quite apart from his achievements in fashion. I was able to watch him sketching and it was quite remarkable. He has a form of genius, but it is a masochistic genius. He spoke to us very frankly about his problems. I was struck by his honesty.'[26]

The Bird Dogs
1991–1992

On Sunday afternoons François Mitterrand often enjoyed a post-prandial stroll by the Seine, and the photographers of *Paris-Match* and *L'Express* knew that their best chance of snatching a shot of the President of the Republic relaxing was to wait beside the Seine bridges in case he came by. More often than not a short, stocky man with wiry grey hair would be walking beside him, listening intently to what the president was saying, sometimes breaking off into a rollicking guffaw. It was Pierre Bergé, whom the magazines' readers had come to recognize as one of President Mitterrand's closest friends and, as Jacques Chirac the Gaullist leader put it, 'the first and fore-most member of the *gauche caviare*'.

After a decade of the Mitterrand presidency, the *gauche caviare* had made their mark on France. The gleaming *Grands Projets* had opened in Paris, and local mayors were unveiling their own *Petits Projets* in the provinces, while Jack Lang's largesse drew artists from all over the world to France. Sometimes it seemed as though every famous American passing through Paris was invited to the culture ministry to be awarded the red ribbon of the Order of Arts and Letters. Sylvester Stallone strode into Jack Lang's *salon* with a posse of body-guards and stumbled around Les Bains, the Les Halles nightclub, afterwards muttering about France being the only country that under-stood him. He had obviously not read the press. One columnist suggested that the culture minister had probably confused 'Rambo' with 'Rimbaud', and another that he should have been given the *Croix de Guerre*.

Don Magnifico was in his element: working the room at Parisian private views with hearty cries of '*Mon cher ami*' for friends, and haughty glares at foes, firing off letters of complaint to the organizers of the Cannes Film Festival if he had doubts about his table at the gala dinner. Any journalist with the temerity to criticize Pierre, or anyone else in the Mitterrand circle, risked being subjected to a verbal volley of abuse across Brasserie Lipp, or being pilloried in his weekly *Globe* column. Still active in the AIDS campaign, Pierre was stalwart in his support for SOS Racisme, despite his fury when it opposed François Mitterrand's policy of military intervention in the Gulf War. 'He let us know what he thought,' recalled Harlem Désir, 'and there was a big row, but he continued to give us money. We'd have collapsed without it.'[1] He even published a collection of essays, *Liberté J'Écris Ton Nom*, a title taken from a poem by Paul Éluard.

Much of Pierre's time was spent at the Opéra de Paris, particularly the new Bastille opera house, which had continued to be plagued by problems after its opening. During the first season the orchestra went on strike twice, as did the technicians, and the box office was flooded with complaints about a persistent buzzing from an electronic curtain which made it difficult to hear the music. There was an outcry when ticket prices for the 'people's opera' increased, doubling for some seats, and another row when the culture ministry announced that it could not afford to build the *Petite Salle* needed to stage smaller productions. A year after the official opening Pierre unveiled proposals to merge the management of the new Opéra de Bastille with that of the old Opéra Garnier, only two years after the culture ministry had separated them. When the chief administrator of the Garnier protested, Pierre Bergé fired him.[2]

Somehow he found time for his old fashion industry intrigues, often stirring things up in *Women's Wear Daily*, or the French trade papers, in his role as president of the Chambre Syndicale. If he felt especially strongly about an issue, Pierre did not wait for journalists to call him, but picked up the phone to them. 'He'd launch into these tirades,' said one. 'And there you'd go. A row. A libel writ. He didn't care about the consequences.' Although he sometimes seemed swamped by the hornets' nest he had inherited at the Opéra,

Pierre was as efficient as ever at imposing his views on industry meetings. 'If he decided to back something, it was as good as done,' commented one observer. 'He behaved like a despot. There was no point in arguing if you were on a board chaired by Bergé. Some people tried, but they always gave up in the end. The ones that disagreed with him simply stopped turning up to the meetings. He achieved a great deal for the industry, but it was difficult for anyone in French fashion to know whether to love or loathe him.'

Opinions of Pierre were equally polarized in French business circles, where he had a higher profile after the flotation. His friendship with François Mitterrand stirred up ill-feeling in some quarters, as did his open homosexuality and espousal of the AIDS cause. 'I respected Pierre Bergé for what he'd achieved for that company, but I can't say I liked him or the way he led his life,' commented one senior industrialist. Christophe Girard felt impelled to resign from a prestigious private club in Paris after a fellow member asked him what it was like working for 'ce pédé (that pederast) Bergé'. 'I told him it was fine, just two gays working together,' said Girard, who was homosexual too. 'But I resigned my membership afterwards. I didn't make a fuss about it. It wasn't the fault of the management. But I didn't want to mix with people who thought like that.'[3]

Other business figures liked Pierre personally, as well as admiring his commercial acumen. 'I enjoyed working with him,' observed Alain-Dominique Perrin, the Cartier chairman. 'He's a good manager, he's creative and he's an interesting man.'[4] Jean-Louis Dumas of Hermès remembered something Richard Salomon said when Pierre's name came up in conversation. ' "Whatever anyone tells you about Pierre Bergé, just remember that he's had the same chauffeur for twenty years. That really tells you something about the man." And, of course, he was right.'[5]

Pierre opened a new chapter in his private life by falling in love with Robert Merloz, an assistant in the Avenue Marceau design studio who was thirty-five years his junior. Over the years he had crushes on several male assistants, usually those with the soulful looks he had fallen for in Bernard Buffet and Yves Saint Laurent. 'There was a certain type that we all knew he went for,' said one brief object of Pierre's amorous interest. 'Boys with wavy hair, sensitive faces, and that dreamy, slightly tortured expression. Anyone who looked like Yves Saint Laurent basically.' Merloz was not as handsome as Yves had been at the same age, his features were marred by rather bulbous eyes and a prominent Adam's apple, but he conformed to type with delicate bone structure, foppish brown curls and the fey, forlorn air that appealed to Pierre.

Born in Savoy, Robert Merloz joined Yves Saint Laurent in 1985 when he was twenty years old and had completed his studies at the Chambre Syndicale school. After working alongside the other assistants, he was put in charge of the fur collection where Pierre was convinced he displayed an extraordinary aptitude for design. He proudly confided to friends that he had found another exceptional talent, as he had with Yves thirty years before. Since his departure from rue de Babylone, Pierre had been seen around Paris with a number of young men, but none with whom he seemed as besotted as Robert Merloz. 'He was potty about him,' said a friend. 'Pierre had always talked about how it had been love at first sight with Yves, and here he was falling in love all over again. Robert was a sweet enough boy, and he seemed crazy about Pierre, hanging adoringly on his every word. It was obvious to me that he'd never match up to Yves as a designer, but Pierre didn't seem to think so.'

Eager to introduce his new discovery to a wider audience, Pierre had arranged a special presentation of the Yves Saint Laurent fur collection during fashion week in March 1991. Furs were hopelessly out of fashion, considered an anathema by most of the ecologically-aware younger generation. The hipper magazines banned fur advertising, and some supermodels, such as Christy Turlington, refused to wear them. The annual Paris fur presentations were usually low-key affairs for small audiences of specialist buyers and older *couture* clients: but on this occasion the YSL press office was instructed to invite a full complement of fashion journalists, who were already in the city for the *prêt-à-porter* shows. Clara Saint and her assistants rustled up a respectable turnout. 'There was a three-line whip,' said one employee. 'And the journalists came.' The Saint Laurent set treated the event as a social outing. Pierre arrived with Ficelle bundled under his arm, while Betty Catroux and Marie-Hélène de Rothschild were there to cheer on the young designer, and Yves watched proceedings discreetly from a seat tucked away on the back row.

Robert Merloz's designs were certainly more inventive than the usual run of fur collections, if a little *too* inventive for some spectators, who cringed at the sight of a grey cape with 'Fur For Ever' emblazoned on the back in diamond studs, and at a jacket in the shape of one of Yves's signature pea-coats made from minks' paws dyed navy-blue.[6] Nonetheless the show ended with a warm round of applause for Robert Merloz, before the audience filed out for a postmortem. 'I hadn't realized what was really going on until afterwards,' said one woman in the audience. 'I walked out with a male fashion editor who was part of that high camp fashion circle. And he said "Well! So that's the *dauphin*." Suddenly it all seemed to make sense.'

For years there had been rumours that Yves might be quietly pushed aside, to make way for a young successor: but Pierre Bergé had denied them, just as he squashed the stories that Yves was dying of AIDS, or any of the other illnesses he was said to have contracted. On any objective analysis it would have been prudent for Pierre to plan ahead for Yves's eventual departure, particularly after the stock market flotation when he not only had the future of the company's employees to safeguard, but the shareholders' interests too. Yves was clearly in a fragile state, psychologically as well as physically, as illustrated by his breakdown the previous year. Reviews of his collections were often openly hostile,[7] and his behaviour hardly helped. One American reporter remembered being sent backstage to snatch a comment from Yves after the show to see him standing in a *mêlée* of models and make-up artists with a white powder 'moustache' of cocaine smeared around his mouth. 'The atmosphere at his shows was horrid,' said an English fashion editor. 'Half the audience blindly idolized him. And the other half was so cynical that you got the impression they'd only turned up in case they missed a front-page story if he dropped dead on the catwalk.'

Once Pierre had refused even to entertain the prospect of what would happen to the company after Yves's death or retirement, but by then it was evident he had given some thought to the matter. In recent interviews he had threatened to close the *couture* house, rather than trying to revive it as Alain Wertheimer had done at Chanel.[8] The clear implication was that its other activities, including Rive Gauche, would continue, presumably with a *dauphin* in charge of design. Robert Merloz's ascent convinced the Paris gossips that Pierre had decided to precipitate events, by replacing Yves with the younger designer who happened to be his new lover.

The spring and summer rolled by, but there was no *dauphin* announcement from Pierre Bergé. He and his new protégé were still visibly very much in love, but Merloz's role remained that of the company's fur designer. Meanwhile the Avenue Marceau staff were instructed to prepare for a gala at the Opéra de Bastille to mark the thirtieth anniversary of Yves Saint Laurent on 3 February 1992, which Pierre Bergé was determined would be a landmark event, to celebrate three decades of Yves's *haute couture* designs.

A week before the gala Yves unveiled his sixty-first *haute couture* collection. Over the years, even at the depth of his depressions, he had always been able, if he bestirred himself, to create collections of tremendous virtuosity and this was such an occasion. The designs encompassed his greatest gifts, masterful mixes of colour and impeccable proportions, in clothes from his classic repertoire which were exquisitely stitched and finished by the Avenue Marceau *ateliers*. The English designer, Vivienne Westwood, had made a special request for a seat and joined the *fidèles* as they raced backstage, a conspicuous figure with her peroxided hair and surreally-cut tweeds, but she adored Yves's designs, telling him they were 'fantastic, so chic, such wonderful technique, so perfectly judged in every detail'.[9] Suzy Menkes praised the show in the next day's *Herald Tribune* as 'the work of a designer at peace – at last – with himself and his rosy-tinted view of femininity'.[10]

Scores of the journalists who had come to Paris for *couture* week stayed on for a few extra days to go to the thirtieth anniversary gala, as did Yves's *couture* clients, who usually flew home, or headed for the ski slopes, immediately after their fittings. Nearly three thousand people had been invited to the gala, including coachloads of YSL factory workers and their spouses, all the staff from the Avenue Marceau *couture* house and Rive Gauche's headquarters on Avenue Georges V, together with the artisanal button-makers, silk-weavers and embroiderers who supplied them.

Coaches deposited the factory workers on the white steps of the opera house and the paparazzi took up their positions to snap the celebrities as they arrived. Danielle Mitterrand, the French first lady, stepped out of her limousine in a dove-grey YSL trouser suit, followed by Jack Lang and Rudolf Nureyev, still handsome despite being visibly ill with full-blown AIDS. He wrapped a Slavic woollen shawl around his suit for the night, and wore a jaunty beret to cover his head, with a whisper of grey goatee on his chin. Zizi Jeanmaire showed off her legs, still long and lovely at sixty-eight, in sheer black stockings under a dashingly short skirt; and Paloma Picasso sported an equally daring red satin shirt slashed open to her waist. Yves's escort, Catherine Deneuve, wore a pea-green sequinned jacket over a long turquoise satin skirt. Even J. Mack Robinson and his family had flown in to Paris from Atlanta especially for the occasion.

After the guests settled into the auditorium, the gala began with film clips of Yves and his work over three decades, including footage from his second *couture* show at Hôtel Forain. The soprano, Katia Ricciarelli, and baritone, Dmitri Hvorostovsky, sang a selection of his favourite arias accompanied by the Opéra orchestra, before the curtain came up to reveal the vast stage, cleared of props and scenery. Slowly a model dressed in one of Yves's black *smokings* became visible to the audience, as she paced the length of the stage, with another four models, also in black *smokings*, appearing behind her, and five more behind them. One by one the most influential designs from Yves's thirty-year career came on: the 'bare-breasted' sheath of black silk chiffon with an ostrich feather trim that had caused such a scandal in 1968, the triumphant *Ballets Russes* designs, and the $100,000 Van Gogh *Iris* and *Sunflower* beaded jackets he unveiled after 'Black Friday'. The clothes were grouped in themes, as they had been for Diana Vreeland's retrospective at the Metropolitan Museum nearly a decade before, and some of the sequences included pieces designed ten or twenty years apart, but because Yves Saint Laurent's collections had become synonymous with what the audience regarded as 'classics' they blended together perfectly.

For the finale, all the models formed a phalanx on either side of the stage, while a black model pirouetted past wearing a white sheath dress decorated with the silhouettes of Picasso's doves, another white 'dove' on her head and long white ribbon streamers dangling from her wrists. Yves appeared behind her in a brusque black business suit, his silhouette looming larger as he paced along the stage to thunderous applause. Catherine Deneuvre stepped forward to stand beside him on his left, with Pierre Bergé at Yves's right. After an introduction from Pierre, Yves was handed a microphone and slowly, unsteadily started to speak, beginning with an apology. 'I beg your pardon, but I am not as eloquent as Monsieur Bergé.' His speech was slurred, as though it was a great ordeal for him, and after a few words of thanks, he paused so uncertainly, his gaze falling to the floor, that there was an uneasy minute of silence before the applause began again. During the ovation Pierre prodded Yves gently in the back, telling him when to bow.

Yves was led backstage where he was surrounded by models clapping and cheering, smearing his cheeks with the cupid bows of congratulatory kisses. Catherine Deneuve cleaned him up for the cameras, dabbing off the lipstick with brisk strokes of her fingers. The models sang a chorus of '*Happy Birthday*', and one of them kissed him again. Catherine Deneuve whisked a crisp white handkerchief out of her bag, moistened a corner of it and wiped the lipstick firmly off Yves's face. He murmured a few words. 'No, it's not funny, not funny at all,' she scolded, as a mother might a wayward child. Putting the handkerchief back in her bag, she snapped it shut with a matronly click, and smiled agreeably as she chatted to Pierre Bergé. Neither made any attempt to draw Yves, still standing between them, into their conversation.

Gina Newsom, a British television producer, was backstage with her camera crew filming the event for a BBC documentary. 'It was chaos. The models were clapping and kissing Saint Laurent, saying "Wonderful. Wonderful." "Beautiful. Beautiful." Suddenly Yves noticed that one of them was missing. God knows how. There were so many girls around him I don't know how anyone could have known what was happening. But he kept on saying "Where is she? Where is she?" until they found her. It made me realize that although he always seemed so out of it, he was actually very aware of what was going on.'[11]

The guests filed out of the auditorium into the foyers and bars encircling the opera house, where waiters were hovering with trays of champagne beside tables of elaborately arranged food and flowers. Yves and his entourage slipped into an ante-room behind a velvet rope *à la* Studio 54, where he sat between Catherine Deneuve and Rudolf Nureyev at a table including Loulou, Thadée, Zizi and Jacques Grange. On an adjacent table Pierre Bergé chatted animatedly to

Danielle Mitterrand, whom Yves approached with a smile. A giant chocolate birthday cake in the shape of a heart was wheeled in with 'Love 1962–1992' piped in gold on the chocolate icing and he was led away to cut it, watched by Deneuve, Pierre and the beaming Zizi. Photographers and camera crews circled around them, seizing a rare chance to snap a picture of Yves Saint Laurent off the catwalk.

The thirtieth anniversary of Yves Saint Laurent was one of the most elaborate events the fashion industry had seen. The bill for remaking the clothes for the Bastille show came to well over a million dollars: then there was the cost of food, the champagne, the models, the flowers, even the Opéra orchestra. Valentino and Givenchy had celebrated important anniversaries the previous summer: Valentino marked his thirtieth year in business with a ball in Rome, and Hubert de Givenchy commemorated the fortieth year of his *couture* house with the opening of a retrospective in Paris. Both had thrown grand, glamorous parties for their famous friends and clients, but neither invited their factory workers, even laying on coaches to ferry them from the provinces, as Yves Saint Laurent had done.

Everything about the evening epitomized the idiosyncratic nature of the YSL group. It was a touching tribute to Yves and the artistry of his *couture* creations, but was paid for by the profits from the licensed socks, sunglasses and cigarettes that he had probably never seen. By then, the Paris *couture* industry employed around two thousand people to make bespoke clothes for roughly the same number of clients, and many of Yves's peers accepted that the only reason why the *couture* collections continued was to drum up publicity for their perfumes and licences. Karl Lagerfeld seemed to relish the irony, once opening a Chanel show with a *tableau* of supermodels Naomi Campbell and Claudia Schiffer preening themselves beside a giant bottle of Chanel No. 5, and mocking *couture* conventions by playing blaring rap music on his soundtracks. Yet Yves cherished the *haute couture* traditions, as did Pierre Bergé, who firmly believed that the *raison d'être* for selling licensing rights and launching perfumes was to keep the *couture* house going, not the other way around. 'The only reason why this company exists,' he insisted, 'is so Yves can continue to create *couture* – there's no other.'[12] Yves Saint Laurent's thirtieth anniversary gala looked like an extravagant attempt to prove that *haute couture* had a higher purpose than generating publicity for the name of a man who by then was too isolated to communicate with his friends and family, let alone with scores of unknown journalists in the Bastille auditorium.

Karl Lagerfeld had no patience with it, dismissing the anniversary celebrations to *Vanity Fair* as 'a nightmare' that looked 'as if all these people were going to their own funeral'.[13] As for Yves. 'Look, you want his life? Of course not, eh? I mean. I hear Yves is suffering, but you cannot suffer and bring out the same collection every six months.'[14] On the day that the Saint Laurent set wallowed in nostalgia at the Opéra de Bastille, Lagerfeld was in New York collecting an award at the Council of Fashion Designers of America's annual dinner. If the YSL anniversary reeked of nostalgia, the CFDA's night out was unrelentingly contemporary with a cast-list that included a movie star in Anjelica Huston, a starlet in Uma Thurman, and a guard of honour from the Gotham City motorcycle club. Woody Hochswender of the *New York Times* likened the event to 'something out of the *Day of the Locusts*'.[15]

Yet Lagerfeld had a point. Who would want Yves's life? After the Bastille gala, Holly Brubacher wrote in the *New Yorker* that during the evening her mind 'kept straying from the vigorous young man in the film to the broken-down man in our midst'.[16] Yves claimed to have kicked his alcoholism after his last course of treatment at the American Hospital, and now brandished glasses of Diet Coke or orange juice with pitiable pride, but he was physically frail, and so melancholic, that even his mother kept her distance at times. 'He adores me,' said Lucienne in an interview with *Femme* magazine. 'He calls me his *mamouche* (a pet name for mummy), he covers me with presents, with jewellery that is so sumptuous I couldn't possibly wear it.'[17] But the woman who adored Yves, and had pampered him all his life, was reduced to telephoning his *valet de chambre* to check up on her only son. 'I just say that I'm here, that's all. I ask for news of his dog, or leave a message to be passed on to the chauffeur.'[18] *Femme* followed Lucienne's interview with an essay by the French writer, Gonzague Saint Bris, entitled '*Yves Saint Laurent, ou l'honneur de souffrir*'; 'Yves Saint Laurent, or the privilege of suffering'.[19]

That summer Yves's suffering erupted in public when Robert Merloz presented a *prêt-à-porter* collection at the height of *couture* week in July. The Paris gossips had got it wrong. Merloz did not become Yves Saint Laurent's *dauphin*: instead Pierre Bergé set him up in business, using $2 million of the company's money to launch the Robert Merloz label. Convinced the new venture would be a successful investment, Pierre planned his new protégé's debut with the rigour hitherto devoted to Yves Saint Laurent. A dozen members of staff were delegated to work on the Merloz line, and for his show the company hired the pretty glazed gallery of the École des Beaux Arts on rue Bonaparte, where Karl Lagerfeld often staged Chanel's *couture* presentations. The collection was to be *prêt-à-porter*, but would be shown during *couture* week, and this time the YSL press office did not need to resort to a three-line whip. None of the journalists gathered in Paris for the *couture* shows wanted to risk missing what was billed as the debut of the next Yves Saint Laurent, and the clients were as eager to see Pierre Bergé's new boyfriend as they were to inspect the clothes. 'By then Pierre and Robert were very much an item on the Paris social scene,' said one observer. 'Pierre didn't try to hide it. Wherever they were – at the opera, or a party, in a café – he'd sit gazing moonily into this young boy's eyes.'

On the day of the show, Pierre put the models through their paces, while Robert Merloz fussed over his designs, and the audience streamed into the École des Beaux Arts gallery from the steamy heat of the sandstone courtyard. The Saint Laurent set was there *en masse*. Paloma Picasso fanned herself gently from a front-row seat, beside her husband Rafael Lopez-Cambil; and Loulou's mother, Maxime de Falaise, arrived with her grand-daughter, Lucie. Even Lucienne attended, looking splendidly cool in a cream-coloured YSL *couture* suit with golden sunflower earrings, her face heavily made-up and hair dyed a similar shade of brunette to that of her son who, as the more perceptive spectators had already noted, was *not* present.

Pierre Bergé ran his eye around the room to make sure the right people were in the right seats before signalling to the models that it was time to start. The production was as elegant and efficient as for an Yves Saint Laurent show, but the clothes were not. The audience shuffled uncomfortably as models walked along the runway wearing skimpy tunics and toga-style dresses, some with scarves knotted jauntily around their necks. For the finale Robert Merloz, joyful tears tumbling, embraced a pregnant model in a blue hooded tunic and slipped a wedding ring on to her finger in a mock 'marriage', which caused the same embarrassment among the audience as the spectacle of his mink-paw 'pea-coat' at the fur show. The ripple of applause as Merloz took his bow was barely polite.

It struck a stark contrast with the rapturous ovation that greeted the end of Yves's debut thirty years before, when he and Pierre had pulled off a *succès d'estime* by cobbling together a collection with very little money under arduous circumstances. Robert Merloz's efforts were bolstered by the financial and administrative resources of what was generally regarded as the best-run fashion house in Paris, but the response to his work was tepid at best. 'It was like seeing an untrained actor sent out on stage too soon,' said Marion Hume, the British fashion journalist. 'There was something very cruel about sending this poor little chick out in public when half the room was from the Saint Laurent camp. But he just wasn't up to it.'[20] As the spectators filed out of the gallery into the courtyard, Lucienne was surrounded by reporters and camera crews, and wasted no time in expressing her opinion of the event. The efforts of this 'young man', as she insisted on referring to Merloz, could not possibly be compared to those of her son who, she confided, was *'effondré'* (in anguish) about the day's events, while she personally was furious with Pierre Bergé for financing the label with the company's money, rather than his own.[21]

When the reviews of the collection were published a few days later, Robert Merloz's fate was sealed. Suzy Menkes dismissed his designs as 'fey and whimsy' in the *Herald Tribune*,[22] and Bernadine Morris wrote in the *New York Times* that although the show 'may have sounded like a good idea ... it was not.'[23] The reaction from store buyers was equally discouraging. The hottest looks for that season were the stringy slip dresses inspired by the angst-ridden music of the Seattle grunge bands, Nirvana and Pearl Jam, the Adidas and Nike sportswear of rap and hip-hop stars, and the independent films of new American directors such as Quentin Tarantino and Gus Van Sant. Even hardened fashion victims were adding thrift store finds to their designer wardrobes, and when American *Vogue* published a special centenary issue that spring, the cover featured a crop of models wearing white cotton Gap T-shirts. The improbably perfect supermodels had been eclipsed by the 'waifs', a new breed of models barely out of adolescence with elfin faces and urchin haircuts – Kate

Moss, Amber Valetta, Shalom Harlow and, Yves's favourite, Lucie de la Falaise – who were splashed across the covers of *Vogue* and *Harper's Bazaar* which was being revived under the editorship of Liz Tilberis, after she moved there from British *Vogue*, and her creative director Fabien Baron. Fashionable young designers, Jean Touitou, the man behind APC in Paris and the Canadian shoe maker, Patrick Cox, stuck to simple styles and prided themselves on selling at comparatively low prices. Robert Merloz's brand of conservative French chic was hopelessly out of tune with the times and few stores ordered his togas and tunics, with the exception of Barney's New York which agreed to buy the line in a package including Rive Gauche, but sent the Merloz consignment back to Paris when the Rive Gauche part of the deal fell through.

Why did Pierre Bergé do it? 'Love is blind,' suggested one of his friends. 'It's the only possible explanation. There'd been a couple of other men after Yves, but nothing very serious. Along came Robert Merloz, he fell in love and thought he'd found another genius. Number one was Bernard Buffet. Number two was Yves Saint Laurent. So, third time lucky. Or so he thought. But he was wrong. I didn't think Robert Merloz had much talent when he was doing the furs and he certainly wasn't capable of doing a full collection even with the resources of YSL behind him. But the worst thing about the whole business was that it hurt Yves very, very badly.'

Yves was in despair. All his life he had been the centre of attention, first from his parents and then, for the past thirty-five years, from Pierre Bergé. Having been the unrivalled receptacle of his mother's affections throughout his childhood, it seemed only natural to be treated in the same way in adulthood, and he had taken Pierre's obsessive love virtually for granted. Suddenly he had been supplanted by another man, first in Pierre's personal life and now, it seemed, in his professional domain. Yves had found it difficult when Pierre first became distracted by his responsibilities at the Opéra de Paris, but to be publicly usurped by Robert Merloz was unbearable. Pierre had used the company's money, and its employees, to launch his new boyfriend in business, as though Yves no longer mattered and, worst of all, he was too debilitated to do anything about it.

Certainly he was too distressed to concentrate on his *couture* collection, which was due to be shown four days after the Merloz presentation. Even Yves's smallest *couture* presentations included at least a hundred outfits, but this time he only managed fifty. He did not make a wedding dress, so sent out one of his models as a masked bride wearing a silk *faille* gown in a fiery, furious shade of scarlet. Some members of the audience interpreted the colour as an elegant riposte to Robert Merloz's 'marriage' to his pregnant 'bride', and an apt expression of Yves's feelings for Pierre Bergé.[24]

At the end of the show the spectators rose to their feet to treat Yves to a standing ovation of stinging claps, rousing cheers and even more fluttering handkerchieves than usual. A triumphant Lucienne led the rush backstage, where she planted a dozen kisses on her son's cheeks in front of the paparazzi lenses. 'I think anguish must be good for him,' she proclaimed, a sharp eye on the surrounding journalists, who were scribbling her words down in their notebooks. 'Look at the result: it was sublime, perfect, a wonderful surprise.'[25] Her offensive had worked. Yves was cast as the wronged hero of the hour, Pierre Bergé as the villain, and Robert Merloz as the dupe. The *fidèles* were worried about Yves, dismissive of Robert Merloz's efforts and indignant that Pierre Bergé could have placed their favourite in such a painful position.[26]

Yves was taken away to Château Gabriel in Normandy to stay there with Moujik until the end of the summer, and after his return to Paris that autumn, he and Pierre gradually patched things up. 'They had to,' said a friend. 'They'd be lost without each other, even with Robert Merloz on the scene.' Yet Pierre continued his love affair with Robert Merloz, and continued to back his label. They opened a boutique on rue de Grenelle, one of the chic shopping streets south of Place Saint-Germain des Prés, and Robert Merloz presented a second collection the following season, albeit in a smaller venue with fewer spectators than the first, but to such a lukewarm reception that the gossip about him being Yves Saint Laurent's *dauphin* fizzled out.

By then the issue was irrelevant. It would have been impossible for Pierre to have replaced Yves with another designer, even if he had wanted to, because while the fashion world was distracted by the embarrassment, and expense, of the Robert Merloz episode, Pierre Bergé was secretly negotiating to sell the company, and it would be impossible for him to sell it without Yves Saint Laurent.

The President's Men

1992–1993

In October 1991, nine months before the first Robert Merloz show, Pierre Bergé had convened a meeting with the senior directors of a Paris bank. He knew them all well, as they had advised him in 1986 when he joined forces with Carlo de Benedetti to buy Charles of the Ritz. At that time the bankers were working for the French subsidiary of Crédit Suisse First Boston; they had since left to set up a Paris office for Wasserstein Perella, one of the whizzier New York investment banks. Pierre Bergé had an intriguing project to put to them – he asked Wasserstein Perella to find a buyer for Yves Saint Laurent.

For eighteen months Pierre had borne the financial burden of the $99 million he borrowed in his and Yves's names to buy Carlo de Benedetti's shares, and meeting the interest payments on those debts was becoming difficult, even for men of their wealth.[1] As the months went by and the recession deepened, his chances of selling the shares diminished, and Alain Minc, now advising Pierre in his new role as a consultant, suggested that the prospect of buying 100 per cent of Yves Saint Laurent might be more enticing. It was a bold suggestion, and one that appealed to Pierre, but *only* if he could keep control of the company.

He told Wasserstein Perella exactly what he expected from the deal. The asking price for Yves Saint Laurent was to be $1 billion, including a substantial sum for Yves and himself as a *quid pro quo* for dismantling the *société en commandite par actions* mechanism. Pierre wanted to be paid in cash, not shares, and insisted on a guarantee that he would be given complete autonomy to run Yves Saint Laurent, both the fashion and beauty businesses, until he retired at seventy. Pierre Bergé was then sixty-one.

The sale of Yves Saint Laurent was an important project for Wasserstein Perella. As a newcomer to the French financial field, it had often lost out on prestigious deals to established Paris banks, such as Paribas or Lazard Frères. The YSL dossier was the type of high-profile project it needed to make its mark, and a heavyweight figure, Jean-Pierre Halbron, was hired to take charge of the transaction. A cordial man of fifty-five, Halbron had excellent connections throughout French finance and industry. He was a *Sciences Po*' graduate who held senior positions at Rhône-Poulenc, the chemicals company, and Total, the oil giant, before becoming a banker at Banque Edmond de Rothschild. Finding a buyer for Yves Saint Laurent was to be his chief concern at Wasserstein Perella, and he wasted no time in contacting Pierre Bergé.

Only a few years before the acquisition of Yves Saint Laurent would have been an attractive proposition. It was one of the most famous brand names in the then-buoyant luxury market with best-selling perfumes in Opium and Paris, and a successful chain of ready-to-wear boutiques in Rive Gauche. Even its *couture* collection made money, albeit not much, at a time when most other fashion houses, with the probable exception of Chanel, were running theirs at a loss.

But by early 1992, the luxury industry looked less appealing, as did Yves Saint Laurent. For the first time in thirty years, Pierre Bergé was running a company which was contracting, rather than expanding. Some of the Rive Gauche boutiques had closed, and sales of Opium and Paris were declining.[2] The scare stories about Yves's health, coupled with critical reviews of his collections, had tarnished the brand name, as had the plethora of cheap YSL pens and polyester shirts on sale in discount stores. In the 1980s the investment community had praised luxury companies like Saint Laurent for exploiting the full financial potential of their licensing rights, but now its role models were Chanel and Hermès, which imposed rigorous control over the use of their brand names, keeping them at the most exclusive end of the market.

In the circumstances Jean-Pierre Halbron suspected that Pierre's demands were excessive. One obstacle was his insistence on retaining control, which would prevent the new owner from merging the YSL products with their own, thereby cutting costs by pooling resources in areas such as manufacturing, raw material sourcing, marketing and distribution. Any prospective buyer calculating whether they could afford the acquisition would rely on those savings to improve profitability, and without them, the company would seem more expensive. 'It was a problem,' admitted Halbron. 'The deal only made sense financially for most companies if they had complete control and could do what they wanted.'[3]

He also realized that it would be more difficult to sell the fashion and beauty businesses together, rather than separately, an option which Pierre Bergé refused to entertain. 'It would definitely have been easier just to have been looking for a buyer for perfumes and cosmetics,' he said. 'That was the part of the company everyone wanted. They didn't understand fashion and weren't interested in it. And I mean, who'd want to have to manage Yves Saint Laurent himself?'[4]

Halbron was certain that Pierre's $1 billion price tag was too high, with good reason, given that the YSL share price had almost halved in value since its peak of 1,219 francs at the beginning of January 1990, to 699 francs two years later. 'I said "Pierre, it's very difficult, asking someone to invest $1 billion and still not get control of the company." I said, "The timing isn't good. Two or three years ago it would have been possible to get that . . . but in 1992 the atmosphere is just not right."'[5]

Undeterred, Pierre courted his contacts, convinced that the opportunity to acquire 100 per cent of Yves Saint Laurent would be too good to miss. One of the first companies he approached was Cartier, which still owned six per cent of the YSL group. Alain-Dominique Perrin turned down the chance to buy Carlo de Benedetti's 14.9 per cent stake, when Cerus first put it on the market, and now he rebuffed Pierre's offer to sell him 100 per cent. 'We did look at the deal,' he acknowledged. 'But we weren't really interested. Yves Saint Laurent is involved with fashion and that isn't an area that appealed to us. It didn't fit in with our long-term plans.'[6] Another of Pierre's old allies, Seiji Tsutsumi of Seibu-Saison, also said 'no': he was preoccupied by his company's problems in the depressed Japanese market.

A more promising candidate was Orcofi, the luxury conglomerate founded by Henry Racamier after he was edged out of LVMH. Having backed the launch of Inès de la Fressange's boutiques and liaised with L'Oréal to relaunch Lanvin, Racamier still had some spare capital and was seriously tempted by the prospect of buying Yves Saint Laurent. 'It's a fantastic business, one of the best brand names in the industry, probably the best,' he said. 'Yves is very creative and they've built up an excellent company. It's a prestigious name and the perfumes are of very high quality. We considered it for a couple of weeks. But the price was very high. We'd have had to have paid in cash and when we added it up, it was an awful lot of money.'[7]

When Pierre had exhausted his contacts, Jean-Pierre Halbron made overtures to other possible bidders. The number of companies interested in buying luxury brands had thinned out since the 1980s. Avon and Revlon were hampered by leveraged buy-out debts, and Investcorp was wrangling with Maurizio Gucci over Gucci's financial difficulties. Shiseido, like Seibu-Saison, was concerned about the economic situation in Japan, and had decided to build a European beauty business from scratch, rather than acquiring one, hiring Chantal Roos to run it. Halbron made overtures to Unilever and Colgate Palmolive, but both declined; as did Elf Sanofi, the pharmaceuticals arm of Elf Aquitaine, the state-controlled oil group. Sanofi already owned the Nina Ricci and Oscar de la Renta perfumes, and Halbron thought it might be interested in expanding its beauty business. 'There wasn't even a negotiation,' he recalled. 'They just said they weren't interested.'[8]

One group was definitely interested: L'Oréal, the world's largest cosmetics company. Founded eighty years ago by the chemist, Eugène Schueller, at a laboratory in the Parisian suburb of Clichy, L'Oréal had dominated the hair-care and sun-protection markets for decades. During the 1980s it diversified into the luxury business, buying the rights to Giorgio Armani's and Ralph Lauren's perfumes, and relaunching Lancôme, a skin-care brand it had owned since the 1960s, with Isabella Rossellini, the daughter of the movie star, Ingrid Bergman, and the Italian film director, Roberto Rossellini, as its 'face', a successful strategy that culminated in the launch of the best-selling Trésor perfume.

The architect of the new L'Oréal was Lindsay Owen-Jones, nick-named 'OJ' by his executives, who became chairman in 1988 at the age of forty-two. One of the few foreigners with a senior position in French industry, Owen-Jones was a Briton, who graduated from Oxford University and studied for an MBA at Insead, the French business school, before joining L'Oréal in 1969. A protégé of François Dalle, then chairman, he was put in charge of Cosmair, its North American arm, before being recalled to France to be primed for the chairmanship. An energetic man, who competed in Formula One motor races as a hobby, Owen-Jones was proud of L'Oréal's competitive culture. The company's staff were expected to generate a constant stream of ideas for new products, and if their suggestions were accepted they were summoned to the 'Confrontation Room' to be questioned about them by their seniors, sometimes by 'OJ' himself.

An alliance with L'Oréal was very attractive to Pierre Bergé. L'Oréal had the financial strength to launch new YSL perfumes, and could provide research resources for his latest venture, the launch of a skin-care range. For L'Oréal, the acquisition offered a rare opportunity to acquire one of the hallowed trio of French fashion brands – Christian Dior, Chanel and Yves Saint Laurent. When Lindsay Owen-Jones was told that Pierre Bergé was looking for a buyer, he leapt at the chance. 'Of course we were interested,' he affirmed. 'I see the dossiers on every company that comes on to the market in this business and any brand name of Yves Saint Laurent's size and stature is of interest to us. A Saint Laurent deal would have made a lot of strategic sense for us – at the right price.'[9]

But price was a subject they could not agree on. Discussion began on an informal basis between Lindsay Owen-Jones and Pierre Bergé that winter, and were then left to their advisers. L'Oréal was keen to do the deal, but not at the price Pierre Bergé wanted. Owen-Jones thought he was asking too much for the business and, in any case, his ability to make acquisitions on that scale was complicated by L'Oréal's ownership structure.

Although L'Oréal was quoted on the stock market, the majority of its shares were owned by Gesparal, a holding company belonging to Liliane Bettencourt, the daughter of Eugène Schueller, the group's founder, and Nestlé, the Swiss food giant. Liliane Bettencourt held just over fifty per cent of Gesparal's stock, which gave her control of that company and, hence, of L'Oréal; while Nestlé had the right of first refusal if her shares were sold. There was no prospect of Nestlé taking over during her lifetime, as Bettencourt, then in her early seventies, had pledged not to sell the shares, but the situation after her death was less certain, and in the meantime Lindsay Owen-Jones and the rest of L'Oréal's management were reluctant to risk upsetting the delicate balance of power with either of their main shareholders.

Acquisitions were a sensitive issue. Most publicly quoted companies could choose to finance acquisitions in cash, or by issuing new shares, but L'Oréal always had to pay cash, as both the Bettencourt family and Nestlé refused to permit Gesparal's holding to fall below its current level of fifty-one per cent. If Lindsay Owen-Jones had paid the $1 billion that Pierre Bergé wanted, he would have had to borrow at least part of the money, and the interest payments would reduce L'Oréal's earnings per share for a year or so after the deal. The L'Oréal board was nervous about Gesparal's reaction to that, but when Owen-Jones pressed Pierre to accept a lower price, he refused, and 'when it became clear that we wouldn't be able to acquire the company at the price he wanted without diluting our earnings, the talks broke off.'[10]

There was, however, another reason why Lindsay Owen-Jones decided not to go ahead with the acquisition: the political implications of buying a company like Yves Saint Laurent. 'Everyone in France knows how close Pierre Bergé is to President Mitterrand. That meant that the sale of Saint Laurent was bound to stir up political controversy. I couldn't risk that.'[11] By the early 1990s L'Oréal was already embroiled in a storm over revelations that some of the company's executives had links with the Nazis during the War, and more recently it had come under fire in the United States for allegedly illegally complying with an Arab boycott of Israel. The last thing Lindsay Owen-Jones needed was another political scandal, which would have been inevitable if L'Oréal was involved in a deal linked, however loosely, to François Mitterrand.

Not only was President Mitterrand close to Pierre Bergé, he was also an old friend of Liliane Bettencourt's husband, André, and of L'Oréal's former chairman, François Dalle. After World War II when Mitterrand was campaigning for election to parliament, Dalle gave him a job at L'Oréal, as a director of *Votre Beauté*, one of its magazines.

He worked there for a year, resigning the post as soon as he was elected. 'François Mitterrand has known François Dalle and André Bettencourt since they were at school,' said Owen-Jones. 'They even slept in the same dormitory. Can you imagine what the press would have said if we'd done the Saint Laurent deal? It would have exposed us to such a controversy. I just didn't want that.'[12]

Pierre Bergé was stymied. When L'Oréal withdrew from negotiations in late spring 1992, Yves Saint Laurent had been unofficially up for sale for six months, and no other serious bidders had emerged. He and Yves were still paying interest on their expensive loans, and Pierre was concerned that the banks might press him to repay part of the capital. If necessary he could sell some of their YSL shares on an *ad hoc* basis, but there was a limit to the amount of money he could raise that way, and the sales might depress the share price.

Meanwhile conditions in the luxury market were worsening. Orcofi and L'Oréal closed Lanvin's *couture* operation that January, and a few months later Ronald Perelman cancelled plans to float Revlon on the New York stock market because share prices were so weak. Calvin Klein's empire came close to collapse when a block of bonds came up for redemption and he did not have enough money to buy them. Eventually he was rescued by his friend, David Geffen, the billionaire music mogul, who bought the bonds for $30 million. Yves Saint Laurent's financial difficulties were minor compared to Calvin Klein's, but even so, it was under pressure.

The crux of the company's problems was that the slowdown in sales came at a time when it needed to make substantial investments. Pierre planned to introduce a new women's perfume in autumn 1993, and had invested in a new factory and laboratory to develop the skin-care range, due to be launched that autumn with an advertising campaign featuring Catherine Deneuve, shot by the fashion photographer Jean-Baptiste Mondino. He and Jean-Francis Bretelle had also started upgrading the YSL licensed products, by weeding out weaker licensees and imposing tighter controls on the rest by becoming more involved in design and marketing. It was a sensible long-term strategy to protect the brand, but one which would involve lower licensing income and higher costs in the short term. There was also the $2 million bill for the launch of the Robert Merloz label that July which, at the time, Pierre hoped would rejuvenate the company's image and eventually provide a new source of sales. He realized that the combination of recession, and these heavy investments, would make it even harder to attract investors.

By early summer Jean-Pierre Halbron and his other advisers had convinced him to modify his demands. 'I told him we had to look at other options,' said Halbron. 'You've always got to be flexible in a deal like this.'[13] They decided to resurrect the plan to sell the 14.9 per cent stake that Yves and Pierre had bought from Carlo de Benedetti, which would at least raise enough money to placate the banks. Pierre had already tried, and failed, to sell that holding, but he had made informal approaches to personal contacts, and Wasserstein Perella felt that it might have more success if it marketed the stake on a formal footing. Pierre agreed, even conceding that the deal could include rights of first refusal over his and Yves's other shares, and Wasserstein Perella started contacting likely bidders in July.

Meanwhile Pierre set about raising capital to placate the banks by selling *ad hoc* stakes in Yves Saint Laurent. He sold 16,500 of his shares in the company on 31 July 1992 through Banque Morval in Geneva and on 7 August he sold the same number of shares through Banque Rothschild in Geneva. On 11 September he sold 85,000 shares belonging to Yves and 2,000 of his own shares through Banque Julius Baer. By the end of the transactions, he had raised a total of $18 million.

Wasserstein Perella's marketing efforts soon flushed out one company interested in the minority stake – LVMH. 'Arnault called me and said he wanted to talk to me, would I come to lunch?' recounted Pierre. 'He said, "What are you doing? What are you up to? I hear you are selling fifteen per cent." He said, "You know I'm interested – I'll take the fifteen per cent. We will make a great company: you will have freedom, you will have anything you want." I said, "Good bye. I will think it over."'[14] Not for long. One reason why Pierre had borrowed so heavily to buy the De Benedetti shares in the first place was the fear of them being auctioned off to Bernard Arnault. Pierre responded to Arnault's approach by suggesting that they merged Yves Saint Laurent, Christian Lacroix, Hubert de Givenchy and Christian Dior into 'a real luxury company' with himself as chairman. 'And the answer was no, of course. He wouldn't do it. That was no surprise to me.'[15]

Another of Wasserstein Perella's prospects was more promising. One of the first companies Jean-Pierre Halbron went back to that summer was Elf Sanofi, which had turned down the original deal the previous winter, but now claimed to be interested. Sanofi was an unusual company, founded in 1973, when it was spun off from Elf Aquitaine to buy businesses outside the cyclical oil industry. It had since made nearly two hundred acquisitions, mostly in pharmaceuticals, but like other drugs groups, notably Squibb, it had bought some beauty brands, the best known of which was L'Air du Temps, the Nina Ricci scent which had been a best-seller since its introduction in the 1940s.

Despite its expansion Sanofi had never succeeded in emerging from the shadow of Elf, its powerful parent company. An intensely political entity, Elf was a state-controlled concern whose chairmen, like those of other nationalized groups, were appointed by the government of the day. Sanofi, by contrast, usually managed to stay out of the political firing line and its chairman, Jean-François Dehecq, had held on to his job under the socialists, despite being a supporter of Jacques Chirac, the Gaullist leader. 'Dehecq wasn't really seen as being political at all,' said a senior Sanofi executive. 'But nor was Sanofi itself. It was run separately from Elf and it was in a different business with a different culture. Sanofi's managers were always a bit more gung-ho, less plodding and civil-servanty than Elf's.' The fifty-two-year-old Dehecq conformed to the cliché, cutting a flamboyant figure among the *Grandes Écoles* graduates who ran other French large companies. A bank clerk's son from Nantes, he was a jocular man of basketball player proportions who was proud of being the same height – six foot five – as his political hero, General de Gaulle. After working as a maths teacher, he joined Elf as an engineer and was seconded to Sanofi when it was founded, becoming chairman in 1985. 'Dehecq was an exhibitionist, a bit of a cowboy,' commented one of his competitors. 'He'd made a lot of acquisitions for Sanofi over the years and was off on an ego trip.'

Most of Dehecq's acquisitions had been in pharmaceuticals, an industry where he was well known and Sanofi was a force to be reckoned with. So far he had shown little interest in developing the beauty division, and by the early 1990s it was so much smaller than Unilever's or L'Oréal's that, like Yves Saint Laurent, it risked being relegated to the industry's second division, with its brands gradually being dropped by department stores and duty-free shops. Sanofi had approached the point where it needed to decide whether to get out of the beauty business, or become a much bigger player; if the latter, then liaison with a prestigious international brand such as Yves Saint Laurent made perfect sense. Together the two companies would create the world's third largest beauty group.[16]

Yet Jean-François Dehecq had spurned the chance to bid for Yves Saint Laurent when Jean-Pierre Halbron first approached him six months before. One consideration was that Elf was under acute financial pressure because of the decline in the oil price since the Gulf War. If Sanofi paid the $1 billion in cash for Yves Saint Laurent that Pierre Bergé wanted, its earnings per share would have fallen, and Elf would not have sanctioned a reduction in its income from Sanofi at a time when it core oil interests were so unstable. Like Lindsay Owen-Jones, Dehecq thought Pierre was asking for too much money and, at the time, the YSL chairman showed no sign of being willing to compromise either on price or on the issue of control. 'The price Pierre Bergé wanted then was too high,' he recalled. 'He was insisting on cash and on keeping control. It didn't look like a good deal.'[17]

Elf was still under pressure when Jean-Pierre Halbron approached Sanofi again that summer; if anything its problems were worse. The oil price was still depressed and French petrol sales were hit by a decline in demand for diesel because of a lorry drivers' strike. But Pierre Bergé's position had changed. Not only was he opening the door to negotiation by offering to sell Carlo de Benedetti's minority stake rather than a straight 100 per cent, but he might, or so his advisers hinted, be prepared to be more malleable about other aspects of the deal.

Jean-François Dehecq met Halbron in late July, and told him that Sanofi might be interested in the minority stake, but that they would have to wait before starting negotiations as he was leaving for the annual French summer holiday in August. When Dehecq returned to Paris in early September, Halbron arranged for him to meet Pierre Bergé for lunch. Convinced that he had found a buyer, Pierre revealed in an interview with *Le Nouvel Économiste*, the French business magazine, that the old De Benedetti stake was on the market and that he expected to have sold it by the end of the year.[18]

Talks rumbled on until early December when Dehecq produced a new proposal. 'I went to see Pierre Bergé and told him that we didn't want a minority stake but wanted to buy everything. I really thought he'd say no.'[19] And so he did at first because by 'everything' Jean-François Dehecq meant control of the entire company. 'Then I explained that we'd take the perfume and cosmetics, but he and Yves could keep the *couture*. He said it was worth thinking about. A few days later he said he was still looking at it. I was still convinced he'd say no. I thought it was the last conversation we'd have on the subject.'[20]

The terms Sanofi was offering were not ideal. Jean-François Dehecq had not yet specified his exact price, but it was evident that he had no intention of paying $1 billion for Yves Saint Laurent. He was also insisting on paying in shares, not cash, which would leave Yves and Pierre with a large block of Elf Sanofi stock. They could sell those shares but would have to be careful about doing so for fear of depressing Sanofi's share price and reducing the value of their own investment.

Moreover Pierre was loth to give up control of the perfume company, and risk a repetition of the conflict with Squibb, even though he accepted that the only way Sanofi, or any other bidder, could make the acquisition pay was by merging the YSL products with their own beauty brands. However, he realized that Saint Laurent needed the backing of a larger group to develop its beauty brands, and whereas parting with the fashion house would have been unthinkable, as he and Yves had sole control of it since 1972, they had only owned the perfume and cosmetics since 1986. 'Sanofi was very clever,' commented Halbron. 'They had to have control of the YSL perfumes if they were going to make money from the deal. So they offered to let Pierre Bergé keep control of the fashion as a "concession". Of course it wasn't really a concession at all. They didn't want the *couture* house in the first place. It was the perfumes and cosmetics that interested them.'[21]

Besides, as Sanofi and its advisers were well aware, Pierre was running out of options. The company had been up for sale for over a year and Sanofi was the only buyer in sight. 'We only ever had two real contenders: L'Oréal and Sanofi,' he later admitted. 'We talked to L'Oréal for a long time, but it didn't work out. Then we talked to Sanofi.'[22] Meanwhile the YSL share price was plummeting. On 21 September 1992, Pierre announced that the company's profits during the first half of the year had been much lower than expected, and warned of a further reduction during the second half.[23] The entire company had been badly affected by the recession, the initial response to the skin-care range had been disappointing and, by then, it was obvious that the Robert Merloz label was *not* going to meet Pierre's commercial expectations.

Yves Saint Laurent's shares fell from 805 francs on 21 September 1992, the day of the profits warning, to 520 francs by early December, when Dehecq started discussing terms to buy the whole company. The shares carried on falling during the first two weeks of the month, reaching 476 francs on 15 December. The stock market value of Yves Saint Laurent had almost halved in less than three months from 3.14 billion francs to 1.86 billion francs.

Pierre accepted Sanofi's terms. 'Pierre Bergé's a proud man, but he's a realist,' observed Jean-Pierre Halbron. 'Whenever we came up against a problem, I'd explain the situation to him and he quickly understood what was happening. He mightn't have liked it, but he'd soon accept that we had to find a way round.'[24] By Christmas, Pierre and Dehecq had agreed on the outline of a deal whereby Sanofi would pay between $600 million and $700 million in shares for Yves Saint Laurent, taking full control of the beauty division, and leaving Yves and Pierre with managerial control of the fashion house until the year 2001. Yves would also retain the right of veto over the marketing of all the YSL products, including the perfumes, that he had with Squibb. 'What Monsieur Bergé really wanted to make sure of was that he should retain control of the company's image and that Yves Saint Laurent should have total freedom to create,' said Dehecq. 'That seemed fair enough to me.'[25]

There were still issues to be resolved. The level of Yves's and Pierre's salaries had yet to be decided, as had the terms on which they would cede control of the fashion business to Sanofi in the year 2001 and dismantle the *société en commandite par actions*. The question of the *commandite* was particularly sensitive as Pierre expected that he and Yves would be paid a substantial sum in return for relinquishing their right to control. This was standard practice in such transactions, but Sanofi was concerned about the risk of complaints if

Yves and Pierre were seen to be making much more money from the sale than the company's other shareholders.

Another obstacle was the YSL share price which, having fallen steadily during the autumn, suddenly rose in mid-December. The shares started climbing on 16 December, when they crept from 476 francs to nearly 480 francs, and jumped again to 482 francs the following day. By the end of the month they were worth 525 francs. It was no secret that Yves Saint Laurent was in talks with Sanofi – the De Benedetti stake had been publicly up for sale since a *Le Nouvel Économiste* article in late September, and subsequent reports had cited Sanofi as a possible purchaser – but no one had suggested that Sanofi was negotiating to buy the entire company, nor was anyone supposed to suspect it.

The increase in the share price was too high to be attributable to the prospective sale of a minority shareholding that had been common knowledge for months. The only people who had anything to gain by buying YSL shares were those who knew about the Sanofi deal, and expected to be able to make a profit by selling the shares at a higher price after the acquisition was announced, or who wanted to drive up the share price to inflate the eventual value of that deal. Given that Sanofi planned to pay with shares, the higher the YSL share price, the more of its own shares Sanofi would have to issue. By Christmas the Commission des Opérations de Bourse, the body that polices the French stock market, was so concerned by the apparently inexplicable rise in Yves Saint Laurent's shares that it began an insider trading investigation into the price movements during December and the previous summer.

The bankers and lawyers representing Sanofi and Yves Saint Laurent worked through Christmas and New Year to complete the deal, and by the second week of January the two sides had agreed on final terms. Jean-François Dehecq and his team arrived at 55 rue de Babylone for a formal meeting with Pierre Bergé, Yves Saint Laurent and their advisers. It was the first time that Dehecq had met Yves who, as usual, had played no part in the negotiations, leaving everything to Pierre. After a brief conversation, Yves, Pierre and the Sanofi chairman each signed seven copies of the fifty-page contract, and Yves Saint Laurent became a subsidiary of Elf Sanofi.

The final terms obliged Sanofi to exchange four of its shares for every five YSL shares. This would involve issuing so many new shares that Elf Aquitaine's majority stake would be reduced from sixty-one per cent to just over fifty-one per cent. When the acquisition was announced Sanofi's share price was 1,087 francs, against 630 francs for YSL's. This meant that Sanofi would be paying shares worth $650 million for Yves Saint Laurent, the equivalent of 870 francs a share, 38 per cent higher than the market price, but significantly less than the 950 francs Pierre paid Carlo de Benedetti two years before.

Yves and Pierre were to retain control of the fashion house until the year 2001, as previously agreed, and to receive annual salaries of $2 million.[26] However, they would relinquish their rights to royalties on sales of the YSL perfumes, thereby saving Sanofi several million dollars each year, as their share of Opium's royalties alone was around $2 million.[27] As compensation for relinquishing those rights, and other financial entitlements, and for dismantling the *société en commandite par actions*, Yves and Pierre would receive $65 million in shares, in addition to the Sanofi shares they were getting for their 43.7 per cent stake in Yves Saint Laurent.[28] The entire deal, including the arrangements for ceding the *commandite*, was to be voted on by the YSL shareholders at a special meeting which should, in theory, have defused any complaints that Yves and Pierre had received preferential treatment by enabling the shareholders to decide whether to accept Sanofi's offer. In practice, the outcome of the vote was a foregone conclusion as Yves and Pierre personally controlled nearly fifty per cent of the shares. 'Dissolving the *commandite* with a shareholders' vote was a brilliant idea,' acknowledged Lindsay Owen-Jones. 'I must admit it hadn't occurred to me.'[29] In the meantime the Commission des Opérations de Bourse insisted that a formal warning to shareholders be attached to the public document spelling out the terms of the deal, drawing their attention to the *commandite* premium.

On the morning of Monday 18 January 1993, Sanofi and Yves Saint Laurent announced that they were suspending their shares and holding a press conference the following afternoon. At the press conference Jean-François Dehecq announced that Sanofi was buying the entire YSL group. He was at pains to stress that the acquisition was 'the culmination of a twenty-year strategy' for Sanofi in the beauty business,[30] while Pierre Bergé emphasized how anxious he had been to find 'a French solution' to the question of YSL's future ownership.[31] Yves did not appear at the press conference; he was completing the fittings for the following week's *couture* show, which was dedicated to Rudolf Nureyev, who had died earlier that month. The journalists and investment analysts were not surprised by his absence, as by then they were accustomed to dealing with Pierre Bergé on financial matters. Besides, their attention was diverted by the presence of another figure on the podium, Loïk Le Floch-Prigent, chairman of Elf Aquitaine.

Le Floch, or 'Flock of Pigeons', as his employees called him, was François Mitterrand's appointee as Elf's chairman. A staunch socialist, he had been a senior aide to Pierre Dreyfus, the industry minister in Pierre Mauroy's radical early 1980s government, before being made chairman of Rhône-Poulenc, the state-controlled chemicals company, in 1982, only to be ousted by Jacques Chirac's new centre-right government four years later. The socialists returned to power in 1988 and Le Floch was given the top job at Elf the following year. No one had any doubt that it was a political appointment, and he was often described in the press as being close to President Mitterrand. 'That wasn't strictly true,' observed one senior Elf executive. 'Le Floch knew Mitterrand and he was part of the socialist camp. But he wasn't really intimate with the president, in fact he wasn't even in the second circle. It's just that people thought he was and, at the time, it suited Le Floch to let them think it.'

The chairmanship of Elf Aquitaine was regarded as the plum job in French industry. As France's largest company, Elf owned numerous minority shareholdings and its chairman would automatically be appointed to the boards of other large companies, and be consulted by other industrialists on important issues. Past Elf chairmen had been bastions of the business establishment, but Le Floch was viewed as an outsider, as a doctor's son from Brest who studied engineering at a college in Grenoble, rather than going to an élite *Grande École*. 'He always had a bit of a chip on his shoulder about that,' said one of his colleagues. 'And it's fair to say that his rivals didn't let him forget it.' Fairly or unfairly, Loïk Le Floch-Prigent never succeeded in convincing the investment community that he was up to the Elf job. 'He was a political appointee but so are all Elf's chairmen,' observed a senior Paris banker. 'It didn't really matter whether he was left wing, right wing or middle wing. The bottom line was that

Le Floch wasn't the man to lead Elf Aquitaine into the twenty-first century and everyone knew it.'

Le Floch's presence at the press conference was interpreted as a tacit admission that he had a hand in Sanofi's acquisition which, given his presumed intimacy with François Mitterrand and the political sub-text to so many of Elf's activities, fuelled suspicion that the sale of Yves Saint Laurent was a political deal orchestrated by the President of the Republic to help his friend, Pierre Bergé. 'God knows why Le Floch turned up that day,' groaned one of his associates. 'There was no reason for him to be there. He'd known about the YSL deal all along, of course he had. Sanofi couldn't make a big acquisition like that without getting its majority shareholder's consent. But Dehecq had done all the negotiating. He's a straightforward guy. Everyone knows that. He's got no connection to Mitterrand. He's a Gaullist for God's sake. If Le Floch hadn't been there, the whole thing would have been seen as Jean-François Dehecq's deal and things would probably have been very different. But Le Floch made an error of judgement in going to that press conference and it stirred things up for everyone.'

The earliest reports of the deal speculated as to whether it had been influenced by Pierre Bergé's political connections.[32] Pierre made matters worse by being quoted in Le Figaro as saying 'it's a good deal for me', and tactlessly telling Women's Wear Daily that 'I still don't know what we're going to do with it all (the money).'[33] The speculation intensified as YSL's shares rose from 630 francs to 765 francs two days after the announcement, while Sanofi's fell from 1,087 francs to 969 francs, and stock market traders dubbed the deal 'le coup Bergé', 'Bergé's masterstroke'.

Political intervention in industry was not unusual in France. The fact that the state either owned or controlled so many large companies made it easy for politicians to meddle in industrial affairs. Sometimes they did so directly, by issuing instructions to the management; mostly it was done indirectly by putting political appointees in charge of state-controlled companies. The positions of the state-appointed chairmen were reviewed every three years, which meant that if they displeased their political mentors, they could be replaced. This system, which was called 'the chairmen's waltz', ensured that many of France's most powerful industrialists, like Loïk Le Floch-

Prigent, owed their jobs to the government of the day, and knew exactly what was expected of them. Such blatant political intervention in industry would have been considered scandalous in Britain or North America, but in France it was regarded as perfectly normal.

François Mitterrand's socialists were no more interventionist than the previous right-wing governments, as illustrated by the speed with which Jacques Chirac's administration removed Loïk Le Floch-Prigent from Rhône-Poulenc in 1986. But *le coup Bergé*, and the huge profits made by Yves and Pierre, struck a nerve, and rather than dying down after a few days, as similar scandals had done, it continued. The usually restrained *Le Monde* entered the fray on 27 January 1993 in a front-page story entitled 'Saint Laurent at Any Price' in which it quoted an unidentified 'intimate' of the president as describing the deal as 'a political affair'.[34] The article questioned whether the sale of Yves Saint Laurent was '*un cas de copinage*', which roughly translates as a 'conspiracy among friends', whereby a state-controlled company had given a 'gift' to one of the President of the Republic's closest friends by buying his company for an inflated price in a deal announced two months before the next parliamentary elections in March, which the socialists seemed certain to lose.[35] Some investment analysts were quoted as saying that Sanofi had overpaid for Saint Laurent, given the level of its debts and the depressed state of the luxury market. They also suggested that Sanofi would have been better advised to focus on its pharmaceutical interests, as it had appeared to be doing with the acquisition of Sterling Winthrop, an American drugs group, in 1991.[36]

The story was followed up by other French newspapers and business magazines, and by foreign publications, including the *New York Times* and *Vanity Fair*, which considered the affair to be of greater interest to their readers than the usual round of French business scandals because of the glamour of the Yves Saint Laurent brand name. No firm evidence was discovered to suggest that Loïk Le Floch-Prigent had engineered Sanofi's acquisition of Yves Saint Laurent at François Mitterrand's behest, so why did the allegations of '*un cas de copinage*' rumble on for so long?

One explanation is that the French press seized on *le coup Bergé* as an opportunity to criticize François Mitterrand, who had previously been seen as too powerful to attack, but was weakened by the prospect of the socialists' defeat in the March 1993 parliamentary elections. The president's popularity peaked during the Gulf War, and had fallen steadily as the economic situation worsened. Mitterrand would stay on as president until the end of his eight-year term of office in May 1995, even after the Left lost its parliamentary majority, but he risked being marginalized by the right in a *cohabitation* government. During the last bout of *cohabitation* from 1986 to 1988, he had out-manoeuvred Jacques Chirac, but this time he would be older, at seventy-five, and physically feebler, having recently had an operation for prostate cancer. Only a few years before the French public would probably have been willing to ignore accusations of nepotism against a popular, powerful president like François Mitterrand; but now he was weaker and politically isolated. The President of the Republic was perceived as being vulnerable, as were his friends, including Pierre Bergé, and the press felt able to be more critical of them than in the past.

Another factor was that a number of Sanofi and YSL rivals, including L'Oréal and LVMH, were stoking the controversy, apparently convinced that it was a politically orchestrated transaction. 'There's no doubt that they were, shall we say, pouring oil on the flames,' said a senior French financial journalist who covered the deal. 'It was all done in a softly-softly manner. It was a case of someone connected with one of LVMH's companies taking you on one side after a press conference and suggesting you might look a little further into a particular aspect of the deal. Or maybe there'd be a couple of apparently casual comments at a dinner. "You don't seriously believe that the President of the Republic wasn't involved, do you?" That sort of thing.'

Did François Mitterrand ask Loïk Le Floch-Prigent to engineer a deal for Sanofi to salvage Yves Saint Laurent? Pierre Bergé and Jean-François Dehecq have both consistently denied it. 'That sort of talk is crap and I don't care who says it,' barked Pierre to *Women's Wear Daily* while the controversy was raging.[37] 'It's absolute rubbish,' insisted Dehecq. 'Mr Le Floch-Prigent never asked me to start the negotiations. Anyone who knows me well knows that I am not the sort of person who responds to orders. It was a sensible acquisition for the company that turned us into a force in perfume and cosmetics. We were given a good opportunity and we took it.'[38]

In strategic terms the YSL deal was undoubtedly a 'sensible acquisition' for Sanofi, given that it needed another prestigious beauty
brand, and greater critical mass, if it was to remain competitive in
an increasingly consolidated industry. Even its competitors admitted
that the transaction made commercial sense. 'It was an important
deal for Sanofi, much more important than it would have been for
us,' observed Lindsay Owen-Jones of L'Oréal. 'We were already the
world's largest cosmetics company: but for them it was a major
opportunity to become a force in the luxury world.'[39]

A more sensitive issue is whether Sanofi was interested in building
up its beauty business at that particular time. The last of its beauty
acquisitions was in the heady late 1980s when it was fashionable for
companies to expand. Stock market trends had changed, with investors looking more favourably on companies that concentrated on
clearly defined areas of expertise. Dehecq had always seemed more
interested in pharmaceuticals, and the theme of his most recent
presentations to investment analysts was that Sanofi intended to
concentrate on that side of the business. They would have been less
surprised had he announced that Sanofi was selling its beauty interests, rather than expanding them. Dehecq's explanation is that the
opportunity to acquire a brand of Yves Saint Laurent's calibre was
so rare that it merited a change of strategy. 'We decided to invest
in prestige beauty brands in the late 1980s and, at that time, we
never imagined that one day we'd be able to buy Yves Saint Laurent.
For me there are only three brand names in the world that count –
Christian Dior, Chanel, Yves Saint Laurent – and they all seemed
inaccessible. Suddenly we had a chance to buy one of those three
brands so we took it.'[40]

Why then did Jean-François Dehecq pass on the opportunity to
acquire that brand when Wasserstein Perella first approached him
in spring 1992? It is true that Elf, Sanofi's parent company, had
financial difficulties at the time, but Elf's problems were worse during
the summer when Jean-Pierre Halbron made his second approach.
Again Dehecq had a perfectly plausible answer in that, although
Elf's financial position had not changed, Pierre Bergé's negotiating
stance had. If Sanofi had paid $1 billion for 100 per cent of Yves
Saint Laurent, its earnings per share would have fallen, a prospect
which would have been unacceptable to Elf. By buying a minority

stake, as Halbron suggested that summer, or paying $605 million in shares for 100 per cent of the company, Sanofi could make the acquisition without depressing its earnings per share, and hence its contribution to Elf's profits.

Pierre Bergé's 'flexibility' enabled Jean-François Dehecq to buy Yves Saint Laurent for $605 million, two thirds of the original asking price, and the fact that the deal was paid in shares, not cash, makes the price seem more reasonable, as share transactions are usually slightly more expensive than cash ones. On an objective analysis, the price Sanofi paid for Yves Saint Laurent was high compared to the share price, but not ridiculously so, particularly as it was acquiring control by dissolving the *commandite*, the existence of which would have slightly depressed the market value of the shares. Moreover, as Pierre had given way on the control issue, there were cost savings to be made by pooling production, distribution and research resources; and it was exempted from paying the standard five per cent royalty on the sales of the YSL perfumes which would add several million dollars a year to its profits.

Sanofi was also buying Yves Saint Laurent at a sensible time, at the bottom of the luxury cycle, when the industry was depressed and prices were low. Even *Le Monde*'s original *cas de copinage* article quoted investment analysts saying that Sanofi had got a bargain,[41] and that was the consensus among its commercial rivals. 'Saint Laurent is a very, very good business,' observed Henry Racamier of Orcofi. 'And the price isn't so high if you pay in shares as Sanofi did. It was a very good acquisition for them. They needed another prestigious name and they don't come any better than Yves Saint Laurent.'[42]

Given the gravity of Pierre's and Yves's financial difficulties, Jean-François Dehecq might have been able to beat them down to a lower price, but it is unlikely that he or his advisers realized the full extent of their debts. What he did know was that the deal represented a rare opportunity to buy one of the best brand names in the beauty business and that 'there were a couple of companies waiting in the wings hoping our negotiations would fall through'.[43] If Sanofi did not buy Yves Saint Laurent, Dehecq was certain that one of its competitors, possibly LVMH, would do so.

Another consideration is that, despite the allegations that Jean-François Dehecq was pressured into doing the deal by Loïk Le

Floch-Prigent, he had nothing to gain by pandering to the Elf chairman. When Sanofi started talks with Yves Saint Laurent in autumn 1992, the socialists were doing so badly in the opinion polls that they seemed sure to lose the parliamentary elections the following spring, which meant that the new centre-right government would be bound to force Loïk Le Floch-Prigent to leave Elf Aquitaine, just as it had fired him from Rhône-Poulenc. By autumn 1992 Le Floch was finished at Elf, and all his executives knew it. If Jean-François Dehecq was bullied into doing the YSL deal, all he needed to do was play for time by exploiting legal or financial technicalities until after the March elections, knowing that he would then be able to use his political connections with the new government to persuade the next Elf chairman to abandon it.

Instead Dehecq pressed ahead with the acquisition. His own senior executives, as well as those of Elf and even President Mitterrand's staff at the Élysée are convinced that it was a straightforward commercial transaction, conceived and executed by Sanofi. 'I'm absolutely sure of that,' said an Elf man. 'There was never any evidence, not the slightest hint, that it was ever anything else.' When Le Floch had previously been involved with politically sensitive transactions at Elf, he had called in senior colleagues beforehand to discuss plans for a 'damage control' exercise to defuse the controversy. If either he, or François Mitterrand, were involved with the YSL acquisition, Le Floch would have realized it was bound to be controversial and implemented his usual 'damage control' measures, but he did not do so. '

'It was no secret that Le Floch was Mitterrand's man and that from time to time he did deals for political reasons, but this wasn't one of them,' said an Elf executive. 'Whenever something sensitive was happening, there were meetings and briefings. We'd be warned to expect trouble and told how to deal with it. Nothing like that happened with Saint Laurent. There were none of the usual indications that there was anything peculiar about it. It was a commercial deal for Sanofi in one of its existing businesses. If Pierre Bergé hadn't been a friend of President Mitterrand and Le Floch hadn't been puffed up into one by the press, no one would have made a fuss about it.'

The Sanofi camp was equally convinced that it was an apolitical affair initiated by Jean-François Dehecq, not Loïk Le Floch-Prigent or François Mitterrand. 'At no time was there any sign that it was anything else,' said a banker who advised Dehecq throughout the negotiations. 'Le Floch was told what was going on, but he didn't play any part in the talks. Now, he knew very well that the President of the Republic would be pleased with the acquisition because it was good for Pierre Bergé, but that wasn't the reason for doing it. I sometimes wonder what would have happened if Sanofi had decided to pull out halfway through, maybe there'd have been some political pressure then. But that situation didn't arise, so we'll never know.'

Even François Mitterrand's political opponents eventually concluded that he had nothing to do with the deal. One of Sanofi's senior advisers was François Polge de Combret, Bernard Arnault's friend from New York, who by then was back in Paris as a partner at Lazard Frères, which was advising Sanofi on the YSL acquisition. His links with Sanofi were even closer than with many of his other clients as he had been a member of the board since 1991, and his brother, Bernard, was a senior Elf executive. François Polge de Combret was also well connected with the new centre-right government, as he had been a senior aide to Valéry Giscard d'Estaing during his presidency from 1974 to 1981. Political sources say that both Giscard d'Estaing and Jacques Chirac asked him to find out whether the allegations of President Mitterrand's involvement in the Saint Laurent deal were true, and that he assured them they were unfounded. 'If anyone knew what was going on between Elf and Sanofi it was De Combret,' said one. 'He was absolutely convinced that it was a straightforward deal and that Mitterrand had nothing to do with it. Giscard and Chirac took his word for it. Neither of them said anything publicly about the Saint Laurent sale, nor did any other senior opposition politicians. The only ones who made a fuss were junior figures who didn't know what had really happened.'

Had the right suspected 'un cas de copinage', it could have called a halt to the deal, after its victory in the March 1993 parliamentary elections when a centre-right coalition government was formed with Édouard Balladur, Jacques Chirac's former finance minister, as prime minister. At that stage the sale of Yves Saint Laurent to Sanofi was only agreed in principle and the new government could, if it had wished, have blocked it in the two months before the scheduled completion date in mid-May. It even had a convenient excuse to do so because of the Commission des Opérations de Bourse's investigation into the mysterious movements into the YSL share price and suspected insider dealing. Yet Édouard Balladur and his ministers did nothing.

Don Magnifico's Demise
1993

When Patricia Turck-Paquelier was summoned to Avenue Marceau to discuss the plans for a new YSL perfume she had no idea what to expect. She knew Pierre Bergé fairly well since it was he who had hired her to run the perfume division after Chantal Roos left for Shiseido, but she had only a fleeting acquaintance with Yves Saint Laurent, who was rarely seen by his employees at the *couture* house, let alone by those in other parts of the company. Pierre had called the meeting to start the process of developing the new perfume by defining its image, and asked Turck-Paquelier what she thought. 'I told them that I wanted a perfume that summed up what Yves Saint Laurent was all about. Classic, chic, timeless and daring. When I'd finished Monsieur Saint Laurent said that he'd thought of a name. I wondered, "What's he going to say?" And then he said, "Champagne". Brilliant! It was perfect! As soon as he said it, we knew he was right. It was as simple as that.'[1]

The product development process had been very different at her previous employer, Procter & Gamble, the American multinational which was renowned for acting on rigorous research, rather than flashes of intuition. A lively, attractive woman in her thirties with the fluent English which was *de rigueur* for the new breed of ambitious French executives, Turck-Paquelier had been a rising star at P&G's French subsidiary and a regular target for headhunters, even though she invariably spurned their approaches. 'One day I got back to my office and a headhunter called saying, "Patricia, you must get back to me because this time I've got something really special to tell you about." When I called back they explained that it was running YSL Parfums. Well, I'd grown up hearing about Yves Saint Laurent. My mother loved the clothes and the perfumes. It sounds like a cliché but it was too good an opportunity to miss.'[2]

Dreaming up the name of a new product during a business meeting, rather than subjecting it to the checks and cross-checks of research, was not what Turck-Paquelier was accustomed to, but it was obvious that 'Champagne' was an excellent choice. The industry consensus was that a new perfume should be called by a word which already existed, and was thus instantly recognizable to the general public, but was also appropriate to the product and acceptable in different languages. Only a limited number of words were suitable, and the process of securing the legal rights to them had, like every other aspect of a fragrance launch, become costlier and more complex over the years. When YSL introduced Opium in 1977 it gave a pair of elderly *parfumiers* $200 in exchange for the rights, but when Chanel launched Egoïste, its new men's scent in 1990, it reportedly paid $500,000 to the publisher of a French magazine of the same name.[3] Cosmetics companies had also become more assiduous at protecting their trademarks. When Dior was developing Poison, it registered the rights to similar names, including Hemlock and Venom, and in 1986 Yves Saint Laurent took legal action against Givenchy claiming that the name of its new men's fragrance, Keryus, was confusingly similar to its own Kouros. The matter was settled when Givenchy agreed to rechristen the product Xeryus, but the first batch went on sale with the letter 'X' pasted over the original 'K'.

Anxious to avoid such difficulties for Champagne, Pierre Bergé instructed his legal team to find out whether any perfumes were already using the name. Eventually they found one in Royal Bain de Champagne, launched in 1941 by Parfums Caron, a small French beauty house. YSL then spent $500,000 on buying the name from Caron and registering it as a perfume trademark in 170 countries. By summer 1992 the news leaked out that Yves Saint Laurent was planning to launch a new fragrance called Champagne, and André Enders, director of the CVIC, the organization that represented the champagne industry, telephoned Pierre Bergé's office to arrange an appointment to see him. The two men met at Avenue Marceau in

July 1992, and Enders came straight to the point. 'I told Monsieur Bergé that we wouldn't allow them to use the name Champagne.'[4] Pierre demurred, insisting that if Yves Saint Laurent named its new perfume Champagne, it would raise the prestige of the champagne houses, rather than tarnishing it. 'I explained that wasn't the issue,' said Enders. 'If we allowed one company to use our name, even for something luxurious and expensive, we'd have hundreds of others wanting to do the same thing. Where would it all end? I told Monsieur Bergé that we'd take legal action to stop him if necessary. He was perfectly aware of our position.'[5]

Pierre must have realized that André Enders meant what he said, if only because the champagne industry was renowned for the vigour with which it protected its trademark. Over the years it had mounted, and won, dozens of legal suits against a variety of companies attempting to use the name for anything from sparkling wine to cigarettes, and as champagne was such a prestigious industry, and an important source of French exports, the authorities were generally sympathetic to its pleas.

Determined, as usual, to have his way, Pierre Bergé decided to find a solution. The champagne industry is concentrated in the grape-growing region around the towns of Reims, Épernay and Troyes in eastern France. By far the most powerful force in the industry was Bernard Arnault's LVMH group which owned many of the best-known champagne *marques* including Dom Perignon, Veuve Cliquot and the best-selling Moët-et-Chandon.[6] As the biggest buyer of champagne grapes, LVMH wielded tremendous influence and Pierre knew that if Bernard Arnault swung his weight behind an issue, the other champagne houses would fall into line.

Under normal circumstances Pierre had no reason to expect Arnault to help him. There was little love lost between the two men, who were even at different ends of the political spectrum. Pierre had not taken sides publicly in the LVMH takeover battle, but it was no secret that he would have preferred Henry Racamier to win; and his last encounter with Arnault was when he rejected the LVMH chairman's expression of interest in Carlo de Benedetti's shares with the imperious suggestion that he should take charge of Dior, Lacroix and Givenchy as well as Yves Saint Laurent. Yet in this instance Pierre had a useful negotiating ploy, as Bernard Arnault had recently asked Léon Cligman, Yves and Pierre's partner in Rive Gauche, to manufacture Christian Lacroix's ready-to-wear range. Under the terms of his contract with Saint Laurent, Cligman was not allowed to take on such a commitment without Pierre Bergé's consent. 'I told Cligman that I'd say "yes" as long as I didn't have any difficulties with Arnault over Champagne,' said Pierre, who then arranged a meeting with the LVMH chairman to put the same proposal to him. 'I went to see Arnault. *"Mon cher ami . . ."* I explained everything. And he gave me his word that there'd be no problem over Champagne. So I said it was fine for Cligman to take on Lacroix. I left his office with a promise of neutrality.'[7]

The meeting with Bernard Arnault took place in early 1993, just over six months after André Enders went to see Pierre Bergé, and at around the same time as Wasserstein Perella and Lazard Frères were secretly finalizing negotiations for the sale of Yves Saint Laurent to Sanofi. There was no further communication from the CVIC, and Pierre assumed that the threat of legal action had subsided. By then, the choice of the name, Champagne, was an open secret in the perfume and champagne industries, as was the fact that Yves Saint Laurent planned to launch the product in Europe that autumn and in North America a year later. Pierre Bergé pressed ahead with his launch plans and concentrated on integrating YSL Parfums with the Sanofi beauty division.

Both Yves Saint Laurent and its new parent company desperately needed Champagne to be a success. The fifteen-year-old Opium and ten-year-old Paris seemed dated compared with successful new fragrances, such as Calvin Klein's Escape and L'Eau d'Issey, Chantal Roos's first launch for Shiseido. These new scents, like the latest fashions, had swung away from the opulence of 1980s perfumes to reflect simplicity and minimalism, making the Saint Laurent scents seem heavy and antiquated. Paris, never as successful as Opium in North America, had already slipped out of the top ten, and sales of Opium were sliding.[8] Patricia Turck-Paquelier overhauled the advertising for both fragrances, casting Lucie de la Falaise as the new 'face' of Paris, and her fellow 'waif', Kate Moss, in the Opium campaign, but the YSL portfolio really needed the fillip of an exciting new scent. Meanwhile Sanofi was particularly anxious that Champagne should succeed, as the profits from a new best-selling perfume would help to allay the allegations that it would never make money from its politically sensitive acquisition.

On 7 June Pierre Bergé called a press conference at the Hôtel Intercontinental to announce the details of Champagne's introduction. Yves Saint Laurent had hosted scores of events at the hotel over the years, as well as its six-monthly *couture* presentations, and the management knew the drill. Pierre and his team arrived to find the room arranged exactly as they had requested, with an imposing display of flowers and gilt chairs placed in neat rows in front of the podium. The journalists arrived on cue and slipped into their seats, Pierre Bergé rose to address them and then – chaos.

'Thief! Thief!' came a cry from the back of the room, followed by a shout of 'Saint Laurent is robbing us.' A dozen or so men thrust past the hotel security staff, shouting and chanting as they strode towards Pierre Bergé. The security guards shoved and scuffled the interlopers out of the room, and the press conference stumbled on to its conclusion. 'It was bedlam,' said one of the journalists. 'There we all were in this ever so elegant presentation and suddenly it all went crazy. Bergé was livid. He's never been able to keep his temper, but he really lost it that day. I don't know who was madder, him or the demonstrators.'

The intruders were farmers, grape growers from the Champagne region, who were there to protest against the choice of Champagne as a name for a perfume. France's farmers had a flair for staging headline hitting demonstrations after years of protesting against the European Commission's agricultural reforms. One of their favourite ploys was staging *Opérations Escargots* in towns and cities where they brought the traffic to a standstill by driving their tractors round and round literally at a snail's pace, and a successful recent stunt was *Opération Mickey*, when a group of local farmers sealed off the entrance routes to the Euro Disney theme park, dispersing only after being filmed live for the early morning US television news. Gatecrashing an Yves Saint Laurent press conference was par for the course.

While Pierre Bergé and his executives tried to restore order, Marc Brugnon, president of the CVIC, staged an impromptu press briefing in another part of the hotel. He announced that his organization planned to file suit in the Paris civil court against YSL Parfums and Sanofi for allegedly infringing the Champagne trademark, and to secure an injunction preventing them from using the name. The action was to be based on 1990 French copyright law that forbade the use of an *appellation contrôlée*, one of the certified names which can only be used by wines grown in particular regions, for any other product in a manner likely to debase the original. The CVIC filed suit immediately, although the case would not be heard for a couple of months as it would first be submitted to an investigating magistrate who would decide whether it should proceed to trial. The likeliest date for the start of court proceedings was October, a month after Champagne was scheduled to go on sale in Europe backed by a $17 million marketing campaign.

It was not the first time that the name of a YSL perfume had caused controversy. Opium had provoked a rumpus all over the world, and even the apparently innocuous Paris fell foul of Jacques Chirac's city council, with both fragrances benefiting from a flurry of free publicity. The Champagne affair was different, not least because there was a reasonable chance of the CVIC winning. Sanofi's lawyers intended to argue that the case was groundless as the 1990 law stipulated that the use of the *appellation contrôllée* must imperil the prestige of the original product, a consideration which did not apply in this instance, as association with an expensive Yves Saint Laurent perfume would not detract from champagne's status. But the arguments were not clear cut, the CVIC won a similar case in 1986 to stop Seita, the French tobacco group, from bringing out a Champagne cigarette, and the Sanofi lawyers warned that there was a risk of defeat if the case went to court.

Why did the CVIC wait until June 1993 to start legal proceedings, when it could have filed suit at any time in the eleven months since André Enders delivered his warning to Pierre Bergé? The simplest explanation is that by disrupting the press conference, the farmers ensured that their protest attracted considerably more media attention than a behind-the-scenes battle of lawyers' meetings and political lobbying would have done. By summer 1993 the champagne industry was in a fragile state, as the recession had depressed sales both in France and in its foreign markets, particularly the United States, where wholesalers were sending consignments of champagne back to France to be sold cheaply in supermarkets with their US Customs labels torn off. Many leading champagne houses, including those owned by LVMH, had been forced to lay off workers, and local grape growers faced sharply reduced orders. The publicity generated by the Hôtel Intercontinental protest and the subsequent court case was a way of bringing the industry's problems to the government's attention.

It must also have been obvious to anyone familiar with the workings of the perfume industry that by waiting until June 1993 to file suit, the CVIC would inflict the maximum financial damage on Yves Saint Laurent and Sanofi. Champagne had to go on sale in September in order to be ready for Christmas, a period which accounted for at least half the year's perfume sales. If the CVIC won its October court case, Sanofi would almost certainly have to take Champagne off the French market and relaunch it under a different name, thereby wasting most of the money it had spent on advertising. The situation would have been simpler had the champagne industry started proceedings immediately after André Enders's meeting with Pierre Bergé, or even in early 1993 when Pierre had discussed the choice of name with Bernard Arnault. There would then have been enough time for the court to rule on the issue and, if necessary, for YSL Parfums and Sanofi to choose a new name for the scent before it went on sale, as Givenchy had done in 1986 when it was forced by Saint Laurent from Keryus to Xeryus.

By delaying the start of proceedings until June 1993, the CVIC left Parfums YSL and Sanofi with two equally unpalatable choices: succumbing to the champagne industry's demands by changing the name, or pressing ahead with the launch knowing that if the judge ruled against them Sanofi's initial advertising investment would be wasted. It seems highly unlikely that the champagne houses and grape growers in the CVIC would have grasped the full financial implications of the timing of their legal action, but equally it is inconceivable that a company with such extensive perfume interests as LVMH could not have done so. Nor is it likely that the LVMH champagne houses belonging to the CVIC would have backed the decision to take legal action against Yves Saint Laurent without consulting Bernard Arnault. 'Would Arnault have had a say in what was going on? Absolutely,' affirmed a senior LVMH executive. 'He's an extremely efficient chairman with a tremendous grasp of detail and he makes it his business to know what's happening with all the subsidiaries. There's no way that one part of LVMH would be involved in legal action against a competitor of another division, without checking with him first, particularly if it concerns a high profile competitor like Yves Saint Laurent.'

Bernard Arnault has consistently refused to comment on whether, as Pierre Bergé claims, he gave him an assurance that he would use his influence to squash the champagne industry's opposition to the use of the name Champagne, although LVMH has affirmed that its companies were in favour of the CVIC action. Even if Bernard Arnault was involved, directly or indirectly, in planning the Champagne law suit, he did nothing illegal and was almost certainly acting in the best interests of his businesses. The LVMH perfume division was preparing to launch a new version of Poison, Tendre Poison, in 1994 and planned to overhaul the Guerlain scents, the legacy of a recent acquisition. A successful new Yves Saint Laurent fragrance would have jeopardized the prospects for both projects. Moreover the legal suit was absolutely in keeping with the CVIC's past policy, representing a continuation of its efforts to protect the champagne trademark at a time when the industry was in a parlous state. The CVIC would undoubtedly have sued Yves Saint Laurent over the name of its new perfume whether or not Bernard Arnault was involved, the only aspect of the case where his involvement may have made a difference was in the damaging timing of the action.

Gambling that they would win the court case, Sanofi and YSL Parfums pressed ahead with preparations to introduce Champagne in Europe that September. Even without the CVIC's intervention it was a difficult time to introduce a new fragrance. French exports were under pressure as the franc had risen steeply since the European currency crisis the previous autumn, and a number of other new perfumes were coming out at the same time. Unilever was introducing Calvin Klein's Escape to some European countries, and Eternity to others, including France. L'Oréal was investing heavily in its new scent, Eden, and Chantal Roos scored another success for Shiseido with Jean-Paul Gaultier's first fragrance which was packaged in a bottle shaped like a corseletted female torso and a shiny aluminium can. Champagne seemed almost quaint by comparison, with its classic French name, a bottle modelled on a champagne cork and an advertisement shot by Helmut Newton of a *divaesque* figure in a slinky red sequinned slip flinging up her arms triumphantly beside a theatrical curtain. 'I don't give a damn what the others are doing,' Pierre Bergé barked to *Women's Wear Daily*. 'Those are just trends of the moment and they will pass.'[9] His bravado seemed to be paying off, Champagne achieved sales of $30 million in its first four weeks on the market, nearly as much as it had been expected to sell in the first three months.

But when the legal case came to court on 28 October 1993 the judge found in the champagne industry's favour, ordering Sanofi and YSL Parfums to pay a small fine and to stop using the name Champagne in France. The company was ordered to hand over all the packaging and publicity material to the CVIC for destruction under the supervision of a court-appointed bailiff. Sanofi's share price fell by 22 francs to 999 francs on the news. 'I was so sad when I heard we'd lost,' recalled Patricia Turck-Paquelier. 'Sad and stunned.'[10] She was not the only one to be disappointed. 'Pierre Bergé was very, very involved with the launch,' she said. 'It was his baby. And Monsieur Saint Laurent was really attached to Champagne. He loved it and wanted it to last forever. One time he came into Monsieur Bergé's office and I thought – sniff, sniff – that's Champagne. But it can't be. He's the only other person here. And it was. He was wearing it!'[11]

Sanofi appealed against the decision, and the destruction order was frozen with Champagne allowed to remain on sale until the appeal was heard on 15 December. At the appeal the champagne industry scored a second victory and Sanofi was instructed to stop using the name by the end of the year and to pay the CVIC token damages of one franc. Sanofi's lawyers advised Jean-François Dehecq and Pierre Bergé that there was no point in appealing again, and that afternoon Claude Saujet, head of the perfume division, called a press conference at Sanofi's headquarters on rue Marbeuf, a street running south from the Avenue des Champs-Elysées.

Journalists were ushered into a conference room decorated in a white spacey style that smacked of 1970s kitsch. The conference was conducted by Saujet, a trim figure in his forties with a perma-tanned face and salesman's smile; the only hint of Yves Saint Laurent's involvement was a large black and white photograph of Yves propped up on an easel. Saujet read out a statement saying that Champagne would be withdrawn from the French market on 31 December 1993 and replaced by the same scent in a virtually identical bottle bearing the name Yves Saint Laurent. However, he added, the company still planned to call the perfume Champagne when it came out in North America the following autumn and would continue its fight to save the name in the other countries where the champagne industry had filed suit. The press conference ended in laughter when Saujet invited the journalists to take away a complimentary bottle of Champagne with them. 'We've got rather a lot to get rid of.'

Sanofi's share price fell yet again, by 20 francs to 965 francs over the next two days. The company did what it could to minimize the financial impact of the destruction order which, by chance, came at the least damaging time of year given that perfume stocks were traditionally at their lowest after the busy Christmas season. It even made a joke of its defeat by putting up billboards to advertise the new 'Yves Saint Laurent' perfume with a portrait of Yves and the words, '*Mon parfum, un hommage aux femmes qui pétillent*', 'My perfume, a tribute to women who sparkle', printed in his hand writing.

The publicity over the court case, coupled with the scarcity value of Champagne, helped to increase sales that Christmas. By the day of the destruction order on 31 December, the perfume had been on sale for three months, and during that time it was the best-selling scent in Europe with sales of over $50 million, which meant that Sanofi had already recouped the cost of its $17 million advertising campaign, as well as the $2 million expense of recalling stocks of Champagne and delivering replacement bottles of the new scent. However it now faced the threat of further legal action in other countries and, even if it won those cases, the enforced change of name in France had prevented it from positioning Champagne as a global product with the same name and the same advertising all over the world.

Other perfume companies had faced similar situations in the past. During the 1950s Guerlain had to sell Shalimar as No. 90 in Britain, because another scent was already sold there under the name.[12] If it was difficult for a company to sell a scent under different names in different countries in the 1950s, it seemed virtually impossible to do so in the 1990s. Champagne would only get the full benefit of

Sanofi's marketing investment if consumers in Britain or Australia recognized the name in the advertisements they saw in the American editions of *Vogue* or *Harper's Bazaar*, or on airport billboards. The name change could also cause chaos in the duty-free market. How could an Italian executive who bought her first bottle of Champagne at La Rinascente department store in Milan be expected to know what to ask for when she tried to buy another bottle at the Charles de Gaulle airport duty-free shop?

Whatever happened in the foreign court cases the carefully planned strategy to revitalize the Yves Saint Laurent perfume portfolio and for Sanofi to justify its expensive acquisition was in shreds. In retrospect the sensible course of action would have been to have quietly abandoned the name Champagne, ideally after André Enders made his intentions clear to Pierre Bergé, thereby ensuring that the new product would be launched under the same name everywhere. Even if the name had been changed immediately after the CVIC filed suit in June 1993, there would probably have been just enough time to alter the packaging and promotional material. Yet YSL Parfums and Sanofi stuck to their original proposals and, whether by accident or design, the CVIC's court case turned out to be a masterful revenge for Bernard Arnault against Sanofi for the acquisition of Yves Saint Laurent.

While Pierre Bergé was battling against the champagne industry on one front, he was bickering with his Chambre Syndicale colleagues on another. A row erupted over the dates of the March 1993 *prêt-à-porter* fashion shows, with one faction lobbying for fashion week to be brought forward to February, giving the designers more time to manufacture and distribute their collections, and another camp, led by Pierre, arguing against the proposed change on the grounds that it would not give the *couturiers* enough time to complete their ready-to-wear ranges after *couture* week in January. The sub-text to the battle was the split between the old guard, which was still involved with *haute couture*, and the new guard, which was not and was loathe to allow the constraints of the traditional *couture* trade to prevent them meeting the demands of the modern fashion market. There had been wrangles over the same subject in the past but this time, when the issue went to a vote, Pierre Bergé and his supporters lost. Pierre unearthed a procedural ruse to force the Chambre

Syndicale to reverse its decision, which enraged his critics further. They tasted revenge that February in the elections for membership of the Chambre Syndicale management committee, when his bid for re-election as president was defeated. Pierre Bergé had lost control of the industry body that he had chaired and dominated for twenty years.

When the Chambre Syndicale met again the following month to discuss the dates of the next season's *couture* shows Pierre refused to attend and sent Maurice Cau, managing director of Rive Gauche, to represent him. At that meeting the Chambre voted to bring the *couture* shows forward by a week, and Yves Saint Laurent immediately announced that it would stick to the original dates on the grounds that its employees had already booked their holidays in August, the traditional French summer break, and if the shows were held seven days earlier there would be no work for them to do in the extra week. The argument was logical in principle, but flawed in practice as many of the fashion editors and clients who flew into Paris for *couture* week would not be able to stay on for an extra week to see the YSL show. Pierre's threat might have worked twenty years earlier when Yves Saint Laurent was the undisputed highlight of *couture* week, but by the mid-1990s some of the fashion pack had already adopted a 'See Chanel and Fly' *couture* schedule, leaving Paris immediately after the Chanel presentation and therefore missing Saint Laurent. A month before *couture* week Yves Saint Laurent announced that it had relented and would bring its show date forward in line with the other houses.

'The old Pierre Bergé would never have let all that happen – losing the Chambre Syndicale ballot, letting the industry out-vote him over the *couture* dates and then having to back down publicly,' said one observer. 'He'd been running rings around the rest of them for years. He had all the power and he knew exactly how to use it. But by then there was too much else going on – the political row over the Sanofi sale, the Champagne court case, problems at the Opéra. He took his eyes off the ball.'

Pierre was also under assault from the stock market authorities, as the Commission des Opérations de Bourse completed its investigation into the circumstances surrounding Yves and Pierre's sale of $18 million of YSL shares in summer 1992 and into the mysterious

Pierre Bergé, Grace Mirabella of American *Vogue*, Diana Vreeland, Yves, Catherine Deneuve and models celebrate YSL's twentieth anniversary at the Paris Lido in January 1982. The following year Diana Vreeland curated Yves's retrospective at the Metropolitan Museum.

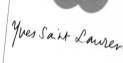

(Clockwise) Château Gabriel in Normandy; the pampered Moujik; a kiss for Catherine Deneuve after a *couture* show, watched by Dominique Deroche *(left)*, Nan Kempner and Susan Train *(right)*.

A Braque-inspired opera cloak from 1988.

From the Parade collection in 1979.

A YSL 'siren' *à la* Loulou in 1979.

(Right) Yves out of control.
(Far right) Robert Merloz
at his ill-fated 1992 debut.
(Below) Les Fidèles treat
Yves and his scarlet 'bride'
to a standing ovation after
the Merloz show; Anna
Wintour, Steven Meisel
and the American *Vogue*
team *(to the right of the
picture)* remain seated.

Friends and foes. *(Below)* Yves sealing the Sanofi deal with Jean-François Dehecq. *(Right, clockwise)* Alan Minc, Bernard Arnault, Henry Racamier, Alain-Dominique Perrin, Jean-Louis Dumas, Lindsay Owen-Jones.

Carlo de Benedetti, *bête noir* of the European corporate establishment, helped Pierre Bergé buy back the perfumes. 'I couldn't have done it without him,' said Bergé, who then had to borrow $99 million to buy de Benedetti's YSL shares.

'ierre Bergé and a woebegone Yves in his Avenue Marceau studio in 1986. Yves's 'Love' images
'r the YSL New Year cards line the wall, and Moujik's basket is under the desk. Some days they
nched together, but at other times the two men couldn't bear being in the same room.

YSL's thirtieth anniversary at the Opéra de Bastille, 3 February 1992. (*Above*) Jack Lang and Catherine Deneuve. (*Top left*) Paloma Picasso, Pierre Bergé, model, Inès de la Fressange, André Leon Talley. (*Lower left*) Jacqueline de Ribes, Alexis de Redé, Loulou de la Falaise, Marie-Hélène de Rothschild.

(*Below*) The *intimes* invited to sit at Yves's table were Jacques Grange, Catherine Deneuve, her charge for the evening, a visibly ill Rudolf Nureyev, with the unfailingly vivacious Zizi Jeanmaire.

movements in the YSL share price then and in December when it was in takeover talks with Sanofi. On 26 May 1993, the COB disclosed that it had abandoned its probe into the December share price rise as it did not have enough evidence to continue, but that it was continuing the inquiry into Yves and Pierre's summer share sales to decide whether to refer the matter to the Justice Ministry. It also announced that it had asked the Justice Ministry to conduct an official investigation into the sale of 80,000 Saint Laurent shares to a private foreign buyer on 17 and 18 September 1992 in preparation for legal proceedings.

The crux of the investigation was to see whether Yves and Pierre had breached insider trading laws dating back to 1967, which forbade people in possession of confidential information about a company's financial position from buying or selling its shares before that information was made available to the general public. In short they were accused of having sold shares at a time when they knew that the company would report a reduction in profits for the first half of the year. The share sales in question took place on 17 and 18 September,[13] and on 21 September Pierre Bergé announced the first half results and warned of a further fall in profits for the second half of the year, thereby triggering a fall in the share price. The COB was also investigating whether the shares sales earlier that summer, the last of which took place on 11 September, had broken a stock market regulation dating back to the wartime Vichy régime which made it illegal to deal in shares of companies quoted in Paris outside the official Paris stock market, as Yves and Pierre had done by selling their shares privately in Switzerland.

On the surface these looked like serious charges, but the case against Yves and Pierre was far from cut and dried. Both rules were weakly worded, somewhat archaic and regularly flouted by large French companies. The wording of the 1967 law was so woolly that it was not clear what the reference to 'market' meant or whether it applied to the YSL transactions, given that they were private sales in Switzerland. The Vichy rule was older and even vaguer, originally implemented to stop investors taking money out of France during the Second World War. The only reason it had not been revoked was to enable the Paris Stock Exchange to continue to collect the *Impôt de Bourse*, the tax levied on each share transaction in Paris.[14]

The *Impôt de Bourse* was widely considered to be an anachronism, and by then so many large French companies were quoted in London, New York or Tokyo, as well as Paris, that 'block trades', or dealings in large quantities of shares, were often executed there to be exempt from it.

Pierre Bergé seemed sanguine about the probes. He had never denied having sold a large block of his and Yves's stock during summer 1992, although he claimed not to know who was behind the sales on 17 and 18 September, or who was responsible for the rise in the share price that December. Besides, the stock market authorities had generally been willing to ignore alleged infractions of such obscure regulations in the past, particularly when one of the protagonists was a close friend of the president of the Republic.

But the political tide had turned against François Mitterrand and his friends, as the president's position had grown increasingly precarious since the socialists' defeat in the March 1993 parliamentary elections. Older and frailer than he was during the last *cohabitation* government, Mitterrand found it more difficult to manipulate Édouard Balladur, the affable centre-right prime minister, than he had the visceral Jacques Chirac. His popularity was also affected by *la morosité*, the gloom that enveloped France as the recession deepened, unemployment soared and the streets were littered with homeless beggars and war refugees fleeing from the former Yugoslavian states. *La morosité* culminated in spring 1993 with the suicide of Pierre Bérégevoy, the former socialist prime minister, who shot himself a few weeks after his party's electoral defeat.[15]

The French media held up the glittering *gauche caviare* as a symbol of everything wrong with contemporary France. Laurent Fabius, the *bon chic bon genre* socialist prime minister from the mid-1980s, was under investigation together with other members of his cabinet over the AIDs blood scandal, in which hundreds of haemophiliacs died after being given blood transfusions tainted with the HIV virus. *Mitterrand and the Forty Thieves*, a book by the right-wing writer, Jean Montaldo, claimed that *Globe* magazine had received over $300,000 to help the socialist electoral campaign, and Jack Lang's munificent arts policies were satirized by the latest Eric Rohmer film, *L'Arbre, Le Maire et Le Médiathèque*, and in *La Comédie de la Culture*, a book by his former dance director, Michel Schneider, who had also criticized the sale of Yves Saint Laurent to Sanofi on French television.

The new government was already moving against members of the Mitterrand circle. Loïk Le Floch-Prigent was ousted from Elf Aquitaine,[16] and replaced by Philippe Jaffré, a long-standing supporter of Édouard Balladur. Then Jacques Toubon, the Chirac loyalist who succeeded Jack Lang as culture minister, announced that Pierre Bergé would not be reappointed as president of the Opéra de Paris when his five year term of office ended in early 1994. Refusing to concede defeat quietly, Pierre railed against Jacques Toubon's arts policies from his monthly *Globe* column, and when he spotted Michel Schneider, author of *La Comédie de la Culture* at a private view of the Henri Matisse retrospective at the Centre Georges Pompidou, he marched across the room and thumped him. 'The bastard insulted us,' he said, by way of explanation, 'so I attacked him.'[17]

In such a hostile climate there was no hope of the stock market authorities being persuaded to taking a lenient stance over the Yves Saint Laurent share dealings. The COB decided to refer its dossier on the summer share sales to the Justice Ministry, and it was then passed to an investigating magistrate, David Peyron, who would decide whether to press criminal charges against Yves Saint Laurent and Pierre Bergé. *Le Point* and *Le Figaro* ran a series of stories on the affair and *Le Monde* followed up its earlier article on the YSL sale to Sanofi with an article entitled '*L'Illegalité Inconnu de l'Affair Saint Laurent*', 'The Legal Secrets of the Saint Laurent Affair'.[18]

On 26 January 1994 the Commission des Opérations de Bourse announced that Pierre Bergé was to be fined three million francs, just over $500,000, for breaching its insider trading rules. The fine was suspended until March when the insider trading charges against him were to be considered by the Court of Appeal. That court upheld the COB's conclusions, but reduced the fine to one million francs. The investigating magistrate was still deciding whether to press criminal charges and, on 30 May, he issued an indictment against Pierre Bergé and Jean-Francis Bretelle for insider trading and for violating the Vichy rule on selling shares outside the Paris market. Yves himself was exempted from both charges, after Pierre assured David Peyron that he had sold the shares using his power of attorney without consulting Yves, who knew nothing about the transactions.

If the case went to court Pierre and Bretelle could be fined up to ten million francs, or sentenced to between two months and two years in prison. 'I really don't give a damn,' Pierre snapped to *Women's Wear Daily*.[19]

The handling of the charges was undoubtedly influenced by the *gauche caviare* backlash but was also affected by a crackdown on corporate corruption across Europe that summer. Italy's jails filled with industrialists and financiers charged with bribery, tax evasion and business fraud in a campaign which would eventually lead to tax charges being brought against a number of fashion designers, including Giorgio Armani. Pierre Bergé was one of over a hundred French businessmen facing allegations of corporate fraud. 'You would think France was a banana republic, thoroughly rotten with fraud and graft,' observed *Business Week* in an article which cited an unnamed COB official as saying that the Saint Laurent charges 'would never have been filed a few years ago'.[20]

'I really felt for Pierre that summer,' recalled one of his old friends. 'There'd been all that trouble over the sale to Sanofi, and the Chambre Syndicale turning against him. Then he lost the Opéra, which he really, really loved. He was passionate about music and he'd adored lording it over everyone as president. Power and position mean so much to the French. He'd had so much and suddenly it all seemed to be taken away. And Pierre's no fool. He knew that all his enemies had just been waiting for the moment when Mitterrand disappeared, and there was no one to protect him any more.'

Le Grand Patron
1994–1996

Glamour was by far the most fashionable fashion magazine in the France of the early 1990s. Its pages were filled with pictures of lithe young things dipping long legs into satin flares as they swapped body-piercing tips and roared off to the Paris flea markets in street-scarred Renault Twingos. The cover girl for May 1994 was Nadja Auermann, the icily androidanal supermodel, wearing a slinky black jumpsuit with criss-cross lacing down the front. The look was perfect for *Glamour*, but the name of the designer seemed somewhat incongruous – Yves Saint Laurent.

Inside the magazine was a six-page article on Yves and his achievements illustrated by a shot of him with Catherine Deneuve at the opening of the first Rive Gauche boutique, a Jeanloup Sieff portrait from 1967, together with a still from *Belle de Jour* and an Andy Warhol silkscreen of Moujik, his dog. The article was entitled *Le Grand Patron*, and dedicated to 'the designer who has transcended fashion'.[1] A glance at the rest of *Glamour* showed why: the fashion pages were filled with sleek, stylized clothes from contemporary designers which looked suspiciously similar to those from the YSL 1960s and 1970s archives.

Only a few weeks before Yves had unveiled his Rive Gauche range to the now customary limp reviews. 'Expecting something great from YSL these days is a little like waiting for Godot,' groaned Cathy Horyn in the *Washington Post*. 'Let's face it, he's just not coming.'[2] When Christophe Girard was introduced to a French banker that spring, she said: 'Oh, so you work for Yves Saint Laurent. How long ago did he die?'[3] But the tide was turning, *Glamour*'s tribute to *Le Grand Patron* was the first of a series of admiring articles. The September issue of *Harper's Bazaar* included a feature in which Sarah Mower catalogued the young designers whose recent collections had rejected the droopy silhouettes of grunge and deconstructivism for the hard-edged glamour of vintage Saint Laurent: Helmut Lang, Anna Sui, Marc Jacobs, Christian Lacroix, Vivienne Westwood and John Galliano. 'Always there, always awesome close-up, it [the signature Saint Laurent style] has also, in the way of monuments, sometimes been taken for granted. Not now.'[4]

Yves Saint Laurent was back. The hippest *prêt-à-porter* collections for autumn 1994 looked like throwbacks to the Rive Gauche rails from twenty-five years before with sleek *smokings* and crisply cut flares. John Galliano showed Dietrichesque trouser suits and bias-cut satin slips in São Schlumberger's abandoned Paris apartment. Helmut Lang and Jil Sander created futuristic versions of Yves's *smokings*. Anna Sui's collection bore the stamp of his 1940s look, and the Saint Laurent influence was very visible in the pared-down designs with which Miuccia Prada was revitalizing her family's luggage firm. The *Independent* newspaper ran a feature entitled, '*Excusez-Moi*, but isn't that mine?' which compared shots of Yves's 1980s reinterpretations of his 1960s and 1970s classics with lookalike designs by Vivienne Westwood, Karl Lagerfeld, Anna Sui and Dolce e Gabbana.[5] 'It was amazing how similar the copies were, almost line for line in some cases,' said Marion Hume, who coordinated the piece. 'And there were so many to choose from. We could have included lots more.'[6] A few months before Pierre Bergé had proved the same point in a Paris courtroom when he successfully sued Ralph Lauren after accusing him of copying a tuxedo dress that Yves had first designed in 1970.[7]

The pages of *Vogue* and *Harper's Bazaar* featured newly glamorized waifs who had cleverly changed their images – Amber Valetta, Shalom Harlow and the English aristocrat, Stella Tennant – shot by Helmut Newton, or the younger photographers inspired by him, such as Nick Knight. Amy Spindler, the *New York Times* fashion editor, suspected a plot hatched by Anna Wintour, editor-in-chief of American *Vogue*, and Liz Tilberis, her opposite number on *Harper's*

Bazaar, claiming that they had taken a tactical decision to promote a glossier, more glamorous style because they were concerned about the effect of the grungey, make-upless look on their advertisers.[8]

Commercial concerns probably did play a part in the Glam revival or, at least, in the glee with which the press publicized it, but the return to the structured forms and sleek silhouettes of Yves's *smokings* reflected a broader shift. Architecture was swinging away from deconstructivism to the refined simplicity of Herzog & De Meuron's work in Switzerland, and furniture design was now dominated by Jasper Morrison's purist forms and Marc Newson's glossy modernism. Grunge's influence over pop culture waned after the suicide of Kurt Cobain, the lead singer of Nirvana, and MTV pumped out 'ghetto glamour' rap and hip hop videos featuring bright, beautiful black kids cruising in convertibles to the Hamptons. There was also a nostalgic sub-text to the new enthusiasm for the 1970s styles that the young designers of the mid-1990s remembered from their teens and early twenties, and for the wild nights at Studio 54 and Le Sept, before the tragedies of AIDS and crack blighted the social scene.

In the days when Yves Saint Laurent was a handsome hippy *de luxe* and the world's hottest fashion designer, John Galliano and Helmut Lang were still at school or college, poring over pictures of his collections in dog-eared copies of *Vogue*. Anna Sui was a stylist who bulk-bought his No. 19 purple lipstick whenever she went to Paris, and Miuccia Prada was a Milanese drama student who tagged along to the Paris collections with her friend, Manuela Pavesi, then a fashion editor on Italian *Vogue*, hoping to persuade Clara Saint to give her a spare seat at the Rive Gauche show. Whereas Yves's peers – Karl Lagerfeld, Gianni Versace and Giorgio Armani – had felt obliged to shake off the Saint Laurent legacy, by the 1990s Yves was regarded as an icon and his collections from the late 1960s and early 1970s were as evocative for the new generation of designers as Lucienne's 1940s look had been for him, and the Belle Époque had for Christian Dior.

Miuccia Prada was typical. A YSL devotee since the late 1960s, she had bought a pink and white puff-sleeved dress at the Rive Gauche boutique when it opened on Milan's via Santo Spirito, and carried on shopping there and at Rive Gauche in Paris throughout the 1970s, as well as scouring the flea markets for antique Saint

Laurent *couture*. By the time she took over the Milanese luggage company founded by her grandfather, Miuccia Prada had been wearing Yves Saint Laurent for well over a decade, and she reinterpreted her clothes in her designs for the Prada collections. 'Why do I admire Yves Saint Laurent?' she said. 'Because he's an innovator, he's a genius.'[9]

The Saint Laurent revival was rooted in the past not the present, yet Yves's persona contributed to it. Having been regarded as, at best, a self-obsessed eccentric in the extrovert 1980s, he now seemed engagingly sincere at a time when the explosion of media interest in fashion had revealed the charades of gay designers hiding behind marriages of convenience, shying away from AIDS benefits and flaunting their 'best friendships' with the supermodels and actors who just happened to be appearing in their advertising campaigns that season. Yves's honesty about his homosexuality and addictions appeared admirable by comparison; as did Pierre Bergé's support for the AIDS and anti-racist campaigns. 'The most important thing about Yves,' observed Anne-Marie Muñoz, 'is that he has always, always been true to himself.'[10]

Predictably Yves's own work was unaffected by the surge of interest in his past designs. 'People are always bringing us things that have been copied from old collections, shoes and pieces that I remember from the 1970s but haven't worn for years, and they ask why Yves doesn't do them again,' said Clara Saint. 'He just doesn't work like that and he never will. The idea of him doing something just because he thinks he'd be able to sell it is crazy.'[11] Yet at the height of Saint Laurent mania Yves staged a virtuoso *couture* show for autumn 1994. It mixed impeccably cut *smokings* and thigh-high leather boots, with a series of mandarin tunics in his improbably perfect colour combinations and a sculpted black-velvet sheath dress so beautifully proportioned that the slightest change in the line would have destroyed it. The bride came on for the finale in a brocade dress topped off with a crown, accompanied by two tiny attendants. 'Hmm. He's looking very healthy,' commented one magazine editor, as a smiling Yves pounded along the catwalk and *les fidèles* rose to their feet to applaud him, hankies in hands. The headline on the front page of the next day's *Herald Tribune* was: 'Yves Saint Laurent Reigns as King Again'.[12]

His confidence lifted, Yves agreed to travel to New York that

September for the North American launch of Champagne, his first visit to the city since the opening of his retrospective at the Metropolitan Museum in 1983. A posse of photographers snapped him and Pierre Bergé as they left the Concorde lounge at John F. Kennedy airport, and a packed schedule awaited them in Manhattan. Fernando Sanchez was hosting a dinner in Yves's honour, and Nan Kempner arranged a special lunch. Yves was scheduled to make a personal appearance at Saks Fifth Avenue, and was keen to see the Mme Grès retrospective at the Met. The trip would end on a solemn note when he and Pierre attended a memorial service for Richard Salomon, who had died that summer, but first there was the Champagne party on the island around the Statue of Liberty to which two thousand guests had been invited.

It was the first time anyone had been allowed to hold a party on Liberty Island, which was lit for the evening by thousands of candles, with red YSL flags fluttering around the waterfront and the Battery Park jetty where boats were waiting to ferry the guests to and from the island. Anxious to arrive on time Yves insisted on setting off so early that he and his entourage had to circle around Liberty Island three times before docking. Even so, they were there long before the other guests. The fashion designers – Marc Jacobs, Bill Blass, Oscar de la Renta and Vivienne Westwood – came to pay their respects; as did Manhattan socialites such as Nan Kempner, Lynn Wyatt, Chessy Rayner, Anne Bass and C. Z. Guest. Betty Catroux wore a black *smoking* with a short skirt and thigh-high boots from the latest *couture* collection, and Loulou de la Falaise arrived in a black, gold and red chinoiserie jacket encrusted with coral, accompanied by her niece, Lucie, in a long ivory brocade coat, and Lucie's fiancé, Marlon Richards, the son of the Rolling Stone, Keith, and the 1960s model, Anita Pallenberg.

The guests tucked into champagne and formal French sandwiches, while gazing at the Manhattan skyline across the water and at the boats plying to and from the red-flagged jetty at Battery Park. Some of them were seen sneaking the sea island cotton YSL napkins into pockets and bags. 'The Americans seemed absolutely fascinated by them, and were taking them as souvenirs, though they didn't get the point of the sandwiches – too French,' recalled Marion Hume. 'But the party was beautifully done – glamorous in the traditional

French style. It was the most wonderful evening and you could see for miles from Liberty Island – the Statue of Liberty, red flags everywhere, and huge candles burning.'[13]

Yves spent the evening cradling a big bottle of Champagne with a wide smile for the cameras, occasionally sinking into a chair to soothe an ache from his sciatica. 'Mr Berge! Mr Berge!' chorused the photographers whenever Pierre Bergé veered into their sights. 'It's Bergé!' he barked back with the emphasis on the acute accent. At 9.45 p.m. a cascade of Grucci fireworks soared above the Statue of Liberty, blazing across the night sky. 'It was a lovely evening – but a most sober one,' reported the *Los Angeles Times*, with the inevitable addendum. 'This was nothing like the wild reverie of sixteen years ago when Saint Laurent launched Opium.'[14]

Champagne sold well in the States, as it had in Europe, if not quite as well as the hottest new perfume of the season, Calvin Klein's CK One, a genderless scent like the ill-fated Eau Libre. Twenty years ago the public had not been ready for a perfume for both men and women, but the concept was perfect for the mid-1990s. The young consumers to whom Calvin Klein hoped to sell CK One had grown up in a society in which 'lipstick lesbians' had become stock characters in soap operas and openly gay icons including the music mogul, David Geffen, the country singer, k.d. lang and fashion designers such as Jean-Paul Gaultier and Yves Saint Laurent were the norm.

Despite CK One's success, the new Yves Saint Laurent perfume seemed to be fulfilling Sanofi's high hopes, but in early 1995 the legal battle against the champagne industry came to a climax when the company lost another court case against the CVIC, this time in Germany. Forced to concede defeat, Sanofi agreed to phase out the name, Champagne, all over the world by the end of 1998. Sales of the perfume had already fallen sharply in France since the name change, and now seemed set to decline in Germany, which augured ill for its prospects in other countries after 1998. Sanofi flung its resources into introducing Opium Pour Homme that autumn and relaunching Opium for women with an advertising campaign featuring Linda Evangelista. Both products sold well, but could not compensate for the untimely demise of Champagne, in which Sanofi had invested so heavily, picking up a $1.5 million bill for the Liberty Island party alone.

Even allowing for the Champagne debacle, Sanofi claimed to be pleased with the progress of its controversial new subsidiary. The company managed to increase its earnings per share in the year after the acquisition, just as Jean-François Dehecq said it would,[15] and the integration of two cosmetics companies seemed relatively smooth. 'We've bought lots of businesses over the years and YSL was in good condition when we took over,' Dehecq commented, 'much better than we'd expected.'[16] The financial strains on Yves Saint Laurent eased as the luxury industry returned to growth when the recession ended in its traditional Western markets and sales soared in South-East Asia, so much so that Condé Nast launched new editions of *Vogue* in Taiwan and South Korea. Gucci, Estée Lauder and Donna Karan all staged successful stock-market flotations. Even the *haute couture* houses found a new source of custom in the *nouveaux riches* Russians who had started luxury shopping in Paris.

Relations between Jean-François Dehecq and Pierre Bergé appeared cordial, although the blustering Sanofi chairman did not look like an obvious successor to the urbane Richard Salomon. 'They might be different in character, but they work together very well,' observed Jean-Pierre Halbron of Wasserstein Perella of the two men. 'Surprisingly well, in fact.'[17] To Pierre's relief it quickly became clear that Sanofi was really only interested in the beauty side of the business, leaving him in sole control of Avenue Marceau. 'Things go on just as before here,' he affirmed. 'It's not at all unusual for us to belong to another company. We're used to it. We had J. Mack Robinson, Charles of the Ritz, then Squibb and now Sanofi.'[18]

For Pierre the *annus horribilis* of 1994, when he faced the political storm over the Sanofi sale, an insider trading investigation and the loss of his prestigious post at the Opéra, had ended with a profile of him in the *New Yorker* entitled, 'The Impresario's Last Act', in which the writer, Jane Kramer, concluded that Pierre Bergé, like the rest of the *gauche caviare*, was 'going out of style'.[19] Unabashed, he added the beaming Richard Avedon portrait that accompanied the article to the clutter of monographs, papers and *objets* in his Avenue Marceau office. Still a *personnage* on the Paris social scene, Pierre made a substantial donation in his and Yves's names to the new American Center, which opened in a Frank Gehry building near Gare de Lyon in eastern Paris, and continued to prowl the auction rooms and antique dealers for treasures for his eighteenth-century house at Saint-Rémy in Provence and his new apartment on rue Bonaparte. When in Paris, he often strolled around the corner with Ficelle tucked protectively into his coat for dinner at Brasserie Lipp or for late night drinks at Café de Flore, where Robert Merloz sat silently while Pierre exchanged greetings with friends, or held forth to the attentive *maître d'hôtel*. He was also spending more time with Yves, going down to Château Gabriel with him in the summer and accompanying him to Hubert de Givenchy's final *couture* show, where they sat side by side in the front row as a gesture of respect while the Saint Laurent set's former foe prepared for retirement.

Politically Pierre found himself pushed on to the sidelines in the 1995 presidential elections, like the rest of the Mitterrand circle, as he had no rapport with the efficient, but uninspiring Lionel Jospin, who stood unsuccessfully as the socialist candidate against Jacques Chirac. There had been talk of Jack Lang standing, but that soon subsided, and Pierre's favourite in the socialist camp was Laurent Fabius, whose hopes of the presidency were scuppered by the AIDS blood scandal. Finally, in January 1996, he lost his political protector, and one of his closest friends, when François Mitterrand died after a long battle with cancer.

One of Pierre Bergé's strengths is his resilience and, having been stripped of his responsibilities at the Opéra, the Chambre Syndicale and even at the YSL beauty business, he flung himself back into running the fashion company with renewed vigour, just as he had in the early 1970s when he and Yves took over from Squibb. Then the priority was to sign scores of licences, now his aim was to rationalize the deals they had already done as, helped by Christophe Girard and Jean-Francis Bretelle, he weeded out the poorly per- forming licensees and imposed tighter controls over the remainder. They liaised with Young & Rubicam, the Parisian branch of the American advertising agency, to create a men's wear campaign with the panache of vintage Yves Saint Laurent advertising. The licensing business even had an unexpected bonanza from the sudden surge in sales of YSL men's shirts among 'casuals', young British football fans who started wearing them alongside other cult sportswear lines such as Tommy Hilfiger, Adidas and Polo by Ralph Lauren.

Pierre still barked at miscreants among the staff, and continued his campaign of attrition against Yves's critics, or suspected critics in the press. Having banned *L'Aurore* from the Saint Laurent shows in the 1960s, the *International Herald Tribune* at various times in the 1970s, and *Women's Wear Daily* in the 1980s, he then clashed with American *Vogue* over Yves Saint Laurent's absence from an article on contemporary *couture* published in its December 1995 issue to mark the opening of an *haute couture* exhibition at the Metropolitan Museum.[20] Anna Wintour and her team were barred from the January *couture* show and, even though the magazine's only reference to the ban was a brief, but polite note in its March 1996 *couture* issue, he barred them from that month's *prêt-à-porter* presentation, too.[21]

To mark the start of a new chapter in the company's fortunes, Pierre decided to redecorate Avenue Marceau, albeit in the same opulent style as Victor Grandpierre's original designs, with the Mies van der Rohe Brnõ and the Eileen Gray furniture still in place. Even so Christophe Girard locked the doors of his office to keep the decorators out, and salvaged the Eero Saarinen table and chairs from Place Vauban, squeezing them into a corner. 'I loved the old style and didn't want to change it.'[22] Yves's studio was sacrosanct, too, so that whenever he returned from Marrakesh he would find it just as he had left it, with the gleaming Jean-Michel Frank fireplace, Christian Bérard's portrait of Diana Vreeland, a Jean-Louis David painting of his ennobled ancestor, Baron Mathieu de Mauvières, above the Louis XV desk on which the baron wrote Napoleon's marriage contract to Josephine, and vases filled with his favourite white orchids.

Most of the old faces would be waiting for him on his return. Anne-Marie Muñoz was still ensconced in the Avenue Marceau design studio, as was Clara Saint at the Rive Gauche press office, although Gabrielle Buchaert retired after thirty years running the *couture* press office. Loulou de la Falaise carried on playing the public 'face' of the company, flying to Los Angeles with her niece, Lucie, for the opening of a new Rive Gauche boutique on Rodeo Drive, and to London with Pierre Bergé for cocktails at the French Embassy to toast its twenty-fifth anniversary in Britain. Catherine Deneuve, Betty Catroux, Charlotte Aillaud and Paloma Picasso continued to come in for their *couture* fittings each season, but not Marie-Hélène de Rothschild, who died in early 1996.

The Saint Laurent revival only lasted a few seasons before fashion moved on to other obsessions. Helmut Lang and Miuccia Prada flirted with futuristic fabrics amid the explosion of interest in digital technology as millions of people signed on to the Internet and the new corporate heroes became 'nerd moguls' such as Bill Gates, the billionaire founder of Microsoft. The next craze was for the 1960s retro look that Tom Ford, the young American designer, devised for Gucci, reworking images of Julie Christie as a mod and Talitha Getty in her hippy *de luxe* heyday, and then for the candy-coloured 'geek' clothes made by Diesel, the Italian casual wear company, and worn by the Britpop stars in Oasis and Pulp. The Paris fashion establishment pinned its hopes on John Galliano, the brilliant but unbridled British designer whom Bernard Arnault had appointed to succeed Hubert de Givenchy, hoping he would rejuvenate *haute couture* as Christian Lacroix did in the mid-1980s.[23] Yet even the most inventive clothes on the Paris catwalks seemed stiff and showy compared with the casual Gap sweats and Nike sports shoes that the 'nerd moguls' wore, and the simple shapes and high-performance fabrics used by experimental sportswear designers such as Massimo Osti in Italy and Sabotage in Germany, who were concerned less with the form of garments than with the materials they were made from. The common themes running through all these 1990s styles were understatedness and a studied simplicity which struck a stark contrast to the ornamental excesses of the 1980s. The mood was summed up by the restless modernism of ads shot by Craig McDean for Jil Sander in which the models were captured in mid-movement, often staring or even striding out of the frame, as though they had far more important cares and concerns than their clothes.

Yves's renaissance might have been shortlived but it reminded the younger generation of designers and journalists of the scale of his achievements. 'These things always play out quickly but it did make him more visible for a while,' observed Paula Reed, fashion director of the *Sunday Times*. 'He designs for women with a real sense of style, who just buy a few classic Saint Laurent pieces which will take them anywhere. It's a fantastically ironic look and the publicity reminded people of that.'[24] After the initial enthusiasm subsided, the reviews of his collections became a little more respectful.[25]

In his private life Yves appeared to have achieved a similar state of stasis, still suffering on his dark days, but generally looking a little sprightlier, and dying his hair a raffish shade of brunette. His health remained delicate, and he had begun 1994 – his renaissance year – in a private room at the American Hospital being treated for pneumonia. After that condition cleared up, he was prey to sciatica as well as the vestiges of his old cortisone and prostate problems, and the cumulative effect of years of substance abuse. When the American writer, Edmund White, interviewed him for the *Sunday Times Magazine* in autumn 1994, he was shocked by Yves's condition. 'He was certainly lucid and had no trouble recalling names and dates, but he seemed heavily tranquillised or perhaps just depressed; enormous silences crept into our conversation . . . More than once Saint Laurent let his head slump onto his chest; I was certain he'd dozed off, but no.'[26]

The old AIDS scare stories about him subsided, but the fashion world remained convinced that Yves had a terminal illness, the favourite theory being Alzheimer's Disease, a degenerative brain disorder which begins with memory loss and ends by destroying the intellect. The company vehemently denied it. 'He hasn't got any illness at all,' insisted Christophe Girard. 'As the head of a big company like this, his health is tested regularly for insurance purposes and there's nothing wrong with him, except for being overweight, because he drinks too much Coca-Cola.'[27]

Yves did seem to have kicked his alcoholism, sipping conspicuous glasses of Coke at the parties he now occasionally attended, or on the nights he accompanied Betty Catroux or Jacques Grange to the Opéra. Once he and Paloma Picasso decided to revisit Le Palace, the nightclub that became their favourite haunt after Le Sept closed. When they arrived the doorman, never having seen them before, refused to let them in. 'Can you imagine?' said Paloma Picasso. 'We had been going there since the day it opened – we launched Le Palace! I even gave a party there for my wedding. I said to him: "How can you not let us in? Don't you know who we are?"'[28] Eventually a manager was summoned and, with abject apologies, they were admitted.

Tentatively, Yves renewed contact with some of the old friends on the fringes of the Saint Laurent set that he had abandoned when the depressions had set in. 'I hadn't seen or heard from him for a long time,' said Jeanloup Sieff. 'Then suddenly he called me in my studio. He wanted me to take a photograph and we chatted. He carried on calling me occasionally after that, just to talk.'[29] Yet Edmund White was struck by his loneliness. During their conversation Yves cited Catherine Deneuve as one of his closest friends. 'She's very protective of me – like a big sister.'[30] But when White spoke to Deneuve she told him that 'she seldom saw Saint Laurent, and didn't really know him very well. I realised how deep his isolation must be . . . Almost as though their friendship was something he elaborated more in his fantasies than pursued in reality.'[31]

Pierre Bergé had a simpler explanation. 'He's not afraid of people. He's simply terribly egocentric. He's simply indifferent to people. When he'll give a dinner party at his apartment, I'll phone him the next morning to find out how it went. "A nightmare!" It's always a nightmare because he had to show an interest in other people, ask them questions about their lives. He doesn't care about other people. I'm the only person he can dine with three times a week. That's because we've known each other nearly thirty-five years! He'd like to see me more often, but I'm not always available. He doesn't have to make an effort with me. He adored our vacation together and told me it was the best time he'd had with anyone in years. Why? Because he feels comfortable with me. We'd eat a little supper together in Honfleur then I'd let him go to bed by 9.30. No demands.'[32]

Yves still spent most of the year in Marrakesh, where he and Moujik pottered around the Villa Oasis gardens, and went for short walks to the Mamounia Hotel each afternoon, sometimes returning there for dinner in the evenings with Bill Willis, Boule de Breteuil, or Betty Catroux, if she happened to be staying. Marie Helvin ran into Yves by chance in the Mamounia lobby one day. 'I saw a man sitting slumped on a chair with his head staring down at the floor. He looked like Yves and I recognised the dog all right. I hadn't seen him for ten years. I wasn't even sure if he would recognise me. I thought, "Well, Marie, you could really embarrass yourself here." But when I went up to say hello he gave me such a big smile. "Ah Marie!" He seemed so happy to see me. We chatted for ten minutes. He was sweet and charming like he'd always been. Then my friends came to collect me. I introduced them to him. He talked politely and then left. The hotel staff said he came for tea at the same time every day, usually alone.'[33]

When in Paris Yves went to work in his studio most days, generally arriving there at half-past ten and returning to rue de Babylone for lunch, sometimes with Pierre, but always accompanied by Moujik. The current Moujik was the third of the three French bulldogs Yves called by that name and he distinguished himself on arrival at rue de Babylone by savaging one of the 'sheep' sculptures that Claude Lalanne had made for Yves twenty years before, then attacking the precious rolls of fabric in the Avenue Marceau studio, occasionally lunging at his master's guests. When the British journalist Lesley White was beginning an interview with Yves for *Vogue* 'a seering pain shot through my leg' as Moujik's fangs sank in.[34] Yves apologetically dragged the dog outside, and the interview recommenced punctuated by the dull thud of Moujik's stocky body as he flung himself furiously against the door.

Yves told Lesley White that, 'my period of total reclusiveness has ended, no more shutting myself away all the time',[35] but his appearances at parties or the opera were still scarce, and when he went out in Paris, it was generally for lunch at Lucienne's, or to dinner with Pierre, Jacques Grange or Betty Catroux. Sometimes he visited Betty and François in their garden apartment on rue de l'Université, or Jacques Grange in Colette's old quarters in the Palais-Royal where he lived with Dolly, his Jack Russell. And from time to time Yves made the journey out to Ury near Fontainebleau to see Claude and François-Xavier Lalanne in the house and studio where they lived and worked surrounded by a prettily wooded garden.

But mostly he spent his time at rue de Babylone, watching favourite Visconti and Bresson films on video in his bedroom, or poring over *À la Recherche du Temps Perdu* in the Mondrian-filled library that Jacques Grange had remodelled as a replica of one at Marie-Laure de Noailles's house in Fontainebleau. Yves was still refining the duplex, redecorating rooms with Jacques Grange and embellishing his art collection. A series of marble and iron bird sculptures by François-Xavier Lalanne were added to the garden, and an imposing tapestry by the English pre-Raphaelite artist, Edward Burne-Jones, loomed over the *salon* beside a beautiful Fernand Léger abstract. Like the Matisses and Mondrians, the Géricault and Goya portraits, and everything else in the art collection, they would eventually join the *couture* designs and sketches in the archive being assembled at Avenue Marceau for the museum that Pierre Bergé planned to open as a monument to Yves Saint Laurent and his work.

Epilogue
Last of the Legends

It seems improbable, if not impossible, that another fashion designer will become so famous that, like Yves Saint Laurent, their name will be known all over the world: not only because his talent is exceptional, but because the role, and perceived importance, of the fashion designer has changed dramatically since Yves shot to fame in the late 1950s.

Yves Saint Laurent owes his fame partly to his innovations, which have changed the way that women dress – even women who could not contemplate buying *haute couture* or *prêt-à-porter*. In the late 1950s and early 1960s, he pushed forward the frontiers of fashion by challenging assumptions of what was and was not acceptable for women to wear, replacing cumbersome *couture* outfits with clothes which were more appropriate to an active, modern life. At Christian Dior, Yves picked up on the leather jackets, polo-neck sweaters and leather boots he saw around him on the Paris streets, and made them seem as luxurious as mink coats and silk *faille* ballgowns. He then achieved the same iconoclastic effect by transforming his visions of Marlene Dietrich in a tailored trouser suit, colonial officials in safari jackets, Zizi Jeanmaire dancing in sheer black stockings, and his mother whirling around a wartime dancefloor in a sharp shouldered *crêpe* dress into what are now regarded as classics. As the first *couturier* to work with models from a wide range of ethnic backgrounds he also helped to redefine conventional perceptions of beauty.

The impact of his innovations was accentuated by the artistry of his work. Fashion is only an applied art, but Yves Saint Laurent's *couture* creations can be so beautiful that they approach art. Perhaps the best analogy is with a Ludwig Mies van der Rohe chair, which fulfils the functional requirements of a chair, but is so exquisitely conceived and executed that it transcends its practical role. 'Saint Laurent *couture* and ordinary clothes are a million miles apart,' observed Sally Brampton of the *Guardian*. 'You can see his dresses coming down the catwalk that look as though no one has ever sewn them because they're so perfect that you can't see a single seam.'[1]

One of his greatest accomplishments is a flair for colour, which he displayed from the Mondrian shifts onwards and refined in the fantastical collections of the late 1970s, starting with the *Ballets Russes* presentation and continuing with the designs inspired by Delacroix's Morocco and Vélasquez's Spain. Katell Le Bourhis, the French fashion historian, believes that Yves Saint Laurent is 'the supreme fashion colourist of our century. Normally I hate it when people make sweeping statements like that. But it's true. No one can challenge it. His mixes of colours are incredible. He knows exactly the right shade of each colour to use.'[2] Another gift is his unerring eye for proportion. 'The first time I saw one of his *couture* shows I was just amazed,' recalled Paula Reed of the *Sunday Times*. 'The clothes were absolutely exquisite, every detail was perfect. You couldn't have added anything, or taken anything away, without spoiling them.'[3]

Yet what truly sets Yves Saint Laurent apart from other fashion designers in his versatility. Even the most gifted *couturiers* are known for a particular style or look, but his body of work spanned the stylized asceticism of the Mondrian shifts and the classicism of his *smokings*, to the theatricality of the *Ballets Russes* and Parade collections. 'There have been other great designers in this century, but none with the same range as Saint Laurent,' observed Christian Lacroix. 'Chanel, Schiaparelli, Balenciaga and Dior all did extraordinary things. But they worked within a particular style. Yves Saint Laurent is much more versatile, like a combination of all of them. I sometimes think he's got the form of Chanel with the opulence of Dior and the wit of Schiaparelli.'[4]

Yet talent, even an extraordinary talent, is not enough on its own and Yves Saint Laurent also owes his fame to fortuitous timing. He founded his *couture* house when there was a lust for something new on the fashion scene, and the burgeoning youth market was receptive to fresh, original ideas. His early success mirrored Andy Warhol's ascent at a time when the art world was tiring of abstract expression-ism, or the Beatles' arrival in the United States on a slow news day when America had ended its mourning for John F. Kennedy's death and teenagers were bored by 1950s rock'n'roll stars. And Yves's luck held out. His business would never have expanded so far, or so fast, without the 1960s economic boom and the youthquake, and then the changes in social and sexual mores that enabled women to attain economic independence, while making it acceptable for men to take an interest in their appearance. Even Yves's self-referential obsession with reinterpreting and refining his established styles struck a chord with the conservative climate of the early 1980s.

Yves Saint Laurent also had the inestimable advantage of Pierre Bergé's efforts to create a commercial environment in which he could nurture his talent. 'Fashion requires a very personal approach to management,' said Lindsay Owen-Jones of L'Oréal. 'Does someone like me at a big company have the time to do it? Of course I don't. I love those crazy creative fashion people. And I respect their talent. But I couldn't be there at the end of the phone every time they needed advice or reassurance. Pierre Bergé has done it brilliantly at Yves Saint Laurent.'[5]

It was Pierre who picked up the phone whenever Yves called, and who saved him from having to struggle for financial support like John Galliano and Vivienne Westwood, both of whom spent long periods of their careers searching for financial backing. Pierre Bergé always found the money to enable Yves to execute his aesthetic fantasies, whether it was the multi-million dollar bill for the thirtieth anniversary celebration or the then-unprecedented sum of $500,000 for the sumptuous *Ballets Russes* presentation. 'The only reason why this company exists is to enable Yves to design his *couture* collections,' he insisted. 'It's up to him how he does it. If he needs anything, he asks for it and I pay the bills.'[6] Thanks to Pierre Bergé, Yves Saint Laurent has enjoyed a level of creative freedom that other fashion designers could only dream of.

Pierre Bergé also ensured that YSL has been as innovative in the business sphere as it was in fashion. Just as Christian Dior defined a new role model for the fashion companies of the 1950s, YSL set the pace in the 1960s and 1970s. It was the first company to develop a coherent strategy for ready-to-wear with the launch of the Rive Gauche chain. The opening of its *haute couture* salon at Seibu-Saison in Tokyo during the early 1960s played a critical part in developing the Japanese market, which was to become one of the largest sources of sales for Western luxury products in the 1980s and 1990s, setting a precedent for other fast-expanding Asian economies such as South Korea and Taiwan in the 1990s. The company was also in the vanguard of the beauty business, where Yves took 'designer marketing' to a new level by posing nude for Jeanloup Sieff to launch his men's scent in the early 1970s and established Opium as a paradigm for the image-oriented fragrances of the 1980s.

Finally, just as Pierre Bergé had the strategic vision to commercialize the Yves Saint Laurent brand name by clinching licensing deals in the 1970s, so he was swift to grasp the implications of the corporate changes that swept through the luxury industry in the 1980s. While the heads of other fashion houses watched helplessly as their lucrative beauty businesses were sold and resold to a motley assortment of parent companies, Pierre Bergé, helped by Carlo de Benedetti and Alain Minc, mounted an audacious bid to buy Yves Saint Laurent's. The liberalization of the financial markets gave him the means to do it, but orchestrating the Charles of the Ritz deal demanded considerable commercial acumen, as well as courage, and he then had the foresight to protect Yves Saint Laurent from being preyed upon by predators, most of whom would have been unlikely to have tolerated the neurasthenic Yves as their chief designer for very long.

Pierre's business record is not flawless. Eau Libre was a mistake, albeit a minor one. The Robert Merloz episode was a more serious misjudgement, as he could have saved himself and his protégé a great deal of embarrassment by financing the launch with his own money rather than the company's. If he had been less distracted by his responsibilities at the Opéra, Pierre might have exerted tighter control over licensing in the 1980s thereby preventing the tarnishing of the brand name. And had he been a little less arrogant when André Enders of the CVIC told him that the champagne industry intended to oppose the choice of the name Champagne for a fragrance, Sanofi may have been spared the dilemma of investing heavily to launch a perfume under one name, only to be forced by the courts to change it to another. Pierre's main misjudgement was burdening Yves and himself with huge personal debts to buy Carlo de Benedetti's shares at such a high price, which ultimately led to them having to sell the company to Sanofi. Yet the alternative of seeing the shares auctioned off to a predator might have been more damaging, and given the casinoesque finances of the beauty business Yves Saint Laurent may well have had to be taken over by a larger company eventually.

But Pierre Bergé's merits as a businessman far outweigh his failings, just as his achievements as president of the Chambre Syndicale – by encouraging the *couturiers* to embrace *prêt-à-porter* in the 1970s and using his political contacts to enhance Paris's prestige in the 1980s – counter the despotic manner with which he exercised his power. He is a rare example of an entrepreneur who had the intellectual agility to make the strategic leap from running a *couture* house, where he literally shouted instructions at each employee, to chairing a multinational luxury goods group. Few industrialists combine the *chutzpah* to barter with rag trade titans like Maurice Bidermann, with the *gravitas* to impress France's leading financial analysts and journalists when floating their company on the stock market. 'Of all the things Pierre Bergé has done, nothing matches the achievement of founding and running Yves Saint Laurent,' observed Franz-Olivier Giesbert, editor-in-chief of *Le Figaro*. 'It's building that business which makes him so fascinating, not having been president of the Opéra, a friend of François Mitterrand's, or any of the rest.'[7]

Trends change in the investment community, just as they do in fashion, and Pierre Bergé's style of running a luxury company is now outmoded. When Investcorp took control of Gucci in 1993, it commissioned Bain, the management consultancy, to study the rest of the industry and to map out a structure for a model modern luxury company. The role model that Bain chose was Alain Wertheimer's Chanel, with a headline hitting designer in Karl Lagerfeld, and a compact range of products manufactured by the company, rather than by licensees. Hence the new Gucci has been reconstructed with the hip young American, Tom Ford, as its design figurehead and a tightly controlled product line, rather than as a labyrinthine licensing empire like Yves Saint Laurent.

Yet it is those licences, rather than the aesthetic *coups* of the *Ballets Russes* collection or the camp iconoclasm of the 1940s line that have made Yves Saint Laurent a household name. The people who own YSL sunglasses, sheets and shirts did not necessarily buy them out of respect to the *couturier* who once showed two dozen versions of his classic *smoking* in the same show, nor out of sympathy with the wreck of a man who struggled for so long against neuroses and addictions. They bought them for the same reason that the Texan who accosted Yves in the Beijing souvenir shop chose a YSL belt, because the name Yves Saint Laurent conjured an abstract image of French good taste and Parisian elegance. Had they been asked what Yves Saint Laurent looked like, they would doubtless have described the tall, slim and bespectacled man they remembered from Yves's portraits in the 1960s; or maybe, like the banker Christophe Girard met in the early 1990s, they might have thought he was dead.[8]

It is almost inconceivable that another fashion designer could achieve the same level of recognition today. One consideration is that fashion receives less media attention than it did in the late 1950s when the twenty-one-year-old Yves shot to fame at Christian Dior. It is taken more seriously as a medium, analysed in greater depth and regarded as a legitimate subject for academic studies, but the reports of the *haute couture* and *prêt-à-porter* presentations no longer command daily slots on the front pages of the *International Herald Tribune*, *Le Figaro* or the *New York Times*, and therefore receive less exposure to general readers who do not pore over the style pages.

Fashion also has less shock value. Attitudes towards dress have changed dramatically since the days when Yves Saint Laurent could hit the headlines by dint of making wealthy women look elegant in tailored trousers, or by revealing a bare breast under a slither of silk chiffon, and most of the old taboos have been broken down. When Yves joined Dior, the Parisian *couturiers* were regarded as style dictators, who defined the fashion for the coming season which was then reproduced by the department stores and discount chains to be sold to the general public. New ideas now come from the street and are appropriated for *couture* or *prêt-à-porter*, not the other way around. Even American *Vogue* dressed the supermodels on its 1992 centenary cover in plain white cotton Gap T-shirts. If there is a creative focus in fashion today it is in sportswear, with the high performance fabrics and technically complex sports shoes that are as structurally sophisticated as an apparently seamless *haute couture* ballgown.

And whereas the old school of *couturiers* conducted themselves like master craftsmen, working with the finest materials and the highest standards of workmanship, *prêt-à-porter* designers work like stylists, identifying concepts for the clothes and liaising with technicians and factories to make them. One of the ironies of Yves's career is that, having pioneered ready-to-wear in the 1960s by making such a success of Rive Gauche, he would not, or could not, make the transition into playing the part of a stylist, which Karl Lagerfeld, who is the same age with the same traditional *couture* training, did brilliantly first at Chloé and thence at Chanel. Lagerfeld revelled in the iconoclastic aspect of the stylist's role, choosing to take it as a compliment when Pierre Bergé referred to him as a 'mercenary',[9] and the next generation of designers accepted it as a *fait accompli*. Miuccia Prada has established Prada as one of the chicest ready-to-wear labels of the 1990s, having trained in drama, not fashion, and has succeeded because of her flair for clothes and sense of what will sell. Fashion need be no less fun, fresh or expressive if it is created by a stylist rather than a master craftsman, but it is less likely to create a household name.

After Yves Saint Laurent's thirtieth anniversary celebration at the Opéra de Bastille, Holly Brubacher of the *New Yorker* drew a parallel between Yves and Paul Poiret whom she described as another gifted *couturier* who had 'outlived his moment' only to die 'penniless as well as forgotten'.[10] In stylistic terms Yves Saint Laurent did outlive his moment, at least for the fashion *cognoscenti*, if not for *les fidèles*, and he had also outlived it conceptually by failing to adapt to the new role of a designer in the *prêt-à-porter* era. Yet he has been able to continue creating his exquisite, if anachronistic *couture* collections, while avoiding Poiret's descent into poverty, because of his fame and the immense wealth created by the licensing empire that Pierre Bergé has built around it.

Whether Yves would have wished to have devoted his career to fashion is a different matter. Pierre Bergé once described him as a 'man of exceptional intelligence practising the trade of an imbecile'.[11] A slight exaggeration, at least on the second count, but he did have a point. Yves swiftly became frustrated by the creative constraints of fashion, as Michel de Brunhoff had warned him, but he did nothing about his plans to give it up whether out of loyalty to his staff, intellectual insecurity, or fear of relinquishing his wealth and fame. By the time he might have slipped into a dignified retirement, as Hubert de Givenchy did, he was too debilitated to do so.

Perhaps Yves Saint Laurent would have fallen prey to the same masochistic cycle had he been free to move on to a more stimulating field, and to live a quieter life as the Lalannes did in Ury, or Jacques Grange in the Palais-Royal. But it is difficult to imagine that his frustration, and the surreal pressure of having to create four fashion collections, and subject them to public scrutiny each year, did not aggravate his personal problems. By the early 1990s Yves claimed to be content with his lot as a *couturier*, saying that fashion would have 'missed me too much', but by then he was weakened and wearied. Or perhaps Anthony Burgess's reading of his palms was correct, and it would have been futile for Yves Saint Laurent to struggle against his fate because his public triumph and private tragedy was already decided for him.

Notes

CHAPTER I   THE BOY FROM ORAN

1. Louis Althusser, *The Future Lasts A Long Time*, p. 34: trans. Richard Veasey Chatto & Windus, London, 1993.
2. Another distant relative, Julie de Saint Laurent, added a raffish note to the Mathieu-Saint-Laurent family history by leaving France for England in the late eighteenth century where she spent nearly thirty years living with Edward, Duke of Kent, the fourth son of King George III, as his mistress. When Edward's family finally forced them to part, Julie went into a convent and lived there until her death.
3. *New York Times*, 3/6/1971, p. 45: 'Criticize Yves Saint Laurent – and It Hurts His Mother'.
4. American *Vogue*, January 1980, p. 207: G. Y. Dryansky, 'Saint Laurent All the Way'.
5. *Le Monde*, 8/12/1983, p. 29: Yvonne Baby, 'Portrait de l'Artiste'.
6. ibid.
7. ibid.
8. ibid.
9. ibid.
10. *Le Figaro*, 11/7/1991, p. 26: Franz-Olivier Giesbert & Janie Samet, 'Yves Saint Laurent: "Je Suis Né Avec Une Dépression Nerveuse"'.
11. American *Vogue*, December 1983, p. 300: Joan Juliet Buck, 'The Strongest Voice'.
12. op. cit. Yvonne Baby.
13. op. cit. Franz-Olivier Giesbert & Janie Samet.
14. The French laws on sexuality were relatively liberal until the Occupation when the Vichy government declared it to be a criminal offence to have sexual relations with anyone under the age of twenty-one. General de Gaulle reaffirmed this law when he took power in 1945. Although that legislation was not aimed specifically at male homosexuals the police used it as a weapon to crack down on them.
15. Laurence Benaïm, *Yves Saint Laurent*, p. 452: Éditions Grasset & Fasquelle, Paris, 1993.
16. Interview with Marie-José Lepicard, Paris, 23/5/1994.
17. op. cit. G. Y. Dryansky.
18. Diana Vreeland ed., *Yves Saint Laurent*, p. 225: Beijing, 1985.
19. ibid.
20. France colonized Algeria in 1830, long before Tunisia in 1881 and Morocco in 1912. The huge efflux of *émigrés* from Alsace and Lorraine in the 1870s and Algeria's physical promixity to Europe meant that by the time Yves

was born in the mid-1930s, one in ten of the Algerian population was of European origin. The proportion of Europeans was even higher in the coastal cities, such as Oran and Algiers, because so many of the indigenous Algerians were dispersed across rural areas inland and in the desert beyond the Atlas Mountains. There was one outbreak of violence during Yves's childhood when a Muslim mob attacked a group of French settlers in the sleepy town of Sétif in the Hodna Mountains on Victory in Europe Day, 8 May 1945. The French forces restored order but only after five days of fighting and the loss of 1,000 lives. The French settlers saw Sétif as an isolated incident, and Algeria then returned to political stability.

21. op. cit. Diana Vreeland.

22. Interview with Janie Samet, Paris, 23/6/1994.

23. *Jardin des Modes*, February 1982.

24. ibid.

25. Paris *Vogue*, December/January 1995/96, p. 30: Susan Train, 'Ils Ont Fait Vogue'.

CHAPTER 2   THE DAUPHIN AT DIOR

 1. Interview with Christian Lacroix, Paris, 15/6/1994.

 2. *New York Herald Tribune*, 25/10/1957, p. 2: Alain de Lyrot, 'Christian Dior'.

 3. Didier Grumbach, *Histoires de la Mode*, p. 43: Éditions du Seuil, Paris, 1993.

 4. Françoise Giroud, *Dior*, p. 3: trans. Stewart Spencer, Thames & Hudson, London, 1987.

 5. *New York Herald Tribune*, 13/2/1947, p. 1: Lucie Noel, 'Christian Dior's New House Sets The Pace': 'They are beginning to flock back to Paris knowing in their hearts that for sheer glamor and excitement the trip is something they must undertake.'

 6. Interview with Katell Le Bourhis, Paris, 27/5/1994.

 7. *New York Herald Tribune*, 6/8/1947.

 8. *New York Herald Tribune*, 8/8/1947. Lucie Noel wrote: '"breathtaking" and "elegant" seem quite mild adjectives.'

 9. op. cit. Didier Grumbach, p. 43.

10. Interview with Katell Le Bourhis, Paris, 27/5/1994.

11. op. cit. Didier Grumbach, p. 43. Christian Dior's sales rose from 1.2 million francs in 1947, to 3.6 million francs in 1948, and 12.7 million francs in 1949.

12. op. cit. Didier Grumbach, p. 77. Over the next four years Christian Dior signed similar contracts with seven other manufacturers and Dior stockings were sold in 2,500 stores worldwide.

13. op. cit. Didier Grumbach, p. 62.

14. American *Vogue*, September 1994, p. 154: Katherine Betts, 'Copy Rites'.

15. Georgina Howell, *In Vogue*, p. 214: Penguin Books, Harmondsworth, Middlesex, 1978.

16. Interview with Susan Train, Paris, 18/5/1994.

17. Interview with Renée Cassart, Paris, 12/4/1995.
18. Interview with Anne-Marie Muñoz, Paris, 12/4/1995.
19. *Glamour*, February 1995, p. 64: Dominique Dupuich, 'Modèles New Look'.
20. Pierre Gaxotte, *Christian Dior et Moi*, p. 163: Bibliothèque Amiot Dumont, Paris, 1956.
21. *New York Times*, 27/5/1967, p. 18: Gloria Emerson, 'Saint Laurent's Latest Creation: A Sadistic Little Lulu'.
22. *Independent on Sunday*, 16/1/1994, p. 32: Marion Hume, 'The Seasoned Customer'.
23. *Glamour*, May 1994, p. 88: Ginette Sainderichin, 'YSL: Le Grand Patron'.
24. Interview with Anne-Marie Muñoz, Paris, 12/4/1995.
25. Diana Vreeland ed., *YSL*, p. 16: Beijing, 1985.
26. *Le Figaro*, 11/7/1991, p. 26: Franz-Olivier Giesbert & Janie Samet, 'Yves Saint Laurent: "Je Suis Né Avec Une Dépression Nerveuse".'
27. *New York Herald Tribune*, 30/7/1957: Art Buchwald.
28. *Femme*, February 1992: Michèle Sider, 'Yves, Mon Fils'.
29. Interview with Anne-Marie Muñoz, Paris, 12/4/1995.
30. *Vanity Fair*, February 1992, p. 68: Maureen Orth, 'Kaiser Karl: Behind the Mask'.
31. *Vanity Fair*, March 1986, p. 76: Javier Arroyuelo, 'Fashion Royalty and the Couture Courts of Paris'.
32. op. cit. Franz-Olivier Giesbert & Janie Samet.
33. Laurence Benaïm, *Yves Saint Laurent*, p. 51: Éditions Grasset et Fasquelle, Paris, 1993.
34. op. cit. Michèle Sider.
35. op. cit. Michèle Sider.
36. *New York Herald Tribune*, 25/10/1957, p. 1.
37. *Le Monde*, 25/10/1957, p. 8.
38. Interview with Susan Train, Paris, 18/5/1994.
39. op. cit. Didier Grumbach, p. 80.

CHAPTER 3   ON THE TRAPEZE

1. American *Vogue*, January 1980, p. 149: G. Y. Dryansky, 'Saint Laurent All The Way'.
2. Interview with Susan Train, Paris, 18/5/1994.
3. *Le Figaro*, 11/7/1991, p. 26: Franz-Olivier Giesbert & Janie Samet, 'Yves Saint Laurent: "Je Suis Né Avec Une Dépression Nerveuse"'.
4. Interview with Anne-Marie Muñoz, Paris, 12/4/1995.
5. *New York Herald Tribune*, 27/1/1958, p. 5: 'The highlight of the series will occur Thursday morning when the house of Christian Dior with twenty-one-year-old Yves Saint Laurent debuting as its main designer, unveils its creations.'
6. Interview with Katell Le Bourhis, Paris, 27/5/1994.
7. Interview with Marie-José Lepicard, Paris, 23/5/1994.

8. Interview with Janie Samet, Paris, 23/6/1994.

9. Diana Vreeland ed., *Yves Saint Laurent*, p. 7: Metropolitan Museum of Art, New York, 1983.

10. *New York Times*, 31/5/1958, p. 1.

11. *New York Herald Tribune*, 31/1/1958, p. 1.

12. *Le Figaro*, 3/2/1958.

13. Interview with Christian Lacroix, Paris, 15/6/1994.

14. Interview with Marie-José Lepicard, Paris, 23/5/1994.

15. Interview with Pierre Bergé, Paris, 11/4/1995.

16. British *Vogue*, November 1994, p. 148: Lesley White, 'The Saint'.

17. Interview with Pierre Bergé, Paris, 11/4/1995.

18. *Tatler*, July 1989, p. 80: Anne Elisabeth Moutet.

19. *The New Yorker*, 21/11/1994, p. 80: Jane Kramer, 'The Impresario's Last Act'.

20. ibid.

21. *L'Express*, 6/2/1958.

22. Interview with Susan Train, Paris, 19/5/1994.

23. ibid.

24. Interview with Pierre Bergé, Paris, 11/4/1995.

25. *Bonjour Tristesse*, the novel that launched Françoise Sagan's career, was published in 1954 when she was nineteen. It tells the story of Cécile, an apparently sophisticated young woman brought up by her father, who like future Sagan heroines is prey to precocious sexual urges and jealousy.

26. Interview with Claude Brouet, Paris, 24/5/1994.

27. Interview with Anne-Marie Muñoz, Paris, 12/4/1995.

28. *New York Herald Tribune*, 1/8/1958, p. 5: Eugenia Sheppard, 'Skirt Lengths Dropped by Saint Laurent for Dior' – 'The Dior collection was hardly over before it became a Grade A controversy in the fashion world. It looks as if Saint Laurent, with his flair for dramatics, has uncovered a cleavage – no reference to necklines – that has been growing wider in fashion for some time. On the one side are the fashion egg-heads with a yen for the youth look and the *avant garde* designers, as against the old line conservatives with their credo of true elegance. It was like Adlai Stevenson switching to the Republican ticket when young.'

29. *Le Figaro*, 28/1/1960, p. 12.

30. *New York Herald Tribune*, 30/1/1959, p. 1: Eugenia Sheppard concluded that the collection's success 'settles for a while the to-be-or-not-to-be question that has hung over the house since Dior's death.'

31. *New York Herald Tribune*, 31/7/1959, p. 1: Eugenia Sheppard, 'Hobble Skirts Revived at Dior'.

32. Georgina Howell, *In Vogue*, p. 210: Penguin Books, Harmondsworth, Middlesex, 1978.

33. Interview with Anne-Marie Muñoz, Paris, 12/4/1995.

34. *New York Herald Tribune*, 28/1/1960, p. 1: Eugenia Sheppard, 'Dior Fashions, Pure, Elegant'.
35. *Le Figaro*, 28/7/1960, p. 11.
36. *New York Times*, 28/7/1960, p. 31: Patricia Peterson – 'It is a rather severe sophisticated vision young Yves Saint Laurent sees for women this fall. There was enough black to keep a horde of merry widows happy.'
37. *New York Herald Tribune*, 8/7/1960, p. 1: Eugenia Sheppard, 'Saint Laurent Shows Collection Which is Cool, Beat, Gone' – 'YSL is a cool kid. In slinks a model wearing a glorified stocking cap and a shiny black motorcycle jacket lined with mink. She looks as if a gold-plated motorcycle were waiting for her at the door.'
38. Interview with Susan Train, Paris, 2/8/1994.
39. Diana Vreeland ed., *YSL*, p. 21: Beijing, 1985.
40. France was condemned by the United Nations for the atrocities committed by the French forces against Algerian civilians after the Battle of Algiers.
41. There were few legitimate ways for men who had completed their studies to avoid conscription unless they were seriously ill or had a widowed mother to support.
42. op. cit. Franz-Olivier Giesbert & Janie Samet.
43. Interview with Susan Train, Paris, 18/5/1994.

CHAPTER 4   THE TEN OF CLUBS

1. *Le Monde*, 22/9/1960.
2. *Paris-Match*, 6/2/1992, p. 90: Victoire, 'L'Année Terrible de Ses Débuts'.
3. Interview with Susan Train, Paris, 18/5/1994.
4. Interview with Pierre Bergé, Paris, 11/4/1995.
5. Interview with Marie-José Lepicard, Paris, 23/5/1994.
6. *Le Figaro*, 11/7/1991, p. 26: Franz-Olivier Giesbert & Janie Samet, 'Yves Saint Laurent: "Je Suis Né Avec Une Dépression Nerveuse"'.
7. ibid.
8. *Femme*, February 1992, p. 11: Michèle Sider, 'Yves, Mon Fils'.
9. op. cit. Victoire.
10. Interview with Pierre Bergé, Paris, 11/4/1995.
11. *Le Figaro*, 27/1/1961, p. 5.
12. *New York Herald Tribune*, 27/1/1960, p. 1: Eugenia Sheppard, 'Marc Bohan's Flapper Show Rated a Smash Hit in Paris'.
13. Interview with Pierre Bergé, Paris, 11/4/1995.
14. *Château en Suède* (Castle in Sweden) was Françoise Sagan's first play, which premièred in 1960 to rave reviews. It is a witty account of the marital problems of an eighteenth-century Swedish couple. The wife routinely seduces any male cousins who visit them in the castle.
15. Interview with Pierre Bergé, Paris, 11/4/1995.
16. op. cit. Victoire.

17. *New York Times*, 15/12/1964: Vartanig Vartan, 'Fashion Means Business to St Laurent's Backer'.
18. Interview with Anne-Marie Muñoz, Paris, 12/4/1995.
19. Interview with Gabrielle Buchaert, Paris, 12/4/1995.
20. Interview with Renée Cassart, Paris, 12/4/1995.
21. op. cit. Franz-Olivier Giesbert & Janie Samet.
22. ibid.
23. Ludwig Mies Van der Rohe, the German modernist architect, designed the Brno chair in 1930 with the interior designer, Lily Reich, for the Tugendhat house at Brno in Czechoslovakia. When Yves and Pierre bought them in the early 1960s the chairs were reproduced by Knoll, the American furniture manufacturer.
24. Interview with Renée Cassart, Paris, 12/4/1995.
25. Interview with Marie-José Lepicard, Paris, 23/5/1994.
26. *New York Herald Tribune*, 26/1/1962, p. 1: Eugenia Sheppard described it on the front page of the *Herald Tribune* as being 'complete, marvelously produced with the first fresh brand new idea this season'.
27. *L'Aurore*, 26/1/1962, p. 12: The text was predictably gushing: 'Chairs flew through the air and champagne flowed. Dior could have prefaced its collection with a proud declaration: "This is fashion".'
28. *W. Europe*, January 1992, p. 18: Barbara Schwarm, 'The House of Yves: Day 1'.
29. *Daily Express*, 30/1/1962.
30. op. cit. Barbara Schwarm.
31. *New York Times*, 30/1/1962, p. 33.
32. Interview with Janie Samet, Paris, 23/6/1994.

CHAPTER 5   THE SCENT OF SUCCESS

1. Morocco was declared independent of France on 2 March 1956, the first of its North African colonies to attain independence. The transition was less traumatic there than in Algeria as the French presence had never been as strong in Morocco and France had left the indigenous governmental system in place, simply supervising it, rather than governing the country directly as it did in Algeria.
2. The OAS staged bomb attacks on mainland France in 1961 and unsuccessfully attempted to assassinate General de Gaulle. But the event that decisively swung the French against *L'Algérie Française* was the bombing of the home of André Malraux, the culture minister, in which a four-year-old child was badly wounded. De Gaulle started peace talks with the Algerians in summer 1961, but those talks were unsuccessful. He ordered a crackdown against the OAS the following January and two months later started fresh negotiations that ended in a settlement.
3. *New York Times*, 31/7/1962, p. 20: Carrie Donovan, 'St Laurent Collections Get First Bravos of Season'.

4. *New York Herald Tribune*, 31/7/1962, p. 1: Eugenia Sheppard, 'Saint Laurent Collection Called Smash Hit'.
5. Interview with Susan Train, Paris, 2/8/1994.
6. Diana Vreeland initially joined *Vogue* as associate editor in 1962, and took over as editor-in-chief in 1965.
7. *Bravo Yves*, p. 14: Yves Saint-Laurent, Paris, 1982. John Fairchild: 'Balenciaga's fashion was on the wane. Givenchy had married the repetitive style of Balenciaga. Chanel was the real dictator of fashion, and Saint Laurent – peering at everything through his large glasses – knew it better than anyone else.'
8. Nicholas Coleridge, *The Fashion Conspiracy*, p. 50: William Heinemann, London, Melbourne, Auckland, 1988.
9. Interview with Marie-José Lepicard, Paris, 23/5/1994.
10. Yasujiro 'Pistol' Tsutsumi made his fortune by buying up land from poor farmers in the 1920s, and from distant relatives of the Imperial Family in the 1940s when they needed money to pay taxes after being stripped of their imperial privileges. An aspiring poet, his son, Seiji was forced into the family business against his will.
11. Interview with Kuniko Tsutsumi, Paris, 21/9/1994.
12. *International Herald Tribune*, Fashion Special Report, 20/10/1989, p. 1: Suzy Menkes, 'A Growing Yen For Luxury Labels'. Pierre Cardin, the *couturier* who was once Dior's chief assistant, went to Japan in 1956 and described it as 'like going to the moon' and 'so difficult that I crossed off every day as though I was doing military service'.
13. Interview with Kuniko Tsutsumi, Paris, 21/9/1994: 'We lost money on it for years. But we had to be sure that we were doing it correctly, if we were going to build up a business for the long term.'
14. One of Richard Salomon's innovations was the 'shop in shop', or concession concept, whereby a cosmetics company ran its own sales unit within a department store with its own clearly identifiable image and sales staff trained to deal with its products. The concept is now commonplace all over the world, but was then an innovation that enabled Charles of the Ritz to control the presentation of its products.
15. Interview with Pierre Bergé, Paris, 11/4/1995.
16. Revlon was the province of Charles Revson, who founded the company in 1933 and turned it into a $200 million concern by the mid-1960s. He called it Revlon with an 'l' in deference to Lachner, his chief chemist. Revson was a self-made man described by one of his own executives to *New York Times* as: 'a tough guy alright. He thinks nothing of calling you in the middle of the night on some minor matter or of forgetting that everyone is entitled to eat lunch every day. The place is a revolving door – any executive who doesn't measure up in a few months is out.' Revlon owned the licensing rights to Pierre Balmain's perfumes: Miss Balmain, Vent Vert and Jolie Madame.

17. Avon was the biggest of the Americans with annual sales of $400 million by the mid-1960s and an army of 'Avon Calling' door-to-door saleswomen, but its make-up and scents were inexpensive, aimed squarely at the mass market.

18. Elizabeth Arden, born Florence Nightingale Graham, trained as a beautician and opened her own beauty *salon* in 1910 on New York's Fifth Avenue, taking her professional name from a friend, Elizabeth Hubbard, and the title of a Tennyson poem, 'Enoch Arden'. Her *salons* evoked a chocolate-box view of feminine beauty with frou-frou pink interiors. Once a suffragette campaigner, she later hired Hedda Hopper, the famous Hollywood publicist, to buff up her image. Yet she was so frugal that, even when a millionairess, she sometimes shampooed the carpets of her *salons* and took sandwiches to work for lunch. Her main indulgence was her stable of racehorses. Blue Grass, her best-selling scent, was named after the grass they grazed on in Kentucky.

19. Helena Rubinstein owned a chain of beauty *salons* in Europe before emigrating to the US in the early 1900s. She adhered to a scientific view of beauty reflected in the businesslike blues of her packaging and the white smocks she insisted her staff should wear in the *salons*. Helena Rubinstein always wore a *couture* suit with a matching hat, often from YSL. She and Elizabeth Arden never actually met.

20. The only one of the old French perfume houses to survive as an international force was Guerlain, largely because of the success of Shalimar, invented in 1921 when Jacques Guerlain accidentally added a new synthetic vanilla ethyl to Jicky, a perfume created by his uncle in 1889. It was the first 'oriental' scent, perfect for the bohemian mood of the 1920s when orientalism was fashionable.

21. *Financial Times*, 'How To Spend It', Autumn 1995, p. 66: Susan Irvine, 'On The Scent Of Liquid Gold'.

22. Joy was created in 1930 from an extremely expensive blend of Grasse's finest *rose de mai* and *jasmine*, which not only gave it a highly distinctive smell but made it genuinely more expensive than most other French perfumes.

23. Interview with Pierre Bergé, Paris, 11/4/1995.

24. Coco Chanel had wrangled for years with the Wertheimers, the family that owned the company which manufactured her perfumes for her and had taken over her *couture* house on rue Cambon when she fled to exile in Switzerland after the War.

25. *New York Times*, 15/12/1964: Vartanig G. Vartan, 'Fashion Means Business To St Laurent's Backer'.

26. Interview with Pierre Bergé, Paris, 11/4/1995.

27. op. cit. Vartanig G. Vartan.

28. *New York Herald Tribune*, 30/7/1965, p. 1: Eugenia Sheppard, 'Saint Laurent's Little Boy Look Cheered', 'Yves Saint Laurent holds Paris in the palm of his hand today.'

29. *New York Times*, 4/2/1964, p. 36: Patricia Peterson, 'Saint Laurent, Givenchy and Castillo Show Collections on a Busy Day', 'This was a big day in Paris and Saint Laurent won it.'
30. Born in Pau, in the Pyrénées region of France in 1923, André Courrèges joined Cristobal Balenciaga's *couture* house in 1950 and worked there as an assistant for the next ten years, until he set up his own business in 1961. His public image was the opposite of the fey, sensitive Yves, as Courrèges was an enthusiastic sportsman who played rugby regularly and was a keen mountain climber.
31. *New York Herald Tribune*, 30/7/1965, p. 1: Eugenia Sheppard, 'Saint Laurent's Little Boy Look Cheered'.
32. *New York Herald Tribune*, 4/8/1964, p. 1.
33. op. cit. Vartanig G. Vartan.
34. Captain Molyneux, a favourite designer of Christian Dior, was one of the few Englishmen to have established himself as a Parisian *couturier*. His heyday was in the 1930s when Pierre Balmain was among his assistants, and Mitza Bricard his 'muse'. He reopened his *salon* after World War II but closed it down in 1950 to retreat to the Riviera where he spent his time painting and tending carnations. His comeback collection was politely reviewed, but he never recovered his old status.
35. *New York Herald Tribune*, 2/2/1965, p. 1: Eugenia Sheppard merely commented that 'buyer reports were conflicting'.
36. American *Vogue*, April 1965.
37. J. Mack Robinson's identity had remained secret, as he had wished, until 1963 when he was 'outed' by *Newsweek* magazine which discovered that he was Yves Saint Laurent's backer.
38. op. cit. Vartanig G. Vartan.
39. Interview with Pierre Bergé, Paris, 11/4/1995.
40. *New York Times*, 19/5/1968, p. 16: Isadore Bramash, 'Cosmetics Makers Putting On New Faces'.
41. *New York Times*, 14/7/1965, p. 28: Gloria Emerson, 'St Laurent Seeks Growth in Prestige, but Not Size'.
42. *New York Times*, 3/8/1965, p. 26: Leonard Sloane, 'Saint Laurent's Backer Spurns Opening in Paris'. Richard Salomon, 'Mr Saint Laurent is one of the most extremely talented young men in the fashion field, and we have great faith in this guy's ability to design fashions in many areas.'
43. *Forbes*, 19/10/1992.

CHAPTER 6 ON THE LEFT BANK
1. *New York Times*, 3/8/1965, p. 26: Leonard Sloane, 'Saint Laurent's New Backer Spurns Opening in Paris'.
2. Interview with Renée Cassart, Paris, 12/4/1995.
3. *New York Herald Tribune*, 3/8/1965: Eugenia Sheppard, 'Saint Laurent Star Rising Again'. Sheppard nobbled Madame Hervé Alphand, the wife of the

French ambassador to the United Nations, when she spotted her lunching with a friend at Maxim's. 'Just what we needed,' said the ambassadress. 'It's young and way-out but not too far.'

4. Interview with Susan Train, Paris, 2/8/1994.

5. *New York Times*, 7/8/1965, p. 11: Gloria Emerson, 'Saint Laurent: Bright, Fresh Clothes for a Baby-Faced Blonde'.

6. op. cit. Leonard Sloane. The orders for that season came to 3.7 million francs, up from 2.4 million francs for the spring line that had been shown six months before.

7. *Time*, 12/12/1983, p. 96: 'The Designer at Home'.

8. Rudolf Nureyev had partnered Fonteyn since 1961 when Ninette de Valois asked them to dance together for a Royal Ballet gala. They were so popular that the Covent Garden crush bar sold three times as much champagne when they were dancing as it did on other nights.

9. Peter Watson, *Nureyev: A Biography*, p. 280: Hodder & Stoughton, London, Sydney, Auckland, 1994.

10. Interview with Clara Saint, Paris, 12/4/1995.

11. ibid.

12. *Paris-Match*, 6/2/1992, p. 89.

13. *Belle de Jour*, Paris Film/Five Film, directed by Luis Buñuel, 1967.

14. Born in San Sebastian, Spain in 1934 as Francisco Rabenada-Cuervo, Paco Rabanne was educated in France and, after graduating from art school, he worked as an accessories designer for Balenciaga, Givenchy and Dior, before founding his own *couture* house in 1967. The collection he designed for the house of Philippe Venet in spring 1966 was a smash hit, with diamond and circular shaped plastic discs linked together by metallic chains.

15. Pierre Cardin was born in San Biagio Di Callala in Italy in 1922 and started off in the fashion industry as a cutter for a men's tailor. He then worked for Christian Dior and established himself as one of the most talented design assistants in the early days of the *couture* house before leaving to set up his own company in 1949. Cardin had a minimalist modern style and received some of the best reviews of his career for his spacey designs in spring 1966. However, he was as well known for men's wear as for women's wear, having launched a men's line in 1960 with collarless suits in cotton and corduroy and unpleated trousers. The Beatles wore his mandarin-collared suits in the mid-1960s.

16. *New York Times*, 5/2/1966, p. 18: Gloria Emerson, 'St Laurent: rue de la West 42nd'.

17. *New York Times*, 6/10/1965, p. 5: Gloria Emerson, 'Saint Laurent to Open a Left-Bank Boutique'.

18. Mary Quant's most famous fashion innovation was the mini-skirt. Her skirts grew shorter each season, until in 1965 when she unveiled the mini, a thigh-skimming skirt that caused a sensation when she and her 'Chelsea girl' models took it on a whistle-stop tour of the United States.

19. Georgina Howell, *In Vogue*, p. 292: Penguin Books, Harmondsworth, Middlesex, 1978.
20. *Women's Wear Daily*, 12/10/1966. The article identified a group of influential young Paris designers, all of whom had chosen to work in *prêt-à-porter*, not *haute couture*. They included Michèle Rosier, Christine Bailly, Emanuelle Khanh, Graziella Fontana, Jacques Delahaye, Daniel Hechter, Jean Cacharel and Yves's friend, Karl Lagerfeld, then working with Rosier at the Chloé fashion house.
21. Interview with Sonia Rykiel, Paris, 21/6/1994.
22. After the War the Chambre Syndicale sent a delegation of members to the United States to study the manufacturing techniques in American factories. But it still refused to embrace mechanization and the only significant change in its rules was the creation of a new category of member, the *couturiers associés*, or associate *couturiers*, in the late 1950s to include those involved solely with ready-to-wear.
23. *Chambre Syndicale de la Couture Parisienne.*
24. Lanvin announced that it would be showing seventy-five outfits in its shows, rather than the usual two hundred, to cut down on labour and material costs.
25. *New York Herald Tribune*, 28/7/1965, back page.
26. Interview with Pierre Bergé, Paris, 11/4/1995.
27. Interview with Katell Le Bourhis, Paris, 24/5/1994.
28. Didier Grumbach, *Histoires de la Mode*, p. 192: Éditions du Seuil, Paris, 1993.
29. ibid. p. 193.
30. Interview with Pierre Bergé, Paris, 11/4/1995.
31. *New York Times*, 5/1/1966, p. 35: Gloria Emerson, 'A Nude Dress That Isn't: Saint Laurent In a New Mood'.
32. *New York Herald Tribune*, 5/8/1966, p. 5.
33. *New York Herald Tribune*, 28/9/1966, p. 5.

CHAPTER 7   THE HIPPY DE LUXE
1. Interview with Susan Train, Paris, 2/8/1994.
2. Interview with Clara Saint, Paris, 12/4/1994.
3. *New York Times*, 3/2/1967, p. 26: Gloria Emerson, 'Saint Laurent Brings Back the Dietrich Look in Paris'.
4. *New York Herald Tribune*, 3/2/1967, p. 5. Eugenia Sheppard: 'Why pay the price of a Broadway musical when the real spectacular is Paris fashion at Yves Saint Laurent? Lots of people in Paris are saying that Saint Laurent's new tailored suits look too much like Lakey in *The Group*. But I don't get the lesbian message. They seem feminine to the point of being costumey.'
5. Interview with Jean-Pierre Derbord, Paris, 12/4/1995.
6. Interview with Maïmé Arnodin, Paris, 11/4/1995.
7. Interview with Betty Catroux, Paris, 17/2/1995.

8. ibid.

9. Warhol met Edie Sedgwick, the daughter of a wealthy Massachusetts family, in early 1965, but they drifted apart as her drug problems mounted.

10. Interview with Betty Catroux, Paris, 17/2/1995.

11. ibid.

12. ibid.

13. *New York Times*, 6/10/1965, p. 5: Gloria Emerson, 'Saint Laurent to Open a Left-Bank Boutique'.

14. *New York Times*, 25/5/1967, p. 18: Gloria Emerson, 'St. Laurent's Latest Creation: A Sadistic Little Lulu'.

15. Yves Saint Laurent, *La Vilaine Lulu*: Éditions Tchou, Paris, 1967.

16. *New York Times*, 1/8/1967, p. 26: Gloria Emerson, 'Saint Laurent Does Chanel – But Better'.

17. Arthur Penn portrayed the gangsters *Bonnie and Clyde*, played by Faye Dunaway and Warren Beatty, an anarchic anti-heroes, which struck a chord at a time when American youth was obsessed with dodging the draft for the Vietnam War.

18. *International Herald Tribune*, 30/1/1968, p. 7.

19. *Dim Dam Dom*, transmitted on 11/2/1968.

20. Interview with Kuniko Tsutsumi, Paris, 21/9/1994.

21. One of William Burroughs' favourites in the 1950s was Eukodol, a synthetic morphine notorious among junkies for its euphoric properties. The German manufacturer withdrew it from the market in most countries when they discovered Eukodol's side-effects, but it stayed on sale in Morocco.

22. David Macey, *The Lives of Michel Foucault*, p. 184: Hutchinson, London, Melbourne, Sydney, Auckland, Johannesburg, 1993.

23. *Vanity Fair*, August 1994, p. 74: Fiametta Rocco, 'Paul Getty's New Life'.

24. Peter Watson, *Nureyev*, p. 298: Hodder & Stoughton, London, Sydney, Auckland, 1994.

25. LSD, or lysergic acid diethylamide, was discovered by chance in 1938 by Albert Hofmann, head of research at Sandoz, the Swiss pharmaceuticals company, during a routine research project looking for a migraine cure. He tested it on mice for five years until he accidentally absorbed a small dose through his fingertips. As he cycled home that night he found himself flung into a fantastical trance. The Sandoz labs continued their experiments with LSD, and in the 1950s Harvard Medical School started testing it on students, paying them a daily fee of $25. Leary took it as part of that experiment.

26. *New York Times Magazine*, 11/9/1977, p. 118: Anthony Burgess, 'All About Yves'. During a lengthy interview Yves told the sceptical Burgess of his conviction that his hallucinogenic experiences had opened new creative avenues in his design work.

27. *International Herald Tribune*, 30/1/1968, p. 7: Eugenia Sheppard wrote a short review describing it as full of 'youth kick'.

28. *New York Times*, 20/1/1968, p. 32: Gloria Emerson, 'Saint Laurent Collection Generates Smoke But Little Fire'.
29. *New York Times*, 30/7/1968, p. 34: Gloria Emerson, 'Buffalo Bill Look Rides High in Paris': 'a beautiful, low key, slightly bored collection'.
30. The protests had started in March 1968 when a student at Nanterre University was arrested after a terrorist attack on an American Express office in Paris in protest against the Vietnam War. The unrest simmered through the spring until Nanterre closed in early May and the demonstrators moved to the Sorbonne in the fifth *arrondissement*.

CHAPTER 8   THE BEAUTIFUL AND THE DAMNED

1. *Time*, 27/9/1968, p. 63: 'Yves in New York'.
2. Interview with Betty Catroux, Paris, 17/2/1995.
3. *Time*, 27/9/1968, p. 63: 'Yves in New York'.
4. Interview with Betty Catroux, Paris, 17/2/1995.
5. *W. Europe*, July 1994: Lorna Koski, 'The Survivor'.
6. Interview with Betty Catroux, Paris, 17/2/1995.
7. Interview with Sonia Rykiel, Paris, 21/6/1994.
8. Interview with Miuccia Prada, Milan, 11/5/1994.
9. Interview with Paul Smith, London, 2/4/1996.
10. *New York Times*, 9/7/1969, p. 40: 'Saint Laurent Shows Maxis, Midis – and Even Some Minis'.
11. *International Herald Tribune*, 2/2/1970, p. 7: Eugenia Sheppard, 'On The Way to Saint Laurent': 'Where does that leave the groom, who can't yet switch to skirts?'
12. *New York Times*, 2/2/1970, p. 36: Gloria Emerson, 'Saint Laurent Hemlines Go From Knee To Ankle': 'Poor Yves Saint Laurent. He is cornered now by his own success. A flop might bring him to his senses. But nowadays his name sells too many clothes.'
13. *International Herald Tribune*, 24/7/1970: Eugenia Sheppard, 'If Dior Is Sensual So Is Aunt Minnie'.
14. Interview with Christian Lacroix, Paris, 15/6/1994.
15. By the end of 1969 there were twenty Rive Gauche boutiques worldwide.
16. Otis Stuart, *Perpetual Motion: The Public and Private Lives of Rudolf Nureyev*, p. 141: Simon & Schuster, New York, London, Toronto, Sydney, Tokyo, Singapore, 1995.
17. *Le Figaro*, 6/4/1971, p. 14: Hélène de Turkheim, 'YSL; "As Chanel Did Her Suits For Herself, I Did My Men's Collection For Me".' Yves Saint Laurent: 'I did my men's line for me, just like Chanel designed her suits for herself. It's full of things that I love or would love to wear, or that please the people around me.'
18. op. cit. Otis Stuart, p. 166.
19. Bob Colacello, *Holy Terror: Andy Warhol Close Up*, p. 60: HarperCollins, New York, 1990.

20. Victor Bockris, *Warhol*, p. 409: Penguin Books, Harmondsworth, Middlesex, 1990. Jed Johnson: 'Andy really liked Paris. He was more accepted in society there than he was in New York, and he loved that. It was glamorous. An artist was more important to the Europeans.'

21. *Harper's Bazaar*, September 1994, p. 404: Sarah Mower, 'The YSL Revolution'.

22. *Le Monde*, 8/12/1983, p. 29: Yvonne Baby, *'Portrait de l'Artiste'*.

23. Interview with Christian Lacroix, Paris, 15/6/1994.

24. Interview with Marie-José Lepicard, Paris, 23/5/1994.

25. *Time*, 15/2/1971, p. 62: 'Yves St. Debacle'.

26. *International Herald Tribune*, 30–31/1/1971: Eugenia Sheppard, 'Saint Laurent: Truly Hideous'.

27. Interview with Christian Lacroix, Paris, 15/6/1994.

28. *Time*, 25/1/1971, p. 54: 'Chanel No. 1'.

29. The son of a tailor, Emanuel Ungaro was born in Aix-en-Provence in 1933 and trained as a tailor in Aix after leaving the local *lycée*, before moving to Paris to work in *haute couture*. He worked for Cristóbal Balenciaga, both in Paris and Madrid, from 1958 to 1964 and then joined André Courrèges as an assistant. Ungaro opened his own *haute couture* house in 1965.

30. Susan Sontag, *Notes on Camp*, 1964: reprinted in *A Susan Sontag Reader*, Penguin Books. Harmondsworth, Middlesex, 1983, p. 105.

31. The Gay Liberation Front was founded in the United States in 1970, the year after Stonewall, and then moved to Britain and France, where the first independent gay protest group, the *Fondation Homosexuel d'Action Révolutionnaire*, was established in 1971.

32. *Time*, 15/2/1971, p. 62: 'Yves St. Debacle'.

33. *New York Times*, 3/6/1971, p. 45: 'Criticize Yves Saint-Laurent – and It Hurts His Mother'.

34. *New York Times*, 19/2/1971, p. 30: UPI, 'St. Laurent Retorts'.

CHAPTER 9   END OF AN ERA

1. Interview with Jeanloup Sieff, Paris, 25/5/1994.

2. ibid.

3. Interview with Claude Brouet, Paris, 24/5/1994.

4. The market for men's scents was still in its infancy; old-fashioned gentlemen bought colognes from their barbers, but other men considered perfume to be effeminate Estée Lauder opened up the market for fashionable men's fragrances in the United States by launching Aramis in 1966, which was successfully positioned as a contemporary scent for modern men.

5. *New York Times*, 6/10/1965, p. 5: Gloria Emerson, 'Saint Laurent to Open a Left Bank Boutique'.

6. Interview with Betty Catroux, Paris, 17/2/1995.

7. Interview with Clara Saint, Paris, 12/10/1995.

8. Virna Lisi was a voluptuous Italian movie star, then in her mid-thirties, who starred in a number of 1960s films including *Casanova*, *How To Murder Your Wife*, and *Signore e Signori*.

9. Interview with Clara Saint, Paris, 12/10/1995.

10. American *Vogue*, November 1971: 'Oasis in Paris'.

11. *New York Times*, 19/2/1971, p. 30: UPI, 'Saint Laurent Retorts'.

12. Didier Grumbach, *Histoires de la Mode*, p. 277: Éditions du Seuil, Paris, 1993.

13. *International Herald Tribune*, 10/8/1971, p. 7: Peggy Massin, 'Saint Laurent: Dropping Out'.

14. There were twenty-three Rive Gauche boutiques worldwide by 1971.

15. Christian Dior introduced a ready-to-wear line called Miss Dior: and Hubert de Givenchy launched the Nouvelle Boutique collection.

16. Kenzo Takada was born in Himeji, near Osaka, and studied at Bunka College in Tokyo before moving to Paris in 1965. He opened the first Jungle Jap boutiques in Galerie Vivienne in 1970 with two friends, Atsuko Kondo and Atsuko Ansaï.

17. Sonia Rykiel started designing for Laura, a boutique owned by her parents-in-law on Avenue du Général-Leclerc in Paris. By the mid-1960s she had devised her own style of 'poor boy' knitwear, a collection of fine skimpy knits that could be worn together as an entire wardrobe, which became commercially successful after one was featured on the cover of *Elle* magazine. She opened a boutique on rue de Grenelle in Saint-Germain des Prés in June 1968, saying that she delayed the opening for a month to participate in the May *événements*.

18. Karl Lagerfeld joined Chloé, which was owned by Gaby Aghion and Jacques Lenoir, in 1963 when he was hired as one of four young designers. By the early 1970s two of the others had left and Lagerfeld was competing furiously to become chief designer against his only remaining rival, Graziella Fontana.

19. op. cit. Peggy Massin. By that time *haute couture* represented less than a quarter of YSL's income.

20. *International Herald Tribune*, 11/8/1971, p. 7: Associated Press, 'Cardin, Courrèges Hint They May Drop Couture'. Robert Ricci, chairman of Nina Ricci and a former head of the Chambre Syndicale: 'Yves Saint Laurent is right. One day ready-to-wear will overtake *haute couture*.' But he criticized Saint Laurent for 'embarrassing' the other *couturiers*. 'We were showing as a group and we should have acted as a group.'

21. *New York Times*, 29/10/1971, p. 34: 'Saint Laurent's Giant Step Away From Couture'.

22. ibid.

23. *International Herald Tribune*, 28/1/1972, p. 6: Hebe Dorsey, 'Paris Couture and How It Has Changed'.

24. ibid.

25. Interview with Julia Kennedy, London, 10/2/1995.
26. Sales of prestige scents and cosmetics rose by roughly ten per cent a year throughout the 1960s.
27. Revlon commanded annual sales of almost $400 million by the end of the 1960s.
28. Estée Lauder founded her eponymous beauty business with her financier husband, Joseph, in New York State in 1946, to market the products developed by her uncle, a Viennese cosmetics chemist. Its first big success was Youth Dew, launched in the 1950s as a brazenly sexy bath oil doubling as a perfume. During the 1960s the company also introduced Aramis, a men's scent, and the Clinique skin-care range. By the end of the decade its annual turnover was about to break through the $100 million mark. The company was still family-controlled.
29. Squibb had agreed that they should open fourteen new Rive Gauche boutiques in the United States and also start manufacturing there.
30. Interview with Jean-Louis Dumas, Paris, 5/9/1994. Jean-Louis Dumas of the Hermès family, a close friend of Salomon's, said that one of his proudest achievements was the launch of Rive Gauche and he often talked about it even after his retirement in the 1970s and 1980s.
31. Yves Saint Laurent for Men had just won the award for the best launch campaign of the year from the Fragrance Foundation in New York.
32. Interview with Pierre Bergé, Paris, 11/4/1995.
33. Yves and Pierre owned a twenty per cent stake in the company, which they were given under the terms of their original deal with J. Mack Robinson. They were also entitled to various fees and royalties on sales of YSL products, including its scents. Richard Salomon arranged for Squibb to give them full ownership of the fashion house and the licensing rights to the Yves Saint Laurent name for anything other than perfume and cosmetics, in return for their twenty per cent interest in the beauty business. They agreed to relinquish all financial entitlements to the YSL scents and cosmetics except for a five per cent royalty on wholesale sales which Squibb would continue to pay them to them. Finally they agreed to pay a sum of $1.1 million to Squibb, which would effectively be treated as a loan being paid in instalments over the next fifteen years at a low rate of interest.

CHAPTER 10   THE NEW CYCLE

1. *International Herald Tribune*, 26/1/1973, p. 7: Eugenia Sheppard, 'Saint Laurent: Clothes Don't Lie'.
2. ibid.
3. *International Herald Tribune*, 6/4/1973, p. 6: Hebe Dorsey, 'Saint Laurent Shines in Paris'. She described the collection as 'beautifully pulled together'.
4. *New York Times*, 6/4/1973, p. 36: Bernadine Morris, 'Saint Laurent Is a Favorite Of Rivals Too'.
5. Interview with Marie Helvin, London, 8/2/1995.

6. ibid.

7. ibid.

8. Didier Grumbach, *Histoires de la Mode*, p. 194: Éditions du Seuil, Paris, 1993.

9. *New York Times*, 8/8/1976, p. 7: Andreas Freund, 'The Empire of Saint Laurent'. The Paris fashion houses boosted their income by 15 per cent to $1.5bn between 1974 and 1975, but almost all the growth came from *prêt-à-porter*.

10. The number of journalists registering for the Paris ready-to-wear shows rose from 374 in 1972 to 459 by 1974, according to the Chambre Syndicale de la Couture.

11. Chambre Syndicale de la Couture Parisienne.

12. Halston's business became so big that he sold it in November 1972 to Norton Simon, the American industrial conglomerate, for $16 million.

13. Interview with Pierre Bergé, Paris, 11/4/1995.

14. *Harper's Bazaar*, February 1995, p. 144: Patricia Linden, 'Fashion's Grande Dame'. A gala was organized by Eleanor Lambert, the American fashion publicist, as a showcase for five French designers – Yves Saint Laurent, Christian Dior, Hubert de Givenchy, Pierre Cardin and Emanuel Ungaro – and five Americans – Bill Blass, Stephen Burrows, Anne Klein, Oscar de la Renta and Halston. Bergé objected to Anne Klein's inclusion on the grounds that, as a sportswear designer, she was not of the same stature as the Paris *couturiers*. Lambert asked Oscar de la Renta, who knew Bergé, to persuade him to withdraw; he agreed, 'as a favour'.

15. Interview with Pierre Bergé, Paris, 11/4/1995.

16. American *Vogue*, January 1980, p. 149: G. Y. Dryansky, 'Saint Laurent All The Way'.

17. By the end of the 1970s the Yves Saint Laurent brand name was applied to one hundred and thirty different products.

18. *New York Times*, 23/11/1972, p. 48: Bernadine Morris, 'With All the Enthusiasm of an American in Paris, Saint Laurent Visits New York'. During an interview in New York, Yves told Bernadine Morris that there was far less scope for innovation than there had been at the start of his career. 'People are closer to reality, especially to the reality of their bodies. The body used to be hidden by all sorts of conventions in clothes. Today it is free. You can't shock anyone any more with anything in fashion.'

19. *Newsweek*, 18/11/1974, p. 74: Lynn Young, 'The King of Couture'. Yves Saint Laurent: 'The greatest change came when I discovered my own style without being influenced by others. It was with the *smoking* and the transparent blouse ... I think women need a certain stability in their clothes.'

20. By 1975 Yves Saint Laurent had the highest turnover of any *couture* house in Paris, generating sales of roughly $1 million each season, with a client-list

that included some 700 of the 3,000 women who patronized the Parisian *couturiers*, including almost all the younger clients.

21. *New York Times*, 10/4/1975, p. 45: Bernadine Morris, 'Saint Laurent: A Classic Mood, A Comfortable Look'.

22. *International Herald Tribune*, 31/7/1975, p. 5: Eugenia Sheppard, 'Saint Laurent Grows Up With Luxury Collection'.

23. op. cit. Lynn Young.

24. Andy Warhol created his portraits by taking Polaroid shots of the subject and then blowing up a negative into a forty-inch by forty-inch square. He snipped out some of the features (generally the least flattering ones) with scissors and enhanced others. The negative was then converted into a silkscreen which was used to print the image on to the first canvas. At that time Warhol charged $25,000 for the first portrait and $5,000 for reproductions in different colours.

25. Bob Colacello, *Holy Terror: Andy Warhol Close Up*, p. 205: HarperCollins, New York, 1990.

26. Interview with Marie Helvin, London, 8/2/1995.

27. Interview with Clara Saint, Paris, 12/10/1995.

28. op. cit. Lynn Young.

29. op. cit. Bob Colacello.

30. *Newsweek*, 9/8/1976, p. 66: Linda Bird Franke & Elizabeth Peer, 'Rags to Riches'.

31. Interview with Susan Train, Paris, 2/8/1994.

32. op. cit. G. Y. Dryansky.

33. op. cit. Linda Bird Franke & Elizabeth Peer. Yves told *Newsweek* that the Vermeer 'reminded me that women like to make themselves beautiful in the evening', and 'it's selfish but I wanted to make heroines like Scarlett O'Hara and Madame Bovary'.

34. Interview with Anne-Marie Muñoz, Paris, 12/4/1994.

35. *New York Times*, 29/7/1976, p. 1: Bernadine Morris, 'A Revolutionary Saint Laurent Showing'.

36. op. cit. Linda Bird Franke & Elizabeth Peer.

37. *New York Times*, 29/7/1976, p. 1: Bernadine Morris, 'A Revolutionary Saint Laurent Showing'.

38. *Time*, 9/8/1976, p. 73: 'The New New Look'.

39. *New York Times*, 30/7/1976, p. 10: Enid Nemy, 'Saint Laurent Impact Seems Certain – but How Much and When?'

40. ibid.

41. American *Vogue*, September 1976: Pierre Schneider: 'Yves Saint Laurent has managed to remind us that fashion at its ultimate, as evinced by *haute couture*, becomes costume. Here we can see just how sophisticated fashion has become in its interpretation of history.'

42. *New York Times*, 31/7/1976, p. 8: Angela Taylor, 'The Rush Is On For Saint Laurent Ready-to-Wear'.

43. *New York Times*, 8/8/1976, p. 7: Andreas Freund, 'The Empire of Saint Laurent'.
44. Interview with Marie-José Lepicard, Paris, 23/5/1994.

CHAPTER 11   A LIVING DEATH

1. Interview with Julia Kennedy, London, 10/2/1995.
2. ibid.
3. ibid.
4. A Napoleonic ban on primogeniture, whereby everything can be left to the eldest son in a family, had a dramatic impact on the distribution of wealth in France. It meant that the fortunes made after the Revolution were widely dispersed among various heirs after the death of their owners, making it rare for anyone, even a Rothschild, to inherit enough money to not have to earn their own living.
5. American *Vogue*, January 1980, p. 149: G. Y. Dryansky, 'Saint Laurent All The Way'.
6. Interview with Pierre Bergé, Paris, 11/4/1995.
7. Under the terms of the original deal Richard Salomon negotiated for them with Didier Grumbach, Yves and Pierre each owned twenty-five per cent of the Rive Gauche holding company, with a percentage of the royalties on sales of the range being paid to the Yves Saint Laurent fashion house, which they owned outright after the 1972 agreement with Squibb.
8. Interview with Julia Kennedy, London, 10/2/1995.
9. ibid.
10. Interview with Christian Lacroix, Paris, 15/6/1994.
11. Interview with Julia Kennedy, London, 10/2/1995.
12. op. cit. G. Y. Dryansky.
13. *New York Times*, 9/11/1977, III, p. 1: Bernadine Morris, 'Parisian Passions: Food and Fashion'.
14. Pat Hackett ed., *The Andy Warhol Diaries*, p. 66: Warner Books, New York, 1989.
15. Interview with Marie Helvin, London, 8/2/1995.
16. *New York Times*, 27/10/1976, p. 27: Bernadine Morris, 'A Rousing Show by Saint Laurent – and Valentino Too'. Yves was described as having 'emerged exhausted but triumphant' after facing 'with some passion the problem of what to do after his epochal *couture* collection in July'.
17. *International Herald Tribune*, 27/1/1977, p. 5: Eugenia Sheppard, 'Saint Laurent in a Low Key'.
18. Interview with Julia Kennedy, London, 10/2/1995.
19. ibid.
20. *Tatler*, February 1995, p. 76: Colombe Pringle, 'New Year's Yves'.
21. Ian MacDonald, *Revolution In The Head: The Beatles' Records And The Sixties*, p. 249: Pimlico, London, Sydney, Auckland, Bergvlei, 1994. The phrase 'Bury my body' was actually taken from Shakespeare, but was only one

of a number of misinterpretations of Beatles' lyrics that were deemed to lend credence to the theory that Paul McCartney was dead. John Lennon's mumbling of 'Cranberry Sauce' at the end of *Strawberry Fields Forever* was mistaken for 'I buried Paul' and another meaningless mumble as 'Paul is dead, man, miss him, miss him'. The fact that McCartney was the only one of the four Beatles to be carrying a black instrument on the *Sergeant Pepper* cover added to the confusion over the symbolism of his 'OPD' badge.

22. op. cit. G. Y. Dryansky.
23. *Le Point*, 25/7/1977, p. 51: Barbara Schwarm & Martine Leventer, 'Saint Laurent: le roi de la mode'.
24. Interview with Julia Kennedy, London, 10/2/1995.
25. ibid.
26. Interview with Betty Catroux, Paris, 17/2/1995.
27. op. cit. Pat Hackett, p. 45.
28. British *Vogue*, September 1977, p. 111: Joan Juliet Buck, 'International Get Together'.
29. *New York Times Magazine*, 11/9/1977, p. 118: Anthony Burgess, 'All About Yves'.
30. ibid.
31. ibid.
32. ibid.
33. ibid.

CHAPTER 12   THE OPIUM WARS

1. The US prestige perfume market grew by around ten per cent a year throughout the 1960s and 1970s reaching $1 billion in 1977, according to the Fragrance Foundation in New York. However, sales of French scents had fallen from twenty per cent of the US market in the early 1960s to ten per cent by the late 1970s.
2. Thanks largely to the success of Youth Dew and Aramis, its men's scent, Estée Lauder's sales rose from $1 million in 1960 to over $100 million by the mid-1970s, when Revlon was also expanding its perfume interests. After launching Norell, a perfume for the fashion designer, Norman Norell, in 1967 as 'the first great fragrance born in America', Revlon then clinched fragrance deals with other American fashion designers, with Bill Blass for a men's cologne and with Geoffrey Beene to market Red as a perfume for women and Grey Flannel for men.
3. Maïmé Arnodin was born in Paris in 1916 and began her career as a fashion journalist, becoming editor of *Jardin des Modes* magazine, before setting up a styling consultancy. Born in Paris in 1923, Denise Fayolle was a champion ice skater before becoming head of design for Prisunic, the supermarket chain in the 1950s and 1960s when it adopted the lively modernist image of Terence Conran's Habitat. They founded their advertising agency Mafia in 1968.

4. Eau Libre was phased out in various countries from 1981 onwards and withdrawn from the market completely by the end of 1983.
5. Interview with Clara Saint, Paris, 12/4/1995.
6. Roy Halston Frowick was born in Des Moines, Iowa in 1932 and educated at Indiana University and the Art Institute of Chicago. He moved to New York in 1957 and worked for Lily Dache, a successful milliner, for a year before joining Bergdorf Goodman as its hat designer. One of his most famous commissions was the pillbox hat that Jacqueline Kennedy wore for her husband's inauguration as president. After opening his own fashion house in 1968, he swiftly made his name with simple, pared-down clothes which were firm favourites of Grace Mirabella, editor-in-chief of American *Vogue* in the 1970s, Liza Minnelli and Bianca Jagger. Halston sold out to Norton Simon, a conglomerate which owned Max Factor cosmetics and Avis rent-a-car, for $16 million in 1973; unlike Yves Saint Laurent he signed away the unconditional rights to the use of his name in the deal.
7. Interview with Maïmé Arnodin, Paris, 11/4/1995.
8. *New York Times*, 5/8/1979, III, p. 3: Jane Friedman, 'France vs US: War of the Noses'.
9. American *Vogue*, August 1994, p. 204: Amy Astley, 'Beauty Clips'.
10. Pat Hackett ed., *The Andy Warhol Diaries*, p. 169: Warner Books, New York, 1989.
11. *Harper's Bazaar*, April 1994, p. 198: Annemarie Iverson, 'Future Scent'.
12. *New York Times*, 18/12/1978, IV, p. 8: Enid Nemy, 'Success and a Bit of Controversy, at $100 an Ounce'. At the annual general meeting Ethel Palmer Morgan, one of Squibb's shareholders, said: 'I don't think Opium is appropriate for your new fragrance. Why don't you call it something else?' To which Richard Furlaud, the Squibb chairman replied: 'Mr Saint Laurent is, I think, a genius in the artistic world. Opium has had a smashing success abroad and the name is part of the concept.'
13. ibid.
14. *New York Times*, 24/4/1979, III, p. 13: Enid Nemy, 'Chinese Americans Join Other Groups in Campaign Against Opium Perfume'.
15. ibid. Franklin Williams told the *New York Times* that he had been 'outraged' while shopping in Bloomingdale's to see a picture of 'a beautiful Caucasian woman (Jerry Hall in the launch advertisement) obviously zoned out – in another world – and a tracery of leaves strongly resembling cannabis.'
16. *New York Times*, 18/12/1978, IV, p. 8: Enid Nemy, 'Success and a Bit of Controversy at $100 an Ounce'.
17. Interview with Maïmé Arnodin, Paris, 11/4/1995.

CHAPTER 13   THE RETREAT TO BABYLONE
1. American *Vogue*, October 1978, p. 353: Barbara Rose, 'The Intimate Yves'.
2. Diana Vreeland ed., *Yves Saint Laurent*, p. 8: Metropolitan Museum of Art, New York, 1983.

3. *New York Times Magazine*, 11/9/1977, p. 118: Anthony Burgess, 'All About Yves'.

4. Interview with Julia Kennedy, London, 10/2/1995.

5. *Bravo Yves*, p. 41: François-Marie Banier, 'Nasty Yves!'. Yves Saint Laurent, Paris, 1982.

6. Interview with Susan Train, Paris, 2/8/1994.

7. *Le Monde*, 8/2/1983, p. 29: Yvonne Baby, 'Portrait de l'Artiste'.

8. Diana Vreeland ed., *Yves Saint Laurent*, p. 15: Beijing, 1985.

9. op. cit. Anthony Burgess.

10. *Le Monde*, 18/9/1977, p. 18: Yves Saint Laurent, 'Testimonial: The End of a Dream'. The tribute to Callas is written in a rich, flowery language that reads beautifully in the original French but does not translate well. 'Miraculous voice, the voice of a genius, with its idiosyncrasies, its flaws, its rawness and its incredible flights, its trills, its warmth, its strength and its anger that bursts forth in flashes of lightning, cataclysm and orgasm . . . Opera! Old opera. Tragic opera brutalized, butchered, surrounded on all sides, I suffer with you. I dream of that time. I dream of her again.'

11. *Bravo Yves*, p. 34: Pierre Bergé, 'The Theatrics of a Lonely Imagination'. Yves Saint Laurent, Paris, 1982.

12. *New York Times*, 2/8/1979, p. 8: Bernadine Morris, 'Saint Laurent: "The Couture is a Dream, Like Opera or the Ballet" '.

13. op. cit. Barbara Rose.

14. *Le Point*, 25/7/1977, p. 51: Barbara Schwarm & Martine Leventer, 'Saint Laurent: roi de la mode'.

15. Interview with Marie Helvin, London, 8/2/1995.

16. Interview with Julia Kennedy, London, 10/2/1995.

17. Pat Hackett ed., *The Andy Warhol Diaries*, p. 261: Warner Books, New York, 1989.

18. op. cit. Barbara Rose.

19. *Time*, 12/12/1983, p. 98: 'The Designer at Home'.

20. Interview with Anne-Marie Muñoz, Paris, 12/4/1995.

21. *New York Times*, 2/2/1979, p. 14: Bernadine Morris, 'Classic Saint Laurent: At The Top of His Form'. Bernadine Morris hailed the spring 1979 *couture* collection as 'classic in the best sense . . . simple, flattering and enduring'.

22. *International Herald Tribune*, 26/10/1977, p. 6: Hebe Dorsey, 'Saint Laurent Looks Back and Returns to the Classics'.

23. *International Herald Tribune*, 25/10/1978, p. 8: Hebe Dorsey, 'Saint Laurent Dips Into Sailor Themes'.

24. Interview with Marie Helvin, London, 8/2/1995.

25. *International Herald Tribune*, 11/4/1979, p. 8: Hebe Dorsey, 'Yves Saint Laurent Sans New Look'. 'Don't quote me,' an anonymous buyer begged the *Herald Tribune*. 'But I feel Saint Laurent cannot pull another of those blousons on us again.' Another buyer complained that the collection was 'not up to par'. 'But this one,' wrote Hebe Dorsey, 'blamed it not on Saint

Laurent, whom everyone agrees is an enormous talent, but on his entourage who have lately been steering him the wrong way. Many feel that one of his assistants, Loulou de la Falaise, who is as exotic as a Brazilian Ara, has been responsible.'

26. *New York Times*, 4/8/1979, p. 8: Bernadine Morris, 'Saint Laurent: "The *Couture* Is a Dream, Like the Opera or Ballet"'. Yves told Bernadine Morris that he found the Bibliothèque Nationale exhibition and that particular period of theatrical design so inspiring because: 'It was the coming together of the arts. Musicians like Satie and Stravinsky worked with the best painters of the time. The mood was thoroughly modern and the arts weren't as separated as they are today.'

27. *New York Times*, 26/7/1979, III, p. 9: Bernadine Morris, 'Diaghilev Inspires Saint Laurent'.

28. *New York Times*, 4/8/1979, p. 8: Bernadine Morris, 'Saint Laurent: The Couture Is a Dream, Like the Opera or Ballet'.

29. Claude Montana was one of the first French designers to specialize in *prêt-à-porter*, rather than crossing over to it from *haute couture*. He was known for the precision of his cut, creating minimalist clothes in sculptural shapes.

30. An exuberant figure, Thierry Mugler, like Montana, was in the vanguard of the *prêt-à-porter* movement. He made his name with flamboyantly futuristic collections, which had echoes of the British punk movement, and was backed by Didier Grumbach, Yves's and Pierre's manufacturing partner in Rive Gauche.

31. Jean-Paul Gaultier, born in Paris in 1952, became an assistant to Pierre Cardin on leaving school at the age of eighteen. He then worked at a number of other companies, including Jean Patou, before returning to Cardin working as a roving stylist in the Philippines. On his return to Paris he teamed up with two schoolfriends, Francis Menuge and Donald Potard, to set up their own company. They financed the production and presentation of the collection on their own for a few seasons and then clinched a licensing deal with Kashiyama in Japan.

32. By the end of the 1970s, some five hundred journalists registered to see the *haute couture* shows, according to the Chambre Sydicale de la Couture Parisienne, compared with over 1,000 for ready to wear.

33. Giorgio Armani was born in Piacenza in 1935, and studied medicine at Milan University before doing three years of military service as a medical assistant. After his army discharge, Armani worked for La Rinascente, the stores chain, and then worked as a designer for Nino Cerrutti for nine years before setting up his own design business with his partner, Sergio Galeotti.

34. Born in Reggio, Calabria, Gianni Versace learnt about fashion from his mother, who earned her living as a dressmaker. When he set up his own company his brother, Santo, took care of financial affairs for him, and his sister, Donatella, was his 'muse' helping with design.

35. Born Ralph Lifshitz in 1939 in the Mosholu Parkway area of the Bronx as

the youngest of three sons of Frank and Freda Lifshitz, he changed his name at the suggestion of his brother, Jerry, who was tired of it being mispronounced in the Air Force reserve. Ralph Lauren majored in business at high school and took holiday jobs in Alexander's and Brooks Brothers, the New York stores. He sold preppie ties for a Boston company, before setting up his own tie business, called Polo, in a tiny office in the Empire State Building.

36. Calvin Klein, helped by Barry Schwartz, his boyhood friend and business partner, had created a $100 million company by the late 1970s and was the only American designer with significant sales outside the States with deals in Japan and with Maurice Bidermann. He made a fortune in the late 1970s from jeans, advertised by the child star, Brooke Shields, with 'Nothing comes between me and my Calvins'.

37. Under the terms of the agreement that Richard Salomon had negotiated for them with Squibb in 1972, Yves Saint Laurent and Pierre Bergé were entitled to a five per cent royalty on the wholesale sales of the YSL scents and cosmetics. That would give him royalties of $2.5 million a year for Opium on retail sales of $100 million, but he was also entitled to other payment for his contribution to Opium's marketing strategy.

38. Interview with Sally Brampton, London, 21/2/1995.

39. ibid.

40. American *Vogue*, August 1980, p. 232: G. Y. Dryansky, 'A Quiet Splendour'.

41. op. cit. Barbara Rose.

42. Interview with Julia Kennedy, London, 10/2/1995.

CHAPTER 14   THE GRAND OLD MAN

1. Interview with Pierre Bergé, Paris, 11/4/1995.

2. ibid.

3. The number of journalists registered for the Paris ready-to-wear shows doubled from 459 in 1974 to 1,057 by 1981, according to the Fédération Française de la Couture du Prêt-à-Porter des Couturiers et des Créateurs de la Mode.

4. Interview with Marie Helvin, London, 8/2/1995.

5. Peter Watson, *Nureyev*, p. 376: Hodder & Stoughton, London, Sydney, Auckland, 1994.

6. Grace Mirabella, *In And Out of Vogue: A Memoir*, p. 179: Doubleday, New York, London, Toronto, Sydney, Auckland, 1995.

7. *Time*, 12/12/1983, p. 96: 'The Designer At Home'.

8. Interview with Marie Helvin, London, 8/2/1995.

9. *Le Monde*, 8/2/1983, p. 29: Yvonne Baby, 'Portrait de l'Artiste'.

10. American *Vogue*, December 1983, p. 302: John Richardson, 'Yves Saint Laurent's Château Gabriel: a passion for style'.

11. Interview with Betty Catroux, Paris, 17/2/1995.

12. *Bravo Yves*, p. 14: Yves Saint Laurent, Paris, 1982.

13. *International Herald Tribune*, 28/1/1982, p. 5: Hebe Dorsey, 'A "Superb" Saint Laurent Show'.
14. American *Vogue*, December 1983, p. 294: Joan Juliet Buck, 'The Intimate Yves'.
15. ibid.
16. Interview with Marie Helvin, London, 8/2/1995.
17. Azzedine Alaïa was born in Tunisia and, at fifteen, he enrolled at the École des Beaux Arts in Tunis, having lied about his age, hoping to study architecture but ending up on a general art and drawing course. He started sewing for a local seamstress to earn some extra money and was taught the basics by his sister before taking a holiday job with a local *couturier* who made copies of designs by Christian Dior and Pierre Balmain. At eighteen he was offered a job with Dior in Paris, but was dismissed after only five days. He then worked at Guy Laroche for a few seasons before eking out a living as a freelance designer in the 1960s, accepting commissions for private clients and occasionally for other designers, including Yves Saint Laurent for whom he made a prototype of the Mondrian shifts, and later Thierry Mugler who encouraged him to stage his own shows.
18. Rei Kawakubo was born in Tokyo in 1942, the daughter of an academic. She worked as a stylist in the Japanese advertising industry until she founded Comme des Garçons in 1973. By the time she started showing in Paris in 1981, she had already achieved iconic status in Japan, drawing hundreds of black-clad groupies to the shows she staged each season in a grey tent outside the sports stadium designed by Kenzo Tange for the Tokyo Olympic Games in 1964. Aesthetically her clothes seemed uncompromising to Western eyes with their monochrome palette, unstructured shapes, un-finished edges and holes in knitwear.
19. Born in Tokyo in 1943, Yohji Yamamoto studied law at university before going on to study fashion at art school. He launched his own company in 1971, two years before Kawakubo, and came to show in Paris ten years later at the same time as her. By that time Yamamoto was working from a design studio in an inauspicious house in a quiet Tokyo suburb, with the upstairs area converted for pattern making. With Kawakubo he was one of the first designers to use older, 'character' models to present his clothes.
20. Pierre Bergé had signed so many licences by the beginning of the 1980s (over 150) that Yves Saint Laurent products were generating sales of at least $270 million a year, leaving Yves and Pierre with roughly $18 million in royalties. Meanwhile the number of Rive Gauche boutiques reached 140 by 1980, against 30 in 1972.
21. By the early 1980s Alain Wertheimer felt ready to invest in the Chanel perfumes and spent nearly $2 million on making lavish commercials – including one for No. 5 directed by Ridley Scott, who made *Blade Runner*, and another for Antaeus, the Chanel men's scent, directed by Roman Polanski.

22. Interview with Maïmé Arnodin, Paris, 11/4/1995.
23. ibid.
24. Diana Vreeland ed., *Yves Saint Laurent*, p. 7: Metropolitan Museum of Art, New York, 1983.
25. *New York Times*, 23/8/1989, p. 1: Bernadine Morris, 'Diana Vreeland, Editor, Dies; Voice of Fashion for Decades'.
26. Interview with Katell Le Bourhis, Paris, 27/5/1994.
27. *Time*, 12/12/1983, p. 96: Martha Duffy, 'Toasting Saint Laurent'.
28. *Time*, 12/12/1983, p. 98: 'The Designer at Home'.
29. ibid.

CHAPTER 15   THE GAUCHE CAVIARE

1. Born in Roubaix in 1949, Bernard Arnault was educated at *lycées* first in Roubaix and then in Lille, before studying at the École Polytechnique. He then worked for the successful building business, Ferret Savinel, that his father Jean Arnault founded first in France, then in the USA.
2. François Polge de Combret was born in Paris in 1941, the son of a wealthy industrialist. He was educated at prestigious Parisian *lycées* before graduating first from *Sciences Po'* and then from the élite École Nationale de l'Adminis-tration. In 1972 he became a senior adviser to Valéry Giscard d'Estaing, the right-wing finance minister, and continued as his aide when Giscard became President of the Republic for two terms from 1974 to 1978 and 1978 to 1981. After François Mitterrand's victory in the 1981 presidential elections, De Combret joined Lazard Frères and was sent initially to work in its New York office.
3. Antoine Bernheim was one of the most powerful partners at Lazard Frères in Paris and a highly influential figure in French finance. Born in Paris in 1924, the son of a wealthy lawyer, he worked for the Wertheimers at Chanel cosmetics and then joined the family property company. He was recruited by Lazard Frères in 1967 and by the time he met Bernard Arnault was a senior partner.
4. Born in Paris in 1938, Jean-Louis Dumas studied at the prestigious Lycée Janson-de-Sailly, before graduating in law and studying at *Sciences Po'*. He served as a lieutenant when conscripted into the army during the Algerian War, and then toured India with his wife in a battered Citroën 2CV, before being sent to New York for a year, while he trained as a buyer at Bloomingdale's. Dumas then applied the lessons he had learnt in the States to Hermès, gradually introducing new products, computerizing production facilities, selling cheaper items, such as ties and scarves, in duty-free stores and hiring a senior executive from Nieman Marcus to build up the business in North America.
5. Born in the Doubs region in 1912, Henry Racamier, an industrialist's son, graduated in law from Paris University and then went to business school. He worked for Peugeot, the motor company, and then became chairman of

Stinox, a steel group, in 1947, holding that post until 1977 when he moved into Vuitton, to which he was connected through his wife, Odile Vuitton.

6. Interview with Henry Racamier, Paris, 6/6/1994. Henry Racamier: 'If we wanted, say, to open a new leather factory, it didn't cost a lot of money so no great investment was required. Our cashflow was so strong that we didn't need external capital. It was like a snowball that got bigger and bigger.'

7. Alain-Dominique Perrin was born in Nantes in 1942, and joined Cartier as soon as he left business school in 1969. He took charge of its new cigarette lighter division in 1972, and having established that business moved on to set up Les Must de Cartier in 1975. He became chairman of Cartier International in 1981.

8. *Business Week*, 16/12/1985: Frank J. Comes, 'For Today's Cartier, Snob Appeal is Not Enough'.

9. Interview with Alain-Dominique Perrin, Paris, 21/6/1994.

10. op. cit. Frank Comes.

11. Interview with Alain-Dominique Perrin, Paris, 21/6/1994.

12. op. cit. Frank Comes.

13. Yves Saint Laurent had signed 190 licensing deals by 1980.

14. The company had planned to call the new perfume Elle or Fleurs, until a friend of Estée Lauder described a sample as smelling 'beautiful' and Estée decreed that *that* would be the name. She procrastinated over the packaging at the eleventh hour, dumping the blue and raspberry-pink box that the company's marketing department had carefully planned and commissioned for plain pink packaging. Beautiful was launched in 1984 with a commercial featuring a dewy-eyed bride in white satin and the song, *You Are So Beautiful*, crooning in the background. Estée Lauder also participated in promotional stunts such as one thrown by a Pittsburgh department store, which hired its own 'bride' and 'groom' who staged a mock wedding ceremony at which they promised to 'love Beautiful perfume for ever' before serving wedding cake to passing shoppers.

15. Elizabeth Arden treated its new fragrance, Calvin Klein's Obsession, to a $19 million launch, including a commercial directed by the fashion photographer, Richard Avedon, that featured a naked woman writhing around a trio of nude men. The controversy over the commercial generated millions of dollars of free publicity, just as the furore over Opium had done five years before, and Obsession achieved sales of $50 million by the end of its first year.

16. Poison was introduced in 1985 by Parfums Christian Dior, then owned by Moët-Hennessy, the cognac and champagne conglomerate chaired by Alain Chevalier. It achieved sales of 500 million francs in its first year on sale in Europe and went on to become Dior's first successful perfume launch in North America.

17. Giorgio was created by Fred and Gayle Hayman, who owned a Beverly Hills fashion boutique of the same name. The Haymans met in the early 1960s

when Fred was manager of the Beverly Hilton Hotel and hired Gale as a cocktail waitress. They divorced in the late 1970s but stayed in business and introduced Giorgio in 1981 at a black-tie party for twelve hundred people in a white and yellow striped marquee pitched on the parking lot next to the boutique. The Beverly Hills High School marching band provided the music and Merv Griffin was master of ceremonies. By 1984 Giorgio had mustered sales of $60 million.

18. Chanel introduced Coco in 1985 with a commercial directed by Richard Avedon starring Chanel's star model, Inès de la Fressange, as 'Coco', in a playlet set in an opera house. It spent $4.5 million on Coco's launch in North America alone.

19. Karl Lagerfeld mounted a sustained campaign to secure the increase in his fee and reputedly also to oust Kitty d'Alessio, the head of Chanel's North American business, whom he suspected of trying to steal his thunder. Lagerfeld refused to take a bow at the finale of the ready-to-wear show that October, thereby fuelling speculation that he had left Chanel and forcing the company to rush out a statement saying that he was staying on as chief designer. Kitty d'Alessio later left Chanel.

20. *Vanity Fair*, March 1986, p. 76: Javier Arroyuelo, 'Fashion Royalty and the *Couture* Courts of Paris'.

21. Nicholas Coleridge, *The Fashion Conspiracy*, p. 192: William Heinemann Ltd, London, Melbourne, Auckland, 1988.

22. *New York Times*, 29/3/1984, III, p. 1: Bernadine Morris, 'Saint Laurent: Polished Professionalism'. Bernadine Morris described the line as 'his usual slick, polished ready-to-wear collection'.

23. *International Herald Tribune*, 29/3/1984, p. 5: Hebe Dorsey, 'Saint Laurent Collection Shows Lack of Sparkle'.

24. Born in 1939 at Mirecourt in the Vosges region, Jack Lang was the son of a businessman. He was educated at a *lycée* in Nancy, before reading law at university in Paris and studying at *Sciences Po'*. In 1963 he returned to Nancy where he founded an International Theatre Festival, which he ran until 1972. Lang alternated his theatrical work with stints as a professor of law in the 1970s and also became active in the socialist party, eventually being appointed minister of culture by François Mitterrand at the start of the first socialist government in 1981.

25. Interview with Pierre Bergé, Paris, 11/4/1995.

26. François Mitterrand was born in 1916 at Jarnac in the Charente region where his father was an agent for the Paris-Orléans railway and then the head of the French vinegar manufacturers' association. Mitterrand graduated in law and worked as both a journalist and a lawyer before the War, becoming member of parliament for the Nièvre region immediately after the Libération in 1946; a year later he joined the cabinet as minister for ex-servicemen. He made his first (unsuccessful) bid for the French presidency

in 1965, only to try and fail again in 1974. He eventually won the presidential elections in 1981 at the age of sixty-four.

27. Interview with Franz-Olivier Giesbert, Paris, 15/7/1994.
28. Interview with Harlem Désir, Paris, 20/5/1994.
29. The number of journalists registered with the Chambre Syndicale to see the
    ready-to-wear shows rose by 500 to 1,610 in the five years to 1985, according
    to the Fédération Française de la Couture du Prêt-à-Porter des Couturiers
    et des Créateurs de la Mode, while the number registering for the *haute
    couture* collections fell from 750 in 1970 to 550 in 1985. However, even
    couture benefited from the clement trading climate of the early 1980s, with
    sales rising from 100 million francs in 1980 to 295 million francs in 1985,
    while the overall turnover of the *couturiers* (also including *prêt-à-porter* and
    accessories) increased from 1.04 billion francs to 2.36 billion over the same
    period.
30. *Washington Post*, 18/10/1984: Nina Hyde, 'France's Fashion Fête'.
31. *New York Times*, 5/10/1985, p. 5: 'Kremlin Chic: Paris Women Take a
    Look'.
32. Interview with Katell Le Bourhis, Paris, 29/7/1994.
33. Other Chinese government initiatives to encourage Western-style dress were
    fashion shows in department stores and education programmes for textile
    workers.
34. *Associated Press*, 7/5/1985. Rick Gladstone, 'Chinese Allegedly Impressed by
    Yves Saint Laurent Fashion Exhibition Held in Peking'.
35. Interview with Katell Le Bourhis, Paris, 29/7/1994.
36. ibid.

CHAPTER 16 BULLS AND BEARS

1. Interview with Pierre Bergé, Paris, 11/4/1995.
2. Interview with Maïmé Arnodin, Paris, 11/4/1995.
3. The rights to the Halston III line were sold to J. C. Penney in 1982, and
   Bergdorf Goodman swiftly announced that it was dropping the main Halston
   line. Norton Simon then sold Halston to Esmark, a company that owned
   Playtex, the lingerie maker, and Esmark was subsequently taken over by
   the Beatrice group of companies. Some Halston lines were sold off and in
   1984 he stopped designing. Two years later Beatrice was sold to Revlon
   which, in turn, was taken over by Perelman.
4. Interview with Pierre Bergé, Paris, 11/4/1995.
5. *New York Times*, 7/1/1986, IV, p. 1: Paul Lewis, 'Italian Enters Paris Fashion'.
6. *Business Week*, 24/11/1986: Frank J. Comes, 'De Benedetti Cuts a Chic Deal
   Modelling YSL'.
7. Interview with George Graham, Washington DC, 21/6/1994.
8. op. cit. Paul Lewis.
9. *Financial Times*, 7/11/1986. Paul Betts, 'De Benedetti buys 25% stake in
   Yves Saint Laurent'. Yves Saint Laurent made net profits of 56.2 million

francs ($8.4 million) in 1985 on sales of 266 million francs ($40 million) with profits of 65 million francs ($9.7 million) forecast for 1986.

10. *Wall Street Journal*, 5/12/1986, p. 1: Philip Revzin, 'Smell of Success'.

11. Interview with Pierre Bergé, Paris, 11/4/1995.

12. Investcorp was founded in 1982 by Nemir Kirdar, an Iraqi-born banker who ran Chase Manhattan's Gulf interests and set up his own bank with Chase colleagues. They structured the company to act as a conduit between investors in the Gulf and Western companies that had fallen into financial difficulty and needed fresh capital to improve their performance. Investcorp's clients agreed to lock their money into the companies while they were being restructured and recovering, with the aim of being paid back when the company eventually went public.

13. Hugh Sebag-Montefiore, *Kings On The Catwalk*, p. 31: Chapmans, London, 1992.

14. *International Herald Tribune*, 29/7/1986, p. 6: Hebe Dorsey: 'With Lacroix *couture* became young and alive again, a feat of sorts. He has been called the Jean-Paul Gaultier of *couture*, which in a way is true. The two have the same irreverent attitude, the same fearless approach to taboos. But Lacroix's wit is more subtle, more *salon* than street.'

15. Interview with Christian Lacroix, Paris, 15/6/1994.

16. Lacroix and Picart hired Lucien Friedlander, the French lawyer who had negotiated Karl Lagerfeld's lucrative $1 million contract at Chanel to handle their side of the talks with Bernard Arnault. The result was a 99-year contract, which gave them annual salaries of $240,000 each, and Lacroix a right of veto over all the products bearing his name.

17. According to the Fédération Française de la Couture du Prêt-à-Porter des Couturiers et des Créateurs de Mode, sales of *haute couture* trebled during the first half of the 1980s, rising from 100 million francs in 1980 to 295 million francs in 1986 and again to 301 million francs in 1987, the year of Lacroix's debut.

18. Nicholas Coleridge, *The Fashion Conspiracy*, p. 64: William Heinemann, London, Melbourne, Auckland, 1988.

19. *New York Times*, 30/7/1986, III, p. 8: Bernadine Morris, 'Ungaro Evokes Balenciaga's Elegance'. This was the same season that Lacroix was congratulated for making *couture* 'young and alive again' by the *Herald Tribune*, but Bernadine Morris dismissed Lagerfeld's *couture* collection for Chanel as being 'schizophrenic'.

20. *International Herald Tribune*, 29/1/1987, p. 8: Hebe Dorsey, 'Saint Laurent, The Giant'.

21. Interview with Christian Lacroix, Paris, 15/6/1994.

22. *International Herald Tribune*, 27/7/1987, p. 1: Hebe Dorsey, 'The Latest Star of Paris Couture'.

23. *Women's Wear Daily*, 27/7/1987, p. 1: 'For Lacroix, A Triumph; For Couture, a Future'.

24. Interview with Christian Lacroix, Paris, 15/6/1994.
25. *International Herald Tribune*, 30/7/1987, p. 6: Hebe Dorsey, 'From Saint Laurent, Designs That Will Please the Faithful'. The report was buried on page six, without a picture, rather than placed prominently on the front page as the article on Christian Lacroix had been.
26. *New York Times Magazine*, 6/9/1987, p. 23: Carrie Donovan, 'The Swagger of Christian Lacroix'. The article estimated that WWD had run over a hundred headlines featuring Lacroix in the preceding year.
27. *International Herald Tribune*, 19/7/1979. Pierre Bergé told the *Herald Tribune*: 'Mr Fairchild is a megalomaniac who wants to prove that he can make or break. I don't like him using Lacroix to destroy Saint Laurent.'
28. Interview with Christian Lacroix, Paris, 15/6/1994.
29. ibid.
30. *Vanity Fair*, February 1992, p. 68: Maureen Orth, 'Kaiser Karl: Behind the Mask'.
31. *Financial Times*, 1–2/8/1992: 'Lean Times for a Man with a Taste for the Grand Style'.
32. He had already repaid part of the $465 million loan package arranged by Crédit Suisse First Boston with the $150 million proceeds of the sale of brands to Revlon in spring 1986 and by selling shares in Rive Gauche that autumn. Léon Cligman, who had come to France as a Russian émigré and become one of the most influential figures in the textile industry, had previously bought out Didier Grumbach's fifty per cent holding in Rive Gauche and that autumn acquired another fourteen per cent thereby raising his stake to sixty-four per cent with Yves and Pierre still owning the rest.
33. *International Herald Tribune*, 10–11/9/1988, p. 18: Suzy Menkes, 'Pierre Bergé: A New Score'. Pierre boasted to Suzy Menkes that there had never been a strike, or even a trade union presence, at YSL even though he admitted that it 'may not be so easy' at the Opéra de Paris, adding: 'I am not a bad manager after more than twenty-five years in business. And since the age of eighteen I am used to being with artists. No one can say of me that I only understand the bottom line.'
34. Interview with Franz-Olivier Giesbert, Paris, 15/7/1994.
35. Interview with Betty Catroux, Paris, 17/2/1995.
36. Bob Colacello, *Holy Terror: Andy Warhol Close Up*, p. 217: HarperCollins, New York, 1990.
37. Laurence Benaïm, *Yves Saint Laurent*, p. 453: Éditions Grasset et Fasquelle, Paris, 1993.

CHAPTER 17   THE BATTLEGROUND
1. Born in Algiers in 1931, the son of a French businessman, Alain Chevalier read law in Paris before going on to study at *Sciences Po'* and the École Nationale de l'Administration. He worked as a civil servant for a few years and then at Moët-et-Chandon, the champagne company, which he turned

into a conglomerate of some of France's most prestigious drinks firms by staging a series of mergers and acquisitions, the theory being that the companies stood a better chance of turning their products into global brands if they pooled facilities such as marketing and distribution. These deals culminated with the Louis Vuitton merger in 1987.

2. Interview with George Graham, Washington DC, 21/6/1994.

3. Under Racamier's management Vuitton expanded dramatically, opening more shops and moving into new international markets. He took the company public in 1986 and then acquired the Veuve Clicquot champagne house as the first step towards constructing a conglomerate of luxury brand names.

4. Interview with George Graham, Washington DC, 21/6/1994.

5. Interview with Henry Racamier, Paris, 6/6/1994.

6. Interview with George Graham, Washington DC, 21/6/1994.

7. ibid.

8. Maurizio Gucci was the main Gucci heir, who owned 50 per cent of the company founded by his grandfather, Guccio Gucci, in 1923. He fell out with his uncles and cousins who owned the remaining shares and invited Investcorp to acquire them. After long and complex negotiations Investcorp finally agreed terms to buy out the other Gucci heirs in 1987.

9. Hugh Sebag-Montefiore, *Kings on the Catwalk*, p. 162: Chapmans, London, 1992.

10. Interview with Christophe Girard, Paris, 12/4/1995.

11. By the end of 1988 Yves Saint Laurent's debt was valued at 2.8 billion francs ($421 million) which was more than twice as much as its equity and lumbered the group with an interest bill of 250 million francs ($38 million) that year when it made operating profits of 439 million francs ($66 million) on sales of 2.63 billion francs ($395 million).

12. The *commandite* would be administered by a management committee composed of Yves Saint Laurent, Pierre Bergé, Alain Minc and Jean-Francis Bretelle, then the YSL finance director.

13. *Financial Times*, 24/6/1989: George Graham, 'Fashion World's Living Legend Goes Public'.

14. Interview with Paula Reed, London, 14/2/1995.

15. *Wall Street Journal Europe*, 7–8/4/1989, p. 1: Philip Revzin and Teri Agins, 'Saint Laurent Remains Idol of French Fashion But He Isn't Immortal'.

16. *New York Post*, 10/4/1989: Liz Smith, 'Spooky News About King Of Couture'.

17. Interview with Teri Agins, New York, 15/5/1994. Agins said that, although there was very little reaction to the original *Wall Street Journal* story there was 'a real stink' when the *New York Post* report broke.

18. Interview with Alain-Dominique Perrin, Paris, 21/6/1994.

19. At the flotation press conference, Pierre Bergé forecast net profits of 175

million francs ($26 million) for the YSL group in 1989, on sales up eleven per cent to 2.9 billion francs ($435 million).

20. Interview with George Graham, Washington DC, 21/6/1994.

21. *Financial Times*, 29/6/1989. George Graham, 'Saint Laurent launches sales drive for flotation'. Henry Racamier, former chairman of Louis Vuitton, told the *Financial Times* that the YSL shares were 'a very good buy'.

22. *Financial Times*, 3/7/1989. George Graham, 'Reform marred by contradictions and confusion'. In an article on the controversy over the decision of some companies, notably Compagnie Générale des Eaux, to introduce *société en commandite par actions* structures, George Graham concluded that Yves Saint Laurent did at least have the merit of having 'come clean' about its intentions to investors.

23. *Wall Street Journal*, 7/7/1989: 'YSL Offering Is Delayed On Huge Demand for Shares'.

24. ibid.

25. The YSL share price rose from the offer price of 653 francs to 945 francs by the end of the first week's trading, and two months later was worth 1,098 francs.

26. The proceeds of the private and public issues would enable the company to reduce its interest bill from just under $38 million in 1988 to $30 million in 1989 and Pierre Bergé then aimed to pay off its debts completely within five years. Before the flotation and private placing Cerus had owned 49.9 per cent of the YSL group; after both transactions its stake would be reduced to 14.9 per cent.

27. Interview with Pierre Bergé, Paris, 11/4/1995.

28. *Washington Post*, 17/1/1989: Edward Cody, 'Storm At The Bastille Opera: Barenboim, Bergé Exchange Volleys'.

29. *The New Yorker*, 21/11/1994, p. 80: Jane Kramer, 'The Impresario's Last Act'.

30. Born in South Korea, Myung-Whun Chung started playing the piano at the age of four and continued with his music after his parents moved to the United States. He studied at the Juilliard music school in New York before assisting Carlo Maria Giulini at the Los Angeles Philharmonic Orchestra. When Pierre Bergé met him in March 1989 Chung had already made his name in musical circles, as had his elder sisters, Kyung Wha, a violinist, and Myung Wha, a cellist.

31. *International Herald Tribune*, 13/7/1989, p. 20: David Stevens, 'Chung: Gambling on Bastille Opera'.

32. ibid.

33. Interview with Alan Robertson, London, 29/3/1995.

34. Interview with Harlem Désir, Paris, 20/5/1994.

35. *International Herald Tribune*, 10–11/9/1988, p. 18: Suzy Menkes, 'Pierre Bergé: A New Score'.

36. op. cit. Jane Kramer.

37. *International Herald Tribune*, 18/3/1989, p. 11: Suzy Menkes, 'A Gentler, Kinder Fashion for the '90s'.

38. *International Herald Tribune*, 20/3/1989, p. 1: Suzy Menkes, 'Romeo Gigli, Time to Take a Bow'. The report of Romeo Gigli's Paris debut appeared on the front page of the *Herald Tribune* with an account of the 'orgy of cheers, tears, clapping and foot-stamping' that marked the end of the show.

39. *International Herald Tribune*, 26/10/1989, p. 1: Suzy Menkes, 'Yves Saint Laurent Shocks Paris – Again'.

CHAPTER 18   DIAMONDS AND SPADES

1. *International Herald Tribune*, 25/1/1990, p. 1: Suzy Menkes, 'Born again Couturier: Saint Laurent Show Is Strongest in 10 Years'.

2. *International Herald Tribune*, 18/3/1990, p. 16: David Stevens, 'Berlioz, Chung and the Taking of the Bastille'.

3. *International Herald Tribune*, 22/3/1990, p. 7: Suzy Menkes, 'Saint Laurent Without Yves: A Reprise of Classic Themes'.

4. *Sunday Times Magazine*, 9/10/1994, p. 30: Edmund White, 'First There Was Yves'.

5. *International Herald Tribune*, 28/7/1990, p. 7: Suzy Menkes, 'A Muted Saint Laurent Show'.

6. *International Herald Tribune*, 25/10/1990, p. 24: Suzy Menkes, 'Deep Into the Casbah With YSL'.

7. Interview with Betty Catroux, Paris, 11/2/1995.

8. Interview with Marie-José Lepicard, Paris, 23/5/1994.

9. Interview with Janie Samet, Paris, 23/6/1994.

10. *Washington Post*, 25/7/1991. Cathy Horyn, 'YSL: New Clothes, Old Hat'.

11. The Cerus camp claimed, though never proved, that Édouard Balladur, the finance minister in Jacques Chirac's centre-right government, had intervened in the bid and asked Paribas to be neutral in order to protect Suez.

12. *The Economist*, 28/4/1990, p. 89: 'Can Carlo come back?'

13. *The Economist*, 24/11/1990, p. 133: '*La Grande Désillusion*'. Cerus's share price had fallen by seventy per cent on the Paris market that year.

14. Interview with Pierre Bergé, Paris, 11/4/1995.

15. Interview with Alain-Dominique Perrin, Paris, 21/6/1994.

16. When Pierre Bergé announced Yves Saint Laurent's financial results on 8 April 1991, he reported that the company had surpassed its forecast at the time of the flotation by increasing net profits by twelve per cent to 252 million francs, or $45.4 million, in 1990 on sales of 3 billion francs, $540 million. He also warned that the Gulf War's impact on duty-free sales would adversely affect the company's performance in the coming year.

17. Interview with Pierre Bergé, Paris, 11/4/1995.

18. Euromonitor Research, 1990. There were over a hundred acquisitions worth $12.5 billion in the beauty business between 1985 and 1990, according to one London stockbroker, which left half the global market in the hands of

five companies: L'Oréal, Unilever, Shiseido, Procter & Gamble and Avon.

19. C'Est la Vie! fell below budget in Europe, and sales were so poor in North America that it was withdrawn from distribution after a few years.

20. *Time*, 16/9/1991, p. 62: Barbara Rudolph, 'The Supermodels'.

21. *Women's Wear Daily*, 24/9/1991, p. 1: Godfrey Deeny, 'The High Cost Of Staying Up On a Catwalk'.

22. Interview with Eleanora Cuinetti, London, 15/4/1996.

23. *The Look*: Freelance Film Partners/BBC, 1992.

24. Interview with Lindy Woodhead, London, 6/4/1995.

25. *Le Figaro*, 11/7/1991, p. 26: Franz-Olivier Giesbert and Janie Samet, 'Yves Saint Laurent: "Je Suis Né Avec Une Dépression Nerveuse"'.

26. Interview with Franz-Olivier Giesbert, Paris, 15/7/1994.

CHAPTER 19 THE BIRD DOGS

1. Interview with Harlem Désir, Paris, 20/5/1994.

2. *Washington Post*, 13/5/1991: Sharon Waxman, 'A Storm In The Bastille: The Backstage Brouhaha At Paris's New Opera House'.

3. Interview with Christophe Girard, Paris, 12/4/1995.

4. Interview with Alain-Dominique Perrin, Paris, 21/6/1994.

5. Interview with Jean-Louis Dumas, Paris, 5/9/1994.

6. *International Herald Tribune*, 16–17/3/1991, p. 15: Suzy Menkes, 'Lagerfeld: the Man With a Midas Touch'.

7. *Washington Post*, 21/3/1991: Cathy Horyn, 'YSL, Saving The Best For Last'. Horyn described the presentation as 'yet another lopsided Saint Laurent show'.

8. *The Times Saturday Review*, 21/7/1990, p. 4: Liz Smith, 'The Three Faces of Yves'. Pierre Bergé told Liz Smith: 'No, we do not have a *dauphin*. We do not have anyone in the closet. There is no short list. But I can assure you, when the time comes I will decide without hesitation to close down the *couture* house. I must do that for Yves. It is a nonsense to carry on without him. Look at Chanel without Mademoiselle Chanel, and Dior without Christian Dior. It is more than a nonsense. It has no integrity. It is a sham.'

9. *International Herald Tribune*, 30/1/1992, p. 5: Suzy Menkes, 'Saint Laurent – 30 Years'.

10. ibid.

11. Interview with Gina Newsom, London, 28/6/1994.

12. Interview with Pierre Bergé, Paris, 11/4/1995.

13. *Vanity Fair*, February 1992, p. 68: Maureen Orth, 'Kaiser Karl: Behind the Mask'.

14. ibid.

15. *New York Times*, 5/2/1992, III, p. 1: Woody Hochswender, 'Ruffle Here, Flourish There As Fashion Honours Its Own'.

16. *The New Yorker*, 24/2/1992, p. 93: Holly Brubach, 'In Fashion: Fanfare in a Minor Key'.

17. *Femme*, February 1992, p. 10: Michèle Sider, 'Yves, Mon Fils'.
18. ibid.
19. ibid.
20. Interview with Marion Hume, London, 7/2/1995.
21. *International Herald Tribune*, 27/7/1992, p. 18: Suzy Menkes, 'Couture Wars: Battling Onstage and Off'.
22. ibid.
23. *New York Times*, 28/7/1992, II, p. 7: Bernadine Morris, 'The Opening Round Goes to Lacroix'.
24. *New York Times*, 30/7/1992, III, p. 1: Bernadine Morris, 'Saint Laurent Overcomes The Anguish'.
25. *International Herald Tribune*, 30/7/1992, p. 8: Suzy Menkes, 'Cut, Color, Class – and Kisses'.
26. ibid. Suzy Menkes said the show could be 'summed up in three words: poetry, simplicity, authority'.

CHAPTER 20   THE PRESIDENT'S MEN

1. The loans were arranged on a short-term basis, with the usual terms attached: a relatively high rate of interest and provision for the banks to demand the repayment of part of the capital.
2. The number of Rive Gauche boutiques had fallen to 110 by the end of 1992, compared with a total of 140 in 1980. Meanwhile, in the perfume division, Paris had slipped out of the top ten best-selling scents by 1991 and, although Opium was still in sixth place, its sales were starting to decline and were down by ten per cent that year.
3. Interview with Jean-Pierre Halbron, Paris, 11/5/1995.
4. ibid.
5. *Vanity Fair*, April 1993, p. 168: Bryan Burrough, 'The Selling of Saint Laurent'.
6. Interview with Alain-Dominique Perrin, Paris, 21/6/1994.
7. Interview with Henry Racamier, Paris, 6/6/1994.
8. Interview with Jean-Pierre Halbron, Paris, 11/5/1995.
9. Interview with Lindsay Owen-Jones, Paris, 24/8/1994.
10. ibid.
11. ibid.
12. ibid.
13. Interview with Jean-Pierre Halbron, Paris, 11/5/1995.
14. op. cit. Bryan Burrough.
15. ibid.
16. In 1991, the year before the negotiations with YSL began, Sanofi's beauty division mustered sales of 1.8 billion francs, compared with 2.5 billion francs for the YSL beauty brands.
17. Interview with Jean-François Dehecq, Paris, 8/9/1994.
18. *Le Nouvel Économiste*, 18/9/1992.

19. Interview with Jean-François Dehecq, Paris, 8/9/1992.
20. ibid.
21. Interview with Jean-Pierre Halbron, Paris, 11/5/1995.
22. Interview with Pierre Bergé, Paris, 11/4/1995.
23. Yves Saint Laurent's group's sales had risen by 6.9 per cent to 1.39 billion francs during the six months to 30/6/1992, but net profits had fallen by 94 per cent to 2.6 million francs, significantly below analysts' expectations. Pierre Bergé warned of a further fall in profits during the second half of 1992.
24. Interview with Jean-Pierre Halbron, Paris, 11/5/1995,.
25. Interview with Jean-François Dehecq, Paris, 8/9/1994.
26. Yves Saint Laurent and Pierre Bergé were to own ten per cent of the shares in the fashion house, but ninety per cent of the voting rights, giving them clear control.
27. Under the standard industry terms, fashion designers generally received royalties of five per cent on the wholesale sales of their perfumes. Opium, at the time, achieved retail sales of roughly $80 million, which would produce a wholesale total of around $40 million, and royalties of $2 million.
28. As a *quid pro quo* for dismantling the *commandite* Yves Saint Laurent and Pierre Bergé were to receive 416,666 shares in the YSL group worth 350 million francs ($65 million).
29. Interview with Lindsay Owen-Jones, Paris, 24/8/1994.
30. *Le Monde*, 20/1/1993, p. 24: Françoise Chirot & Pierre-Angel Gay, 'Elf Sanofi and YSL are going to merge'.
31. *Women's Wear Daily*, 19/1/1993, p. 1: Godfrey Deeny, 'YSL, Bergé Sell Out'.
32. *International Herald Tribune*, 20/1/1993, p. 11: Suzy Menkes, 'Elf Sanofi Buying Saint Laurent'. The article speculated that 'the relatively rich price may reflect Mr Bergé's own connections with the political establishment'.
33. op. cit. Godfrey Deeny.
34. *Le Monde*, 27/1/1993, p. 1: François Bostnavaron & Pierre-Angel Gay, 'Saint Laurent At Any Price'.
35. ibid.
36. ibid.
37. *Women's Wear Daily*, 19/1/1993, p. 1: Godfrey Deeny, 'YSL, Bergé Sell Out'.
38. Interview with Jean-François Dehecq, Paris, 8/9/1994.
39. Interview with Lindsay Owen-Jones, Paris, 24/8/1994.
40. Interview with Jean-François Dehecq, Paris, 8/9/1994.
41. op. cit. François Bostnavaron & Pierre-Angel Gay.
42. Interview with Henry Racamier, Paris, 11/5/1994.
43. Interview with Jean-François Dehecq, Paris, 8/9/1994.

CHAPTER 21 DON MAGNIFICO'S DEMISE

1. Interview with Patricia Turck-Paquelier, Neuilly-sur-Seine, 9/9/1994.
2. ibid.
3. Nicole Wisniak founded *Egoïste* in 1977 and was subsequently its editor-in-chief. She astutely registered the rights to the name to a number of different products.
4. Interview with André Enders, Épernay, 22/5/1995.
5. ibid.
6. The champagne houses within the LVMH group were the products of the acquisitions of Moët-Hennessy and Louis Vuitton before their merger. Together they represented roughly a quarter of all champagne sales.
7. Interview with Pierre Bergé, Paris, 11/4/1995.
8. By 1991 Paris had already left the top ten bestsellers, and although Opium stayed in the top ten its sales fell by 10 per cent that year, according to Patricia Turck-Paquelier.
9. *Women's Wear Daily*, 4/6/1994, p. 4: Sarah Raper, 'YSL Uncorking a Vintage Launch'.
10. Interview with Patricia Turck-Paquelier, Neuilly-sur-Seine, 9/9/1994.
11. ibid.
12. *Women's Wear Daily*, June 1993, p. 8: Sarah Raper, 'What's in a Name? For a Fragrance, Success And Fame'. Guerlain changed the name back to Shalimar in Britain as soon as possible.
13. Pierre Bergé denied having been responsible for the transactions conducted on those dates.
14. French banks and brokers, even the Paris stock market authorities, had long lobbied for the abolition of *Impôt de Bourse*. The finance ministry made no secret of the fact that it was willing to scrap it as soon as the economy picked up and the state no longer needed the additional revenue.
15. A plodding, but palpably decent man, Bérégevoy was said to have been racked with remorse after his party's electoral defeat and haunted by a scandal over a long-standing charge of insider trading levelled against a friend of his and François Mitterrand's. Bérégevoy's friends let it be known through the press that, having spent his entire career loyally serving Mitterrand, he might have felt less depressed had the president paid more attention to him after the election.
16. Loïk Le Floch-Prigent was moved from Elf Aquitaine to EDF/GDF, the electricity and gas boards, of which he was made chairman. He was then made head of SNCF, the French railway, but faced an investigation by the Justice Ministry into allegations concerning his business practices at Elf, but not with regard to the Yves Saint Laurent acquisition.
17. *Women's Wear Daily*, 8/3/1994, p. 4.
18. *Le Monde*, 22/6/1993, p. 22: Pierre-Angel Gay, '*L'Illegalité Inconnu de l'Affair Saint Laurent*'.

19. *Women's Wear Daily*, 1/6/1994, 'Bergé Blasé About Indictment For Insider Trading'.
20. *Business Week*, 25/7/1994: Stewart Toy, 'The real scandal in France'.

CHAPTER 22 LE GRAND PATRON

1. *Glamour*, May 1994, p. 84: Ginette Sainderichin, 'Yves Saint Laurent: *Le Grand Patron*'.
2. *Washington Post*, 9/3/1994: Cathy Horyn, 'Saint Laurent, Short And Missing The Point'.
3. Interview with Christophe Girard, Paris, 12/4/1995.
4. *Harper's Bazaar*, September 1994, p. 404: Sarah Mower, 'The YSL Revolution'.
5. *Independent*, 10/9/1994: Marion Hume, '*Excusez-moi*, but isn't that mine?'
6. Interview with Marion Hume, London, 7/2/1995.
7. Yves Saint Laurent sued Ralph Lauren claiming 5 million francs in damages for counterfeit and unfair competition. The case came to court on 27 April 1994 and the judge delivered her verdict on 18 May. She found Ralph Lauren guilty and fined him 2.2 million francs. The judge also fined Pierre Bergé 500,000 francs for making derogatory remarks about Ralph Lauren in *Women's Wear Daily*.
8. *New York Times*, 27/9/1994, II, p. 13: Amy M. Spindler, 'How Fashion Killed The Unloved Waif'.
9. Interview with Miuccia Prada, Milan, 15/5/1995.
10. Interview with Anne-Marie Muñoz, Paris, 12/4/1995.
11. Interview with Clara Saint, Paris, 12/4/1995.
12. *International Herald Tribune*, 21/7/1994, p. 1: Suzy Menkes, 'Yves Saint Laurent Reigns as King Again'.
13. Interview with Marion Hume, London, 7/2/1995.
14. *Los Angeles Times*, 15/9/1994, E, p. 1: Geraldine Baum, 'All About Yves'.
15. Sanofi treated its investors to a bonus issue of one extra share for every ten after announcing a 16 per cent increase in operating profits to 2.84 billion francs, or $574 million, in 1994 on sales up 11 per cent to 26.1 billion francs. The group's net profits almost doubled, rising from 823 million francs in 1993 to 1.51 billion francs in 1994.
16. Interview with Jean-François Dehecq, Paris, 8/9/1994.
17. Interview with Jean-Pierre Halbron, Paris, 11/5/1995.
18. Interview with Pierre Bergé, Paris, 11/4/1995.
19. *New Yorker*, 21/11/1994: Jane Kramer, 'The Impresario's Last Act'.
20. American *Vogue*, December 1995, p. 246: Katherine Betts, 'The Glorious Tradition'.
21. American *Vogue*, March 1996, p. 378: Hamish Bowles, 'Couture: cult of the Genius'.
22. Interview with Christophe Girard, Paris, 12/4/1995.
23. *International Herald Tribune*, 22/1/1996: Suzy Menkes, 'Galliano's Theatrics

at Givenchy'. Suzy Menkes described the 'much-awaited show' as 'a fashion moment that missed', adding that 'for all its poetry and theater, the shoe did not propel *haute couture* into the next millenium, or define a new image for the house'.

24. Interview with Paul Reed, London, 14/2/1995.
25. op. cit., Hamish Bowles: 'The French ... don't expect someone who has created a great masterpiece once to have to keep on being a genius forever,' wrote Amy Spindler in the *New York Times* after the January 1996 *couture* show, which Suzy Menkes described in the *Herald Tribune* as like 'seeing the pretty young offspring of old friends'.
26. *Sunday Times Magazine*, October 1994: Edmund White, 'First There Was Yves'.
27. Interview with Christophe Girard, Paris, 10/5/1996.
28. *Tatler*, February 1995, p. 76: Colombe Pringle, 'New Year's Yves'.
29. Interview with Jeanloup Sieff, Paris, 25/5/1994.
30. op. cit., Edmund White.
31. ibid.
32. ibid.
33. Interview with Marie Helvin, London, 8/2/1995.
34. British *Vogue*, November 1994, p. 148: Lesley White, 'The Saint'.
35. ibid.

EPILOGUE LAST OF THE LEGENDS
1. Interview with Sally Brampton, London, 21/2/1995.
2. Interview with Katell Le Bourhis, Paris, 29/7/1994.
3. Interview with Paula Reed, London, 14/2/1995.
4. Interview with Christian Lacroix, Paris, 15/6/1994.
5. Interview with Lindsay Owen-Jones, Paris, 24/8/1994.
6. Interview with Pierre Bergé, Paris, 11/4/1995.
7. Interview with Franz-Olivier Giesbert, Paris, 15/7/1994.
8. Interview with Christophe Girard, Paris, 12/4/1995.
9. *Vanity Fair*, February 1992, p. 68: Maureen Orth, 'Kaiser Karl: Behind The Mask'.
10. *New Yorker*, 24/2/1992, p. 93: Holly Brubach, 'In Fashion: Fanfare In A Minor Key'.
11. American *Vogue*, January 1980, p. 149: G. Y. Dryansky, 'Saint Laurent All The Way'.

Acknowledgments

I would like to thank all the people who have worked so hard to help me to write *Yves Saint Laurent: A Biography* notably my editors, Rebecca Lloyd at HarperCollins, London, and Nan Talese at Doubleday, New York, together with the staff of both companies, particularly Mike Fishwick of HarperCollins, whose idea the book was, and my agent, Derek Johns. I am also very grateful for the encouragement and tolerance of my *Financial Times* colleagues during the time I spent researching and writing this book, and for all the pleasure and affection given to me by my friends and family.

My thanks are also due to the staff of the following libraries where I undertook archive research: the Bibliothèque Nationale, the American Library and the library of the *International Herald Tribune* in Paris; the *Vanity Fair* library in New York; and the British Library, the National Art Library at the Victoria and Albert Museum, and the libraries of Condé Nast and the *Financial Times* in London.

During the time that I have been writing *Yves Saint Laurent*, many people have kindly given their time in interviews to help me research the fashion and luxury industries. They include: Giorgio Armani, Bernard Arnault, Naim Attallah, Patrick Bertaux, Béatrice Bongibault, Hussein Chalayan, Terence Conran, Kimberley Delsing, Rolf Fehlbaum, Yukata Goto, Johannes Huth, Françoise Jollant Kneebone, Rei Kawakubo, Donna Karan, Francis Miller, Nemir Kirdar, Georges Klarsfeld, David Lang, Jack Lang, Ralph Lauren, Alain Lompech, Sylvain Massot, Dawn Mello, Jasper Morrison, Loïc Morvan, Jacques Mouclier, Marc Newson, Jean Nouvel, Karla Otto, Mike Perry, Michel Pietrini, Dieter Rams, Serge Rosinoer, Jack Saltzman, Jil Sander, Tom Saunders, Andrew Shore, Ian Schrager, Ettore Sottsas, Philippe Starck, Deyan Sudjic, Koji Tatsuno, Jacques Toubon, Peter Wallis, Gilles Weil, Vivienne Westwood and Xüly-Bet.

I would particularly like to thank the following people who took the time and trouble to help with the research for this book: Teri Agins, Maïmé Arnodin, Pierre Bergé, Sally Brampton, William Bratton, Jean-Francis Bretelle, Claude Brouet, Gabrielle Buchaert, Simon Burstein, Renée Cassart, Betty Catroux, Catherine Chevalier, Nicholas Coleridge, Eleanora Cuinetti, Jean-Claud Dehecq, Jean-Pierre Derbord, Dominique Deroche, Harlem Désir, Denise Dubois, Jean-Louis Dumas, André Enders, Jérôme Faillant Dumas, Pierre-Angel Gay, Franz-Oliver Giesbert, Christophe Girard, George Graham, Jean-Pierre Halbron, David Harrington, Marie Helvin, Marion Hume, Alkarim Jivani, Julia Kennedy, Georgina Knight, Christian Lacroix, Katell Le Bourhis, Marie-José Lepicard, Sarah Moylan, Anne-Marie Muñoz, Eric Musgrave, Gina and Jeremy Newson, Lindsay Owen-Jones, Una Mary Parker, Alain-Dominique Perrin, Miuccia Prada, Henry Racamier, Ariel de Ravenel, Paula Reed, Alan Robertson, Sonia Rykiel, Clara Saint, Janie Samet, Jeanloup Sieff, Paul Smith, Suzanne Tide Frater, Susan Train, Kuniko Tsutsumi, Patricia Turcq-Paquelier, Lucia Van Der Post and Lindy Woodhead.

Finally, thank you to all those who assisted me with this project but preferred not to be named.

List of Illustrations

Bibliography

BOOKS

Louis Althusser, *The Future Lasts a Long Time*, trans. Richard Vestey, Chatto & Windus, London, 1993.

John Ardagh, *France in the 1980s*, Penguin Books, Harmondsworth, 1984

Roland Barthes, *The Fashion System*, trans. Matthew Ward and Richard Howard, University of California Press, Berkeley and Los Angeles, 1990

Laurence Benaïm, *Yves Saint Laurent*, Editions Grasset et Fasquelle, Paris, 1993

Raymond F. Betts, *France and Decolonisation 1900–1960*, Macmillan Education, Basingstoke and London, 1991

Victor Bockris, *Warhol*, Penguin Books, Harmondsworth, 1990

Paul Bowles, *Without Stopping: An Autobiography*, The Ecco Press, New York, 1985

François Caron, *An Economic History of Modern France*, trans. Barbara Bray, Columbia University Press, New York, 1979

Edmonde Charles-Roux, *Chanel*, trans. Nancy Amphoux, Harvill, London, 1989

Bob Colacello, *Holy Terror: Andy Warhol Close Up*, HarperCollins, New York, 1990

Nicholas Coleridge, *The Fashion Conspiracy*, William Heinemann, London, Melbourne and Auckland, 1988

Antony Copley, *Sexual Moralities in France 1780–1980: New Ideas on the Family, Divorce and Homosexuality*, Routledge, London, 1992

Polly Devlin, *Vogue Book of Fashion Photography*, Condé Nast Publications, London, 1979

Claire Duchen, *Feminism in France*, Routledge & Kegan Paul, London, 1986

Elizabeth Ewing, *History of 20th-Century Fashion*, B. T. Batsford, London, 1992

Nadège Forestier and Nazanine Ravaï, *Bernard Arnault, ou le goût de pouvoir*, Éditions Olivier Orban, Paris, 1990

Pierre Gaxotte, *Christian Dior et moi*, Bibliothèque Amiot Dumond, Paris, 1956

Franz-Olivier Giesbert, *François Mitterrand, ou la tentation d'histoire*, Éditions Le Seuil, Paris, 1977

Françoise Giroud, *Dior*, trans. Stewart Spencer, Thames & Hudson, London, 1987

Valéry Giscard d'Estaing, *Démocratie Française*, Éditions Fayard, Paris, 1976

Michael Gross, *Model: The Ugly Business of Beautiful Women*, Warner Books, New York, 1995

Didier Grumbach, *Histoires de la Mode*, Éditions du Seuil, Paris, 1993

Pat Hackett ed. *The Warhol Diaries*, Warner Books, New York, 1989

Dick Hebdidge *Subculture: The Meaning of Style*, Methuen, London, 1979

E. J. Hobsbawn, *Echoes of the Marseillaise*, Verso, London, New York, 1990

Georgina Howell, *In Vogue*, Penguin Books, Harmondsworth, 1978

R. W. Johnson, *The Long March of the French Left*, Macmillan, London, 1981

Leonard Koren, *New Fashion Japan*, Kodansha International, Tokyo, 1984

Ian MacDonald, *Revolution in the Head: The Beatles' Records and the Sixties*, Pimlico, London, Sydney, Auckland and Bergvlei, 1994

David Macey, *The Lives of Michel Foucault*, Hutchinson, London, Melbourne, Sydney, Auckland and Johannesburg, 1993

James F. McMillan, *Twentieth-Century France: Politics and Society 1898–1991*, Edward Arnold, London, 1992

David Mellor, *The Sixties Art Scene in London*, Phaidon Press/Barbican Art Gallery, London, 1993

Grace Mirabella, *In and Out of Vogue: A Memoir*, Doubleday, New York, London, Toronto, Sydney, Auckland, 1994

Leslie Mitchell de Quillacq, *Powerbrokers: An Insider's Guide to the French Élite*, Lafferty Publications, Dublin, 1992

Ted Morgan, *Literary Outlaw: The Life and Times of William S. Burroughs*, Avon Books, New York, 1990

Jocelyn de Nobret ed. *Design: Miroir du Siècle*, Flammarion/APCI, Paris, 1993

George D. Painter, *Marcel Proust: A Biography*, Pimlico, London, 1996

Charles Perrow & Mauro F. Guillén, *The Aids Disaster*, Yale University, 1990

Jon Savage, *England's Dreaming: Sex Pistols and Punk Rock*, Faber & Faber, London, 1991

Christopher Sawyer-Lauçanno, *An Invisible Spectator: A Biography of Paul Bowles*, Weidenfeld & Nicolson, New York, 1989

Hugh Sebag-Montefiore, *Kings on the Catwalk*, Chapmans, London, 1992

Susan Sontag, *A Susan Sontag Reader*, Penguin Books, Harmondsworth, 1983

Susan Sontag, *Aids and its Metaphors*, Farrar, Strauss and Giroux, New York, 1989

Otis Stuart, *Perpetual Motion: The Public and Private Lives of Rudolf Nureyev*, Simon & Schuster, New York, London, Toronto, Sydney, Tokyo and Singapore, 1995

Deyan Sudjic, *Rei Kawakubo and Comme des Garçons*, Fourth Estate, London, 1990

Diana Vreeland ed. *Yves Saint Laurent*, Beijing, 1985

Diana Vreeland ed. *Yves Saint Laurent*, Metropolitan Museum of Art, New York, 1983

Andy Warhol & Pat Hackett, *Popism: The Warhol '60s*, Harcourt Brace Jovanovich, London and New York, 1980

Peter Watson, *Nureyev: A Biography*, Hodder & Stoughton, London, Sydney and Auckland, 1994

Elizabeth Wilson, *Adorned In Dreams: Fashion and Modernity*, Virago Press, London, 1985

Theodore Zeldin, *Anxiety and Hypocrisy: France 1848–1945*, Oxford University Press, Oxford, 1981

ARTICLES*
Le Figaro, 3/2/1958, Jean Fayard 'Diary'
New York Times, 15/12/1964, Vartanig Vartan 'Business Means Business to St Laurent's Backer'
New York Times, 3/8/1965, Leonard Sloane, 'Saint Laurent's New Backer Spurns Opening In Paris'
New York Times, 27/5/1967, Gloria Emerson, 'Saint Laurent's Latest Creation: A Sadistic Little Lulu'
Time, 27/9/1968, 'Yves In New York'
International Herald Tribune, 30–31/1/1971, Eugenia Sheppard, 'Saint Laurent: Truly Hideous'
Time, 15/2/1971, 'Yves St. Debacle'
Le Figaro, 6/4/1971, Hélène de Tukheim 'YSL: "As Chanel Did Her Suits For Herself, I Did My Men's Collection For Me"'
New York Times, 23/11/1972, Bernardine Morris 'With All The Enthusiasm Of An American in Paris, Saint Laurent Visits New York'
Newsweek, 18/11/1974, Lynn Young 'The King Of Couture'
New York Times, 29/7/1976, Bernadine Morris 'A Revolutionary Saint Laurent Showing'
New York Times, 8/8/1976, Andreas Freund 'The Empire of Saint Laurent'
Time, 9/8/1976, 'The New, New Look'
Le Point, 25/7/1977, Barbara Schwarm & Martine Leventer 'Saint Laurent: le roi de la mode'
New York Times Magazine, 11/9/1977, Anthony Burgess, 'All About Yves'
American *Vogue*, October 1978, Barbara Rose, 'The Intimate Yves'
New York Times, 18/12/1978, Enid Nemy 'Success and a Bit of Controversy, at $100 on Ounce'
American *Vogue*, January 1980, G. Y. Dryansky, 'Saint Laurent All The Way'
American *Vogue*, August 1980, G. Y. Dryanksy 'A Quiet Splendour'
Yves Saint Laurent, 1982, Pierre Bergé, François-Marie Banier etc 'Bravo Yves'
Le Monde 8/12/1983, Yvonne Baby, 'Portrait de l'Artiste'
Time, 12/12/1983, 'The Designer At Home'
American *Vogue*, December 1983, Joan Juliet Buck 'The Strongest Voice'
American *Vogue*, December 1983, John Richardson 'Yves Saint Laurent's Château Gabriel: a passion for style'
Business Week, 24/11/1986, Frank J. Comes 'De Benedetti Cuts a Chic Deal Modelling YSL'

* *includes interviews with Yves Saint Laurent and influential articles on him and his business affairs.*

Wall Street Journal, 5/12/1986, Philip Revzin, 'Smell of Success'

International Herald Tribune, 10–11/9/1988, Suzy Menkes 'Pierre Bergé: A New Score'

Washington Post, 17/1/1989, Edward Cody 'Storm At The Bastille Opera: Barenboim, Bergé Exchange Volleys'

Financial Times, 7–8/4/1989, Philip Revzin and Teri Agins, 'Saint Laurent Remains Idol of French Fashion, But He Isn't Immortal'

Wall Street Journal Europe, 24/6/1989, George Graham, 'Fashion World's Living Legend Goes Public'

International Herald Tribune, 26/10/1989, Suzy Menkes 'Yves Saint Laurent Shocks Paris – Again'

The Times Saturday Review, 21/7/1990, Liz Smith 'The Three Faces Of Yves'

Le Figaro, 11/7/1991, Franz-Olivier Giesbert & Janie Samet 'Yves Saint Laurent: "Je Suis Né Avec Une Dépression Nerveuse"'

W Europe, January 1992, Barbara Schwarm 'The House of Yves: Day 1'

Femme, February 1992, Michèle Sider 'Yves, Mon Fils'

New Yorker, 24/2/1992, Holly Brubacher, 'In Fashion: Fanfare in a Minor Key'

Paris-Match, 6/2/1992, Victoire 'L'Année Terrible de ses Débuts'

Le Monde, 27/1/1993, François Bostnavaron & Pierre-Angel Gay 'Saint Laurent à tout prix'

Vanity Fair, April 1993, Bryan Burroughs 'The Selling of Saint Laurent'

Le Monde, 22/6/1993, Pierre-Angel Gay 'L'Illegalité Inconnu de l'Affaire Saint Laurent'

Glamour, May 1994, Ginette Sainderichin 'YSL: Le Grand Patron'

Sunday Times Magazine, 9/10/1994, Edmund White 'First There Was Yves'

The New Yorker, 21/11/1994, Jane Kramer, 'The Impresario's Last Act'

Harper's Bazaar, September 1994, Sarah Mower 'The YSL Revolution'

British Vogue, November 1994, Lesley White 'The Saint'

Tatler, February 1995, Colombe Pringle 'New Year's Yves'

Chronology

1936   Yves Henri Donat Mathieu-Saint-Laurent is born on 1 August to Lucienne-Andrée (née Wilbaux) and Charles Mathieu-Saint-Laurent at the Jarsaillon Clinic in Oran, Algeria.

1942   Birth of a sister, Michèle. Yves starts school.

1945   *Pierre Balmain, a former colleague of Christian Dior at Lucien Lelong, opens his own couture house in Paris.*

1946   Birth of Yves's second sister, Brigitte.
   Marcel Boussac agrees to invest in Christian Dior's couture house.

1947   *Christian Dior unveils his first couture collection, the 'New Look', in Paris to great acclaim.*

1948   Yves attends the Lycée d'Oran, where he will study until he takes his *baccalauréat* in 1954.
   Nina Ricci's L'Air du Temps and Christian Dior's Miss Dior go on sale.

1952   *Hubert de Givenchy, a former assistant at Schiaparelli and Lucien Lelong, opens a couture house.*

1953   Yves Mathieu-Saint-Laurent is awarded third prize in the International Wool Secretariat design competition in Paris. During the trip he meets Michel de Brunhoff, editor-in-chief of Paris *Vogue* to discuss his career prospects.

1954   After passing his *baccalauréat* at the Lycée d'Oran, Yves moves to Paris to start a design course at the Chambre Syndicale de la Couture school and meets Fernando Sanchez there. Yves takes first prize in three out of four categories at that year's International Wool Secretariat competition. The fourth goes to Karl Lagerfeld, for a coat design.
   Coco Chanel returns to Paris from post-war exile in Switzerland to

unveil her first couture collection for 15 years, and sells her business to the Wertheimer family.

1955 Christian Dior hires Yves as a design assistant and the latter starts work in the Avenue Montaigne studio, where he befriends Anne-Marie Muñoz and the star model Victoire. One of Yves's first designs, a white evening dress, is photographed by Richard Avedon for *Harper's Bazaar*.

1956 Yves meets and befriends the choreographer, Roland Petit, and his wife, the dancer, Zizi Jeanmaire.

1957 Christian Dior dies suddenly at Montecatini in Italy and on 15 November, Yves Mathieu-Saint-Laurent is designated as chief designer of the *couture* house.
Pierre Cardin, a former Dior assistant, starts showing haute couture in Paris.

1958 Yves Saint Laurent unveils his first *couture* collection for Christian Dior, the 'Trapeze Line', to rave reviews. He meets Pierre Bergé, his future lover, at a dinner arranged by the society hostess, Marie-Louise Bousquet. Yves's second, more adventurous Dior collection, the 'Arc Line' is less well-received.

1959 After the mixed reception for the 'Arc', Yves wins praise with his classically elegant 'Long Line', but causes yet another furore with the hobble skirts he creates for the next season. He begins a long collaboration with Roland Petit by designing sets and costumes for Petit's *Cyrano de Bergerac* at the Théâtre de l'Alhambra in Paris.

1960 Yves Saint Laurent outrages the conservative Dior clients and executives with the 'Beat Look'. He is conscripted into the French army on 1 September and reports to barracks. After a nervous breakdown, he is admitted to the Bégin Military Hospital at Saint Mandé on 20 September and thence to the Val-de-Grâce mental institution. He is finally discharged from Val-de-Grâce and from the army on 14 November.
Revlon buys the rights to Pierre Balmain's perfumes.

1961   Pierre Bergé rents temporary offices on rue de la Boétie in Paris, while he tries to find capital to launch Yves Saint Laurent in his own *couture* house. He and Yves start living together in an apartment on Place Vauban. Yves wins a legal suit against Christian Dior for unfair dismissal and designs sets and costumes for Roland Petit's *Les Forains* and for a Zizi Jeanmaire revue. After months of searching for a backer Pierre Bergé, signs a contract with J. Mack Robinson, an American businessman, to invest $700,000 over three years.
        Pierre Cardin negotiates the licensing rights to a men's wear line, his Mao-collared suits will later be worn by the Beatles.

1962   On 29 January the first Yves Saint Laurent *couture* collection is unveiled at Hôtel Forain on rue Spontini in Paris to mixed reviews. The Mathieu-Saint-Laurent family flees Algeria to come and live in Paris. Yves executes designs for three Roland Petit ballets, *Les Chants de Maldoror, Rhapsodie Espagnole* and *Le Violon.*
        André Courrèges and Jean-Louis Scherrer also open new couture houses, and Dorothée Bis is launched as a prêt-à-porter boutique in Paris.

1963   Yves Saint Laurent travels to Japan to sign a distribution contract with the Seibu-Saison department store group in Tokyo.

1964   Launch of 'Y' perfume in association with Charles of the Ritz. The success of André Courrèges's all-white 'Space' collection threatens to eclipse Yves Saint Laurent's line, and after buyers skip that season's *couture* presentation, Pierre Bergé bans the press from attending the debut show each season. Yves begins a collaboration with the director, Jean-Louis Barrault, by designing for two of his productions, *Le Mariage de Figaro* and *Il faut passer par les nuages.*
        Estée Lauder introduces Aramis, which becomes the first best selling prestige men's scent.

1965   Richard Salomon, chairman of Charles of the Ritz, buys out J. Mack Robinson's interest in Yves Saint Laurent for $1 million. The rapturous reception for the 'Mondrian' dresses that Yves shows at his July *couture* show restore his popularity with the press and Pierre Bergé lifts his media ban. Yves begins what

will be a long association with the French actress, Catherine Deneuve, by designing her costumes for the Luis Buñuel film, *Belle de Jour*.
L'Oréal invests in André Courrèges's fashion company and Emanuel Ungaro opens a couture house.

1966   The first *smoking* is shown in the spring *couture* collection in January. Yves Saint Laurent and Pierre Bergé befriend Andy Warhol whose 'Pop Art' inspires the controversial YSL autumn *couture* collection. The first Rive Gauche boutique opens in Paris on 21 rue de Tournon on 26 September with Catherine Deneuve as guest-of-honour and Clara Saint as press officer. Yves befriends Betty and François Catroux.

1967   Yves Saint Laurent publishes a book of cartoons, *La Vilaine Lulu*. He and Pierre Bergé buy Dar el-Hanch, 'The House of the Serpent', in Marrakesh, and meet Paul and Talitha Getty. Yves unveils a *couture* collection inspired by Coco Chanel.
Christian Dior and Emanuel Ungaro introduce prêt-à-porter ranges.

1968   The 'safari look' is featured in the spring YSL *couture* collection, which causes a sensation when a model, Danielle, appears bare breasted under ostrich-feather-trimmed silk chiffon. Yves Saint Laurent dedicates his autumn range to the student protesters of May 1968 with a series of duffel coats and fringed jackets. He goes to New York with Betty Catroux to open a Rive Gauche boutique on Madison Avenue.
Sonia Rykiel opens a prêt-à-porter boutique on rue de Grenelle in Paris. Maïmé Arnodin and Denise Fayolle found Mafia, their advertising agency. Balenciaga's couture house closes.

1969   The Rive Gauche men's range is launched. Yves collaborates with the sculptor, Claude Lalanne, on a *couture* collection and designs Catherine Deneuve's costumes for *La Sirène du Mississippi*, directed by François Truffaut. Richard Salomon sells Charles of the Ritz to Squibb. Yves confides to friends that he is thinking of giving up fashion to concentrate on writing and theatrical design. Rive Gauche opens in London.

387

1970   A 'bride' wearing a velvet coat appliquéed with 'Love Me Forever Or Never' closes the YSL autumn *couture* show at which Paloma Picasso appears in a 1940s-style outfit. Andy Warhol spends much of early autumn with Yves in Paris, while his entourage shoots *L'Amour* at Karl Lagerfeld's Left Bank apartment. *Kenzo Takada opens his Jungle Jap boutique at the Galerie Vivienne in Paris.*

1971   Yves Saint Laurent is clouded by controversy after showing a 1940s-inspired *couture* collection which *Time* magazine dubs 'Yves St Debacle'. He poses nude for the photographer, Jeanloup Sieff, to create an advertisement for the first YSL For Men fragrance. Pierre Bergé announces that YSL will stop showing *haute couture* to concentrate on *prêt-à-porter* and the first Rive Gauche show is staged on 28 October. The company introduces Rive Gauche as its new women's perfume. *Didier Grumbach founds Créateurs et Industriels. A group of five American designers – Bill Blass, Steven Burrows, Halston, Ann Klein and Oscar de la Renta – stage a show at the Palace of Versaille with five Parisian couturiers, including YSL. Coco Chanel dies on 10 January.*

1972   Richard Salomon negotiates a deal whereby Pierre Bergé and Yves Saint Laurent buy the fashion house from Squibb for $1.1 million. Pierre Bergé starts selling the licensing rights to YSL products. He and Yves move into 55 rue de Babylone, a 1930s duplex designed by Jean-Michel Frank that they have bought and renovated in Paris. Loulou de la Falaise starts work at the fashion house as Yves's 'muse'. Yves and Pierre befriend Jacques Grange and François-Marie Banier. *Deaths of Cristobal Balenciaga and Elsa Schiaparelli.*

1973   Yves Saint Laurent starts to stage *haute couture* shows again, slipping into the four season fashion cycle of showing *couture* in January and July, *prêt-à-porter* in March and October. He also steps up his theatrical work, designed four productions that year, including Jean-Louis Barrault's version of *Harold and Maud* and Roland Petit's *La Rose Malade*. *Issey Miyake shows in Paris for the first time. Claude Montana and*

Thierry Mugler set up in business. Pierre Bergé forms Groupe Mode et Création to represent prêt-à-porter designers within the Chambre Syndicale and subsequently becomes president of the latter organization. Revlon launches Charlie perfume.

1974   The YSL group moves from its old headquarters on rue Spontini to an *hôtel particulier* at 5 Avenue Marceau. Yves Saint Laurent and Pierre Bergé buy Dar es Saada, a new villa in Marrakesh. Yves Saint Laurent's fashion collections emphasize the classic styles that he will refine for the rest of his career. The Proscenium art gallery in Paris stages an exhibition of Yves's theatrical designs.
       Vivienne Westwood and Malcolm McLaren open the Sex boutique on the Kings Road in London.

1975   A new genderless YSL scent, Eau Libre, is introduced. Despite a blaze of publicity over its advertising, Eau Libre is not commercially successful and is eventually withdrawn from the market.
       Halston introduces his signature scent in the United States, which becomes an instant best seller. Cartier launches its cheaper Les Must de Cartier range of watches.

1976   After a period of fragile heath, Yves Saint Laurent causes a sensation with an autumn *couture* collection inspired by Léon Bakst's costume designs for the *Ballets Russes*. The following season he stages the longest show in Paris fashion history for his 'Carmen' *prêt-à-porter* collection, but almost collapses with exhaustion at the reception afterwards.
       Jean-Paul Gaultier, a former assistant at Pierre Cardin, shows his first prêt-à-porter collection in Paris.

1977   Yves Saint Laurent buys a private retreat on Avenue de Breteuil in Paris and asks Jacques Grange to decorate it for him. Rumours of Yves's 'death' swirl around Paris that spring on the eve of the March *prêt-à-porter* show. Pierre Bergé produces a French version of *Equus* in Paris and acquires the Théâtre de l'Athenée, which he renovates. Loulou de la Falaise marries Thadée Klossowski and Yves celebrates their wedding by throwing a party at Châlet des Îles in the Bois de Boulogne. The YSL group

launches Opium, a new women's fragrance and provokes a furore
with the *'Opium pour celles qui s'adonnent à Yves Saint Laurent'*
advertising campaign.
Henry Racamier becomes chairman of Louis Vuitton.

1978   A range of YSL cosmetics is introduced, the No 19 purple
        lipstick becomes an instant cult hit. Opium makes its debut in
        the United States in September with a party on the *Peking*, a
        Chinese junk moored on the East River after which Yves and
        his entourage go to Studio 54. Despite the glamour of the
        Opium party, Yves is becoming increasingly reclusive and
        henceforth will rarely appear in public.

1979   Yves Saint Laurent is acclaimed for an *haute couture* collection
        inspired by the designs created by Pablo Picasso, Georges
        Rouault and Giorgio de Chirico for the Ballets Russes pro-
        ductions of the 1920s.

1980   Pierre Bergé and Yves Saint Laurent buy Villa Oasis, a 1920s
        house in Marrakesh, and start four years of renovation in collab-
        oration with Bill Willis and Jacques Grange. Yves executes
        theatrical designs for Jean Cocteau's version of *Cher Menteur* and
        Claude Régy's *Wings*. Pierre Bergé signs the 190th YSL licens-
        ing deal.
        Yohji Yamamoto shows his prêt-à-porter in Paris for the first time.

1981   The *smoking* becomes a central theme of the YSL collections.
        Pierre Bergé votes for the right-wing candidate, Valéry Giscard
        d'Estaing, in the French presidential elections won by the social-
        ist, François Mitterrand. He befriends the new culture minister,
        Jack Lang, and moves into the Mitterrand camp. The launch
        of Kouros, a YSL men's scent, is marked at a gala with a special
        performance by Rudolf Nureyev.
        *Rei Kawakubo of Comme des Garçons stages her first prêt-à-porter
        presentation in Paris. Giorgio Armani launches his Emporio Armani
        diffusion range.*

1982   The YSL group celebrates its twentieth anniversary with a gala
        at the Lido in Paris when Diana Vreeland presents Yves with a
        special award from the Council of Fashion Designers of America.

Azzedine Alaïa starts showing under his own name. After discussions with Pierre Bergé, Jack Lang allows the Paris prêt-à-porter shows to be staged in the Cour Carrée of the Louvre Museum.

1983   Yves Saint Laurent creates a *'Noire et Rose' couture* collection to mark the debut of Paris, the new YSL women's scent. Pierre Bergé clinches a licensing deal for women's watches with Cartier. He and Yves buy Château Gabriel, a 19th-century mansion near the village of Bénerville in Normandy which Yves and Jacques Grange turn into an homage to Marcel Proust. Diana Vreeland organizes a retrospective of Yves's career at the Costume Institute of the Metropolitan Museum in New York, its first exhibition devoted to a living artist or designer.
Karl Lagerfeld is appointed chief designer of Chanel and shows his first couture collection at rue Cambon. Vivienne Westwood shows in Paris for the first time. Sybilla founds a fashion house in Madrid, and Romeo Gigli opens one in Milan.

1984   *Bernard Arnault takes control of Agache-Willot, the bankrupt French textile group which includes Christian Dior, after a government auction. Elizabeth Arden launches Obsession by Calvin Klein and Estée Lauder introduces Beautiful perfume.*

1985   Yves Saint Laurent is made a Chevalier de la Légion d'Honneur, one of the highest honours given by the French government, in a presentation conducted by François Mitterrand. After being seen by a million people in New York, the YSL retrospective opens at the Musée des Beaux-Arts in Beijing. Yves Saint Laurent travels there for the opening; he and Pierre Bergé are subsequently made special advisors to the Chinese government.

1986   The YSL retrospective is shown at the Musée des Arts de la Mode in Paris. Squibb puts the YSL perfumes up for sale. Pierre Bergé joins forces with the Italian industrialist, Carlo de Benedetti, who acquires 25 per cent of the YSL group for $38 million, before helping Bergé finance the $630 million perfume deal.
Helmut Lang stages his first prêt-à-porter presentation in Paris.

1987   Andy Warhol dies on 22 February. The YSL retrospective moves to Sydney and the Hermitage in St Petersburg. Yves Saint

Laurent attends Marie-Hélène de Rothschild's Bal des Fées, the coming-out ball she hosts at Hôtel Lambert for her niece, Vanessa. Pierre Bergé is forced to postpone his plans to take the company public after the stock market crash on 'Black Friday'. *Bernard Arnault finances the launch of Christian Lacroix, the first new couture house to open in Paris for over a decade. Lacroix's first collection receives a rapturous reception. Henry Racamier invites Bernard Arnault to buy into the LVMH Group.*

1988   Pierre Bergé campaigns for François Mitterrand in the 1988 presidential elections and, a few months after the socialist victory, is made president of the Opéra de Paris. Charles Mathieu-Saint-Laurent dies in Monaco after a long respiratory illness. Yves Saint Laurent, who has not seen his father for three years, breaks down at the funeral.
After a dawn raid on LVMH's shares, Bernard Arnault is made chairman of the group and begins a battle for control of the company against Henry Racamier of Louis Vuitton. John Galliano shows in Paris for the first time. Martin Margiela opens a fashion business, as does Jean Touitou with APC.

1989   Speculation about Yves's health culminates in inaccurate press rumours about his having AIDS. The YSL group is valued at $500 million after going public on the Paris stock market on 6 July in a heavily over-subscribed issue, following a $180 million private placing of shares among institutional investors, including Cartier. Pierre Bergé causes a furore by firing Daniel Barenboim and Rudolf Nureyev as artistic directors of the Opéra de Paris and Ballet de Paris.
Unilever spends $2 billion on beauty acquisitions by buying Fabergé, Rimmel and Elizabeth Arden. Romeo Gigli shows in Paris for the first time and Rifat Ozbek unveils his all-white 'New Age' collection. Donna Karan launches her DKNY diffusion range and Jean-Paul Gaultier introduces Junior Gaultier.

1990   Yves Saint Laurent unveils a triumphant *haute couture* collection in January, but then breaks down at his house in Marrakesh. On his return to Paris he is admitted to the American Hospital at Neuilly-sur-Seine. Pierre Bergé announces that Yves will be unable to attend the Rive Gauche show in March because of 'overwhelming nervous exhaustion'. His October Rive Gauche presentation is described as looking like a 'downmarket travel brochure'. Carlo de Benedetti warns Pierre Bergé that he will have to sell his YSL shares after a disastrous takeover bid for Société Générale de Belgique.

Gianni Versace shows his couture collection in Paris. L'Oréal launches Trésor de Lancôme perfume.

1991 A special presentation of Robert Merloz's fur collection is staged during *prêt-à-porter* week in Paris. Pierre Bergé issues a formal warning to investors in April that the disruption caused by the Gulf War will adversely affect the company's financial perform-ance during 1991. Having failed to find a buyer for Carlo de Benedetti's shares, he arranges $99 million of bank loans to purchase them in his and Yves's names. Yves Saint Laurent publicly discusses his drug problems and homosexuality for the first time in an interview with *Le Figaro*. Pierre Bergé asks Wasserstein Perella to find a buyer for the YSL group, insisting on raising $1 billion in cash.

Time magazine runs a cover story on the 'Supermodel' phenomenon. Soaring model fees aggravate the financial pressure on the fashion industry at a time when the Gulf War has destabilized the duty free market and demand is weak due to the recession.

1992 The YSL group celebrates its thirtieth anniversary with a gala at the Opéra de Bastille. Pierre Bergé enters into secret, and ultimately unsuccessful negotiations to sell the company to L'Oréal. During the July *couture* shows, Pierre Bergé arranges a presentation of Robert Merloz's first *prêt-à-porter* range. A few days later Yves Saint Laurent, described by his mother as deeply distressed, shows the smallest *couture* collection of his career. The YSL share price falls sharply in September after Pierre Bergé announces a decline in first half profits. That autumn Sanofi secretly starts talks with Bergé over the acquisition of Yves Saint Laurent.

Shiseido introduces L'Eau d'Issey, the first Issey Miyake fragrance. Revlon is forced to postpone its stock market flotation in New York because of sluggish market conditions. David Geffen, the music mogul, saves Calvin Klein's business by buying up a block of bonds due for redemption. Klein subsequently buys them back.

1993   On 18 January, Sanofi announces that it is acquiring Yves Saint Laurent for $650 million in shares. A week later Yves unveils a *couture* collection dedicated to Rudolf Nureyev who has died of AIDS. The Sanofi announcement triggers press speculation that the deal was orchestrated by President François Mitterand. Pierre Bergé is ousted as president of the Chambre Syndicale and, after the socialist's defeat in the parliamentary elections, is told that his Opéra de Paris contract will not be renewed. Champagne farmers disrupt a YSL press conference at which Bergé announces the launch of a women's scent, Champagne, and the company then loses a court case in which the champagne industry challenges its right to use the name.
       Jean-Paul Gaultier launches his first fragrance with Shiseido.

1994   Pierre Bergé fined 3 million francs by the French stock market authorities for insider trading (the fine is subsequently reduced to 1 million francs on appeal). He successfully sues Ralph Lauren for allegedly copying a YSL tuxedo dress. The Saint Laurent revival starts with a series of laudatory press articles about Yves and acclaim for his July *couture* show. He and Pierre fly to New York in September for a Champagne launch party on Liberty Island and to attend a memorial service for Richard Salomon.
       Unilever launches CK One, a highly successful 'genderless' scent for Calvin Klein with an identical product premise to the ill-fated Eau Libre. Patrick Cox introduces Wannabe clothing.

1995   After losing a court case in Germany, Sanofi reaches agreement with the champagne industry to cease using the name, Champagne, all over the world by 1999. That autumn it launches Opium for men and relaunches Opium for women with advertising campaigns. The YSL men's wear line becomes a cult among 'casual' football fans.
       Gucci goes public with a successful share sale in New York, followed by Estée Lauder. Bernard Arnault appoints John Galliano as chief designer at Givenchy to replace the retiring Hubert de Givenchy.

1996   Yves Saint Laurent unveils his July *haute couture* collection to rave reviews before celebrating his sixtieth birthday on 1 August.

Index